Critical Dialogues in Southeast Asian Studies

CHARLES KEYES, VICENTE RAFAEL, AND LAURIE J. SEARS,
SERIES EDITORS

Critical Dialogues in Southeast Asian Studies

This series offers perspectives in Southeast Asian Studies that stem from reconsideration of the relationships among scholars, texts, archives, field sites, and subject matter. Volumes in the series feature inquiries into historiography, critical ethnography, colonialism and postcolonialism, nationalism and ethnicity, gender and sexuality, science and technology, politics and society, and literature, drama, and film. A common vision of the series is a belief that area studies scholarship sheds light on shifting contexts and contests over forms of knowing and modes of action that inform cultural politics and shape histories of modernity.

Imagined Ancestries of Vietnamese Communism:
Ton Duc Thang and the Politics of History and Memory
by Christoph Giebel

Beginning to Remember: The Past in the Indonesian Present
edited by Mary S. Zurbuchen

Seditious Histories: Contesting Thai and Southeast Asian Pasts
by Craig J. Reynolds

Seditious Histories

CONTESTING THAI AND SOUTHEAST ASIAN PASTS

Craig J. Reynolds

UNIVERSITY OF WASHINGTON PRESS
Seattle and London

in association with

SINGAPORE UNIVERSITY PRESS

Published simultaneously in Singapore and the United States.

University of Washington Press
P.O. Box 50096
Seattle, WA 98145, USA
www.washington.edu/uwpress

Singapore University Press, NUS Publishing
AS3-01-02. 3, Arts Link
Singapore 117569
www.nus.edu.sg/npu

ISBN 9971-69-335-6 (Paper)

Library of Congress Cataloging-in-Publication Data

Reynolds, Craig J.
  Seditious histories: contesting Thai and Southeast Asian pasts / Craig J. Reynolds.—1st ed.
    p. cm.—(Critical dialogues in Southeast Asian studies)
  Includes bibliographical references and index.
  ISBN 0-295-98610-7 (pbk.: alk. paper)
  1. Thailand—Historiography. 2. Thailand—Civilization. 3. Southeast Asia—Historiography. I. Title. II. Series.
  DS570.95.R49 2006
  959.30072—dc22
                                                                        2005030907

Contents

THE DIALECTICS OF GLOBALIZATION

Prologue

History writing in Thailand is sometimes seditious, a threat to the regime of the day or injurious to the reputation of powerful individuals. Even when history writing appears to look tame, it can provoke a surprising reaction. In the circumstances, a topic as apparently arcane and innocent as early Siamese epigraphy can draw a huge audience and spirited discussion at university seminars.

For the past fifteen years an inscription of 1292 C.E., in which the Thai writing system was supposedly used for the first time, has been the focus of controversy. The epigraph has been picked apart by linguists, art historians, and political historians, all of whom allege that it is a fake, invented in the middle of the nineteenth century by the Siamese monarch to bolster his standing in the eyes of Western imperialists. In July 2004, Michael Wright, an expatriate British national resident in Thailand for forty-five years, was threatened with deportation, and an eminent Thai art historian of aristocratic ancestry, Dr. Piriya Krairiksh, was threatened with trial for "defaming" the royal author of the inscription, King Ramkhamhaeng. Explaining the position he has taken on Ramkhamhaeng's document, dated by most historians to the late thirteenth century, Michael Wright said, "Inscription One is national myth number one." Demanding that Mr. Wright be deported for his verbal assault on this national icon, Darun Meetes, a former member of parliament who had filed the police complaint, said that the inscription "is a matter of national security. We have already lost the economic war and this is the cultural war."[1]

The idea that a document purportedly written over seven centuries ago should be a matter of national security captures many of the problems I try to grapple with in this book. The discipline of history did not exist when events, catastrophe, or the hubris of the wealthy and powerful created most of these materials. But history was vital to collective memory, to dynastic succession, and to an individual's identification with place. History was a form of political intelligence, another weapon in the arsenal of the well-informed Southeast Asian ruler. It was also a means of assessing enemy strength. The victors in the Siamese-Burmese wars always debriefed the officials and artisans they conquered, and thus genealogies, rivalries for office, and battle tactics surfaced for the historian's scrutiny.

In the Thai public sphere there is no such thing as disinterested history. Even in the contemporary moment numerous examples of biographies, studies of national and regional monuments, and academic research projects could be summoned to defend the proposition. Ancient, premodern, modern, and contemporary history, given the right topic and the right moment, can prick sensitivities about what a proper account of the past should be. Lively and well-attended academic seminars are reported by journalists eager for stories to spice up their newspapers and magazines. Custodians and gatekeepers of particular versions of the past are to be found in the bureaucracy, in the homes of the aristocracy, in university offices, and in the military and the monkhood. In view of history as a battleground, the truth-value of alternative histories has always been less interesting to me than the political, cultural, and social circumstances that created particular accounts, even if it can be demonstrated that the truth-value of those accounts is flawed. Otherwise, why pay attention to the controversy over Inscription One, when the weight of evidence favors the "nationalist" interpretation that protects the inscription's reputation as the wellspring of the language and a noble charter for good government today?

The searching and sometimes bitter debate about the past flowed from political change in Thailand during the 1970s. On 14 October 1973, massive public demonstrations brought down a military government, Thai intellectual life underwent an upheaval whose tremors still reverberate in the country's social and political life, and the security forces engineered a bloody return to power on 6 October 1976. The authorities still refuse to memorialize the loss of life in that tragic event. In that three-year period, history suddenly was no mere classroom subject or academic field but a blunt political instrument and a focal point for debating social ills. Historians and other intellectuals had been imprisoned by the previous military regimes, events had been suppressed or forgotten, and literary life had been stifled. The task of academics and intellectuals was to excavate forgotten pasts and rediscover writers and works now coming back to life after a generation of neglect.

The past was opened up iconoclastically, and history of all sorts—economic, social, intellectual, and political—became a booming discipline, with such critical junctures as the Bowring Treaty of 1855 subjected to intense scrutiny, even parody. An Australian colleague of mine, who was visiting Bangkok in the mid-1970s, recalled seeing street theater in which young Thais played the roles of Bowring and his host, King Mongkut, a skit that would be unthinkable in the country today. Since the events of the mid-1970s have slowly receded into the past, Thai historical studies have undergone a sea change, partly as a result of the professionalization of history within the universities, partly because of a serious attempt to direct the historians' gaze away from the center, and partly because the expansion of the university system required the employment of historians in regional universities. Local history, regional history, Tai history outside of Thailand, economic history, the history of gender, and, lately, post-modernist history all now flourish, and there are signs that university history as a discipline is coming back into favor with students.

Writing history that is engaged with the politics of memory is challenge enough, but another, equally daunting challenge for the foreign historian has to do with being an outsider and a non-native speaker of the language, something I am reminded of every time I pick up a piece of writing in this musical, beautiful, but, for me, terribly difficult language. How is it possible to know Thailand's history from such historical and cultural distances? What steps does the historian take to know that history and what entitles that historian to the knowledge that results? The chapters in this book, written over a thirty-year period and arranged topically rather than chronologically in the order they were written, attempt to answer these questions in various ways.

The first two chapters, on early Southeast Asia and paradigms of the premodern state, address these questions in relation to the region as a whole. Since World War II, Western historiography has struggled to understand the region as a unity, as a domain of comparable if contrasting societies, whose histories are distinct from the histories of the Indian subcontinent and East Asia. The study of early history up to the thirteenth century has been instrumental in defining the region, both because of shared contact across the region with the Indic world and because the geopolitics of the Chinese tribute system gave kingdoms in the early period an external orientation. Western historians of Southeast Asia have crafted tools for this struggle to understand, from the "Hinduization" of the French scholar George Coedès, to the geoenvironmental metaphor of "monsoon Asia" of Paul Mus, to the "man of prowess" coined by O. W. Wolters to characterize the potentials of kingly leadership. "A New Look at Old Southeast Asia" illustrates how historians of the so-called classical period have laid the foundations of the region's distinctiveness *as* a region. In the strongest historical statements about old Southeast Asia it almost seems that the region is deemed unique in world history for some of its distinctive features. It is not so much that histories of the early period argue for the region's unity as they do for the shared historical experience and comparability of the immensely varied cultures and societies within it.

"Paradigms of the Premodern State" puts forward an inventory of models of the premodern state. Two of these—the *mandala* and the theater state or *negara*—are cultural models devised from local words to give them legitimacy and conceptual force. The ship-shape state stresses the mobility and orderly regimes of the coastal and maritime-based polities. Other paradigms, such as the Asiatic Mode of Production and the dynastic state, are conceptual tools found useful in the study of societies elsewhere in the world. There is nothing particularly Southeast Asian about these latter paradigms; they are exogenous models, drawn from theory external to the region. Indeed, as can be seen in the case of the Asiatic Mode of Production, it is the external nature of the paradigm that is its great strength, for it latches onto a global historical narrative. For this very reason the paradigm has from time to time captured the imaginations of Vietnamese and Thai historians.

The second section of the book on seditious histories explores episodes in modern Thai history when writing about the past challenged royal or military authority. Before the end of the absolute monarchy in 1932 the court dominated writing about previous Siamese dynasties. Kings and princes were authorized historians by birthright, and it was almost unthinkable that commoners would write their own versions of that past. When, in the cases documented here, commoners configured their own versions of that past, as in the case of Mr. Kulap at the end of the nineteenth century, or wrote historical accounts that were seen to tarnish the reputation of a military commander appointed by the king, as in the case of Nai Thim in the 1870s, or played with the proper language for describing the past, as in the case with socialist historians of the 1950s, the "authorized" custodians of the past reacted by mocking the historians or punishing them. Chapter 6, on engendering Thai historiography, is seditious history of a different kind, with the implicit message that the way Thai historiography is inflected by gender has made it very difficult to write alternative narratives that do not circle back to mainstream concerns.

The third section of the volume examines the way particular genres of material can be exploited to understand and construct new pasts: a chronicle of 1789; a cosmography, putatively of the fourteenth century; a manifesto of 1867 defending polygamy; and a variety of folk and elite knowledge codified in handbooks. These are examples of what I have called manual knowledge. Deposited in the Thai archive, these diverse materials were not for the express consumption of historians, but to serve power, to articulate a worldview, and to facilitate the transmission of knowledge about how to behave, how to cure disease, how to find the auspicious moment to make war or make love, and how to be modern.

The final section of the book, on the dialectics of globalization, is about the play of the past in the present and the present in the past. "Globalization" is one of the flabby monsters of contemporary social science and cultural studies. Few people want to own up to the term as a helpful analytical category, given its use and abuse in the media and by the merchant heads of government pressing for free-trade agreements. I justify it here on the grounds that in Thailand in the early 1990s it became a buzzword, invoked by its defenders to push along the economic boom or by its detractors to put a brake on internationalizing the economy because of the deleterious conse-quences of hypergrowth. In this section I trace the debate about globalization back to earlier decades when Thai national identity was in a formative phase. In the wake of the 1997 Asian financial crisis, globalization forced Thai leaders and public intellectuals to reexamine what sovereignty means in the present epoch. The responses to the challenges to Thai sovereignty have been conditioned by preoccupations with the meanings of Thai-ness that date back many decades.

The earliest studies in this volume were written in the shadow of my Ph.D. dissertation on the Buddhist monkhood in nineteenth-century Siam. In fact, the topic fit into a series of studies on Siam's response to Western imperialism in the second half of the nineteenth century (Reynolds 1973). David Wyatt's pioneering thesis on the beginnings of modern education in Thailand was completed in 1966, the same year that Fred Riggs published *Thailand: The Modernization of a Bureaucratic Polity*, a study destined to have a wide impact in development studies in other parts of the world (Riggs 1966; Wyatt 1969). There followed dissertations on the modernization of other Thai institutions: provincial administration; Buddhist and provincial education; the army; and finance. These were, for the most part, institutional studies—ministry-specific in many cases—that analyzed the motives, implementation, and impact of the reform enacted from the late 1880s by King Chulalongkorn (r. 1868–1910) and members of his family and the nobility sympathetic to him. Political tensions over the reform had begun soon after Chulalongkorn came to the throne, at the age of fifteen, in 1868. The appointment of the king's younger brothers to head important ministries as the ancient régime of nobles and princes retired or passed away opened up the politics of the Fifth Reign that had been hidden behind the hitherto conventional story of Western advisers employed to carry out the reforms. Hovering in the background of what was then a revisionist history was the notion of a Thai Enlightenment, a this-world orientation that would lead to social betterment.

What propelled this revision of Thai history in English was the modernization theory prevalent in American social-science research for about a decade from the late 1950s. By that time, modernization theory and development studies had become one of the most important justifications for Asian studies in American government and it influenced university funding priorities (Berger 2003: 422). According to the crudest versions of the theory, it was possible to rank societies along a transitional spectrum from tradition to modernity according to social-scientific indicators: population, urbanization, media consumption, media production, literacy, education. A key study with this transition theme prominently on display was based on Turkey, Lebanon, Egypt, Syria, Jordan, and Iran (Lerner 1958). Pioneering societies would lead the way, and follower societies would catch up. Many of the studies were highly programmatic and blatantly Western-centric. Cyril Black's *The Dynamics of Modernization*, for example, set out seven patterns, in the last two of which appeared "the more than one hundred independent and dependent societies of Asia, Africa, the Americas, and Oceania that have experienced colonial rule" (Black 1966: 106). "The functions of modernity are of universal validity," Black confidently declared, "and all societies may be expected to achieve political consolidation, economic growth, social mobilization, and psychological adjustment" (Black 1966: 151). The presumption was common that modernization could only take hold outside the West if the overall Western experience with modernity were duplicated. The administration of President John F. Kennedy proposed a sweeping "Decade of Development" that would build entire new nations (Latham 2000: 57). Political sociologists and political scientists were the main theorists of modernization, and their work left its mark on the other disciplines.

Thailand was a particularly interesting case for modernization theory, because the Siamese dynastic state had never been formally colonized. The factors that induced change in Thailand were of a special kind, not the product of colonial conditions but of the aspirations and apprehensions of an indigenous elite witnessing neighboring dynastic states collapsing around it and emulating some of the strategies and tactics of the colonial powers. Religion was one of the indices under close scrutiny by the modernization theorists, largely because of Max Weber's thesis about the Protestant ethic and the spirit of capitalism. In terms of the sociology and politics of modernization theory, an interesting research question was whether or not religious reform in Siam, which began in the second quarter of the nineteenth century, could be seen as the vanguard of the modernizing process, thus challenging the Weberian presumption that the so-called otherworldliness of Buddhist cultures rendered them "peculiarly unsuited to capitalist modernity" (Pressman 1993: 60). Was it really the case that Buddhism had to be transformed into an ideology replicating Weber's Protestant ethic, because traditional Buddhism and animism were poor ideological vehicles for the transformation (Pressman 1993: 147)? Studies by Robert Bellah had already argued that religious change in Japan was the vanguard of modernization (Bellah 1985 [1957], 1965).

While I was aware of modernization theory, my interest in the dynamics of the relationship between the Buddhist monkhood and the

court soon reached back earlier in the dynasty's history, and I avoided
the question of whether or not Buddhism's otherworldliness challenged
the Weberian thesis. Reacting to the excesses of modernization theory,
I stubbornly avoided the word in the entire dissertation. The late Tom
Kirsch, who had studied with Talcott Parsons at Harvard, was resolutely
opposed to the idea implicit in the modernization writing that Buddhism
was unsuited to capitalist modernity, and he later teased out the
modernizing implications of the "reform" of the Thai Sangha and
published his own arguments with his customary finesse (Kirsch 1975;
Pressman 1993: 44).

Modernization theory passed from the scene long ago, at least
in the paradigmatic form that shaped many dissertations on Thailand
in the late 1960s and early 1970s. "Modernity" still has some theoretical reach, but one is more likely to find studies of the way specific
Southeast Asian communities localize modernity, shaping it in ways
that make sense in local contexts (Taylor 2001). According to Douglas
Pressman's review of the impact of modernization theory in Thai
studies, anthropology lost interest in the Weberian project in the
mid-1970s (Pressman 1993: 65–66). With the singular exception of
Pressman's dissertation more than a decade ago, there has been little
reflection on the impact of the theory on Thai studies, and perhaps
there need not be. By 1978, in a volume on the state of Thai studies
across the disciplines, virtually no attention was paid to modernization
theory, and the volume is now remembered mostly for Benedict
Anderson's charge that, in contrast to the growing scholarship on
other countries by Southeast Asianists, Thai studies in the United States
were conservative, timid, and largely uncritical of power (Anderson
1978). Certainly it was the case that even after the upheavals of
the mid-1970s, American social scientists, in comparison to social
scientists in Britain, neglected class and conflict and instead spent much
effort studying elections, voting patterns, and local administration
rather than the workings of military power or its deleterious and often
violent consequences. There were significant exceptions, such as Thak
Chaloemtiarana's account of Field Marshal Sarit Thanarat's despotic
paternalism (Thak 1979).

For me, the upheavals of the mid-1970s in Thailand brought the
conditions of historical writing into sharper focus and made it impossible
to write history without facing up to the politics that lay behind the

historiography. Marxism and socialism were rediscovered and soon began to inflect historical studies (Reynolds and Hong 1983). The problem of translating Marxist categories made the Thai language itself the object of study. The language sometimes acts like a cell membrane, easing the assimilation of some foreign categories and blocking out others. Thai institutions and individuals—the learned teachers of yore or the public intellectuals of today—have always had a hand in deciding how foreign terms come into the language, and this was the case in thirteenth-century Sukhothai just as it is the case in the globalized world of today. Many of the following chapters worry about words and how language is a space of conflict as well as a medium of communication. Indeed, the Thai language sometimes seems to have a power and genius of its own, independent of its speakers. Its stubbornness and its sheer inventiveness have always been a surprise and a source of pleasure.

Note

1   *Weekly Telegraph* (U.K.), story filed online on July 23, 2004, at <www.telegraph. co.uk>. I am indebted to Professor Charnvit Kasetsiri, of Thammasat University, for this citation.

Acknowledgments

Parts of Chapters 1, 2, and 10 were conceived and researched with the assistance of a grant from the Australian Research Council for a study of state formation in Southeast Asia. This was a collaborative and fruitful project with Tony Day that led to several publications, including Day's own *Fluid Iron: State Formation in Southeast Asia* (2002).

For suggestions on specific chapters, I am indebted to the following. Chapter 1: Nicole Biros, David Bulbeck, John Butcher, Dipesh Chakrabarty, Helen Creese, Jane Drakard, Bob Elson, Victor Lieberman, Tony Milner, and the late Oliver Wolters; Chapter 2: Tony Day, Tony Milner, Ian Proudfoot, and Peter Zinoman; Chapter 3: Tej Bunnag and David Wyatt; Chapter 4: Chalong Suntravanij, Paul Cohen, Tony Day, Tony Diller, Andrew Forbes, Ranajit Guha, Phil Hirsch, Kullada Kesabunchoo, Manas Chitakasem, Antoinette Merrillees, Nidhi Aeusrivongse, Rachaneepon Chanta-aree, Ruth T. McVey, Ruchira Mendiones, B. J. Terwiel, Thongchai Winichakul, Andrew Turton, Wilaiwan Khanittanan, the late Oliver Wolters, and David Wyatt; Chapter 5: Nerida Cook, Ranajit Guha, Hong Lysa, Victor Lieberman, Somkiat Wanthana, and Ruth T. McVey; Chapter 6: Katherine Bowie, Matthew Copeland, Gill Burke, David Chandler, Donald Denoon, Peter Jackson, Jantharakan Jantharachot ("Uwe"), Margaret Jolly, Patrick Jory, Nancy Lindisfarne, Sue Rider, Sitthipong Dilokwanich, David Streckfuss, and Thongchai Winichakul; Chapter 8: David Chandler, Michael W. Jackson and Robert Taylor; Chapter 9: Paul Cohen, Robyn Cooper, and Douglas Miles; Chapter 10: Soraj Hongladarom, Patrick Jory, Nicholas Tapp, Andrew Walker, Thongchai Winichakul, and Aat Vervoorn; Chapter 11: Dipesh Chakrabarty, David Chandler, Matthew Copeland, Tony Diller, Annette Hamilton, Yoneo Ishii, Patrick Jory, Kasian Tejapira, Helen Michaelsen, Maurizio Peleggi, Baas Terwiel, Carol Warren, Jim Warren, and the late Gehan Wijewardene; Chapter 12: Chris Baker, Joel Kahn, Glen Lewis, Pasuk Phongphaichit, Patrick Jory, Phouangthong Rungswasdisab, Sakkharin

Niyomsilpa, Thaveeporn Vasavakul, Tessa Morris-Suzuki, Thomas Kirsch, Maurizio Peleggi, Villa Vilaithong, and the late Oliver Wolters.

I am very grateful to Benedict Anderson, David Chandler, and Annette Hamilton for encouraging me to pursue this project. The University of Washington Press's readers, Charles Keyes and Tamara Loos, suggested detailed and insightful comments that made a pleasure out of the burden of revision. Michael Duckworth and the Press's editorial staff have been prompt and helpful correspondents from the moment I proposed the volume. Andrew Walker offered invaluable advice on the manuscript, as did David Chandler and Maurizio Peleggi, and the local collegial friendships of Andrew Walker, Nicholas Farrelly, Chintana Sandilands, and Aat Vervoorn have sustained me over the duration of the project. I am especially grateful to Jacob Ramsay for assistance both editorial and intellectual in the final stages, and I wish him well on his new career. As always, Vacharin McFadden's knowledge of the Thai materials at the National Library of Australia has been of inestimable value to my research.

Sources

Previously published chapters of this book are reprinted unchanged or with minor revisions. If substantially revised, the chapter's earlier version is cited.

Chapter 1: *Journal of Asian Studies*, 54.2 (May 1995), pp. 419–46. Reprinted with permission of the Association for Asian Studies, Inc.

Chapter 2: Published for the first time in this volume.

Chapter 3: *Journal of the Siam Society*, 61.2 (1973), pp. 63–90.

Chapter 4: *Thai Constructions of Knowledge*, ed. Manas Chitakasem and Andrew Turton (London: School of Oriental and African Studies, University of London), 1991.

Chapter 5: *Feudalism: Comparative Studies*, ed. Edmund Leach, S. N. Mukherjee, John Ward (Sydney: Sydney Association for Studies in Society and Culture), 1985.

Chapter 6: An earlier version appeared in *South East Asia Research*, 2.1 (1994), pp. 64–90.

Chapter 7: *Perceptions of the Past in Southeast Asia*, ed. Anthony Reid and David Marr (Singapore: Heinemann Educational Books (Asia) Ltd. for the Asian Studies Association of Australia), 1979.

Chapter 8: *Journal of Asian Studies*, 35.2 (1976), pp. 203–20. Reprinted with permission of the Association for Asian Studies, Inc.

Chapter 9: An earlier version appeared in volume 2 of *Proceedings*, Seventh IAHA Conference (Bangkok: Chulalongkorn University, 1979), pp. 927–70.

Chapter 10: Published for the first time in this volume.

Chapter 11: An earlier version appeared in *National Identity and Its Defenders: Thailand Today*, ed. Craig J. Reynolds (Chiang Mai: Silkworm Books), 2002.

Epilogue: An earlier version appeared in *Southeast Asian Identities: Culture and the Politics of Representation in Indonesia, Malaysia, Singapore, and Thailand*, ed. Joel S. Kahn (Singapore: Institute of Southeast Asian Studies), 1998. Portions are reproduced here with permission of the Institute of Southeast Asian Studies.

STUDYING SOUTHEAST ASIA

1

A New Look at
Old Southeast Asia

What interest do today's historians have in studying early Southeast Asia? What are they looking for in the early past? An essay by F. R. Ankersmit, in which he talks about what the modern reader brings to evidence from the past, serves as a point of departure for my answer. Rather than labor at accumulating more and more evidence about the past, historians should reflect on the difference between our own mentality and that of an earlier period. The past acquires point and meaning "only through confrontation with the mentality of the later period in which the historian lives and writes." The experience of confronting this mentality Ankersmit calls "the historical sensation," "which is accompanied by the complete conviction of genuineness, truth" (Ankersmit 1989: 146). "A phase in historiography has perhaps now begun," he says, "in which meaning is more important than reconstruction and genesis."

> The wild, greedy, and uncontrolled digging into the past, inspired by the desire to discover a past reality and reconstruct it scientifically, is no longer the historian's unquestioned task. We would do better to examine the result of a hundred and fifty years' digging more attentively and ask ourselves more often what all this adds up to. The time has come that we should think about the past, rather than investigate it.
>
> (Ankersmit 1989: 152)

Many historians, particularly of early Southeast Asia, would question Ankersmit's bold assertion that the reconstruction of what has happened in the past is no longer the historian's unquestioned task. The thrill of discovery is a motivation of intellectual endeavor not to be sneered at, and scholarship always relishes new data. Early Southeast Asian historiography has been all the better for a little digging, real digging in the case of historical archaeology (e.g., Bulbeck 1992; Manguin 1993).

Anticipating the criticism that he devalues fact-finding in the historian's craft, Ankersmit quickly affirms that historical truth and reliability are not obstacles to a more meaningful historiography. But he does argue that the metaphorical dimension in historiography has now become more powerful than the literal or factual dimensions, forcing the historian to confront the incongruity between present and past. The focus is on the language used to mediate the past in order to transcend the difference in mentalities. Attending to the way the past is textualized leads the historian to think about the activity of remembering and to be conscious of the historical sensations that arise from confrontation with earlier mentalities.

The *Cambridge History of Southeast Asia* devotes three hefty chapters to early history but pays little attention to the activity of remembering, apart from the first chapter, "The Writing of Southeast Asian History," written by John Legge (Tarling 1992). A survey of historical writing in European languages from prehistoric to modern times, this chapter tells of late-colonialist historiography; the debate in the early 1960s about the autonomy of Southeast Asian history; the influence of the social sciences on historians of Southeast Asia; and various other paradigms, conceptual models, and theories, including poststructuralism and deconstruction, all of which have had a bearing on the writing of Southeast Asian history. By entrenching itself in the conventional distinction between history and historiography that is being vigorously questioned by the theoretical interventions of cultural studies, feminism, poststructuralism, and postcolonialism, the *Cambridge History* closes off scholarly debate about the nature of the historian's enterprise. Approaches, paradigms, and models are put to one side in order to pave the way for the consolidation of knowledge that is unambiguously accountable.

A central question not confronted in the *Cambridge History* has to do with who is doing the remembering as much as what is to be remembered. Is it really possible, for example, to survey this field of knowledge without taking into account the histories of early Southeast Asia in vernacular languages? Are vernacular histories simply sources for European-language history, culturally delimited and therefore culturally relativized perceptions of the past? Does knowledge about early Southeast Asia in English pretend to know more than what Southeast Asians themselves can know? Southeast Asia, mostly a Euro-Japanese construct, has only recently become a domain meaningful for study within the region where national histories have been of primary concern. The regional bloc, the Association of Southeast Asian Nations, which now includes all of the nation-states, has prompted one Western historian to argue for Southeast Asia as an indigenous concept, but this state-level identity has not displaced older skepticism about the meaning of Southeast Asia as a label for an academic field (Reid 1999; Keyes 1992).

History has been important to nation-building within Southeast Asia no less than in other regions of the world. The classical kingdoms located in the Red River Delta of Vietnam, Pagan in Burma, Angkor in Cambodia, Sukhothai in Thailand, and Majapahit in Java are woven into the narratives of the modern nation-states of the region. Their material remains are sites for the production of myths about the nation-state: its long pedigree; a heritage of which citizens can be proud; a glorious past to impress the international tourist. A certain grandeur attaches to the ruins of these kingdoms, a grandeur whose history is traceable to the French, British, and Dutch colonial archaeological services. After independence the fledgling nations used this knowledge to identify noble pasts for themselves.

The age of the state, the longevity of settlement sites, and the inventiveness of early bronze or ceramic technologies have been of vital importance to contemporary national communities, an importance that is translated into issues for today's scholars. Inside the many linguistic worlds of the region, there exists a politics of early Southeast Asian history, as Southeast Asian nationals in universities, the national archaeological services, and public life debate the construction and meanings of the early past they have inherited. Researchers may pit new archaeological and ethnographic data against nationalist historiography. This has been happening in Thailand, for example, where scholars have argued that the Zhuang people of Kwangsi, in southern China (significantly, outside the boundaries of the Thai nation-state), possess the "oldest" culture, predating the period of contact with Sinic and Indic Asia (Srisakr and Pranee 1993). Debates about ancient technology and settlement can stir emotion, and memory of even the distant past can be hurtful.

I recall a conversation in 1969 in Bangkok with a young Mon man from Burma who was agitating for a separate Mon state. Wanting to show off my knowledge of the sixteenth century, when the Burmese ruler King Bayinnaung swept southward and imperialized the Mon principalities in lower Burma, I managed to display a total lack of sensitivity to ancient historical wounds by asking the Mon man his opinion of Bayinnaung. The reply was as ruthless as it was concise, as if Bayinnaung were towering over us with a sword poised to strike. "We hate him," said the Mon youth. Do such emotions and polemics belong in the field of early Southeast Asian history? It would seem from what has been produced so far that they rarely have been included. Academic history in Western universities tends to regard contentious debates within Southeast Asian public cultures as impediments to the scientific collection of data.

Do older Southeast Asian discourses of the past or oral traditions about foundation heroes have a place in modern historical science, where fact is judiciously separated from the collective memory of the community? By older discourses, I mean perspectives on the past lodged in earlier times. I do not have the linguistic resources to deal adequately here with the indigenous historiographies that could be brought to bear in answering this question. A volume of 1979, self-consciously preoccupied with the questions about Southeast Asian historiographies, contained articles by Charnvit Kasetsiri, Supomo, and O. W. Wolters that addressed some of these historiographies (Reid and Marr 1979), and Wolters's work has been largely concerned with older discourses of the past (e.g., Wolters 1976, 1988). But generally I find that European-language historiography, particularly that of Western scholars, is reluctant to incorporate indigenous, older historiographies.

So just how is Ankersmit's plea to think about the past rather than investigate it to be translated in practical terms to early Southeast Asian historical writing in English? The quantity of early history scholarship and its vitality in Southeast Asia itself offer a clue that early Southeast Asian historiography helps to define the contours of Southeast Asian studies as a field of knowledge. As I hope to show, there is a mutually validating relationship in this scholarship between knowledge and region, and the most fruitful way of discussing the historical writing is to look at the way it authenticates Southeast Asia as a region of study and a field of knowledge. This motivation to authenticate Southeast Asia as a region and field of study is connected to modern, contemporary anxieties about authenticity. I want now to look closely at the preoccupations in this historical writing about origins, agency, and difference, for it is these three historical sensations, to use Ankersmit's language, that help today's historian to write with conviction. By framing the discussion in terms of origins, agency, and difference, I hope to establish an understanding of what the historiography purports to say and of why the historiography of early Southeast Asia has been paradigmatic for the study of later periods.

Origins

The discipline of history, like the disciplines of geology or archaeology, in which time is a variable, is a discourse about origins. Colonial knowledge of Southeast Asia produced by the Dutch, French, and British archaeological services appropriated the entire colonized entity, especially the ancient past, where the origins of the colonized entity resided. In the post–World War II period, as new nations emerged from independence movements, the concern for origins in Western historiography helped to give voice to the "birth" of those new nations. At the same time, to provide a pedigree for the independent nation-state, Southeast Asian nationalist historiographies exploited colonial knowledge that had done so much to pursue, locate, and document the state's origins.

In the face of this complicity of colonial and nationalist historiography in documenting origins, modern history textbooks more often than not see early Southeast Asia as an originating tradition or system that was disabled or thrown out of alignment by European intrusion, which in turn marks the onset of the modern period (e.g., McCloud 1986; Steinberg 1987). This intrusion was once signified by the Portuguese conquest of Malacca in 1511, when Europeans first began to disturb indigenous patterns and continuities. Western premodern historiography, exemplified by A. J. S. Reid's study of what he calls "the age of commerce," emphasizes this European rupture now more than ever, and, in fact, Reid pushes the symbolic date of rupture back into the fifteenth century (Reid 1988b).

Historians of early Southeast Asia strive to transcend the European rupture to find the echt Southeast that exists on the other side of the European divide. Terms such as "dawn," "birth," and "origins" are not uncommon in the titles of works on early history. In this light, the historian's desire to return to a past as yet untrammeled by European intervention may have resulted in an overly benign view of early Southeast Asia. This was a time when the region seemingly experienced little conflict and was not so warlike nor so ridden by social, economic, and environmental problems as in more modern periods. The return to the early past involves a search for origins that will enable Southeast Asia to "write back" against the European intrusion. Early Southeast Asian historiography is thus engaged in a postcolonial and an anti-colonial project.

What are the elements of this original, this echt Southeast Asia? French and Dutch Oriental scholarship, each of which has its own genealogy of origins, bequeathed to Anglophone historiography the notion of a cultural matrix along a broad band stretching from pre-Aryan India through island and mainland Southeast Asia into southern China. An important element in the matrix was bronze technology, and so the Dong Son culture-complex with its famous bronze drums took a prominent place in efforts to define what was distinctive about the region. The French epigrapher and historian George Coedès made a fundamental contribution to this notion of the cultural matrix by endorsing a cultural substratum that featured wet-rice technology, important roles for women, and other distinctive social features and mythologies (Coedès 1968: 8–9). Of course, Coedès was not solely responsible for formulating the features of this cultural matrix, but his willingness to speak of "this unity of culture" underpinned the consolidation of Southeast Asia as a field of study.

In a brief, stimulating essay, Paul Mus first wrote in 1933 about "a religion of the monsoon zone of Asia," the fundamentals of which lay in worship of the energies of the soil personified in a god. The chief, or delegate of the human community, was the medium of the divinity, and "in him, by delegation, resides the power which assures the fertility of animals and plants, and in general the good fortune of the group" (Mus 1975: 15). For Mus, the cult of the god of the soil, which he identified as male, embodied an interdependence between the soil, divinity, and authority over the human community that ran deep in Southeast Asian culture.

The notion of a Southeast Asian cultural matrix or cultural substratum has never died and has continued to be a linchpin in the formation of knowledge about Southeast Asia. Wolters called the first chapter of his 1982 volume "Some Features of the Cultural Matrix" (Wolters 1999). The lineage of this matrix is plain in H. L. Shorto's reconstruction from fragmentary sources of the sociopolitical organization of the Mons, the early mainland people responsible for transmitting wet-rice technology and Theravada Buddhism to later arrivals such as the Burmese and Siamese. In two densely packed articles, Shorto (1963, 1967) examined the Mon prototype for the Burmese spirit cult of the thirty-two *nat*, a cult that drew together divinity, territory, and political authority. Relying on analogies with Chinese and Cham cults, and picking up on Mus's suggestive essay, Shorto proposed that the Mon cults were sites where human communities tapped the spiritual powers of deceased ancestors. Shorto saw the local cults as units that were transformed into "higher" forms of political organization. The Indic numerological framework (thirty-two or thirty-six) functioned as a design for the integration of clan- or lineage-based groups into more complex centralized polities. Because of the widespread cluster of elements in the cult—kinship, ancestor worship, and territorial control—Shorto speculated that the Indic manifestations of the cult were transformations of older politico-cultural forms. Other examples of cultural processes that condense this cluster of elements defining the cultural matrix abound in the literature. Stanley O'Connor has ingeniously decoded a puzzling sculpture at Candi Sukhuh in central Java by suggesting how the stone relief may be read as depicting spiritual transmutation. As two men forge a weapon, they engage in a rite of ancestor worship for the liberation of souls (O'Connor 1985).

This notion that an indigenous cultural matrix gave identity to the region is to be found in historiography from the eastern to the western limits of Southeast Asia. Arakanese society was receptive to Indian religion, because it "was familiar in its substratum of beliefs developed in the same monsoon-dominated environment" (Gutman 1976: 320). In his deconstruction of the "Indianization of Southeast Asia" as a confusion of categories, Ian Mabbett suggested that the dichotomy between an autonomous, local Southeast Asia and a civilizing, Indic culture was a false one (Mabbett 1977a). But the indigenous cultural matrix, expressed as general "features" or as the "substratum," persists. In the Western Visayas, animism is seen to have affinities with Coedès's cultural substratum, Mus's religion of monsoon Asia, and Shorto's territorial cults (McCoy 1982). The importance of genealogy has been suggested as one of the autochthonous elements, Khmer kingship being a case in point. In putting forward claims to the throne, claimants used matrilineal as well as patrilineal kin relations to gain the widest possible network of allies and supporters (Kirsch 1976). A bilateral system of kinship reckoning gave women in the aristocracy special influence in dynastic politics, even if the throne itself was a male preserve.

The region encompassing Vietnam and southwestern China has been seen to mark a distinctive cultural-ecological continuum of a very different kind, "neither entirely Chinese nor completely Southeast Asian" (Tai 1988: 91). Keith Taylor, who has been a persistent critic of formulations that omit Vietnam from the formation of knowledge about Southeast Asia, proposed that Vietnamese animist cults were "folded into" a cult of royal authority in the eleventh century, which he calls "Ly dynasty religion," in a way that corresponds to the ancestor divinization/territory/chiefly authority nexus found elsewhere in Southeast Asia (Taylor 1986a, 1986b). The metaphor driving these analyses is stratigraphic. Underneath layers of subsequent—and foreign? —accretions lies a bedrock of the echt Southeast Asia. Moreover, it is this real Southeast Asia that provides the agency in historical processes.

Urbanism has also preoccupied early historians concerned with documenting origins. Ancient words in Southeast Asian languages, pre-Indic and pre-Sinic, that signify "center," "nucleus," or "settlement" and that later came to mean "capital" or "city" may be residues of Southeast Asian urbanism. I am thinking, for example, of Burmese *kharuin*, which also means "heartwood"; Thai *muang*, which meant "fortified settlement"; and Javanese *kraton* (royal residence), which derives from Austronesian *ratu* (or *datu*), meaning "chief." These terms refer to the core areas that gave rise to principalities, kingdoms, and empires. Pressure from the affiliated disciplines of anthropology and archaeology, in which urbanism was a favored paradigm in the 1960s and 1970s, pushed scholarship along certain lines. In the case of Srivijaya at Palembang, the presumed "lateness" of urbanization in insular Southeast Asia skewed attempts to fit archaeological series against written history (Bronson and Wisseman 1976). The first modern excavations for material evidence of Srivijaya failed to find anything significant. The history of Srivijaya, a maritime empire presumed to have been the first known large-scale state in island Southeast Asia, has been substantiated as a result of excavations that have themselves led to a new set of exciting questions (Manguin 1993).

The historical geographer Paul Wheatley, who pioneered the structural history of the Malay Peninsula from Chinese toponyms, outlined a schema for urban genesis in an essay that he later expanded into a book (Wheatley 1979, 1983). Using concepts from American social theory and comparative work on Africa, the Middle East, and Middle America, he came up with criteria for urbanism that suggested "urban imposition" for the Sino-Viet territories during the period of Chinese overlordship and "urban generation" for the Indic territories. Such a schema bifurcated Southeast Asia, thus excluding Vietnam from sharing the region's history. A critical review of Wheatley's 1983 book by Keith Taylor argued that Wheatley had misunderstood the degree of Sinicization experienced by early Vietnam and had denied Vietnamese historical agency (Taylor 1986b). In fact, Wheatley's schema of urban genesis was a way of getting at the problem of the state and its genesis. Some historians see urbanization as a feature of late state formation (Kulke 1991). Others are more skeptical that urbanization and state formation go together, preferring to see an upper limit to population growth beyond which settlements tended to fissure and disperse. This is certainly an argument that has been made for central and east Java (Christie 1991).

The question of state formation intervenes in Southeast Asian historiography in the early centuries A.D. because the history of the region, narrowly defined here as study of the past from documentary materials, begins when Southeast Asian polities come into view through the medium of sources that already bear traces of contact with India and China. The time before this moment is the region's prehistory, although the distinction between history and prehistory is an arbitrary one created by the specializations of modern knowledge.

Archaeology, the methodology used to study prehistory, is employed well into the historical period, often to support interpretations from written sources. Manguin's excavations at Palembang, studies of material remains on South Sulawesi, and Higham's archaeological analysis of Angkor to the end of the twelfth century may be read as a reply to Hutterer's criticism that archaeologists had yet "to break the logjam that has been obstructing access to the early social history of the Southeast Asian region" (Manguin 1993; Macknight 1993; Higham 1989). Hutterer once called on archaeologists to fit archaeological sequences to the narratives that historians fashion from chronicles, traveler accounts, inscriptions, and other written materials (1982). The disciplinary collaboration between prehistory and history is now a matter of course.

Prehistorians and historians alike have worked hard to define the moment when chiefdoms, "paramountcies," or "tribal societies" (Wheatley's terms, 1983) "on the verge of statehood" (Christie's phrase, 1990) crossed the threshold into "true states" (Bronson's term, 1977: 40). Understanding chiefdoms in the very early historical period is essential to understanding kingship later, at Angkor, for example, where the role of kings has been overstated (Vickery 1998, chap. 8). For Kenneth Hall, Funan was Southeast Asia's "first state" (1985, chap. 3). The question of the threshold is not specific to early Southeast Asia; comparative prehistory suggests there is a "structural cork" between the two phases (Miksic 1990: 92). Manguin's formulation is typically nuanced, stressing the long-term socioeconomic change that seems to have taken place. He speaks of economies crossing over the border between tributary modes of production and wider ranging networks connected to world economies (Manguin 1991: 54).

In the pre-Hispanic Philippines, the largest sociopolitical unit was the *barangay*, or village, over which the chief (*datu*) presided. The chief's status was determined locally, rather than by "attachment to a structure of authority emanating from another realm" (Rafael 1988: 141; Scott 1982: 96–126). Spanish descriptions of early Tagalog society do not mention "elaborate mythologies" connecting the cosmic and human orders or "meticulously compiled genealogies" that might privilege one group or family over others (Rafael 1988: 146). The *barangay* were politically autonomous until they were gradually but incessantly brought within reach of the colonial state apparatus. The vocabulary of state formation does not appear to be apposite for the pre-Hispanic Philippines, and this is one reason the Philippines often drops out of the premodern historiography of Southeast Asia.

The transition that historians have sought to document is not unlike the one traced for India as lineage society evolved into "state" (Thapar 1984). On the one hand, the vast comparative, conceptual literature on the relationship between trade and state formation that was popular in the 1970s (e.g., Webb 1975) has had an enduring impact on early Southeast Asian studies, leading to the proposition that early state formation was trade-dependent (Glover 1992; Hall 1985; Hall and Whitmore 1976; Kathirithamby-Wells and Villiers 1990). Burma is the exception that proves the rule (Aung-Thwin 1990). The more stimulating studies of what was once called Indianization (e.g., Mabbett 1977a; Wolters 1974) emphasized that exchange networks were highly valued not only because they led to the accumulation of wealth but also because they acted as hubs for the spread of knowledge and ideas as well as of goods and raw materials. The trade routes served as a communications net along which material objects traveled to stimulate artistic innovation. Religious images might be bartered and thereafter become models for local artisans to copy and modify. Some of the exchanges that took place undoubtedly enhanced prestige, status, and power and came to have political consequences. Another source of the trade-state formation connection was late-colonial writing—Dutch historiography, for example, with its distinctive economistic orientations (van Leur 1967). But the relationship between state and trade, between king and merchant, was not unambiguous. It was not always and everywhere mutually reinforcing. The two had "a conflictive rapport," and out of this conflictive environment arose trade-based political myths that testify to the tension (Manguin 1991: 51).

An equally scientistic kind of explanation has been sought in a socioenvironmental "trigger" for the mechanisms that transformed chiefdoms into kingships. Wheatley suspected that this trigger was socioenvironmental stress manifested in agricultural innovation such as wet *padi* as a staple grain crop (Wheatley 1983: 277–78). Prehistorians still associate wet-rice cultivation with a certain level of social integration and military power throughout Southeast Asia— in south Sulawesi, for example (Macknight 1983). Wet-rice cultivation required an intensification of cultivation and a greater relative investment in agricultural labor, which led, in turn, to competition for wet *padi,* social differentiation, and hierarchy.

In a stimulating essay that for a long time was ignored by early historians, Michael Dove challenged the thesis about wet *padi,* arguing that wet rice does not favor the individual cultivator and could not in itself trigger the change that took place (Dove 1985). Cultivators did not change to wet rice because it was more productive per capita. It was not. They would have gradually changed to wet rice because ancient rulers held out the offer of statuses, honors, and other induce-ments to local overlords to make the land more productive per unit area and thus more remunerative for exploitation by the court.

Historians who dared to offer an explanation for the "structural cork" are few and far between, but they have been rewarded. When Kulke charted the trajectory of the early Southeast Asian state through its local, regional, and imperial phases (i.e., chiefdom, early kingdom, and empire), his explanation was flexible enough to be placed as the initial essay in an important volume of essays on the classical period (Kulke 1986). But his thesis stressing synthesis, comparison (Java, Cambodia, Burma), and comprehensive generality was largely undercut by the essays that followed it, although he maintained his interpretative framework of consecutive phases in later work (1991). However, his discussion of the dynamics of local-regional-central relations in their details was more interesting than the proposition that the core areas of early Southeast Asia had undergone an "overall (though not homogeneous) process of state formation" (Kulke 1986: 5). What gets lost in a framework that conceives time developmentally is the sense that, even in the early stage, tiny centers had a sense of geopolitical significance and looked outward to the world, and that, even in the later stage, empires took care to pay homage to the local loyalties that rooted them to a specific place and sustained them.

Kulke's analysis also betrays a preoccupation with structuralist formulations and evolutionism typical of European scholarship (Kulke 1986: 17). The same can be said of Renée Hagesteijn's structural-functionalism, even as she tries to adapt it to Southeast Asian cultural realities (Hagesteijn 1989; Reynolds 1992). Historians have been encouraged to avoid such structuralism, because its formalism renders opaque the cultural characteristics that give the region its character, a view that is as distinctively American as the other is European (Bentley 1986). Substituting "spiral" for linear trajectory as the shape of early Southeast Asian time further complicates the geometric metaphors (Aung-Thwin 1991).

Christie's revisionist readings of Old Javanese inscriptions have been healthy for early history by taking issue with the way the state has been studied, for she has directed attention to wider aspects of early Southeast Asian social formations. Using the epigraphic evidence to illuminate social structure and the religious and social duties of officials, her interpretive methods have strong links with a generation of Dutch scholarship influenced by structural anthropology (e.g., de Casparis 1986; Pigeaud 1977; van Naerssen 1977). Her extensive work on *sima* grants—transfers of tax rights by the king or local petty ruler, which were the basis for religious foundations—have provided a much-needed social dimension to early Javanese history (Christie 1983; Jones 1984, chap. 2). This work articulates the way religion, economics, and politics cluster together, a conjunction that modern historical science tends to overlook. It would seem that the temple— more to the point, the foundation grant—not the state, is the category that repays ardent inquiry. It was through the *sima* grants that the early Javanese kingdom took its form and function—spread out, yet strong enough and impressive enough in its representations to make local authorities mindful of its presence.

The thrust of Christie's research was to broaden and deepen the focus of study beyond the royal base (*kraton*). She proposed that the early Javanese state was a dispersed entity. Moreover, the "diffuseness and mobility of political and economic foci" extended down to the Javanese village (*wanua*) (Christie 1991: 31). The dispersed nature of early Javanese society stemmed from the dynamics of demography, once the population reached a certain level. Excess population did not aggregate into urban centers but, instead, formed into small residential units, a process that was underway in central Java as early as the ninth century (1991: 34–35). Although Christie placed her work in the context of early state formation, the thrust of it was to push dynastic events to one side and to display an almost granular texture of early settlement and social relations.[1] A volume of translations from the epigraphy published in 1984 allows the English-language reader to sense the richness of the early Javanese material (Jones 1984). There are clearly methodological obstacles to using epigraphy or the Javanese and Balinese *kakawin*—epic poetry written in Indic meters—to write social history. For example, the presence or absence of women may be a function of a highly stylized genre rather than an index of social fact. Historians are now confronting such methodological questions directly (e.g., Creese 1993).

An example of a study in which the modern historical imagination plays self-consciously with the memory of the origins of the Southeast Asian nation-state is Keith Taylor's *The Birth of Vietnam* (Taylor 1983). The book's title is not merely one conceived by the publisher to attract readers but reflects a particular kind of interest in early Vietnamese history, the real Vietnam that emerged after its Chinese overlordship. In this reading, the Chinese phase, however important in shaping Vietnamese state and society, was primarily a foreign phase. "Independence," the title of Taylor's last chapter, finally triumphed in the tenth century, and a genuinely Vietnamese state emerged. By the late fourteenth century, Vietnamese "wild" histories were celebrating cultural confidence and redrawing boundaries in light of Vietnamese, rather than Chinese, proprietary interests (Ungar 1986).

What is at stake in this metaphor of birth is nothing less than the self-determination of a Southeast Asian people as the integument of foreign overlordship falls away or, as was the case from 1946 to 1975, is thrown off by force. In this modernist reading of Vietnam's ancient history, a reading that vivifies the ancient Vietnamese past in recognizable terms, the spirit of Taylor's account reminds me of Gordon Luce, who found in the early history of Pagan "a thrilling moment of birth and awakening" when the seed of the modern national community was planted (Luce 1969: 97; Reynolds 1992: 149–50). Similarly, Michael Aung-Thwin subtitles his study of Pagan *The Origins of Modern Burma* (1985). There is no gainsaying the present-mindedness of this enterprise, undertaken in the long afterglow of tumultuous independence movements. Early Southeast Asian historians affirm their duty to reconstruct ancient societies, because these societies bequeathed a sociocultural heritage to the nation-building process (Kulke 1986: 17). The study of early Southeast Asian history involves an emotional investment, as historians reclaim a past overridden and devalued by Western imperialism.

Agency

The identification of Southeast Asian agency is closely linked to the trope of origins, whether it be of kingship, cities, or state that motivates the writing of early history. In discussing the way prehistorians and historians have configured the Southeast Asian cultural substratum, I have already suggested that these scholars look for the echt Southeast Asia underneath layers of influence. One of the central problems of origins is that they may have been Indic or Sinic and hence inauthentic. In a word, they are "colonial," but not Western colonial, as anything from outside is deemed external and therefore "colonial." The key processes in the historiography that give voice to agency are "domestication," "vernacularization," "indigenization," and "localization." These are the names historians give to the processes by which Southeast agency may be traced. These processes are the traces of Southeast Asian agency, the consequences of Southeast Asian will. They are evidence of the capacity of Southeast Asian societies to shape change. The stress on localizing agency shifts the focus onto Southeast Asians and their future, away from their suspect origins as mere borrowers and culture brokers.

The idea of the autonomy of Southeast Asian history has a long and distinguished pedigree, its most famous expression in English being an essay of 1961 by the late John Smail. The essay, long hailed as seminal, has been highly regarded largely because it has been fundamental to the rationale and funding strategies for Southeast Asian area studies in the United States (Smail 1961). A fundamental aim of the enterprise has been to differentiate Southeast Asian studies from South Asian or East Asian studies. Mindful of the false dichotomies and confusions of the terms Europe-centric and Asia-centric, Smail nevertheless was intent on encouraging "a general domestic history of the area" that still remained hidden. In doing so, he called for attention not only to "the autonomous and mutually exclusive thought-worlds" of Southeast Asians in all periods of their history but also to the thought-world of the modern Southeast Asian historian writing about her or his own past. Although "modern Southeast Asia" is explicit in Smail's title and the "autonomy" of Southeast Asia has continued to be a motive force for all periods of historical inquiry, early Southeast Asian historiography has had a special role to play in documenting this autonomy.

But Smail did not invent the idea of autonomy, and it is hardly coincidental that, as a student of Indonesian history who knew Dutch, his first footnote is to J. C. van Leur, the historical sociologist.[2] Basically, Smail, who was critical of van Leur but also inspired by him, was calling on modern Southeast Asian historians of his time to finish what van Leur had begun. Speaking about the history of Indonesia, Van Leur had uttered an eloquent and memorable statement that forged a connection between origins and agency. Foreign cultures and world religions—Hinduism, Buddhism, Islam—had, said van Leur, exerted "weak" influence.

> They did not bring any fundamental changes in any part of Indonesian social and political order. The sheen of the world religions and foreign cultural forms is a thin and flaking glaze; underneath it the whole of the old indigenous forms has continued to exist—with many sorts of gradations appearing, of course, according to the cultural level.
>
> (van Leur 1967: 95)

The operative terms here are "sheen," "thin and flaking glaze," "the whole," "old indigenous forms," and "cultural level." The idea that world religions and foreign cultural forms are a mere veneer, "a thin and flaking glaze," has been modified, refined, and even challenged. And van Leur's writings have been subjected to trenchant criticism for embodying the very Eurocentrism for which he criticized others (Biros 1992). In an early critique of the historical discourse Smail inherited from van Leur, Tony Day pointed out how van Leur's image of the ship entrenches the exteriority of the Western observer. From the ship's deck, the Westerner—sea captain, colonial adminis- trator, or twentieth-century scholar—peers through the gray and undifferentiated fog of colonial historiography to pick out the multi- tudinous world of Southeast Asia as the eye wanders "from one delightfully exotic fact to the next." The Dutch scholar's Orientalist theoretics of representation entrenched the exteriority of the Western observer and thus worked against the Southeast Asian autonomy he sought to establish (Day 1984: 149–50).

Van Leur's formulation is still demonstrably present in how historians think about the early period, for it brilliantly employs two metaphors that contradict each other. One is the stratigraphic one ("the cultural level") I have suggested is omnipresent in early historical writing. The other is the inside-outside Southeast Asia distinction that is embedded in the historiography. The aim was to displace colonial historiography—Smail spoke of van Leur's having "reversed" that historiography—which had once seen the destiny of Southeast Asian societies determined by the British, French, or Dutch East India trading companies, administrations of governors-general, and colonial regimes. Southeast Asia and its history would no longer be the creatures of colonial will and management. Southeast Asian agency would "write back" against the constructions of colonial historiography. Indeed, as is clear from van Leur's statement, Southeast Asian agency was required to write back against any and all external "influences," including Sinic and Indic.

The question of agency in early Southeast Asian historiography intersected with debates in the social sciences generally, particularly in structural anthropology, which were informed by Marxist problematics of agency (e.g., Comaroff 1982: 145–46). The debates centered on the question of structure versus subject. To what extent did human will (or consciousness), individually or collectively, contribute to the making of history? To express Smail's argument in this other language, one could say that autonomy of another thought-world or culture was a metaphor for agency. In historiography these problematics have generally concerned the colonial and postcolonial periods, but the axis along which the debates have taken place—"traditional" society versus "capitalism" centered elsewhere that renders "traditional society" dependent—is clearly visible in the early historiography of Southeast Asia.

What is the character of this Southeast Asian agent, this prime mover, that has the capacity to work change? H. G. Q. Wales called it "local genius" that was alive and active, particularly in Java, Champa, and Cambodia. The pre-Indic civilization "survived in the 'subconscious' of the Indianized peoples," and "the people responded to this stimulus" of Indic cultural influences "in the light of their local genius, the continuing effect of their repressed previous civilization" (1957: 111). Wales proposed a theory of influence to explain why some foreign cultural elements survived while others were sloughed off (Wales 1951: 196–97). The tangled theories from Freudian and behavioral psychology were too mechanically applied for Western historians, and his work is not taken very seriously today. But "local genius" lives on. In 1984, the government of the Republic of Indonesia sponsored a forum on "Local Genius and Indonesian Culture" in connection with its efforts to promote a clearer definition of national identity (Sudradjat 1991). In Southeast Asia "local genius" is taken to be something that needs to be both respected and nurtured. In the region today it is represented by local knowledge, a buzzword that has become the rationale for a rhetoric of self-reliance in rural development and autonomy in the harsh conditions of the globalizing epoch.

The notion of "layers" of influence, the "inside-outside" dichotomy, and the all-important role of "the local" are as prominent as ever in the early historiography. Even if not named as such, "local genius" has been a regular motif in political, economic, and cultural studies of the earlier period. The definitive work on indigenous monetary systems to A.D. 1400 anticipates its conclusion in its subtitle, *The Development of Indigenous Monetary Systems*. Coinage is everywhere localized, with a dichotomy throughout much of Southeast Asia between local valuational systems for exchanges and other systems for extralocal trade (Wicks 1992). Wolters has contributed to the development of the theme of localization as much as anyone, from his now classic study on the origins of Srivijaya originally published a half-dozen years after Smail's essay to his 1982 essay on the general features of Southeast Asian history and culture and his work on Vietnam. The success of Srivijaya stemmed from the substitution of Indonesian products of comparable value for Persian products bound for the Chinese market. The shippers as well as the products were increasingly Indonesian (Wolters 1974, chaps. 9–10). Wolters, once a colonial official who as an academic historian did his part to reconstruct the echt Southeast Asia, here implanted an element of Southeast Asian cunning in his reconstruction of early Indonesian commercial strategies.

With an emphasis on process and consequence rather than on agency, as such, Wolters later put forward what amounts to a theoretical statement about how local cultural statements can be studied to see the effects of Southeast Asian agency.

The term "localization" has the merit of calling our attention to something else outside the foreign materials. One way of conceptualizing "something else" is as a local statement, of cultural

interest but not necessarily in written form, into which foreign
elements have retreated.

(1999: 57)

The historian's task is to "broach a process for restoring the effects of
foreign fragments when they retreat into local cultural ambiences"
(Wolters 1999: 65).

Wolters here pulls back from what Wales was eager to talk about,
namely, the character of Southeast Asian agency. Instead, in a
postmodernist turn, we are directed to the "local statement," which
may or may not be written. It may be a Visnu image on peninsular
Siam, or the Indic bas reliefs on the ruins of a temple in eastern
Java, or the Chinese legal code in fourteenth-century Vietnam. The
rather backhanded way Wolters phrased the concept—"a local statement ... into which foreign elements have retreated"—betrayed his
reluctance to be too specific about the mechanics of the process or,
in contrast to Wales, the psychology of the agent(s) responsible for
the process. He was taking care to avoid the sloppy language that
often accompanies discussion of Southeast Asian cultural diversity—
"mixing," "blending," "syncretism," "eclecticism"—which makes a
complex historical process sound like a fisherman's catch. Localization became for Wolters one of the "distinctive" features of the
region. In early times, Sanskrit or Chinese loanwords did not just
rename existing categories, although they were often admitted into
local languages precisely because they did this and thus elevated the
status of existing categories. They also wedged themselves into the
structure of local languages and created new spaces, new relationships.
Early historians can use the process of localization to "write back"
against the foreignness—of "influences" or of evidence—that must
constantly be negotiated because of the nature of the sources for
early history.

In the case of the early historiography of the Philippines, this
"writing back" against what is foreign is particularly problematic. No
indigenous accounts antedate the Spanish conquest of the sixteenth
century. Spanish missionary writers of the early seventeenth century
described a local script called *baybayin*, a supplement to learning the
correct voicing of Tagalog. Although the script never completely
disappeared during colonial rule and there is a "wealth of documentary

testimony spread across four centuries," the Spanish marginalized *baybayin* by introducing romanized phonetic writing as a medium for conversion to Christianity (Rafael 1988: 44–45). The Spanish regarded the script as "inadequate, incomplete and unintelligible." The monumental work of William Henry Scott was devoted to the issue of Filipino agency, to the possibilities and limitations of writing the "history of the inarticulate" (Scott 1982, 1984).

The question of agency has also been acute with respect to Vietnamese historiography, because of Chinese political domination and the use of Chinese language in the Vietnamese court. Modern Vietnamese-language historiography has pushed the dating of a distinctively Vietnamese polity back to the seventh century B.C., centuries before the Chinese incorporated northern Vietnam into their provincial control in the interest of establishing an authentic, pre-Chinese polity (Ungar 1986: 184). After long exposure to Chinese overlordship, the Vietnamese went through a period of conscious "desinicization and nationalization of Vietnamese culture," in the words of a modern Vietnamese historian (Tran 1986: 272). Ceramic production during the Ly and Tran dynasties (eleventh to fourteenth centuries) can be seen to demonstrate that Vietnamese culture was anything but the "pale reflection of Chinese culture" earlier studies presumed it to be (Guy 1986).

The very ability of Southeast Asian societies to bend foreign cultural elements to their own use, to domesticate them, to resist them, or to localize them brings to notice a related feature attributed to the earlier period. This feature is adaptability. Again, examples from Vietnam are instructive. The Vietnamese succession in the later Ly period was open to all sons of the emperor, and the royal clan admitted privileged members of the aristocracy. Whitmore labels this kinship system "fluid" and sees this fluidity as characteristic of Southeast Asia as a whole (Whitmore 1986: 125). The unspoken opposite of this attribute is the supposed rigidity and inflexibility of the Chinese system. China was a severe and stern teacher, says Tran Quoc Vuong (1986: 272). But the Confucianism we find at the late-fourteenth-century Vietnamese court, for example, is a Vietnamese Confucianism. "The Confucian canon had always been fragmented in Vietnam to lend weight to specific Vietnamese statements about themselves" (Wolters 1988: 39). In order to fragment the canon, the Vietnamese Confucian advisers had the capacity to resist its all-encompassing system of relationships and to utilize it in a way that was meaningful to them.

Southeast Asian agency is seen to have the capacity, the inventiveness, the genius to adapt, and this capacity is what makes localization, indigenization, and vernacularization work. One even gets the sense that historians are attributing tolerance or adaptability to the region's character, although these words might give the impression of a receptor-like passivity if used in a lazy manner. But it does seem that this attribute of tolerance is a clear manifestation of the Western liberal imagination projected onto the region's past.

The source of this tolerance, in the archipelago and in the mainland port polities upriver from the coasts, stems from an outward-looking attitude and openness. Importance was attached to being up-to-date or contemporary. "Now" was the time that mattered. In Wolters's words, "The possibility of being 'up-to-date' was often linked to and sustained by the sense of being an integral part of the whole of the known 'world' rather than merely belonging to one's own patch of territory" (Wolters 1994: 4). Such an attitude was hospitable to merchants and overseas trade, and Manguin has used Malay folktales and histories to testify to it (1991). There was always, it seems, a dynamic interdependence with the rest of the world typified in the great trading empires (Biros 1992: 464). One may detect here quite a shift from the earlier notion of autonomous history, if that means a separate history. The adaptability of Southeast Asian agency that saw itself as part of the whole known world could make sense of just about anything that was originally "foreign."

I have traced the genealogy of Southeast Asian agency and various signifiers that express it not to be reductive, nor to suggest that the concern for agency has inhibited scholarship or constrained inquiry. On the contrary. The persistent appeals to local inventiveness, if now much altered from Wales's confused formulations nearly forty years ago, and the call for "autonomous history," which has left its traces in the historiography but is also expressed differently nowadays, have been very productive. I have invoked agency to suggest that it has been instrumental in keeping the formation of knowledge about the early Southeast Asian past continuous and intact. The theme of indigenous agency has been essential to the project of defining Southeast Asia as a field of study.

Difference

It is through difference that Southeast Asian agency can be glimpsed and brought to life. The historian's task is to identify, document, and communicate differences among Southeast Asian societies or between a particular society and Western historical experience. While a line of inquiry may be driven by concepts and theories that come from social science or the literature on comparative civilizations (e.g., "state formation is trade-dependent" or "urban generation is stimulated by external cultures that are more complex"), the task of the historian of early Southeast Asia is to domesticate concepts in specific Southeast Asian contexts.

One obvious way this is done, by no means unique to early history, is to explicate terms in Old Mon, Old Javanese, medieval Chinese, Sanskrit, and so forth in indigenous inscriptions, chronicles, and foreign accounts. These are the terms italicized in the Anglophone historiography. Key terms for leadership, units of social organization, and religious terminology are examples of the kinds of things historians focus on in an effort to distinguish Southeast Asian experience and make it culturally specific. They are aids for the imagination to immerse itself in other worlds. Mabbett is at pains to show that *varna* in Angkor was hardly the same social category as it was in early India (1977b). Similarly, the English term "slave" misses out on the way early Cambodian "slavery" was embedded in relations of patronage and clienthood (Mabbett 1983). To call a tenth-century Javanese settlement a *wanua* is to evoke a pattern of population dispersal and a form of social organization that "village" does not quite capture (Christie 1991). Much of what Christie has had to say about the *sima* foundation grants also underscores this general point.

Enlarging the canvas, we can see this concern for culture-specific meanings in the way historians explain worldviews, kinship systems, religious orientations, and so forth. Keith Taylor advances the notion of "Ly dynasty religion" to persuade us that the Ly dynasty wielded a "peculiar type of authority" that was unlike the Chinese-style dynastic institution with its bureaucratic administration (Taylor 1986a: 141). Jim Fox argues that the early Javanese kinship system was Austronesian, not Indic (Fox 1986). Belief systems and cosmologies are vital indicators of Southeast Asian difference, as Michael Aung-Thwin has shown for old Burma (1985). In the phrase Khmer "Hinduism," the quotation marks tell us that some kind of change has been wrought that made Southeast Asia different from ancient India, as early Cambodian rulers and priests textualized Hinduism in their own environment (Wolters 1979b). Indeed, single terms, some of which are the phantom generalizations against which Wolters warned, become in Western scholarship windows through which we see early Southeast Asia. Mabbett's 1969 essay on the *devaraja* in early Khmer society was somewhat eclipsed by Kulke's 1978 study, but his proposition about what the term signified is characteristic of the early historian's efforts to contextualize categories by unpacking the meanings of words in ancient languages.

> We are better equipped to translate the language of Khmer religious symbolism if we regard it as the language of a society, employed to formulate ideas that were important to that society, rather than as the propaganda of a succession of megalomaniacs.
>
> (Mabbett 1969)

Here Mabbett has glossed *devaraja* as a keyword in "the language of Khmer religious symbolism," but his gloss draws us away from the word itself to an entire system of signifiers about connections between the divine and the human.

This particular comment on why it is important to distinguish early Cambodian kingship from caricatures of rulers that can creep into the historiography illustrates that the documentation of difference has an important polemical purpose. Like the "man of prowess" trope, Mabbett's gloss on *devaraja* may be read as a rebuttal of the Oriental despot that dates from the Western Enlightenment and can be traced through nineteenth- and twentieth-century European, especially Marxist, thought. Like the "man of prowess" trope, welcomed by historians, prehistorians, and archaeologists alike, Mabbett's gloss on *devaraja* shows how Western scholarship is still intent on writing against the stereotypes of an orientalizing knowledge of Southeast Asia. Mabbett, and Kulke even more so, have tried to cut the *devaraja* down to size and to give it cultural specificity rather than attribute to it powers to unify and integrate that it could not have possessed (e.g., Sedov 1978). The ancestral elements of the cult with the Indic name are manifestly embedded in the Cambodian cultural substratum, in the "common ideology" of peasants as well as the elite, which predated the "Sanskritic" tradition of the cult (Nidhi 1976). Thus "godkingship," the English calque of *devaraja*, must never be equated with "oriental despotism," insists Ian Mabbett (1985: 78).

In one sense, there is nothing exceptional in this concern for documenting difference in early Southeast Asian history. Other area studies, for that matter, must also meet demands to recognize difference by documenting cultural specificity. And all historians are trained to analyze what is particular and specific about the moment of the past that concerns them. Most historians take for granted that documenting difference is one of their essential tasks. But in the name of what is this difference being documented and specified? Despite Christie's criticism that indigenous concepts of the state such as *negara* and *mandala* reify long-standing Orientalist prejudices about distinct Eastern and Western mentalities, historians immersed in early source materials on the whole prefer such a vocabulary precisely because it keeps Southeast Asia distinct from other social formations. Glossing terms as keywords need not, they would argue, constitute an act of totalizing Southeast Asia as a distinct "civilization."

Nevertheless, I see the project of documenting Southeast Asian difference as part and parcel of the project of tracing origins and identifying agency. Transcending the period of European intervention in Southeast Asian life to document the echt Southeast Asia, pushing back the dates of the earliest polities, scrutinizing cultural products to discover how they belong to Southeast Asia and nowhere else: these all belong to the same enterprise.

Conclusion

I have taken refuge in Ankersmit's admonition to think about the past rather than investigate it, in part because space and my own technical limitations prevent me from doing otherwise. The next step would be to look into the dynamics of indigenous Southeast Asian historiography in the vernacular languages of the region. I do believe that in their eagerness to carve out a topic of expertise for themselves, early historians writing in English have often overlooked the connections their work has with lines of inquiry elsewhere in Southeast Asian studies and beyond. I have been suggesting that, while early Southeast Asian history attracts scholars with proficiency in old and difficult languages, the research protocols are driven by themes and polemics that pre-occupy historians of more modern periods. I have grouped these themes and preoccupations under the headings of origins, agency, and difference and tried to show how these emphases are discernible in the historiography of early Southeast Asia.

What is at stake in this enterprise is nothing less than the authenticity of Southeast Asia. The preoccupations with origins, agency, and difference have to do with the effort to authenticate Southeast Asia as a region and a field of study. As such, the effort is very much a Western, postcolonial project. A few Southeast Asian nationals have discovered Southeast Asia as a field of knowledge while studying in the West, and Singapore, whose academic pretensions have distinct colonial residues, boasts an Institute of Southeast Asian Studies devoted to Southeast Asian studies across the map. But, basically, the identity of Southeast Asia as a region and Southeast Asian studies as a field of knowledge are newly imported into Southeast Asia itself.

Just why authenticity should be such an abiding concern is a complex question of general interest outside of Southeast Asian studies. The philosopher Charles Taylor has proposed that authenticity is a moral ideal, prominent in modern society, that has been trivialized and demeaned even as it has been encouraged by certain tendencies in contemporary life. An ideal worth struggling to refine and aspire to in the effort to confront the "ever-deepening hegemony of instrumental reason," authenticity is expressed in our desires for self-exploration, self-discovery, and self-fulfillment. We strive for the ideal in a dialogic engagement with others in order to develop a unique and identifiable self. Through recognizing and accepting diversity, we come to have a clearer sense of our own identities. The rhetoric of difference and diversity is central to the contemporary culture of authenticity (Taylor 1991: 7). We cherish diversity, whether biological or cultural, for its value in authenticating the self.

Taylor's meditations are related to some of these themes. I see in the historiography of early Southeast Asia more than a pale reflection of the contemporary anxieties about authenticity of the self to which Taylor alludes. It would be simplistic to say that in their endeavors to authenticate early Southeast Asia historians are engaged in a project of self-exploration, self-discovery, and self-fulfillment, but at the same time, study of the early past is not driven purely by dispassionate inquiry. As is clear from some of this scholarship, the project of authenticating the ancient past is a feature of public culture within Southeast Asian societies today. The nation-state's origins; its capacity to act independently of outside "influences," whether it be with regard to human rights or trade; and its difference from others, its uniqueness, are all familiar themes in contemporary life, and it is little wonder that these themes have found their way into the historiography. There is nothing new in the collaboration between history and the nation-state.

We can see the connection between authenticity and knowledge formation when Southeast Asian studies is most self-conscious, such as when the academy reviews itself. At these moments, disciplinary, institutional, and funding pressures demand attention, and when the American academy, which has the critical mass of scholars and the funds, periodically publishes its deliberations, the results are quite specific to the American educational culture. It has been pointed out that, by European standards, "Southeast Asian studies in America is something of a freak" (Hirschman et al. 1992: 2). There is only one Southeast Asia center in the educational culture in which I work (Australia); elsewhere, "Asian studies" or "Oriental and African studies" may be the preferred institutional arrangement.

In one penetrating reassessment of Southeast Asian studies in America, participants expressed much concern about the "peripherality" of area studies, of how the disciplines will always marginalize area studies. What was interesting was the passionate call for the estab-lishment of Southeast Asian studies as "an intellectually viable interpretive community." Because of the "obvious diversity of historical and contemporary civilizations and cultures," there is a need for the "interpretive community" to generate and disseminate knowledge about this diverse region. The knowledge called for should supply "a set of indigenous texts that are recognized as classics," particularly religious and literary texts, in order to compensate for an absent "orientalist tradition." Is this to be a textual canon that authenticates the field of knowledge? Such knowledge should also "identify common patterns" in Southeast Asia (Hirschman et al. 1992: 60–62). Here is a statement explicitly expressing the mutual validation of regional identity and the formation of a field of study. Create the knowledge and the regional identity will take shape. Declare the region's existence as a patch of the earth's surface, and the knowledge will follow. Despite the fact that a 1989 assessment of Southeast Asian history in the United States failed to take note of early history as such (Lockhard 1989), and the American review barely makes mention of history at all (Hirschman et al. 1992), the sheer quantity of the early-history scholarship is an indication that early historiography helps to define the contours of Southeast Asian studies as a field of knowledge.

James Scott once opined that Southeast Asian studies has overemphasized stasis and continuity (Hirschman et al. 1992: 7). He thought the reason for this is that the source material and the foci of study have been overwhelmingly elitist and based on formal texts. Actually, the fundamental cause of the overemphasis on stasis and continuity is worry about holding the region and the field of study together. The famed diversity of Southeast Asia that defeats all attempts to unify it and sets teams of historians to work on books that can claim coverage of the region puts pressure on the academy to produce a certain kind of scholarly product that emphasizes lineages of development from early times.

The discipline of history, with its finely honed craft of documenting specificity, has been fundamental to building and maintaining Southeast Asia as a field of study. In its preoccupations with origins and agency, the historiography of early Southeast Asia has played a particularly important role. As Nordholt has put it, citing Ruth McVey, it was especially in the early and premodern period that "an interconnected and more coherent Southeast Asia was located" (Nordholt 2004: 42). But more thought could be given to where this body of knowledge has come from, what holds it together, and how it might be liberated for wider use. The implications of Donald Emmerson's essay (1984) on Southeast Asia as a contrived identity, reified by scholars, publishers, and educational institutions in the West, have never been pursued. This is doubtless because, notwithstanding the worries expressed in reviews of the region as a field of study, funding bodies, professional associations, and the federal government recognize Southeast Asia studies as a category.

Fields of inquiry are never naturally given, as John Comaroff has put it. "The question of the 'unit of study,' far from being a methodological nicety, is a consequential theoretical matter" (Comaroff

1982: 144). I suspect that the most trenchant critiques of Southeast Asian studies, the body of knowledge to which the early historiography has given so much, will come from the new anthropology and from cultural studies. This is already happening, as academics with little or no Southeast Asian-language training step onto the stage from what we think of as nowhere to make smart, useful remarks about what is happening in the region today. And it is already happening in the work of scholars new to "the field" (a concept I have tried to problematize here), who arrive with reading and interpretive methodologies that have been slow to gain ground precisely because they challenge the principles and strategies fundamental to the formation of knowledge about Southeast Asia. This new kind of history attends to how texts mean, whether they be songs, documents, inscriptions, or secondary sources, as well as to what they mean (e.g., Biros 1990, 1992).

The polemics of interpretation and the theoretics of representation thus exposed will call the project of authenticating Southeast Asia further into question, and the ensuing debate will generate a galaxy of questions that could make Southeast Asian studies more accessible to newcomers. One of the basic questions would be whether, in its energetic efforts to winnow out the echt Southeast Asia from the Eurocentric concepts that have encased it through the colonial and postcolonial periods, the early historiography has met Ankersmit's challenge that historians should be thinking about the meaning of the past rather than merely investigating it. I have tried in this essay to suggest that the historiography has already thrown up meanings. We might begin to reset the research agenda by dwelling on them skeptically for what they purport to tell us about ourselves as well as about the Southeast Asian past.

Notes

1.   Studies of early Burma and Cambodian society using a similar approach have built up a picture of social and economic life (Aung-Thwin 1976, 1979; Luce 1969; Mabbett 1977b, 1983).
2.   The long history of Dutch debates about agency in Indonesian history, especially with respect to Indic cultural history, are summarized in Sudradjat 1991: 25–35.

2

Paradigms of the
Premodern State

T he high-modernist state is a global phenomenon, an all-seeing, omnipotent entity that dominates societies everywhere in the world. This leviathan had its origins in changes wrought by the Enlightenment, when society was discovered and studied scientifically as an object separate from the state (Scott 1998: 91). One consequence of this attention during the Enlightenment was a critique of despotic power, and as far as what was known about Asia in the seventeenth century was concerned, this critique focused on the Oriental Despot.

Emerging from the Enlightenment, the works of Max Weber and Karl Marx have been central to study of the state and state-society relations in the fields of political theory, comparative politics, political sociology, and political anthropology. From Weber has come a definition of state that emphasizes the legitimate use of force over a given territory, an administrative apparatus regulated by legislation, and binding authority over all persons in the area of the state's jurisdiction. From Marx has come a concern for economic domination and class interests. While for Weber the state has an institutional form in its own right, for Marx the state is an epiphenomenon, an effect of class conflict that is illusory.

For historians of Southeast Asia, the state is elusive and difficult to define (Nordholt 1996, chap. 1; Vickery 1998: 322–23). Typically, state formation in the region's history is seen as something introduced from the outside by Western expansion in the colonial period (Nordholt 1996: 334). Nevertheless, social scientists have pursued the state and searched for its origins within the region. Where and when did the "first state" appear? Political scientists and political sociologists establishing a lineage of the modern nation-state have demanded an answer to this question from historians of earlier periods.

31

Yet, with its connotations of rationality, order, and omnipotence, "state" sets up false expectations when the term is applied to pre-modern Southeast Asia. The result of the search for "state" is often the discovery of an entity with shortcomings. In the words of an economic historian of the region, "states were characteristically weak" and exhibited a "bureaucratic and infrastructural primitiveness" (Elson 1997: 28, 33). Lacking both bureaucracy and infrastructure, premodern states were unable to assert themselves beyond the immediate environs of the royal base. To measure "strength" and "weakness" in terms of bureaucracy and infrastructure, however, is to judge the premodern state anachronistically according to twentieth-century models. Colonial administrators did just this, finding the multiplicity of rulerships awkward to administer. They viewed the autonomy of the smaller chieftainships as evidence of weakness and aversion to authority.

How have historians responded when pressed for an indigenous definition of state? What can these entities be called if "state" is a category of external, Western origin? The discussion that follows addresses these questions by reviewing the definitions or models of the state in Southeast Asia that have emerged over the past three decades or so. By tracing the genealogies of these paradigms, I hope to show how they have guided thinking about the past and set agendas for historical inquiry. Finding an indigenous paradigm that successfully counters the unwelcome implications of "state" derived from Euro-American theory is almost impossible, but the search has led to creative interaction among the disciplines. The first of these paradigms, the Asiatic Mode of Production, is arguably the oldest, harking back to a Marxian theory of social formations.

Mode of Production

Some premodern Southeast Asian kingdoms were port polities based on maritime trade, both regional and long-distance. Some were inland agrarian states dependent on wet-rice cultivation for whom trade was less important in the maintenance of royal power than it was for the acquisition of luxury items to display status. Still other, smaller polities depended on local products, such as tin, gold, animal hides, or forest produce, that were traded with the larger agrarian or maritime states. Thus, the economics of royal wealth has been central to many studies of early and premodern Southeast Asia, when merchant kings monopolized maritime trade and local trading networks.

Lacking the power and administrative capacity to extract surplus produce from far-flung provinces, the premodern state relied on tax farming to acquire revenue (Butcher and Dick 1993). Another source of royal gain was tribute, paid by cultivators or merchants to regional overlords or to royal centers. Eric Wolf used the term "tributary mode of production" to express the economic aspects of these hegemonic relations between peasant and overlord (Wolf 1982: 92). The "tributary mode of production" purports to explain how surplus produce was passed up the line to local overlord or provincial ruler, and, finally, to the ruler as a sign of loyalty and deference. Homage to a superior and respect for authority were not merely social values but were indicative of material exchange.

One ready-made model of economic relations that has had direct and indirect impact on the writing of Southeast Asian economic history is the Asiatic Mode of Production (AMP). This is hardly an indigenous model of the state, having its origins in the writings of Marx and Engels and in notions of Oriental despotism to be found in European treatises on the state written in the sixteenth and seventeenth centuries (Anderson 1974: 462–549; Bailey and Llobera 1981, part I). But it is a model that has been exploited by twentieth-century historians in the region in an attempt to account for lagging economic development. The AMP has three characteristics: (1) the absence of private property in land; (2) the controlling power of a centralized state that provided the conditions of production, such as irrigation and communication; (3) scattered settlements in the countryside in the form of villages that are cohesive and self-sustaining, but isolated. In the AMP schema, the state intervened in the production process and formed a part of the productive base for those domains within its reach (Sawer 1977: 52). Kinship, custom, religion, and the law—what Marxist historians once referred to as the superstructure of the state—enabled the state to extract wealth as tax or tribute by applying the sanctions of custom, religion, and the obligations of kin and kinlike relations.

The genealogy of the AMP in Southeast Asian historiography can be traced along two pathways. One is through the accounts of aristocratic European travelers and envoys to Southeast Asia, such as Simon de la Loubère's *The Kingdom of Siam* of the seventeenth century. These accounts are heavily laden with the seventeenth-century aristocratic critique of royal absolutism and its supposed similarities to the bureaucratic despotism of Oriental society, the legacy of which is the predatory or exploitative state. The AMP is thus implicit in many premodern European sources on Southeast Asia, which describe royal absolutism in the region as arbitrary and tyrannical. Historians who rely on these sources run the danger of transferring the trope of absolutism cum despotism to their own work where it does not belong. Although A. J. S. Reid assiduously avoids use of the term despotism in his account of royal absolutism in Southeast Asia during the sixteenth and seventeenth centuries, his reliance on European sources has reproduced some of the characteristics of the European discourse of despotism. Merchant kings could intervene directly in the market, and there were few institutional checks on royal authority. In contrast to contemporary Europe, absolutism in Southeast Asia "was not accompanied by institutions or even theories" that might empower other elements of society (Reid 1993, chap. 4). Yet, apart from Sultan Agung (Java), Iskandar Muda (northern Sumatra), and Narai (Siam), all of whom ruled in the seventeenth century, there were few absolutist rulers in the region who were able to exercise the power implied by royal absolutism.

The other path by which the AMP has been favored is via quasi-Marxist theories of state and society. Here the AMP is of service in the work of modern historians as an economic explanation for political power. It is an appealing model in a narrative of linear development, and it has been taken up by historians and social scientists working within the region because it explains why "Asiatic" states and societies were trapped in static social formations. But when applied as a meta-paradigm to explain centuries of history, the AMP seems inflexible and teleological, even when the analysis has an ample empirical base (Tichelman 1980).

The AMP has also contributed to a debate in Southeast Asian historiography about the autonomy of the village, given the stereotypical view of villages in the AMP as scattered and isolated. One implication of the idea that the village was isolated and autonomous is that it lacked the dynamism to propel it to higher stages of development. Marx's AMP presumed that the dynamism for change had to come from outside forces, such as those unleashed by the colonial process.

While Marx himself pointed out the collective solidarity of village life, he also saw rigidity and stasis in "this undignified, stagnatory, and vegetative life." It was a social foundation at peace, but, given the lack of a real past, it was the peace of the graveyard. This view of peasants and their worlds as constricted and confining is at odds with numerous historical examples of rebellion, resistance, and migration, forced and otherwise, and the AMP consequently became a target of revisionist historical writing (Breman 1988: 7–8).

The role of the center in supervising irrigation works at the village level, which is one of the three characteristics of the AMP, has given focus to a debate on the role of irrigation in royal power and, by extension, on the significance of so-called hydraulic society for state-society relations. While few historians take seriously the preposterous formulations of Karl Wittfogel in his 1957 book on Oriental despotism, the ruler's role in the planning and control of irrigation works, even if only at a symbolic level, has continued to stimulate research.

In the early period, extensive irrigation works found at a number of Southeast Asian sites have led archaeologists and historians to presume that the ponds and reservoirs, the moats and canals, performed a double function. They had symbolic meaning in the epics and myths of Hindu-Buddhist cosmology; they also served to irrigate fields for wet-rice cultivation, what is called in Java *sawah* cultivation. The French scholarship on Angkor embraced this interpretation of the double function of hydraulic works but emphasized the importance of the control of irrigation for royal power, in other words, "despotism." This direct connection between royal power and the hydraulic system is also to be found in Soviet scholarship on state and society at Angkor (Sedov 1978: 114). The historian currently most generous about the AMP and its possibilities for studying early Cambodian society is Michael Vickery, who gives persuasive reasons for using the paradigm, calling it by a different name perhaps to rid it of historiographical baggage and reconfiguring it theoretically (Vickery 1998: 7–17).

The evidence that the reservoirs and moats surrounding the temple complexes at Angkor also formed an irrigation network for wet-rice cultivation is not persuasive (Acker 1998; van Liere 1980). There is little evidence that the moats led out to irrigation canals in the countryside. The vast patchwork of ancient ricefields visible in aerial photographs seems to have been irrigated by terracing and dam construction at the instigation of individual cultivators. Thus the waterworks at the center served mostly as symbols by coding the terrestrial kingdom in the language of Hindu-Buddhist myth. Water, as it passed through the sculpted representations of Hindu-Buddhist myth, was imbued with the king's symbolic omnipresence and omnipotence (Day 1994: 196). The purpose of the immense reservoirs may simply have been their immensity (Acker 1998: 36).

In a number of early Southeast Asian states, royal initiative and village labor combined to build or repair irrigation works, accomplishments that, according to the elitist evidence, reflected favorably on the ruler's reputation (van Naerssen and de Iongh 1977: 41, 56). In early Burma, pagodas and spirit shrines were built along weirs and dams, providing a string of sightlines in order to estimate water levels (Aung-Thwin 1990: 15–16). The religious monuments were constructed not just to sanctify water and the social hierarchy associated with it but also to contribute to the operation of the irrigation system.

Similarly, hydraulic engineering was incorporated into Balinese bureaucracy through the local organization of irrigation societies, or *sekaha subak*, evidence for which can be dated at least three centuries before the Majapahit period in ancient Java (c. A.D. 1222–1451). These associations, possibly prehistoric in origin, regulated ground and water rights and empowered an official to supervise adherence to the rules and customs that allocated access to water. Geertz sees the *subak* officials not as rice-field rajahs acting on behalf of lords but as functionaries who served the interests of the irrigation-association members by arbitrating disputes over water. This kind of interpretation of the evidence tends to dispute the AMP paradigm, for it suggests that hydraulic agriculture did not necessarily centralize power (Geertz 1980: 168–69).

What is at stake in this debate of kings versus villagers as hydraulic engineers is that village initiative and local enterprise have a hidden history in state-sponsored irrigation works. A minor Khmer official, who entered royal service as caretaker of the sacred buffaloes in the second half of the eleventh century, expresses pride in the initiative he took to construct tanks, dikes, canals, and bridges (Day 2002: 45–46). The gross systems of the imperial centers, which can be glimpsed from epigraphy and aerial photography, mask smaller systems that preexisted the larger ones and formed the actual productive base. The imperial center possessed resources of "man-management," to use one of Wolters's terms, not so much to intervene in the productive process as to link together the lesser hydraulic systems into larger networks of religious and economic exchanges. But in achieving this feat and promoting its accomplishment, the imperial center laid claims to the parentage of the production systems that developed in its environs, claims that the provincial elites and peasants who actually constructed the systems might have regarded as false.

In historical writing within Southeast Asia, the AMP has had a mixed reception. It flourished briefly during the tumultuous 1970s in Thailand in a debate about periodization and the causes of under-development, a debate sparked by Marxist historiography and by renewed interest in economic history (Reynolds and Hong 1983: 87–91). Chatthip Nartsupha, a prominent Thai economic historian who participated in that debate, has written about the Thai village economy in a way that suggests the persistence of self-sufficient village economies well into the twentieth century (Chatthip 1999). His self-sufficient village economies sound a lot like the AMP. In Vietnam, where historians were deeply influenced by Soviet and Chinese historiography, the AMP was unpopular through the mid-1950s because of Stalin's *Dialectical and Historical Materialism*, published in 1938, which periodized history into five modes of production that did not include the Asiatic Mode of Production (Pelley 2002: 55). In the Democratic Republic of Vietnam, constraints on discussion of the AMP lasted longer than for European Marxist historians, and it continued to be dismissed until the early 1960s, when arguments over the circumstances of two Vietnamese states breathed new life into study of the past. Vietnamese historians turned to the AMP because it explained "the power and centrality of the state and made class conflict irrelevant" (Pelley 2002: 58). Indeed, the AMP in most applications strikes a sharp contrast between the state as the most important historical agent and the village as "outside" of history, static and incapable of change.

Finally, it can be said that the AMP paradigm draws peasant cultivators into the ambit of the state in two distinct ways. The vast majority of peasant cultivators were outside the state's control, living on subsistence agriculture and making crafts for home use. By contrast, those peasants within the state's reach were conscripted for labor on the irrigation system, which formed the basis for the "despotic" rule of the king. Peasants have a part in the AMP in contrast to some of the other paradigms that follow, such as the *mandala*, where they are mostly invisible, or the theater state (*negara*), where they are spectators.

The Mandala

In keeping with the stress on the autonomous history of Southeast Asia, which sought to challenge colonial history and to write against neocolonial Western categories, the thrust of Southeast Asian historiography in the 1970s was to find alternatives to these external concepts of state. Weber and Marx were targets, but so were other external models of Indic or Middle Eastern origin. In the world of the Minangkabau in Sumatra, for example, the Alam was "a unit quite unlike a state, whose central concern lies in the political affairs of a society and which ultimately rests on coercive power" (Reid and Castles 1975: 77). Similarly, in a study of the Batak people, "state" means central authority, and state formation "under the influence of outside pressures and models" occurred only on the fringes of the Batak country. "Looked at from the inside, Batak society did not need any state" (Reid and Castes 1975: 75). The aim of the 1975 volume was to indigenize concepts of the state before colonial rule in order to locate the dynamics, maintenance, and dissolution of state within Southeast Asia itself. But what were these entities or polities to be called if "state" was an external category of Western origin?

One paradigm, which has been taken up by historians as well as by anthropologists and political scientists, is the *mandala*, a "variable circle of power centered on a ruler, his palace, and the religious center from which he drew his legitimization" (Stuart-Fox and Kooyman 1992: 85). The *mandala* applies to the entire premodern period until indigenous kingdoms were gradually replaced by territorial states with defined borders.

The paradigm has a tangled pedigree but emerged most distinctly in 1980 in a small book by O. W. Wolters on early Southeast Asia (Wolters 1999). Although Wolters was characteristically nonpolemical, he invoked the *mandala* as a term appropriate to the dynamics of early Southeast Asia in order to counter the aping of foreign models and the Eurocentric connotations of "state." Moreover, describing the ruler at the center of the *mandala* as a "man of prowess," a notion that sounds distinctly like the "big man" of Pacific political culture, allowed Wolters to find indigenous roots of leadership that preceded Sinic and Indian models. The *mandala* paradigm, which works as well for the seventh-century maritime empire of Srivijaya as for the Vietnamese Ly dynasty in the eleventh century, dispensed with "Indianization" as a historical process in the early centuries. In this sense, Wolters's early history of the region can be seen as a revisionist treatment of the classic study by George Coedès, *The Indianized States of Southeast Asia* (Coedès 1968). Wolters also eschewed any interest in Hindu-Buddhist cosmology that had correlates elsewhere in the world (Heine-Geldern 1956; Mabbett 1983). *Mandala* and "man of prowess" allowed Wolters to transcend the division of the region into island and mainland and to conceptualize Southeast Asia as a unity with an innate cosmopolitanism that owed nothing to India and China.

The political field in early Southeast Asia was pictured as a patchwork of overlapping *mandala* or circles of kings.

> In practice, the *mandala* represented a particular and often unstable political situation in a vaguely definable geographical area without fixed boundaries and where smaller centres tended to look in all directions for security. *Mandalas* would expand and contract in concertina-like fashion. Each one contained several tributary rulers, some of whom would repudiate their vassal status when the opportunity arose and try to build up their own networks of vassals.
>
> (Wolters 1999: 27–28)

Rulers jostled for supremacy if they were strong and ambitious, and for security and protection if they were weaker and dependent. The "men of prowess" who dominated this political space possessed spiritual and leadership resources that enabled them to mobilize their kinsmen and build wider networks (Wolters 1999: 18–19, 112–13). A later gloss by Martin Stuart-Fox made the important point that *mandala* were shaped differently by the transcultural religions of Hinduism, Buddhism, and Islam to which they were exposed (Stuart-Fox 2000).

Mandala has also been defined as an Indic topographical formula for a contained core "that provided a design for the integration of clan or lineage-based groups into more complex centralized polities" (Hall 1985: 9). This definition suggests programmatic capacity, as if the *mandala* were a blueprint or instrument for integrating kin groups, though it is unlikely that social practices could actually stem from its use. According to Wolters, it was the ruler's flexibility, resourcefulness, and powers of improvisation that explained his success in exerting his authority within the *mandala*. Similarly, Higham's stress on *mandalas* as "centralised state-like polities" was at odds with Wolters's notion of dynamic, unstable, constantly shifting alliances (Higham 1989: 240). However these entities actually worked, Wolters came to believe, they were not centralized, for they lacked the institutional supports that would maintain stability indefinitely (Wolters 1999: 108).

The term *mandala* had a religious etymology in the Indic world. In Sanskrit, the term means "circle," in the sense of "a centered space" and also in the sense that "it is a totality, a whole formed by an association of parts" (Snodgrass 1985: 104–5). In Buddhism, it is, more specifically, a "configuration of forms" that communicates "perfect equilibrium and symmetry within the Dharma Body of Vairocana," one of the Buddhas (Snodgrass 1985: 106–7). The symmetry of the circle is a compelling geometric form that served as the template for the *stupa*, the reliquary found throughout the Buddhist world, and for this reason, in Tibetan, Chinese, and Japanese Buddhist art and architecture, the *mandala* is a powerful icon.

But the dynamics of the actual workings of *mandala*, both within and between *mandala*, were hardly conducive to the harmonious whole pictured by the strictly sacred connotations of the term. On the contrary, the dynamics suggested unstable, constantly shifting relationships that called for improvisation and expedients rather than programs or doctrines to solve problems. For Wolters, the inspiration for the *mandala* as a trope for prehistoric and early Southeast Asian kingdoms came from an Indic treatise on interstate relations, the *Arthasastra* of Kautilya, the so-called Indian Machiavelli, which Wolters first applied to his understanding of the diplomatic strategies of the sixteenth-century Siamese hero-king Naresuan (Wolters 1968). Also within Southeast Asia, epigraphic evidence from Angkor suggests that *mandala* was a metaphor for kingdom. Rajendravarman's *mandala*, for exmple, was rich and without faction (Mabbett 1978: 37). But the question of whether the *mandala* depicted in Kautilya's *Arthasastra* was a concept known to early Southeast Asian rulers, or a heuristic device that a twentieth-century historian used to make sense out of varied and grudging documentary materials such as inscriptions and Chinese dynastic records, is probably unanswerable.

In a series of studies that roughly paralleled those of Wolters, S. J. Tambiah tested the "representational efficacy" of *mandala* in an attempt to give it greater comparative sweep and theoretical power. Using Thai, Burmese, Mon, and Javanese material in a method of exposition he called "totalization," Tambiah proposed another term, the "galactic polity," which immediately brings to mind the expansion and contraction of early polities "in concertina-like fashion." Tambiah saw the recurring pattern of *mandala* in the cosmological, territorial, politico-economic, and administrative aspects of "the state." One feature that Tambiah's galactic polity shares with Wolters's *mandala* is the highly unstable character of its politics: "circles of leaders and followers that form and reform in highly unstable factions" (Tambiah 1985: 281). But Tambiah did not limit the galactic polity to the prehistoric or early historic period. It continued up to the nineteenth century, when contact with the West began to alter the form and function of the state. The ensuing, sometimes violent, confrontation between these different conceptions of space and the worldviews and technology for mapping space that accompanied them can be seen in the history of Siam, where the bounded state, which has been coined the geo-body, emerged (Thongchai 1994). Emphasizing the non-Western features of the Southeast Asian state, one Thai historian has availed herself of both galactic polity and *mandala* to show the compatibility of the two models and, by implication, their shared lineage (Kobkua 1988: 4–30).

The *mandala* and the galactic polity would seem to be cousins in an extended family of cultural models of the state that bear strong resemblances to the segmentary state, a concept borrowed from anthropological work on Africa and utilized by historians of premodern India (Stein 1980: 274; Sunait 1990). "The Indian king was an overlord, not a manager. He demanded submission to his claim of superiority, rather than obedience to his orders" (Stein 1975: 77). These arrangements were durable, because chieftainship or kingship was sacral. The state was incorporated ritually rather than administratively (Stein 1980: 275). Territorial sovereignty was

recognized but limited and essentially relative, forming a series of zones in which authority is most absolute near the centre and

> increasingly restricted towards the periphery, often shading off into a ritual hegemony. There is no centralised government, yet there are also numerous peripheral foci of administration over which the centre exercises only a limited control. There is a specialised administrative staff at the centre, but it is repeated on a reduced scale at all the peripheral foci of administration.
>
> (Stein 1977: 9)

The more or less autonomous satellite units, the segments, did not transfer all or even most of their agrarian surplus to the ritual core (Subrahmanyam 1986). These details, most of which are echoed in the *negara* and *mandala* models, make the segmentary state look familiar in the Southeast Asian landscape.

Only a few historians of Southeast Asia have used the segmentary state or are even aware of it, despite the fact that it has the potential to identify similarities between inland agrarian states and maritime trading states. James Warren's work on the Sulu archipelago drew on an anthropological typology of the Sulu sultanates as segmentary states, and he pictures the Jolo sultan's territorial sovereignty as strongest at the center, shading off into "ritual hegemony in distant areas" (Warren 1981: xxiii). Christie mentioned the segmentary state for the early period in Java but denied its applicability on very narrow grounds (Christie 1986: 73). Kulke, who came to Southeast Asian studies from South Indian studies, was more alert to the possibilities of the model for the early period, and indeed found his initial exposure to Southeast Asian materials enriched by the controversy over the segmentary state that he had encountered in South Indian studies (Kulke 1986: 4–5). Though he welcomed the model, especially for the early period of chieftaincies, he was generally averse to models of the state, because they were too static and ahistorical to describe the structural changes he saw taking place (Kulke 1986: 5).

Two other paradigms of the state belong to the *mandala* family. "The contest state," drawn from early Java and Burma, seeks to decenter the state, or at least highly qualify royal absolutism. Adas defines this form of "political organization" as "rule by a king or emperor who claims a monopoly of power and authority in a given society but whose effective control is in reality severely restricted by rival power centers among the elite" (Adas 1981: 218). The contest state is a conflictual model, and on this score it recognizes more explicitly the constant presence of warfare than does the *mandala* as expounded by Wolters. The contest state is not free of the familiar Weberian overtones, however. Conditions of low population-to-land ratio, poor communications, and weak administration "gave rise to politics in which there was a constant struggle between ruler and the nobility" as well as cleavages at other levels. Here is the familiar refrain of the premodern Southeast Asian polity as "weak."

The "network state," coined by Nagtegaal in his study of the Dutch East India Company and northern Java, has the virtue of emphasizing fluidity and the phoenixlike survival of the state through times of chaos and violent disturbances (Nagtegaal 1996: 51–55). The network state recognizes the personalized structure of power, and it makes a virtue of what appeared to the Dutch as "disarray." Relations between the regents on the north coast and the Mataram ruler inland varied greatly from person to person, and regents acquired their position through power struggles. There seemed to be many officials who enjoyed overlapping responsibilities. In many respects, the network state differs little from the *mandala*. Indeed, both the contest state and the network state try to capture what strikes most historians about the premodern state in Southeast Asia, namely, the looseness and fluidity of relationship between rulers, ministers, nobility, and provincial lords.

The Theater State (*Negara*)

The genesis of this model may be found in Clifford Geertz's studies of the symbolics of power in Morocco and nineteenth-century Bali (Geertz 1977, 1980). Other scholars were exploring the nature of power and Southeast Asian royal ceremony about the same time, notably Anderson, whose 1973 essay on the Javanese concept of power could be read as an analysis of political leadership that drew its force from earlier, pre-legal rational forms of authority in the Javanese past (Anderson 1990, chap. 1). Milner, who prefers "ceremonial polity" to "theater state," also contributed to this scholarship on the indigenous concepts of power, by extensively glossing the Malay term *kerajaan*, variously translated by European lexicographers as "state," "kingdom," or "government" (Milner 1982: 114; Milner 1995: 24). In his study of Bali, Geertz built up a picture of what he called the theater state and only hinted at claims for its application anywhere else, although the model was immediately seen to have wider explanatory value and was quickly applied to other parts of Indic Southeast Asia (Gesick 1983).

Geertz mobilized his theater state as an indigenous construct against definitions of the state propounded by Weber, Marx, and the sixteenth- and seventeenth century European theorists of state such as Machiavelli, Hobbes, and Locke. In the "great fraud" views of the state (Marx and his epigones), material interests and material conflicts were concealed or mystified to enable the ruling class to extract what it wanted at will. In the "great beast" views of the state, such as that of Hobbes, power was conjured up by the threat of force, thus striking awe and fear in a submissive citizenry (Geertz 1980: 122). Another target of Geertz's analysis was the notion of the Oriental despot, which was rooted deep in Western thinking about Asian leadership and in modern times given its most striking expression in Karl Wittfogel's polemic against Chinese authoritarianism (Wittfogel 1957). Against these European models, the theater state might be read as an Asia-centric trope for charismatic authority.

A culture of ceremonialism acted as a magnet at the center, exerting a pull on the subject population, thus explaining political authority and the obedience of subjects without reference to bureaucracy or economics, or to violence and coercion. Geertz's concept of power is not one of command-and-obedience but one that privileges the capacity of pomp, ·drama, and display to order human affairs. Ceremony puts people in their places, particularly in relation to divinity, and thus orders their existence. The larger purpose of governing a population is also served, although it becomes indistinguishable from devotion to divinity. Ceremony, drama, and display are not illusory; they do not conceal the ordering function of the state. They enact it. In Geertz's words, "the state drew its force, which was real enough, from its imaginative energies, its semiotic capacity to make inequality enchant" (Geertz 1980: 123). The enchantment of inequality, it could be argued, helps to explain the attraction of monarchical authority and of public office throughout Southeast Asian history.

Geertz's theater state generated an enormous critical literature from both historians and anthropologists. One criticism directed at the theater state is that it is decontextualized and ahistorical. Geertz's model "lacks a dynamic and historical character," says Christie, adding that early Javanese kings were "not ritually potent enough to qualify them for the lead in a 'theatre state' as defined by Geertz" (Christie 1986: 85). Geertz's analysis pictures the Balinese ruler in an "overly flat, static, immobile, and ritualized" way that seems drawn from aged Balinese informants or from engrossing but "dated" Dutch accounts (Tambiah 1985: 336). Similarly, Pemberton argued that Javanese ceremonialism in the nineteenth and twentieth centuries must be read as a product of colonial as well as indigenous forces (Pemberton 1994: 34–35, 70). By ignoring the impact of Dutch colonialism, Geertz's study unwittingly accepted as "classical" what is, in fact, a product of the colonial past (Nordholt 1981: 474). Geertz recapitulated what Dutch colonial officials said and thus fails to take into account indigenous discourses of leadership and authority (Wiener 1995: 10).

Geertz's model has also been criticized for its failure to demonstrate how the elite extracted the surplus product from the producers. Taxation was "no less explosive in classical Bali than it has been elsewhere in the world," but the realities of slavery and revenue collection receive only glancing attention in *Negara* (Shankman 1984: 268). The harsher realities of political and social life recede into the background in favor of the semiotics of power that "prettifies" Balinese society. In the words of one historian, the theater state "leaves little room for the conflicts and the violence inherent in Balinese society," although, contrary to these criticisms, Geertz did acknowledge the role of coercion in prying support from producers and promising violence to recalcitrants (Nordholt 1996: 7; Shankman 1984: 268). As an example of how the same scholars can read diametrically opposing meanings into the same work, Robinson credits Geertz with restoring a measure of realism to the description of the precolonial Balinese polity, which was characterized by internal division and "the steady hum of political violence" (Robinson 1995: 23n.18).

Geertz's argument about the "ordering force of display, regard, and drama" could be pushed further. Exemplary symbols, ritual, and ceremony at various levels of the hierarchy were more than mere symbols. There is an element of coercion even in ceremony and ritual, as social norms and values compel onlookers to participate. Regard for authority entails deference and awe, thus subordinating the participant. Semiotics, politics, and economics should be integrated rather than compartmentalized if the expression and exercise of power is to be understood realistically (Vickers 1986: 74).

The Shipshape State

The previous models are almost entirely devoted to capturing the distinctive features of state formation in land-based, agrarian societies, particularly inland societies. Yet from early times much of Southeast Asian history must be understood in terms of the sea that connected Southeast Asia to China and Japan on the one side and to the Indian subcontinent, the Middle East, and Europe on the other. Indeed, the port polity might be argued to be a paradigm of its own. Even kingdoms that were primarily agrarian, such as the Burmese from the sixteenth through the eighteenth centuries, depended on maritime commerce for their economic health (Lieberman 1984: 117–27).

The sea was a source of livelihood, in terms of food as well as trade and the wealth it brought, and the sea connected Southeast Asia to the rest of the world. Riverine traffic put upriver communities in touch with this seaborne trade and the information that came with it. In the maritime world, the state traveled wherever people could navigate. As Wolters put it, on the Sumatran rivers "where no implement was more important than the paddle, ... signs of the royal presence, the messengers, were mobile" (Wolters 1979c: 17). Maritime trade in a polity that was primarily a port meant that in the Malay world leading port officials such as the *syahbandar* could be members of the royal council, as was the case in Banten on Java (Kathirithamby-Wells and Villiers 1990: 111). The early maritime kingdom of Srivijaya, on Sumatra, exploited trading networks and commercial acumen, which it passed on to Melaka on the west coast of the Malay Peninsula, which was in a sense succeeded by the Johore Sultanate. Later, the colonial port of Singapore built its reputation from its strategic geopolitical location on the Straits of Melaka (Kwa 1998).

In premodern Malaya, the river played a vital part in the spatio-ecological conception of the kingdom (Gullick 1988: 21). The Malay ruler needed to possess a firm grip on the *ulu*, or upstream part of the river where the subsistence agrarian villages were located. Downstream (*hilir*) was the *istana*, the authority, court etiquette, and elite culture that would be threatened if the *ulu* were neglected. *Ulu* was also the term for the handle of a kris and of farming implements, thus inscribing the spatio-ecological setting of the river-based kingdoms with the shape of the Malay warrior's weapon (Airriess 2003: 90–91).

The ever-present ships in the world of island Southeast Asia provided an organizational metaphor for the state. The command hierarchy on a ship was suggestive to Pierre-Yves Manguin, who was trying to get away from the notion of a fixed, structural idea of state and find a model of the state that applied to insular and maritime Southeast Asia. He integrated the ship motif as part of a symbolic discourse and elaborated it into a metaphor for the ordered social group (Manguin 1986: 187). In the Malay, Tagalog, and Cebuano languages, a close relationship exists between boat vocabulary and social systems. The Malay sultanates, for example, were "quite fond of fully fledged boat metaphors to express their own perception of political institutions" (Manguin 1986: 196). In parts of the island world, villages were conceived as groups of people safely protected as if they were passengers on perahus. People of south Sumatra utilized the ship as a major structuring principle. It appears as the basic conceptual form for houses and ceremonial processions.

Manguin considered the abundant evidence of ship symbolism in the island world and proposed that the symbolism constitutes a maritime correspondent to the Indic cosmologies and hierarchies of inland agrarian states. The boat symbol is "a metaphor for hierarchical levels or social and cosmological systems" (Manguin 1986: 200). Strict hierarchies govern the way ships are crewed and piloted. The spatial order of ship construction provides a reservoir of shapes and relationships that people of maritime societies have adapted to express their relationship to each other and to the cosmos (Manguin 1986: 201).

While the previous models have all been territorial-minded, the ship-shape state draws on the historical experience of maritime Southeast Asia and emphasizes mobility and fluidity. In this model, the state need not have a fixed center; the center was located wherever the ruler happened to be. But as is clear from Manguin's gloss, the ship motif also implies hierarchies that give structure to social systems and governments.

The Dynastic State

Much of early Southeast Asian history relies on the use of Chinese records, particularly in the period to 1500, so the Chinese view of what a state should look like has influenced the Western historiography on

Southeast Asian state formation. The Chinese thought that a state properly so-called should be centralized under the just and ethical rule of an emperor who possessed superior virtue (*de*). The custom of dynastic succession ensured that rulers were replaced in an orderly way, and states had fixed boundaries. The earliest Chinese envoys to Southeast Asia commented on the territorial extent of the kingdoms they visited and measured distance from what they perceived to be the frontiers of those kingdoms (Wheatley 1966: 16–17).

Of all Southeast Asian states in contact with the Chinese imperial court from early times, Vietnam heeded the principles of Chinese statecraft most assiduously, adopting and adapting these for Vietnamese purposes. Vietnam, which at first sight does not fit the *mandala* model very closely, did not expand and contract in concertina-like fashion. "Borders, once acquired, changed only to be pushed forward," and the center at Thang Long, the site of Hanoi, was permanent (Wolters 1999: 144). In the seventeenth and eighteenth centuries, the Vietnamese dynastic state in the north advanced southward by means of military colonies, comprised of soldier peasants, Ming supporters, and Qing prisoners of war, which opened up the frontier and established territorial control (De Koninck 1996).

While the Vietnamese did not exactly emulate the Chinese state, the education of Vietnamese government officials in the Chinese classics ensured that some of its basic features became a measure of success in statecraft. Vietnamese rulers regarded the learning of antiquity embodied in Chinese classical literature as "an encyclopedia of recorded wisdom" that they could consult in "ways that seemed relevant in recognizing specific situations" (Wolters 1979a: 84). The thirteenth-century Vietnamese historian Le Van Huu, for example, made critical judgments about the performance of rulers according to their abilities to arrange their succession in times of crisis and to avenge attacks across Vietnamese borders (Wolters 1976, 1979a). Orderly succession, ethical rule based on a reading of the past conduct of emperors, and protection of borders were criteria Vietnamese historians used to assess the performance of rulers.

Despite certain ideals of Chinese imperial rule that impressed Vietnamese court officials, Wolters describes the style of government in Vietnam, as late as the Tran dynasty (1226–1400), as decidedly Southeast Asian in its relaxed and informal court behavior. This behavior was much condemned by a later Vietnamese court historian who measured good government in terms of the discipline, rites, and regulations prescribed in Chinese texts (Wolters 1999: 144–45).

In the course of southward expansion, an increasingly polycentric and polycultural field developed that made it more and more difficult from the late sixteenth century for the imperial court in the north, and later the center, to prevail. By the nineteenth century under the Nguyen dynasty (1802–1945), personal relationships and family ties connecting the ruling family to the outside, particularly to residual loyalists of the Lê dynasty (1427–1788) in the north, threatened to undermine Nguyen primacy over the newly unified kingdom. In the early 1830s under the second Nguyen king, Minh Mang (r. 1820–41), the court at Hue turned to Chinese administrative models to impose order on this heterogeneity and to centralize its rule (Woodside 1971). Recent historical research, however, has questioned the extent to which efforts at re-Sinification, even before the nineteenth century, achieved a neo-Confucian, single Vietnam.

By the middle of the seventeenth century, the Red River Delta had ceased to be the only center of Vietnamese civilization. This happened three generations after Nguyen Hoang, a general who fought the Chinese-sponsored Mac in the Lê restoration, departed south to assume control over the southern protectorate of Thuan Hoa in 1558. Hailed as the ancestral founder of the Nguyen dynasty in nineteenth-century court historiography, Nguyen Hoang (1525–1613) displayed a style of leadership more in tune with the "man of prowess" in the *mandala* than with the Confucianized emperor in Thang Long. Nguyen Hoang "lived by his wits," in effect rejecting the traditional definition of a "good Vietnamese." Talent and ability would now count for more than birth and position (Taylor 1993: 64). Nguyen Hoang trusted his own lineage and rewarded his lieutenants lavishly; right up to the middle of the nineteenth century, his descendents surrounded themselves with officials and advisers with strong connections to the ancestral province of Thanh Hoa (Cooke 1998: 148). Under the Nguyen lords (Chua), a new Vietnamese politico-cultural space emerged in the south: a creature of local geography with abundant land and Cham and Khmer cultural residues. Here Vietnamese referred to their cultural space as the "inner region" (Dang Trong), or "Cochinchina," in contrast to "outer region" (Dang Ngoai), or "Tonkin," which was the north (Tana

1998: 12). Nguyen Dang Trong was not an economic extension of the north but something new, neither a diluted dynastic state nor a *mandala*.

The model of the dynastic state properly so-called does not apply only to Vietnam, however. In the wake of European expansion into the region, colonial regimes in the East Indies, Malaya, and Vietnam created European-style "dynasties" from indigenous elites as a complement to their bureaucratic style of rule. They insisted on orderly succession in royal families in order to remove what they saw as looseness and unpredictability of the existing social hierarchies. In the East Indies, in 1854, the Dutch instituted a heredity principle that reinforced the more established dynasties and curtailed the flexibility and fluidity of established hierarchies (Sutherland 1974: 24). In Sumatra and Bali, dynasty-like structures were imposed on relations of power to facilitate Dutch rule (Dobbin 1983; Robinson 1995). In mainland Southeast Asia, borders became important, as they had been for Chinese geographers, when the European colonial powers brought with them a conception of territory and its administration that had not previously existed. Even Siam, which was not formally colonized, responded to the new requirements of territorial-based sovereignty by installing the rule of primogeniture at the end of the nineteenth century.

Until modern times, primogeniture was the exception rather than the rule for most of Southeast Asia, however. Descent and bloodline were important in claiming a right to the throne, but genealogies in the Malay, Javanese, Tai, and Cambodian worlds tended to be inclusive rather than exclusive. The genealogies were used to incorporate families through the maternal line, as in the extensive solar and lunar dynastic lines claimed by Cambodian kings. The significance of the dynastic state in the colonial period is that European administrators imposed "proper" dynastic succession in order to facilitate control of their colonies.

Conclusion

With the exception of the AMP, these cultural models of the premodern state in Southeast Asia share several things in common. They assume the prestige and power of a monarch, but they seek to avoid the language of Euro-American political theory about despotism or absolutism. These paradigms were invented to confront the implications of a modernist, Weberian model that emphasized bounded, territorial sovereignty buttressed by the rule of law. One of Weber's ideal types was charismatic leadership. The theater state and the *mandala*/galactic polity might be seen as attempts by late-twentieth-century scholars to revisit the nature of premodern leadership without resorting to the more mystical, ineffable meanings associated with charismatic leadership.

The Weberian model also posits weakness when it is applied to premodern Southeast Asia, and it is this weakness that the cultural models were mobilized to contest. As with Stein's characterization of the Indian king as an overlord rather than a manager and the state incorporated ritually rather than administratively, the Southeast Asian king did not command the infrastructure that would allow tight control of resources or people. Royal power is based on the personal characteristics and "prowess" of the ruler rather than on institutional or legal supports. By their very nature, however, the personal characteristics of the ruler were visible only in a very limited domain. Not far from the center of these kingdoms, the personal reach of the ruler ebbed away to be replaced by the authority of regional and provincial overlords who could call upon their own personal resources and networks. The cultural models in the inventory above do not deny the absence of modern infrastructure in terms of communications and transportation networks. They simply say that the nature of royal power was different. It cannot be described and assessed in terms of a political theory reliant on Weberian criteria.

Centers were of defining importance in these premodern kingdoms, but the polity was not centralized. The dynastic state in northern Vietnam—and later in the colonial state—was an exception to this generalization, because the localization of Chinese Confucian statecraft by the Vietnamese mandarinate allowed the center to exert a tighter hold on manpower and resources. Only after the expansion of the Vietnamese state southward from the fifteenth century did the dynastic center find its control ebbing as the state discovered the cultural and religious heterogeneity of the southern regions.

Elsewhere in Southeast Asia, the center shifted according to pressure from rivals and to commercial and trading opportunities thrown up by Chinese, Indian, Arab or Western contacts. In Burma, the royal base oscillated between the north-central region and the coast on the Bay of Bengal. In Cambodia, the center moved around the Great Lake area during the early centuries when Angkor flourished but then was pushed eastward as Thai power increased after the fourteenth century. In the Tai world itself, the political field was polycentric (Luang Prabang in the early centuries, Chiang Mai, Ayudhya, Sukhodaya). In the archipelago, any entrepôt with an enterprising rajah and access to commodities suitable for export could become a center. These movable centers and the fluidity of politics within the court and in relation to tributary rulers were "read" by Western colonial administrations as weaknesses that needed to be rectified by determining the correct royal line and by installing the rightful heir.

"Fluidity and instability" is another way of saying that rulers with imperial ambitions expanded by force of arms. The dynastic histories of almost all premodern kingdoms are filled with succession disputes: princes who were half brothers and advanced their claims on the throne by force; boy-kings who were propped up by senior relatives; interdynastic conflicts among powerful families when the succession was in question. The history of warfare is a much-neglected subject, and if the technology of warfare were better understood, the cultural models might have to be adjusted.

Because of the grudging nature of the evidence in epigraphy, chronicles, and court records, the peasantry is also a neglected topic. Royal endowments of religious institutions and land grants occasionally bring peasant cultivators into the historical record, but for the most part, the peasantry enters history only as it is about to disappear with cash-cropping in the colonial period. The Asiatic Mode of Production, whose popularity has waxed and waned with indigenous historians according to local circumstances, incorporates the peasantry but only as an undifferentiated mass.

The historians and other social scientists who have advocated the cultural models of the state in Southeast Asia have mobilized their efforts against Eurocentric stereotypes that can be traced to political theories of the Western Enlightenment and to the prejudices of colonial administrators. The preoccupation with authoritarian regimes throughout the region in the period after Southeast Asian countries gained their independence further stimulated academic scholarship to find ways of talking about political leadership that explained authoritarianism and, at the same time, did not demonstrate its inevitability.

SEDITIOUS HISTORIES OF SIAM

3

Mr. Kulap and Purloined Documents

Throughout the period of the absolute monarchy until 1932, the writing of Siamese history centered around the court. Kings, princes, nobles, and high-ranking monks were the historians of the Siamese past. Of the monarchs in the Bangkok period, King Mongkut (r. 1851–68) and King Chulalongkorn (r. 1868–1910) expressed an especially intense interest in the past at the very moment when internal reform, pressures from the Western powers, and reactions to Western ideas brought the past into question and thus sharpened historical consciousness. Mongkut deciphered the inscription of the best-remembered monarch of the Sukhothai period, King Ramkhamhaeng, and supervised the revision of an Ayutthayan chronicle (Griswold 1961: 37). King Chulalongkorn composed an exhaustive history and description of festivals and edited a text written in the reign of King Rama III (1824–51) (Chulalongkorn 1963, 1939). Princes Damrong, Narit, and Wachirayan, to name but a few, all concerned themselves with the past, and numerous members of the nobility and the Sangha also contributed to Siam's historical literature.

Since historians were rulers and administrators, study of the past related directly to the science of government; utility motivated much of the quest for historical knowledge. During King Mongkut's reign, Siamese officials presented French diplomats with a chronicle of Cambodian history to substantiate Siamese rights to Cambodia (Osborne and Wyatt 1968: 191). Siamese officialdom was not alone in such uses of the past for contemporary, political purposes. In the eighteenth century, when victorious Burmese carried off Siamese nobles and royalty after the fall of Ayutthaya, the captors interrogated the Siamese not on military stratagems or fortifications but on Siamese history and customs.[1] History was a kind of political intelligence. Kings would review the historical record for the guidance it provided to royal conduct and governing (Breazeale 1971: 45).

But in the second half of the nineteenth century, circumstances also permitted, even encouraged, the writing of history outside the court. As the arena of historical research widened and its boundaries were redefined, one might expect that the process awakened official sensitivities toward figures outside the court whose new acquisition of literary and technological skills enabled them to publish historical works and make them available to a larger audience. One such figure who zealously and conspicuously pursued investigation of the past, and in doing so challenged royal prerogatives, was K. S. R. Kulap, a commoner who lifted himself from an obscure background to take a prominent place in the history of Siamese journalism. He fed his passion for history by collecting books, unpublished manuscripts, and bits of printed matter, from which he fashioned historical essays. Controversy arose over the accuracy of these essays, many of which concerned monarchical history, and the royal family was sufficiently alarmed to respond officially to Kulap's activities. As a commoner, K. S. R. Kulap would never have left such an enduring impression on Siamese historiography had he not mastered the new medium of printing, which gave him authority and power.

The circulation of literary works remained small until the end of the nineteenth century, when the widespread use of printing replaced the former methods of copying on palm leaf or on *samutthai*, bark folded in accordion pleats and inscribed with black or yellow ink or white chalk (Gerini 1912: 255–67). Metallic type and a printing press first entered Siam in 1835 with the American missionary Dr. D. B. Bradley, who produced the first printed work in Siam in June 1836.[2] For some forty years, knowledge of printing technology remained predominantly the property of the missionaries and the Siamese elite, the latter quick to experiment with the opportunities afforded by the technology. King Rama III (r. 1824–51) published laws prohibiting the importation of opium in 1839, and Mongkut used a press to publish Pali texts in a script of his own invention.

The name of Dr. Bradley, associated with much of the cultural and technological exchange with the West until his death in 1873, was also linked with the publication of the first periodical in Siam, the

Bangkok Recorder, which appeared in July 1844 (Lingat 1935: 203). Although the four pages in each issue were almost entirely in Siamese, the reading public was not adequate to support the venture and the monthly closed in fifteen months. This first periodical avoided Christian proselytization and printed articles on physics, chemistry, philology, and medicine, as well as news of Europe, America, China, and Singapore. An edition entirely in Siamese appeared again in the fourth reign on 29 April 1865. From 1859, Bradley also edited and published in English the *Bangkok Calendar*, first published by the Baptists from 1847 to 1850 (Khajorn 1965: 26; Lord 1969: 115). This annual periodical contained news of shipping arrivals and departures, commercial information, consular appointments, and a host of other miscellaneous notes useful to the historian of this period.

For the purpose of understanding the career of K. S. R. Kulap, the list of kings in 1860, the *kathin* ceremonies, and the triennial Pali examinations are of special interest, for these articles heralded the appearance of published writing in Siam about the kingdom's customs and history. That Bradley received the list of kings from a court scribe, Phraya Sisunthornwohan, underscores the importance that King Mongkut attached to printing as a way of acquainting the foreign community with the kingdom. Bradley, ever watchful for ways to utilize his Siamese type, purchased the copyright of Mom Rachothai's *Nirat London*, the journal of the first Siamese diplomatic mission to London. The date of publication, 1861, marks the beginning of the book trade in Siam (Suthilak 1966: 244).

Those intrigued by the new technology and who grasped its utility for the kingdom included the lowborn as well as the highborn. The press on which Bradley published the *Bangkok Recorder* was located in the palace of Prince Wongsathiratsanit, and it was on this press that *nai* Mot Amatyakul, a commoner who later acquired the noble title of Phraya Kasapkitkoson, illegally printed an edition of the Siamese laws in 1849, bringing him a reprimand from the king (Schweisguth 1951: 242–43). The new technology was an irresistible attraction. Bradley found upon examining the motives of one potential Christian convert that he merely wanted to learn the printer's trade (Lord 1969: 115).

Bradley had competition for his news journals and historical literature. Samuel Smith—who had been personal secretary to Phra

Pin Klao, Mongkut's brother who was the Front Palace Prince—
had founded a press when the latter died in 1865 and printed
Buddhist sermons commissioned by Jaophraya Thiphakorawong
(Khajorn 1965: 70). Thiphakorawong's *Kitjanukit*, possibly the first
book printed entirely with Siamese sponsorship, appeared in 1867
and may very well have been printed on Smith's press. In 1869, Smith
began to publish the *Siam Weekly Advertiser* and a monthly, *Siam
Repository*, and, from 1882 to 1886, a Siamese language periodical,
Sayamsamai, which had news on education, foreign affairs, taxation,
and royal ceremonies.

These publishing enterprises gathered momentum, and by the last
quarter of the century, the printing press had become indispensable
in disseminating news, government announcements, and opinion.
King Chulalongkorn established a Royal Printing Office, which in
1874 began to produce the *Royal Thai Government Gazette*, a
publication with which Mongkut had experimented some fifteen years
previously. In 1873, King Chulalongkorn came of age and undertook
his first tentative reforms with the backing of his brothers and half
brothers, who published a newsletter in 1875. Another journalistic
effort, *Darunowat*, the first Siamese-managed newspaper, began in
1874 with notices of world events, European monarchies, and commentary on King Chulalongkorn's Privy Council along with many
other subjects (Wyatt 1969: 45). A number of periodicals flourished
about this time, periodicals that offered a means of communicating
international and domestic news as well as historical and literary essays
(Damrong 1929b). Some of these journals, unable to find a readership
or having tested the limits of acceptable discourse, closed down after
a brief run.

The journal *Wachirayan wiset* (weekly, 1884–94), later called
Wachirayan (1894–1905), enjoyed the longest life, having grown out
of the establishment of the first public library by King Mongkut's
children. Nobles of literary talent joined with Prince Damrong, the
king, and other members of the royal family to write on biography,
poetry, travel, epic literature, proverbs, history, and foreign affairs.
Publication of these texts, which included some by the late King
Mongkut, provided nineteenth-century readers with Siam's written and
oral traditions until 1904, when the royal family adopted the practice
of issuing printed books at cremations (Damrong 1966: 162). In effect,

the works in *Wachirayan* and the shorter-lived periodicals meant that texts previously confined to court reading were appearing in the public domain for the first time and that works passed down orally from generation to generation would now be committed to written form. Printing enlarged the readership for these historical materials and provided access to historical works for literate commoners as well as for nobles and royalty.

A Bumptious Commoner

The royal family and nobility could not dominate the pursuit of the past forever, for the printing press made it possible for commoners to present history to the public. By the 1880s, one commoner in particular, K. S. R. Kulap Kritsananon, was publishing works as fundamental to Siamese literature as those appearing in *Wachirayan wiset*. In one year alone, 1889, he published no fewer than five books, including the classic Siamese poem *Khun chang khun phaen*.[3] K. S. R. Kulap lived history with the same kind of intensity as the royal family; he consumed history as if it were his only source of nourishment. As an enterprising publisher and writer, he earned his reputation not only for publishing Siamese classics but also for his own historical tracts, which drew him into confrontation with the royal family. The ensuing controversies tested the limits of the royal family's forbearance and granted Kulap a permanent place in modern Siamese historiography.

Self-promotion through the press was one of this writer's characteristics, and nowhere is this revealed more explicitly than in his autobiography, a document rare at this time for a commoner.[4] Born in 1834, during the reign of Rama III, K. S. R. Kulap, who may have been part Vietnamese, traced his lineage through his mother and maternal grandmother back five generations to an Ayutthayan noble of the *phra* rank from the northeastern principality of Nakhon Ratchasima (Sawat 1966: 168). This man's grandson had served as a minor civil servant in the first reign (1782–1809), and K. S. R. Kulap began preparation for a similar career at the age of eleven, serving in a special contingent for children of the Royal Pages Bodyguard Regiment. In his autobiography, Kulap confined most of his early recollections to his teachers. He claimed to have studied with Princess Kinnari, a daughter of Rama III; at the age of thirteen, he went to study with Phra Ratmuni at Wat Phrachettuphon, a monastery closely connected to the royal family in the early Bangkok period.

At fourteen, he began to study the *Jindamani* grammar and to learn Buddhist teachings from Prince Paramanuchit, a monk at the same monastery and uncle of King Mongkut, who was to become supreme patriarch in the following reign. He entered the monkhood as a novice under Prince Paramanuchit, taking the ecclesiastical name of Kesaro, an Indic rendering of *kulap* (rose), which precedes his name in initialed form (K. S. R.). When he left the novitiate in the reign of King Mongkut, he entered the Royal Pages Bodyguard Regiment and also managed to acquire a "smattering" of Latin, French, and English from the French apostolic vicar, Mgr. Jean-Baptiste Pallegoix, who had taught King Mongkut. Contrary to Siamese custom, Kulap received ordination as a monk at the age of twenty-six, a year after marrying. In the monkhood, he again studied at Wat Phrachettuphon, learning how to compose poetry, and "how to summarize and how to elaborate" in prose. He also added Sanskrit to his linguistic accomplishments. He studied old law and administrative practice with Phraya Sisunthornwohan, a distinguished nobleman of letters who served as an adviser to King Mongkut.

The next stage of his career after he left the monkhood in about 1860 veered away from this ideal education to which every young man in the kingdom would have aspired. For the next fifteen years, he took a series of jobs with foreign firms run by English, Americans, and Germans, mostly as a clerk in steam rice mills.[5] No doubt he learned more English during this period. Successive positions brought him increases in salary, from 20 baht to 250 baht per month. His employers favored him with trips to Singapore, Penang, Sumatra, Manila, Batavia, Macao, Hong Kong, Calcutta, and Europe. His travels even took Kulap to China, with stops in Saigon and Japan as interpreter on a purchasing expedition for the cremation pyre of Queen Sunanthakumarirat, who had died in 1880. For the exhibition of 1882 celebrating the centennial anniversary of the founding of Bangkok, Kulap was invited to display his collection of more than 1,000 volumes of old Siamese books and received for his efforts a souvenir medal and two royal autographs. Knowing that he was "fond of books," the princes thought well enough of Kulap's bibliographic expertise to grant him membership in the Vajiranana Library on

21 August 1884 (Damrong 1966: 145). About the same time, Kulap began official service as "adjutant" under Jaophraya Norarat in the harbor police, his seven-year service eventually earning him commendation from the king in the form of a medallion imprinted with images of the five Bangkok kings.[6] When a dinner for the royal family, the diplomatic corps, and merchants was held to welcome the king home from his European trip in 1897, Kulap and his family received an invitation to attend. Kulap's professional life did not prevent him from being a model father by nineteenth-century standards. His twelve wives bore him seventeen daughters and one son.

However difficult the autobiography is to substantiate, its claims tell us much about nineteenth-century respectability: lesser noble lineage, monastic education, tutelage by distinguished figures close to the crown in the most renowned monasteries, contact with Europeans including Bishop Pallegoix, knowledge of Western and Indian classical languages, and travel abroad. Except for the global tour, Kulap's upbringing might very well have been that of King Mongkut, and had King Chulalongkorn not visited Batavia and India in the early part of his reign? By his own account, Kulap's education was the best obtainable at the time, an education fit for a king. In his publications, he proudly printed invitations he had received to join learned societies, invitations to lecture, and announcements of royal awards for his service.[7] Socially and professionally, Kulap perceived for himself the same opportunities and rewards as those enjoyed by the highest-born in the kingdom. In a variety of ways, he tied the events of his life to the royal family whose aura exerted a pull on him, shaping his ambition, but despite his accomplishments and aspirations, he was never a part of the court world. His bumptious attempts to prove his social status in his publications only underscore the fact that he was not a member of the social and political hierarchy. Yet his career in publishing did pave the way for his successors in journalism to become a mirror for that hierarchy after the turn of the century.

In one field, however, Kulap challenged royal prerogative, for in the second half of his life he became a master of the craft of printing and an amateur historian who managed to gain access to sources in the royal archives. In his zeal to discover the past, K. S. R. Kulap rewrote his sources in such a way that King Chulalongkorn, Prince Damrong, and others questioned his integrity and motives.

Purloined Documents or a Creative Historian?

Kulap's path crossed that of the royal family when he first met Prince Damrong in 1882 at the centennial celebration of the founding of Bangkok. By that year, Kulap had demonstrated a connoisseur's interest in printing and had accumulated a notable collection of handbills, copies of royal announcements, commercial circulars, first-edition printed books, and other odd bits of printed matter. He had considerable skills as a cataloguer, enabling him to locate books quickly in his large collection (Sawat 1966: 171). Fortunately for Kulap, the room adjoining his contained royal manuscripts entrusted to the private care of Prince Bodinphaisansophon, then head of the Department of Royal Scribes, while the Royal Scribes' library in the Grand Palace underwent renovation.

The accessibility of these manuscripts to Kulap sparked his curiosity, and out of his love for old writings, he paid daily visits to admire the most ancient books in the kingdom. Naturally, he desired copies for himself, his passion for old books guiding him around any obstruction. According to Prince Damrong's account of the episode, based on conversations with Kulap's accomplices, he circumvented the prohibition on public access to such documents by persuading Prince Bodin to lend the texts overnight one at a time (Damrong 1966: 138–41). With a manuscript in his possession, Kulap then rowed across the river to the Thonburi bank to the famous monastery, Wat Arun or Wat Claeng. There, in the portico of the monastery, Kulap spread out the accordion-pleated text its entire length, and members of the Royal Pages Bodyguard Regiment, hired by Kulap to assist in this venture, were then each assigned a section of the manuscript. In assembly-line fashion, they managed to complete the transcription within the allotted time. Kulap then rowed back across the river to return the original with the prince apparently none the wiser.

In this way, Kulap acquired original sources, which he used to write many of his historical essays, but he did not merely circulate or publish these texts verbatim. He elaborated, emended, and corrected them; he altered them with his own insertions and speculations. He also published some of them before they had been published by the royal family and without the royal family's permission. Kulap offered manuscripts out of this treasure of adulterated documents to the

Vajiranana Library, manuscripts that astonished the princes who were themselves constantly searching for new historical sources (Damrong 1966: 146–47). Prince Damrong confessed that he had never before seen books from the Royal Scribes' library and, having no standard by which to judge Kulap's copies, could not at first identify their origins. The princes were only temporarily perplexed, however, and began to suspect the authenticity of the texts. Prince Sommot, who at that time administered the library with Prince Damrong, acquired Kulap's history of the third reign and compared it with the library copy. Kulap's revisions became obvious. The king, notified by the princes, took no punitive measures but wrote teasing remarks of censure where Kulap had altered the original.

The origin of another text was not so easily established and defied explanation for some three decades. In 1883, shortly after the centennial celebration, Kulap published a document at Dr. Samuel Smith's press entitled *Testimony of Khun Luanghawat* that purportedly contained testimony on history and customs given by Siamese nobility and royalty to their Burmese captors after the fall of Ayutthaya in 1767. Distortions cast doubt on the authenticity of the work, and since copies of such a document should have been in Burma, the princes first presumed that uncaptured Ayutthayan survivors must have compiled the text in the early Bangkok period (Damrong 1966: 142–44, 1914, preface). King Chulalongkorn joined the debate on the text's origin, observing that he had seen a similar text in the Department of Royal Scribes' library and recalling that King Mongkut had used the Royal Scribes' text to compose inscriptions (Chulalongkorn 1963: I, 244).

Only many years later did Prince Damrong realize what had happened. In 1911–12, with the assistance of Dr. Frankfurter and Taw Sein Ko, Prince Damrong obtained a Burmese text resembling Kulap's, traced its origins to the Burmese Grand Palace, which the British had attacked in 1886, and had it translated with the title *The Testimony of the Ayutthayans* (*Khamhaikan chaokrungkao*).[8] Also, about 1911–12, the original Royal Scribes' text fell into the hands of the library's governing committee and the mystery was unraveled. For paleographic reasons, this text was dated to King Mongkut's reign, and although it bore the title *A Chronicle Translated from Mon*, this was soon changed to *Testimony of Khun Luanghawat* when the princes recognized it as Kulap's source. Kulap had seen the text long enough to rewrite, and revise it, but the royal family had lost track of its location until 1911–12. In the various versions of the prefaces to *The Testimony of the Ayutthayans*, Prince Damrong discusses Kulap's adulterated text but never mentions its author by name.

Shortly after this confusion was settled, Prince Damrong in his preface to *The Testimony of the Ayutthayans* reported King Chulalongkorn's admonitions against compilers who failed to identify their own revisions and alterations. The king welcomed new interpretations and corrections, but these should not stand as truth without further examination, and a compiler should declare how he or she had modified the original. Then, "if alterations are made and one turns out to be wrong," said the king, "nothing is lost. What person never knows error?" (Damrong 1914: viii). Criticism of Kulap's methods and the charge of tampering with royal texts pursued Kulap his entire life, but the text published in 1883 had launched another stage in his career.

It was early in the 1880s, while the princes and the king puzzled over the text's origins, that Kulap entered official service and became a library member, his reputation much enhanced as a person knowledgeable in ancient studies and one who possessed old manuscripts. On 3 December 1897, Kulap commenced publication of his own journal, *Sayam Praphet*, which ran at least until 1908 and reproduced the texts he had revised from royal manuscripts and other sources. In the second issue (January 1898), Kulap announced a circulation of fifteen hundred and cited five hundred subscribers in Bangkok, eight hundred in the provinces, and more than fifty in Europe, America, and Cambodia. Subscriptions at that time were six baht per year. The title page defined the publication as "eloquent advice," a collection of "various texts displaying keen knowledge for the moral and worldly progress of the future generations of mankind." The publications sold so well that three years later Kulap and his two sons were able to produce another journal, a weekly, "to provide alms of knowledge" to monks and poor people.[9]

Kulap proudly saw *Sayam Praphet* as a companion to the other journals of the period, which published historical texts and essays. No doubt the most important model for this type of journal was the Wachirayan Literary Society publication produced by the princes and the king. *Sayam Praphet* brought Kulap additional respect and popularity; many people began to use the honorary title for teacher or learned man, *ajan*, when speaking about him (Damrong 1966: 148).

Many of the articles which appeared over the years were pedagogical dialogues consisting of questions addressed by Kulap's son to his father. Historical problems were raised and resolved. The son might cite contradictions among various texts and the father would discuss alternative answers, arguing a position on chronology, titulature, nomenclature, traditional practice, administrative organization, and any number of other subjects. Kulap's essays covered the introduction of steamships into Siam, the founding of provincial capitals, canal construction in Bangkok and Thonburi, Chinese secret societies, and monastery histories. Just as the Siamese kings viewed the historical record as political intelligence, so Kulap viewed his reading of chronicles and ancient documents "as a device for suggesting how we may view ways of doing things which can be employed in new situations."[10] The reader of his journal would also encounter "unusual and surprising" episodes for the first time, but the articles were not at all a journey into the fabulous. The son might ask if King Chulalongkorn was the first Asian monarch to visit Europe. Kulap scoured thousands of pages, including books in French and English, and concluded that a Persian monarch had preceded King Chulalongkorn. He apologized for not having time to reproduce a photograph of the Persian monarch and his harem in Europe. Many of the problems posed were provocative and the categories of discourse were often the same ones employed by Prince Damrong when he wrote his own histories.

In his enthusiasm to display his erudition and his texts, however, Kulap committed excesses which embroiled him with the royal family. In a number of incidents, his writings alarmed King Chulalongkorn to the extent that the king reprimanded him publicly.

In terms of the punishment meted out to Kulap, the first incident was the most serious and occurred about 1897 or 1898. Once Kulap had exhausted his supply of royal manscripts, he, according to Prince Damrong, turned to creating sources of his own, including a chronicle of the Sukhothai period when Sukhothai submitted to Ayutthaya's superior power and fell into vassalage (Damrong 1966: 148–54). In Kulap's chronicle, a Sukhothai king called "Phra Pinket" was succeeded by his son, "Phra Chunlapinket," but the heir was incompetent and led the kingdom to dishonor and defeat. King Chulalongkorn saw mischief in the story. By means of wordplay in the names of his fictional monarchs, Kulap had associated Chulalongkorn with the misfortunes of the incompetent heir.[11] The allusion offended the king, and he sentenced Kulap to seven days of labor in the asylum (*rong ba*). For a man who had been granted trust by the princes on the Vajiranana Library committee, this punishment was extreme, but it did not deter him from further acts of his irrepressible imagination.

A few years later, in 1900–11, an article in Siamese appeared in the *Bangkok Times* describing the cremation ceremony for Crown Prince Vajirunahis, who had died on 4 January 1895. The Siamese-language editor of the *Bangkok Times* was none other than Kulap's son, and an article citing sixty-five to seventy volumes of old manuscripts and elaborating on the newspaper account promptly appeared in *Sayam Praphet*, Kulap's journal. But members of the royal family present at the ceremony could not recognize many of the details reported in these accounts. Concerned that the readership would be misinformed on cremation customs, the king then ordered the minister of the palace, Prince Phitthayalap, to question Kulap on the sources he had consulted. Prince Phitthayalap's report, published in the *Royal Thai Government Gazette*, disclosed that Kulap, when pressed to defend his account with substantiating evidence, retreated.[12] He conceded that the manuscripts were not old texts but merely accounts of cremations he had collected from chronicles of Jaophraya Thiphakorawong, the only verifiable sources he had used. Such matters as participation of members of the royal family in various stages of the ceremony and the protocol involved in lighting the pyre were based on Kulap's conjectures and speculations. The minister of the palace concluded his report by warning readers of Kulap's unreliability and by discrediting him as an accurate chronicler of the kingdom's traditions. Casual habits of reportage had blemished an important dynastic event, the cremation of the crown prince, whose early death had saddened the kingdom, and had thereby required this strongly worded public expression of royal displeasure.

Unauthorized Biography

By far the most extensive investigation into Kulap's writings coincided with Prince Phitthayalap's inquiry and overshadowed it. Kulap composed a cremation biography of Supreme Patriarch Sa, abbot of Wat Ratchapradit, who had died on 11 January 1900, and submitted two thousand copies of it to King Chulalongkorn for distribution at the cremation. While not of royal blood himself, Supreme Patriarch Sa through his association with King Mongkut and King Chulalongkorn had been teacher and spiritual counselor to many members of the royal family. The king was thus disturbed to receive a copy of Sa's biography filled with rather novel facts about his life, which was well known at the time.

This senior monk, one of the most respected in the nineteenth century, received his first religious education from his commoner father, who had been a renowned preacher while a monk. Sa then completed the nine grades of Pali study at the age of eighteen while he was still a novice, a feat accomplished by only a handful of monks in the early Bangkok period (Damrong and Sommot 1923: 140–52; Praphat 1962: 286–325). He was ordained as a monk about 1833 at Wat Rachathiwat, where King Mongkut had studied at the beginning of his twenty-seven years in the monkhood. Sa soon became attached to King Mongkut's entourage as one of ten "royal followers" in the Thammayuttika order and then followed King Mongkut to Wat Bowonniwet, where the latter had been appointed abbot by Rama III in 1837. After being appointed by Rama III to the highest ranking class of senior monks, the Phra Rachakhana class, Sa disrobed, possibly without Mongkut's permission, only to be persuaded by the king to reenter the Sangha and be ordained again (Praphat 1962: 293). During his reign, King Mongkut built a new monastery, Wat Ratchapradit, exclusively for the Thammaytittika order, which he had founded, and invited Sa to be its abbot. Further increases in ecclesiastical rank brought this monk, in 1893, to the pinnacle of the Sangha, the position of supreme patriarch. In one of the appointment decrees King Chulalongkorn cited Sa's knowledge of Khmer, Siamese, Sinhalese, Mon, Sanskrit, and Pali, languages that Sa put to use in compiling a large number of books for Buddhist instruction. Indeed, King Chulalongkorn had good reason to express deep respect for him, since he had officiated at the king's own ordination.

For a monk of such stature to be honored with anything less than an impeccably truthful biography was an affront not only to the late patriarch but also to the Sangha. Faced with the inaccuracies and distortions that had crept into Kulap's account, the king declined permission to distribute the book at the cremation ceremony, and acting as he had after reading Kulap's misinformed account of the late crown prince's cremation. Chulalongkorn ordered an investigation "because the words are not credible, and people will be deceived by Kulap's mixing of falsehood and truth."[13] A commission, consisting of members of the royal family and nobility who had experience pertinent to Sa's life, was appointed to separate fact from error. The nominal chairman was Prince Wachirayan Warorot, half brother to the king, head of the Thammayuttika order, abbot of Wat Bowonniwet, and subsequently supreme patriarch himself in the following reign. Prince Naret Worarit and Phraya Sisunthornwohan assisted Prince Wachirayan as deputy chairmen.

The investigating commission met for less than a month, beginning on 5 March 1901 with the hearing of testimony, and ending on 27 March 1901 with an announcement of its findings.[14] The commission undertook its assignment methodically and rigorously. Despite its brief existence, it called a wide range of witnesses, including members of the royal family, the nobility, the Sangha, and relatives of persons mentioned in the biography. Dates were checked, genealogies were reconstructed; wherever possible, facts were checked against independent controls. By 23 March, the commission had finished gathering evidence and testimony, portions of which were not made public out of deference to the late patriarch and individuals interviewed by the investigators.[15]

Many of Kulap's sources and assertions collapsed under close scrutiny. The commission spent considerable time attempting to examine Kulap's principal written source for the biography, a large collection of *samutthai* entitled *Mahamukkhamattayanukunlawong*, which utilized a number of works including a genealogy of the Bang Chang line. In tracing the history of this document, Prince Wachirayan and the others learned that Kulap had revised an original manuscript by adding his own speculations and suppositions but had then lost the original volumes of *samutthai*. Having established the nature of Kulap's basic source, the investigators then challenged his argument that a certain noble in the Ayutthaya period, Jaophraya Chamnanborirak, was the founder of the line that produced Supreme Patriarch Sa. They calculated the ages of Sa's ancestors and discovered that ages given by some of Kulap's oral sources were improbable. After exploring the web of kin ties and acquaintances surrounding the late patriarch, the investigators concluded that Kulap's genealogy of Sa's line was faulty. Even facts in Kulap's own life, as he told it, did not withstand the tests. The commission doubted, for example, that a renowned patriarch, Prince Paramanuchit, had officiated at Kulap's ordination. The copper nameplate supposedly in Kulap's possession, which would have confirmed this claim, had become corroded and Paramanuchit's name was now illegible. Much of Kulap's evidence seemed to disintegrate before the inquiring eyes of the commission in just this manner. When asked to demonstrate his command of Sanskrit and Latin, Kulap could only pronounce a few words.

Kulap referred to a number of individuals who had contributed data for his biography of Sa, and the commission interviewed these witnesses to ascertain their reliability. Prominent among them was Thianwan, or T. W. S. Wannapho, a commoner who was distantly related to the Ayutthayan noble cited by Kulap as the founder of Sa's line. The most provocative social theorist and reformer of his time outside official life, Thianwan was imprisoned for seventeen years beginning in 1882 for a legal petition submitted to the king that had been judged seditious (Sangop 1967: III, 13). After release from prison, Thianwan circulated his ideas through a fortnightly journal, *Tunlawiphak photchanakit,* which ran from 1902–3 to 1906–7, and in a monthly, *Siriphotchanaphak,* which ran briefly in 1908–9 (Chai-anan 1972, 1979). Thianwan and Kulap were peers in terms of age and social class, but although they also shared the same position vis-à-vis the monarchy and royal prerogative, the extent of their personal association is difficult to discern (Sangop 1967: XXI, 13–14). Thianwan had at least seen portions of Kulap's biography, however, and the investigators took his testimony seriously. Much of the evidence given by Thianwan in interviews was acceptable; some of it could not be verified from other sources, thus weakening Kulap's case even further (Damrong 1929a: 9, 21–23, 28–29).

Kulap himself appeared before the commission to defend his biography. Statements about his written sources made in *Sayam Praphet* conflicted with the biography, and his own account of what his oral sources had told him contradicted their versions (Damrong 1929a: 15–16). Kulap submitted two confessions, but Prince Wachirayan had serious doubts about the sincerity of both and felt that Kulap was still concealing the truth (Damrong 1929a: 4). In the second confession, however, Kulap admitted to many of the charges. He conceded that he should have submitted a draft of the biography to the Royal Secretariat for review, that he had used his written and oral sources uncritically, and that he was a person easily influenced by the assertions of others (Damrong 1929a: 10–11). He did not, however, admit to being "untruthful," by which he meant that the inaccuracies were not deliberate. Indeed, much of the subsequent comment by Chulalongkorn and Damrong indicates that they did not take Kulap's distortions to be prevarications so much as the errors of a misled man.

On 27 March 1901, the investigating commission submitted its report to the king, finding Kulap blameworthy in seven ways:

1. He misrepresented himself, such as by boasting of texts he did not possess, so that others would believe in him.
2. He fabricated material, thereby deceiving others. For example, he composed passages that had no basis and cited this or that text that did not exist. Sometimes he inserted passages in books written by others.
3. He destroyed previously established truth. For example, he made statements that contradicted the evidence, or he took statements that people had spoken or written and cast doubt on them.
4. He does not look after his books. None of the volumes in his possession is well preserved.
5. He speculates freely when he is ignorant. In reporting on the death of the supreme patriarch, he saw monks carrying flasks of water and assumed they were going to bathe the corpse after the civil officials.
6. He goes beyond the evidence to supplement the facts. Kulap wrote, for example, that when *phraya* Sisunthornwohan (Fak) was in the monkhood, he officiated at the second ordination of the supreme patriarch. This is a fact, but Kulap adds that it occurs in an ancient text.
7. He is careless with language. For example, he referred to *krommamun* Bowonrangsisuriyaphan as *krommamun* Bowonrangsisuphanthawong. He did not begin by thinking carefully in order to be precise.[16]

The commission concluded that the biography of the supreme patriarch contained three kinds of error:

1. Falsehood with no factual basis, such as the lineage of Jaophraya Chamnanborirak.
2. Falsehood mixed with truth. That is, the root of the matter is false, but a portion is true. For example, he tied the lineage of the supreme patriarch to the family of Jaophraya Chamnanborirak.
3. Truth mixed with falsehood. That is, the root of the matter is true, but a portion is false. For example, he wrote about the supreme patriarch reaching the ninth grade of Pali study when only a novice. This is true, but the statement that Rama III gave him a congratulatory pat is false.

The commission expressed concern that even if the biography were not distributed at the cremation, it would acquire the reputation of an accurate account. At best, it would not be proven false, and Kulap would seize the opportunity to enhance his reputation as he had done on similar occasions in the past.

The king acknowledged the work of the investigating commission on 9 April 1901 and pondered its findings for another month before issuing an announcement of his judgment (Chulalongkorn and Wachirayan 1929: 244–47; Damrong 1929a: 48–49). People with sufficient knowledge would be able to distinguish fact from error, but others would accept everything Kulap wrote as truth. Since the supreme patriarch was a preeminent figure in Siamese society and a "refuge" for Siamese people, the deviations from the truth in Kulap's biography were inappropriate, and the public was forbidden to believe in the account. Although the king felt that such conduct deserved imprisonment, he suspended the sentence owing to Kulap's advanced age of sixty-eight at the time of the investigation.[17]

King Chulalongkorn had a final encounter with Kulap in 1908–9 when Kulap distributed handbills claiming he possessed a copy of the Siamese laws dating from the early eighteenth century in the Ayutthaya period. Kulap's claim suggested a rare document and aroused interest in official circles, leading Prince Damrong, then head of the Vajiranana Library, to send a noble to verify it (Damrong 1966: 151–54). The noble reported that someone had tampered with the date, an observation Prince Damrong could confirm when he learned that the year in the animal cycle did not correspond to the calendar year. In characteristic fashion, however, when requested to submit the *samutthai* to the king, Kulap changed the number of the calendar year back to 1804–5 in the early Bangkok period before the manuscript reached the king's hands. The king opened the book only to find the date in its correct form. When informed of Kulap's ruse and the carelessness of the official sent to obtain the book, Chulalongkorn could only exclaim with a laugh, "You have been tricked by Mr. Kulap!" Just how Kulap had acquired a royal copy of the laws remained a mystery until Prince Damrong in the course of buying up ancient manuscripts met a man who had sold Kulap the texts.[18]

The trade in ancient manuscripts continued through the first two decades of the twentieth century, and Kulap was not the only individual to acquire royal manuscripts. Untrustworthy followers of Prince Bodinphaisan concealed a number of copies belonging to the Royal Scribes' library and sold them upon the death of their patron.[19] One of Prince Damrong's tasks as head of the Vajiranana Library was to purchase as many of these manuscripts as he could, often for a bargain price if the owner did not realize the value of his possession. After 1932, all the books previously stored in the Royal Scribes' library were transferred to the Vajiranana Library and, in addition to the volumes that Prince Damrong had faithfully collected from private owners, almost the entire original collection was reconstituted.

A number of factors contributed to the accelerating pace of recovery and preservation of ancient texts during the reign of King Chulalongkorn, and the confusion in record-keeping highlighted by the Kulap episodes was surely one such factor. Prince Damrong's experiences with Kulap no doubt helped spur him to locate manuscripts and to find a suitable location for them. In fact, Kulap had outwitted the princes so easily because the care of ancient manuscripts was uncoordinated. Copies were scattered in the homes of nobles and princes as well as in several government buildings, and no one maintained an inventory of the royal holdings.

Furthermore, confronting a historian who willfully corrupted his texts and then represented them as authentic forced the court to reflect on the standards of its own scholarship. Kulap's works became a measure of irresponsible scholarship. Prince Damrong thought so little of them that he omitted *Sayam Praphet* from his bibliography of newspapers and periodicals published in Siam. While editing the letters of Princess Narintharathewi, King Chulalongkorn encountered problems of authorship and dating and cited Kulap's journal of corrupted texts, thereby making an invidious comparison (Chulalongkorn 1939: 35). Both the king and Prince Damrong used a term for "faked" (*ku*) to describe Kulap's textual alterations (Damrong and Naritsaranuwattiwong 1961: XI, 10). The question raised by Kulap's revisions was briefly captured in the title of the volume containing the commission's testimony: *riang ru taeng?* Did Kulap *compile* or did he *compose?* In writing chronicles and annals, historians should compile, put in order, arrange in sequence (*riang*); they should not assume the task of correcting or embellishing (*taeng*). At the time the commission undertook its work, this distinction was important in defining acceptable historical writing.[20]

Conclusion

The confrontations with the crown, formal reprimands, and publicity resulting from Kulap's revisions of royal manuscripts discredited Kulap as a historian, but it remains for future historians to conduct their own evaluations of his books and articles. These controversies aside, what was the extent of his expertise? Were his categories of historical discourse innovations in Siamese historiography? What in his writing derives from Prince Damrong and Jaophraya Thiphakorawong? Until each of Kulap's works has been compared with the original documents, these questions are difficult to answer. Even if the final verdict portrays him as a popularizer, his books and articles deserve a place in the history of Siamese historical writing. He seemed particularly intrigued by the process of assimilation, and in one essay conceived of Ayutthayan society as a multiethnic mix of Siamese, Chinese, Hindu, and Muslim peoples, each headed by a prominent family (Kulap 1913). He used French sources for his accounts of the seventeenth century and pointed out to his readers the value of European sources (Kulap 1913: 35–36). Some of his publications are valuable compendiums of data, despite the fact that they may be derivative works.[21] His magnum opus, *Mahamukkhamattayanukunlawong*, which had served as a source for Sa's biography, was a most intricate genealogy of the Bunnags, a noble family that had grown to unrivaled power during the nineteenth century.

Evidence exists, moreover, that he had a part in awakening nationalist sentiments, speaking sometimes as a cultural nationalist by criticizing the European handkerchiefs, Egyptian cigarettes, Swedish matches, and imported whiskey in which faddish residents of Bangkok indulged (Wacharaphon 1963: 45). His reaction was not one of xenophobia so much as dismay at the lack of confidence in Siamese ways.

Kulap's work is interesting for the variety of insights it offers into Siamese society during his lifetime. To dismiss him as an unscrupulous copyist would be to overlook his place in late-nineteenth- and early-twentieth-century history. As a journalist, for example, he explored and refined techniques in printing, using the medium effectively to carry him to a wide range of readers in the kingdom. He was, above all, a media man. Just as the editor of a mass-circulation daily, he understood the impact of illustrations. Drawings of coins, reproductions from seventeenth-century French texts, a medallion of Pope Innocent XI, swords and battle-axes, and a mysterious man on horseback appear in his books. The reader's eye was fixed on certain passages by the imprint of a hand with index finger outstretched, pointing to important paragraphs. Kulap knew instinctively how to exploit the nature of a printed work to capture the attention of his audience.

He was also a gifted salesman. In his books and in *Sayam Praphet*, he announced forthcoming publications from his press, offering prospective purchasers such inducements as a pocket calendar and a chance to win one thousand baht.[22] Purchase of one particular volume entitled the owner to visit Sayam Praphet Press and to view original illustrations from French books. In addition to encouraging readers to inspect invitations to social functions, Kulap also proposed to give away five thousand baht if he did not really possess a certain French text and another one thousand baht if certain French books did not contain illustrations as claimed (Kulap 1913; Damrong 1966: 151).

To a certain extent, this commercial shrewdness typified the times. The enterprise and energy embodied by Kulap reflect the possibilities and increasing prosperity for the subjects of King Chulalongkorn. In publishing, no less than in commerce and official service, opportunities beckoned the ambitious man. Much of Kulap's publicizing was an attempt to validate his qualifications as a historian and as a collector of old texts. In this context, one should recall his background. Such qualifications were new for commoners, and in the eyes of a self-made man, readers needed convincing proof.

Kulap's attempts at self-validation helped to create a cult of personality about the man, which must have been abrasive to some people. One of the illustrations employed in his books depicted Kulap inside a rose with the caption, "K. S. R. Kularb (or Rose)." He thrust himself on his readers. Yet his popularity did not derive only from his mastery of the printing medium and his natural talent for projecting himself through his writings. In several ways, he struck a responsive chord with commoners in whose class he was ultimately rooted. He operated a genealogical service where Bangkok residents desiring to know if they had noble lineage could obtain a reconstructed family tree. His knowledge was encyclopedic; it was said that he could reply to anything that was asked him (Sawat 1961: 171). These attributes as well as his publishing ventures earned him a reputation as a sage.

For others, however, his purported wisdom was a sham, and they mocked him publicly as a charlatan and a fool. In reporting the irregular sale of the law books, the *Bangkok Times Weekly Mail* in 1909 referred to Kulap as a patent-medicine seller, a label which Kulap's promotional instincts had encouraged. Several years earlier he had been photographed "active and hearty at 71" with his son in a newspaper advertisement for a product known as Dr. Williams' Pink Pills.[23] This aggressive personal quality also subjected him to criticism and ridicule from the princes. They saw him as a man seeking fame for himself (Damrong 1929a: 11–13). He foisted falsehoods on the public to gain the public's respect, and, worst of all, he had no shame about it when caught (Chulalongkorn and Wachirayan 1929: 242). To a certain extent, the princes were reacting to the way Kulap conducted himself, since, in the words of a modern author, "he knew too much to the point where he incurred the enmity of some princes who said he was excessively pretentious" (Sawat 1966: 169). One prince was not outraged so much as amused, and engaged himself in writing parodies of *Sayam Praphet*, which he distributed for the entertainment of the other princes.[24] The parodies focused on Kulap's manner of presenting himself in his publications.

The controversies, then, centered on more than the accuracy of his historical works. The court was also discovering the degree of diversity and variability it could tolerate before its identity and prerogatives were called into question. Kulap was testing this identity by imperfectly imitating courtly scholarship and courtly skills. The most imposing model for *Sayam Praphet*, the journal of a commoner, was *Wachirayan*, the journal of princes, but Kulap's publication was far from an exact copy. Like a curved mirror, he reflected a distorted image of the monarchy back on itself. Even the name of his journal echoed the name of the kingdom, *sayam prathet*, in a near homophony.

Finally, one other example suggests how Kulap must be seen in relation to the court and the official hierarchy. K. S. R. Kulap along with such men as T. W. S. Wannapho used initials before their names to set themselves apart from other Siamese. Although the royal family used initials to indicate the generation of royalty (M. C. for Mom Jao, M. L. for Mom Luang), this usage by Kulap and Wannapho was probably an affectation of European convention, expressing their "classless" position. Kulap and Wannapho, like the Bangkok Europeans who owned the steam rice mills or who served as Christian missionaries, found themselves outside the official hierarchy of noble and royal lineages. These men, living by means of the talents required by new technologies and economic activity, represented a new type of figure in Siamese society, "classless" in the sense that it did not fit into the traditional social framework. Furthermore, the usage of initials, widespread among journalists in recent Siamese history, may indicate that these authors were declaring themselves nonconformists with respect to the norms that govern Siamese behavior. In the tradition of K. S. R. Kulap and T. W. S. Wannapho, the author who employs initials in his signature gives notice that he is assuming a critical stance toward convention.

K. S. R. Kulap lived at least until 1913,[25] his long life touching a number of themes in nineteenth- and early-twentieth-century Siamese history. His journal brought the subjects that interested him—ethnic assimilation, genealogy, and moral improvement, among others—to literate commoners. His historical imagination, force of personality, mastery of printing technology, and passion for antiquity propelled him into conflict with the world of the court, conflict that has earned him a place in Siamese historiography, journalism, and cultural and social history.

Notes

1. Prince Damrong in his preface to the records of these interrogations (Damrong 1914: iii) states that Siamese versions of Burmese chronicles consist largely of information obtained in this manner.

2. Low's Siamese grammar of 1828 had been printed in Calcutta; Bradley's type arrived by way of Burma and Singapore. In Burma, the Baptist missionary Judson and a printer named Hough had used the type for Siamese held as captives from the fall of Ayutthuya (Khajorn 1965: 2–7).

3. David K. Wyatt, personal communication, 19 February 1973.

4. P. Wacharaphorn (1963: 44) makes this point about the uniqueness of the autobiography, which appears at the beginning of the lengthiest of his writings, *Mahamukkhamattayanukunlawong* (Bangkok, 1905). K. S. R. Kulap's reputation as an inaccurate reporter makes this autobiography difficult to use. Some of his statements are confirmed in other sources, but a number of recollections were challenged.

5. From D. B. Bradley's *Bangkok Calendar* of 1865 and 1867, the employers cited in Kulap's autobiography can be identified as Franklin Blake, manager of the American Steam Rice Mill, established in October 1858; Pickenpack of Pickenpack Thies and Co., established in January 1858; A. Markwald, manager of a German rice mill, established in 1858; A. Redlich, a partner in Windsor and Co., established in 1870. Damrong (1966: 138) confirms that he worked for Markwald. The managers of most of these firms served as consuls to various European countries.

6. Sawat (1966: 169–71) lends credence to this service in the harbor police as does Prince Damrong. It is possible, of course, that the elderly noble interviewed by Sawat recalled this episode from his reading of Kulap's autobiography, but the noble's account is more detailed than Kulap's recollections on this point.

7. Kulap explained that he printed these letters, invitations, and rewards to offer gratitude and to remind his children and relatives of the king's majesty. Anyone doubtful of the authenticity of the letters was invited to inspect them; *Sayam praphet*, 1.2 (January 1898).

8. 1911–12 is a notation indicating that the Buddhist Era year, which began in April, did not coincide with the Gregorian Era year.

9. *Sayam praphet*, 3.32 (Oct. 1900). Its circulation was 1,000 copies per month. The foreign press translated the title literally as "alms of knowledge" and pointed out that Kulap was the first to offer such alms, *Bangkok Times Weekly Mail*, 12 Sept. 1900.

10. *Sayam Praphet*, 1.3 (Feb. 1898).

11. An English translation in the *Bangkok Times Weekly Mail* on 3 June 1899 of one of Kulap's articles, "The Origin of the Siamese," mentions King Pin Ket. *Pinket* was synonymous with *jomklao*, Mongkut's coronation name; Chulalongkorn's coronation name was *junlachomklao*. Presumably, the sensitivity was to the pressure from France and Great Britain. Kulap's son worked for the *Siam Observer*, a European owned newspaper that took a strong irredentist position toward the French after 1893 (Khajorn 1965: 70).

12. *Ratchakitchanubeksa* [Royal Thai Government Gazette], 17.53 (31 March 1901).
13. See King Chulalongkorn's letter of 28 February 1901 in Chulalongkorn and Wachirayan 1929: 240, charging the investigators with their responsibilities. As is clear from the strong language in the following letter of 21 March 1901 (1929: 241) about Kulap's writings, the king was losing his patience. Kulap later published a version of the biography in *Sayam Praphet* 4.10 different from the one submitted to the king.
14. See Damrong 1929a for the prince's full account of the investigation, including minutes of the commission meetings.
15. Damrong 1929a: 4, 7, 8. As Damrong notes in his preface, publication of the Chulalongkorn-Wachirayan correspondence finally precipitated the publication of the commission's inquiry, which had been withheld for almost three decades. Detailed transcripts of the testimony were printed in *Ruang nai kulap editoe sayam praphet riang ru taeng prawat somdetphrasangkharat* [On whether Mr. Kulap, editor of Sayam Praphet, compiled or composed the biography of the Supreme Patriarch] (Bangkok n.d.). This publication presents comparisons between the two versions of the biography, tables showing inconsistencies and contradictions in witness testimony, and a genealogy constructed according to that testimony.
16. Chulalongkorn and Wachirayan 1929: 244–47. A previous letter of 12 March 1901 (1929: 242–43), answering the king's letter of 21 March with equally strong language about Kulap's character, outlined what the findings would be. See also Damrong 1929a: 40–42.
17. The investigation may have had a bearing on the formulation of a copyright law decreed by the king in *Ratchakitachanubeksa*, 18.20 (18 August 1901). Books published in *Wachirayan* had been pirated without acknowledgment (Damrong 1969: 28). In his subsequent writings, Kulap publicized his obedience to the law by stating on the title pages, "copyright according to royal decree."
18. Burnay 1930: 136 refers to the 1901 investigation of Kulap and alludes to the loss of two volumes of law books that were offered to "local amateurs" for sale. Both volumes were returned to the king, who put them in the Vajiranana Library. An English account at the time reported that the manuscripts had been offered to a foreign legation, which declined to buy them; *Bangkok Times Weekly Mail*, 27 January 1909, "Tampering with a Manuscript—A Passion for Antiquity."
19. Damrong 1966: 155–56. One member of the royal family bought up many of these manuscripts, fearing they would fall into the hands of Europeans and leave the country. One that escaped him was an illustrated text on Buddhist cosmology; fortunately, though, one copy remained in Siam. Prince Damrong personally inspected Siamese-language holdings in Western libraries when he visited Europe (1966: 169–74).
20. For the meanings of these terms during the nineteenth century, see Pallegoix 1896.
21. Kulap 1939 consists of selections from Kulap's writings first printed in 1918. It contains the ranks, personal names, names of parents, and short biographies of ministers at the beginning of the Bangkok period.
22. The free pocket calendar was an inducement to buy *Nangsu bamrung panya prachachon* [A book to improve people's minds] (2 vols.; Bangkok, 1909). An

extensive list of publications available for sale at the Sayam Praphet Press appears at the end of volume 2; David K. Wyatt, personal communication, 25 January 1973.

23. *Bangkok Times Weekly Mail,* 21 November 1905.

24. Prince Prachaksinlapakhom wrote and personally financed twelve issues of the parody journal, called *Sayam praphut tuayang nangsu sayam praphut khong krommaluang prachaksinlapakhom* [An example of Prince Prachaksinlapakhom's magazine, Sayam Praphut] (Bangkok 1925).

25. An introduction to his biography of Jaophraya Aphairacha published in 1913 gave his age as eighty-one, but according to his age calculated from his autobiography, he would have been only seventy-nine.

4

A Seditious Poem and Its History

D uring the 1980s, the charge of sedition, signified in English by an anglicized French term, lese-majesty, became more frequent as the incumbent Thai king's reign lengthened and experienced the stresses and strains that one might expect of a constitutional monarchy sharing the political stage in the late twentieth century with a series of military and civilian regimes. Even today King Bhumibol Adulyadej gives no indication of abdicating, but his advanced age raises the question of his successor and, therefore, of the future of the monarchy, making comment on the institution a delicate matter. From time to time the authorities charge people with lese-majesty in what is interpreted as an accusation of disloyalty not only to the monarchy but also to the national Thai government.

Because of the way it relates sovereign power to speech and writing, lese-majesty raises questions about the relationship between power and language. The charge is leveled at someone for saying something in public, as in the case of a former cabinet minister who said that if he could choose to be born, he would prefer to be born in the Grand Palace (FCCT 1988: 162). Or it is leveled at an author for remarks about the monarchy in print, as in the 1984 case of Sulak Sivaraksa, a well-known essayist and social critic (*The Nation* 1984). In one case, in December 1987, leaflets sullying the name of the crown prince were distributed at busy Bangkok intersections (Sukhumbhand 1988). These leaflets, circulated by "Thai Patriots" and other groups, attacked the integrity of the crown prince by alleging impropriety in his minor wife's education credentials: such behavior, the leaflets warned, threatened "to destroy the monarchy." As is sometimes the case in Thai radical politics, criticism was made in the name of defending and strengthening the monarchy, but such fugitive printed material that circulates comment on the royal family can be, in any case, quite virulent and derisive. Produced by crude printing technology, this fugitive material resembles, in the vehicle of its dissemination if not in its content, the underground and subversive *samizdat* literature of the Soviet Union in the heyday of its hegemony.

The ruling elite, and palace officials in particular, are mindful that prosecution of the crime of lese-majesty tarnishes the country's image in the eyes of foreign governments and human rights organizations. In October 1987, as if to prepare the way for more lenient treatment of those charged with lese-majesty, one of the king's private secretaries gave an interview to a Thai journalist suggesting that prosecutions for lese-majesty would gradually diminish and might very well disappear altogether if the country were going to progress satisfactorily to a democratic form of government. Then, in November 1987, in an amnesty just prior to the king's sixtieth birthday, a prominent political prisoner charged with lese-majesty was granted a royal pardon and released (*FEER* 1987), a case along with others that had been publicized worldwide by Amnesty International. The interview by the king's private secretary sparked a roundtable discussion on the lese-majesty law in the criminal code involving a privy councilor, a noted human rights lawyer, and many distinguished legal scholars at the Siam Society on 1 December 1987, a mere four days before the king's birthday (*Pacarayasara* 1987). This kind of public debate on an issue of such sensitivity was unprecedented in Thai history.

Just how the crime of lese-majesty has been used in the twentieth century to protect the monarchy, or, by extension, its supporters, or to silence opponents of military regimes, or to maintain public order has almost never been an object of serious academic study, perhaps because lese-majesty is a subversive discourse and a sensitive issue that threatens to cross the thin, sometimes invisible, and constantly shifting line separating academic pursuit and political action.[1] In the discussion that follows, I am proposing not so much to excavate the deeper roots of lese-majesty in an earlier period of Thai cultural and political history as to set out some terms in which lese-majesty might be discussed. The terms I have in mind include poetics, the construction of knowledge, the authority for cultural production, and the way in which political legitimacy was signified in the Thai state a little over one hundred years ago.

Although free of direct colonial rule, the Thai state in the nineteenth century was undergoing changes very similar to states elsewhere in Southeast Asia that had become colonial possessions in European empires. Local environments, which had been relatively autonomous, were being drawn into the orbit of the center politically, culturally, and economically. These local environments consequently became more fragmented, more heterodox, and more closely linked to larger networks—particularly the international economic network—than had been the case in premodern, precolonial times (Chatthip 1986, 1999). Moreover, the power of the center was increasing at the expense of the local. As McVey puts it, "this was not simply a matter of transferring power from one centre to another, but of an increase in the power available to any centre at all" (McVey 1978: 12).

Along this line of argument, it would not be an exaggeration to say that the nineteenth-century Thai state must be viewed as a colonizing state whose expansion to secure territory and thereby realize its own geobody compromised the relative autonomy of its provincial outposts and former tributary states. From a Lao perspective, for example, Thai expeditions against the Ho bandits in the last quarter of the nineteenth century would certainly look like colonialist maneuvers and encroachments (Chaiyan 1994, chap. 4; Thongchai 1994: 103–4). In the least successful cases, the attempted extension of central authority resulted in the compulsory cession of tributary states to France in 1907 and to Great Britain in 1909. From hindsight, historians living in the Thai nation-state have termed such forced cession as "loss" of territory, which is an anachronistic perspective. Before the nineteenth century, the central Thai state did not have a clear sense of itself as a bounded entity with a fixed perimeter (Thongchai 1994, chap. 7). How could it "lose" what did not clearly belong to it, at least in modern, i.e., European, cartographic terms? The very effort to reach and permanently hold these distant territories, at first by armed force and mapping techniques and later by reformed public administration, is an excellent illustration of how, in McVey's formulation, the center could wield greater power than ever before.

Other major changes were taking place in the nineteenth-century Thai state in terms of social and class relations. Economic change and the introduction of new technology, particularly the printing press, created new occupations and vocations, new kinds of local environments, new groups, new voices, and new modes of thought that began to interact with the center and the elite in unexpected and provocative ways (Sathian 1982: 62–63). Producers of knowledge began to move outside the court and the monasteries, creating a problem of how knowledge was to be authorized, and testing the boundaries and conventions that separated commoners from the aristocracy. Struggles broke out for rights and privileges between the aristocracy and the more outspoken of the new voices (Reynolds 1994: 10–11). In one incident, a poetic account of a military campaign to the northeastern frontier in the mid-1870s invited the wrath of a Bangkok nobleman who leveled the charge of lese-majesty—a direct attack on the monarch as the sovereign power of the state—at the poet and called for his execution. In the end, the king agreed there had been an offense but desisted from executing the poet and instead had him flogged and imprisoned, a humiliating if not death-dealing punishment.

As the suppression and censorship of the poem in question, *Nirat Nongkhai*, has for Thai intellectuals today come to symbolize conflict between writers and the state, persistent reflection on the incident has spawned a distinguished historiography. In a long essay on the poem written in 1961 while he was a political prisoner, the poet and scholar Jit Poumisak analyzed all the documents on the case he could find. His study placed *Nirat Nongkhai* in a lineage of literary works that had challenged the standards of literary value upheld by the premodern, feudal ruling order, and most historians of political literature rely on Jit's interpretation of the poem (inter alia, Bamrung and Chusak 1980: 184–85; Rungwit 1982), an interpretation I will evaluate below. In the mid-1970s, Thai critics rediscovered an interest in social realism, and Jit's work along with that of other writers and critics of the 1950s was unearthed and reprinted (Sathian 1982: 417–61). Jit's study of *Nirat Nongkhai* was published for the first time in 1975 along with the Fine Arts Department's censored edition of the poem and was reprinted in the same year (Jit 1975). Among the historians to pay serious attention to *Nirat Nongkhai* was Natthawut Sutthisongkhram, who in 1962 told the story of the 1878 suppression of the poem (had he known then of Jit's as yet unpublished work on the poem?), producing a fuller account fifteen years later, in both cases with the interpretation in terms of class and ideology favored by Jit filtered out (Natthawut 1962, 1977). In what follows, I want to reopen the lese-majesty case of *Nirat Nongkhai* as an opportunity to investigate how the composition, publication, and suppression of Nai Thim's poem illustrate the relationship between power and language in the nineteenth-century Thai state. I suggest that what was at stake in this case entailed an assault on the theory of literature and reading endorsed by the state. I call this theory of literature and reading "state poetics."[2]

The Poem, Its Author, the Genre

The author of *Nirat Nongkhai* was Nai Thim Sukkhayang (1847–1915), a man of humble origins who by the end of his life held the noble title of Luang Phatthanaphongphakcli (Damrong 1955). His father, a petty trader, put his son in the care of a nobleman, Jaophraya Mahintharasakthamrong (Pheng Phenkun), who provided patronage and, eventually, employment. Nai Thim was ordained as a monk and spent three years at Wat Ratchaburana, a monastery along the river where his father moored his trading boat. After he disrobed as a monk in 1870 and until Pheng died in 1894, Nai Thim served as a resident writer in the entourage of the elder nobleman.

Pheng Phenkun, himself a man of apparently humble birth, judging from the absence of a family history in his official biography, was a kind of foster son and attendant of King Mongkut from the age of twelve, making his way up the ladder in official service by means of his diplomatic and military skills (Fine Arts Department 1969b). So trusted was the nobleman that Mongkut summoned Pheng to his bedside as he lay dying in 1868. Along with other senior noblemen and princes loyal to Mongkut's branch of the royal family, Pheng helped the boy-king Chulalongkorn survive the 1868 accession and the Front Palace coup attempt in 1874 and was rewarded in that year with the highest noble title of Jaophraya. Natthawut says that Chuang Bunnag, the regent from 1868 to 1874, bitterly opposed this promotion, thus highlighting personal differences and rivalry that would later explain the course of events as the controversy over the poem unfolded (Natthawut 1962: 1333–35).[3]

Archival evidence suggests a more complex relationship between the two men. Chuang had backed Pheng's appointment to a key manpower post in the early part of the reign (Kullada 1988). But certainly Pheng was close to the young king, just as he had been close to the late king. He was both a councilor of state and a privy councilor in Chulalongkorn's early efforts to formalize broader elite participation in royal decisions. Strengthening these ties of service and loyalty in adversity was a marriage alliance: Chulalongkorn took Pheng's daughter as one of his concubines. This knot of reciprocal obligations between Pheng and the royal Jakri family that had built up over two reigns is seen by all historians of the incident to explain not only the leniency that Chulalongkorn showed Nai Thim but also the vehemence with which Nai Thim's poem was criticized by Chuang Bunnag, the minister who stood to lose a great deal if Chulalongkorn were to become powerful on the throne and independent of Bunnag influence.

Nirat Nongkhai was composed during a military expedition to the distant northeast frontier at Nongkhai in 1875—to the "boundary" of the Siamese state (*krung*), says the first line of the poem (NN 1955: 1.1). Directed from the capital by Chuang Bunnag and led in the field by Pheng Phenkun, the expedition to Nongkhai took place only a few months after the crisis of the Front Palace coup attempt had ended, Chuang and Pheng having taken opposing sides in the dispute. The campaign of the mid-1870s was the least successful of three efforts (the others were in 1884–85 and 1885–87) to suppress marauding Haw bandits who had made their way into the Lao states from China and were molesting and plundering the local people. Haw in northern Southeast Asia referred to Yunnanese Chinese (though many of them were Muslim) who conducted a caravan trade between Yunnan and markets outside of Yunnan (Atwill 2003: 1088). The few Haw who actually appear in *Nirat Nongkhai* seem to be hapless figures caught in a military sweep (Jit 1980: 248–51). Yet another poem about the expeditions in the 1870s and 1880s was composed in 1887 (*Nirat Tangkia* [Tongkin]), notable for its detailed descriptions of Saigon, Haiphong, and Hanoi, though it has never enjoyed the notoriety that has surrounded *Nirat Nongkhai* (Manas 1972: 166).

The sequence of campaigns against the Haw was serious for the Bangkok court because of French designs on what is now Cambodia and Laos. The territory of what was to become the Siamese nation-state was not yet defined, let alone secure, and French intervention was a likely consequence if the Bangkok court could not pacify the Mekong principalities. The purpose of the campaigns, as with other skirmishes elsewhere on the fringes of the realm, was to eliminate ambiguity about sovereignty as much as to quell a nuisance rebellion (Thongchai 1994: 106). The Lao country on both sides of the Mekong River thus had considerable strategic rather than economic value; the Lao economy had fallen behind the economy of other parts of Thailand more affected by the international, European-organized trade (Wilson 1987: 175). What the Bangkok court wanted of the Lao states was allegiance, not booty or commodities.

The expedition was something of a disaster, however, not least because other Thai-led troops already in the northeast reached Nongkhai and subdued the Haw before the army from Bangkok could rescue the endangered town. But for the Thai troops conscripted to march and fight, the expedition was disastrous, because it was conducted at the peak of the rainy season, leaving Bangkok when the rivers were swollen with water and the jungle rife with fever. Along the forested pass up to the plateau and the northeastern gateway town of Khorat, the rainy season was the malaria season. In telling the story of the campaign, the poet reports the grievances of the foot soldiers, their crowded camp conditions, their inadequate food supplies, their apprehension of the jungle and the ferocious Haw, and their fear of illness and death. As he says sardonically when the army is still at Saraburi, the cunning Haw would kill off the Bangkok soldiers by fever rather than force of arms, a remark Jit Poumisak thought was particularly galling to Chuang Bunnag because it made him out to be more stupid than the bandits (Jit 1980: 191; NN 1955: 15, 18–19). Before the army even entered battle, there were more than a hundred deaths from malaria and food poisoning (NN 1955: 56.17–18). And so nervous were the soldiers about the Haw that upon hearing gunfire while still many days' march from Nongkhai, they scrambled to prepare to fight only to find that they had mistaken villagers holding a midnight religious festival for an enemy attack (NN 1955: 44.116).

A straightforward chronological narrative, *Nirat Nongkhai* is virtually a diary of the expedition's fortunes, and it thus identifies itself as belonging to the genre of poetry known as *nirat*. Alongside each date appear place names and a description of their distinctive natural and cultural features. The poem takes on the character almost of a word map of the route to the besieged city, a travelogue in verse. In April 1988, I took a train journey and retraced the path of the march along the railway as far as the troops had ventured. I found the poem to be a reliable guide to the stations from Saraburi to Khorat: Kaeng Khoi, Hin Lap, Muak Lek, Chan Thuk, Si Khiw, Sung Noen, Kut Chik. The jungle on either side of the deep cut through the escarpment leaves no doubt even today of the hazards that faced the armies and trade caravans that had traveled this well-worn but forbidding route to the northeast by elephant and oxcart before the rail line was constructed.

Apart from the poetic rendering of place-names, *Nirat Nongkhai* has another element prescribed by Thai literature manuals for the *nirat* genre, namely, the place names en route remind the poet of his loved ones back home (Manas 1972: 148, 157). A *nirat* poem should encompass "movement and separation" (Wenk 1986: 182). The probable futility and danger of the venture before him make Nai Thim yearn all the more for his spouse, his kin, and his friends. Thorn Bush Swamp (Kut Phak Nam), for example, stimulated his imagination to compare the pain of separation to a thorn in his heart; if only he could see his lover, the thorn would drop away (NN 1955: 39.9–12). To ease his melancholy while walking through a forest just before Thorn Bush Swamp, he works his way through twelve lines of tribute to the *wan* family of plants, a virtuoso performance that should earn him an honorary membership in the Wan Society of Thailand devoted to the identification and study of these medicinal aids (NN 1955: 37–38).[4] Throughout, the novelty of new places, new things to eat, and new ways of life to learn of is offset by the ache of separation from his familiar surroundings and loved ones. Such Thai terms as *awon* and *alai*, which appear frequently in the poem, render this emotion of yearning and worry for loved ones far away. Alienation of place and person is thus built into the fabric of this kind of poetry, a genre whose themes oscillate between homesickness and the living reality that is pressing itself against the poet's senses.

The *nirat* genre was much changed by the last quarter of the nineteenth century, largely as a result of the verse of Sunthorn Phu, who composed a great many *nirat* (Manas 1972: 151–52; Wenk 1986). In fact, there developed during the course of the nineteenth century two distinct types of *nirat*. One, written usually in *khlong* verse, was closer to the Ayuthaya *nirat* and emphasized separation and yearning; the other, written usually but not always in *klorn* verse, arose from the merging of *nirat* and *phleng yao* (Nidhi 1984: 200–202). This second, hybrid type of *nirat,* which sometimes had no reference at all to

separation from loved ones, took the form of a travelogue, a documentary account (*jotmaihet*) of a journey. Although there are some
exceptions in which the poet indulges in fantasy, the *nirat* enjoys a
reputation for realism that stems from a concern to record the natural
and social landscape actually seen and experienced during the journey
(Jit 1980: 168). Jit Poumisak described this evolution of the *nirat* as
moving from "subjective romanticism" to "naturalism" to "realism"
(Jit 1980: 170–71). It is worth noting that *Nirat Nongkhai* marks
itself in the first line as belonging to this second, hybrid type, as the
poet announces that he is going to provide a documentary account of
the story of the journey to Nongkhai (NN 1955: 1.1). The theme of
separation and yearning appears throughout the poem with almost
predictable regularity.

The start of the expedition to the northeastern frontier was
auspicious enough. A flotilla of boats embarked from Bangkok on 22
September 1875, replete with music and pomp, blessed by aged
Brahmans blowing conch shells, and bid farewell by Chuang Bunnag,
the general who directed the expedition, and by the king himself. A
host of people witnessed the departure, including attractive young
women who watched seductively from the river banks, an early test
of the poet's resistance to temptation (NN 1955: 5.18–19). The boats
made their slow journey up the Chaophraya River through the provinces
of Nonburi and Prathumthani to Bangpa-in and Ayuthaya, where
Pheng paid homage to various historic and religious monuments. The
Pasak River carried the expedition on to Saraburi, after which beasts
of burden transported the army along the old trade route up to the
Khorat Plateau (Chai 1979: 275–77). This route, which to a certain
extent can be plotted according to an early-nineteenth-century indigenous
map of central and northeast Thailand, was well trodden under the feet
of previous Siamese armies sent to pacify the Lao territories (Kennedy
1970). The enormous effort to move the men and supplies from low-
lying Bangkok to the Khorat Plateau may be gauged both from the
duration of that part of the journey (two months) and the numbers of
animals (170 elephants, 500 oxen, and innumerable horses), many of
whom perished in the ascent to the Khorat Plateau. The Lao world to
the north and northeast had always taxed Bangkok's ability to provide
logistical support in the mountainous terrain (Battye 1974: 61–62).
And this was an army raised before the modernization of Thai military

forces that would take place later in the century; the Haw campaign of the mid-1870s was being fought "by the old militia under provincial and tributary state officials and chiefs" (Battye 1974: 211n.7).

On the march up to Khorat, Pheng and his men performed meritorious works. The soldiers joined with villagers to repair the chedi at Wat Klang in Khorat where they enshrined a tooth relic of the late King Mongkut; they enshrined another tooth relic at the ancient site of Phimai on the outskirts of Khorat (NN 1955: 58–60, 82). These pious works were carried out with much gaiety and goodwill from the local people—Chinese, Thai, Mon, and Lao—who donated food and labor to the cause. To commemorate the occasion, the Bangkok troops constructed a splendid pavilion and performed an episode of the Ramakian in masked drama (*khon*). They displayed their theatrical skills again after Pheng was invited to cut the tonsure of the Khorat lord's grandson (NN 1955: 68–69). In Saraburi, on the date of the death of his late king and patron, Pheng had sponsored a performance of the Vessantara Jataka (NN 1955: 22).

Several points about these episodes in *Nirat Nongkhai* are worth noting. The style in which Nai Thim recounted the march to the northeast is very much the style of a royal progress. Although Pheng was a military man and senior statesman, his relationship with King Mongkut and his son, the young King Chulalongkorn, conferred on him a special status virtually equal to that of a prince (Jit 1980: 228). The acts of merit recorded by his poet—his generosity to indigent local people, his ability to organize food and shelter for hungry and weary soldiers, his personal attention to their health, his just decisions in arbitrating conflicts between the troops and local women and in suppressing bandits—all these are the virtues a loyal client expects of a protective patron, a retainer of his lord, or a loyal subject of a benevolent monarch. Through its imagery, the poem tells us that this behavior is esteemed and valued. Sovereign authority itself, as well as military leadership, is what is celebrated in this account. Moreover, while "the local" reacts to "the center" in the person of Pheng and his army, what is being described in the poem is more an instance of "the center" moving through "the local." The grandest display of virtue is through the example of Pheng, the field commander of Bangkok troops, and the most lavish construction of religious monuments is undertaken by means of his energy and resources. Pheng and his army are rather like a traveling exhibition of central-Siamese culture. Only a few local customs creep into the text of the poem; here and there Nai Thim observes quizzically that northeastern ways deviate from Bangkok norms (e.g., NN 1955: 69.13–16).

The counterpoint of this hymn to benevolent and decisive leadership and to the civilizing norms of court culture being propagated in distant provinces is a mournful wail of complaint and frustration at the folly of a campaign in the rainy season, against which the ancestors had always warned. "The rainy season was no time to fight a battle," Nai Thim says emphatically (NN 1955: 15.15). Time and again in dispatches sent to the field, Chuang insisted that the expedition proceed—at one point he traveled by steamship up the river to make a personal appearance—even when it transpired that the object of attack, the main Haw force at Nongkhai, had already been defeated. Indeed, the biggest battle scene described in the poem is not Pheng's army pitted against the Haw but another general's rout of the Haw, and the fighting is not witnessed "live" but reported as hearsay from a returned scout (NN 1955: 61–67). This battle stands for the real thing, as it were. It is the battle Pheng should have fought had not time and circumstance denied it to him. Still many days' march from Nongkhai, Pheng received a dispatch from the Bangkok command finally summoning him home. In the end, Pheng's mission did not require him to demonstrate the qualities of a warrior at all, and the main body of the army returned to the capital without having fired a shot at the enemy.

From the first lines of *Nirat Nongkhai*, Nai Thim sounds the theme of resistance to this expenditure—the term "waste" is outside the poet's frame of reference—of men, animals, and supplies. The debt slaves and bonded men levied by the generals to form the army did their utmost to avoid conscription, and the lesser nobility responsible for the labor power cheated the system by reporting that their charges had fled; they did not want to lose the labor power to a long military campaign. For every three men levied only two could be located, many of the missing having bought their way out of the obligation (NN 1955: 1–2). In the tributaries, when the lord of Nongkhai levied Lao men to fight the Haw, the statistic was even worse: only one in three made it into the army (NN 1955: 62.15–16). The alternative to the army other than flight was either to pay the Haw protection money or to serve them "like beasts of burden" (NN 1955: 62.14).

The conditions in which the soldiers march and bivouac on their way to the battle they will never fight are miserable. While they are still in the lower Menam Valley at Prathumthani, they spend the night in a flooded monastery, the men squeezed together onto the few available dry spots (NN 1955: 8.19–22). All along the route, food and shelter are inadequate. Pheng's resources are soon exhausted, and the army must rely on the efficiency of Bangkok's communications and standing with local authorities to supply them with rice and fish. Near Khorat, the rice price has increased in anticipation of a hungry army (NN 1955: 41.15–18). Corrupt officials extort money from peasants and supply unhealthy oxen that are all skin and bones (NN 1955: 77.15–22). Planning for the expedition in Bangkok neglected warm clothing for the cold northeastern nights (NN 1955: 57–58).

Apart from recording the physical misery experienced during the ill-conceived campaign, Nai Thim also relates relations between the army and local peasants, particularly women. The young Bangkok soldiers womanize at every opportunity, forcing their way with Lao women around Saraburi (NN 1955: 18.10–13). Lao families had been brought to this area and resettled after Thai armies had conquered Vientiane in 1778 and 1779 (Wyatt 1963: 20, 30). When the army reached Khorat, the *jao* feared that the soldiers would make off with his female retainers and posted a guard. Some women of menial status were put in chains to prevent their elopement—or was it flight from bondage?—with Bangkok troops (NN 1955: 70.9–16). Finally, the gates of the city were closed to keep women from being carried away, and any soldier found with a local woman was required to redeem or return her (NN 1955: 74.15–20). The incident that led to this measure involved a servant woman, I-Phum, who was identified as having delivered soldier's clothing to a concubine of the Khorat *chao* so she could dress up as a man and escape with the army. Instead of punishing the favorite concubine who instigated the ruse, the *chao*, incensed at disloyalty, had the servant flogged almost to the point of death. Eventually, I-Phum disappeared, and as escape was difficult in the circumstances, Nai Thim muses that perhaps the *chao* had her killed (NN 1955: 70–74). As this is the only instance in the poem in which the name of a subaltern-class person is actually given, perhaps it is in itself evidence of Nai Thim's belief that she had, indeed, been killed.

Such graphic accounts of human cost and human misery chart another terrain of experience and values quite different from the one I outlined above that pertained to Pheng's virtues as a leader and governor. With its simultaneous referents in elite and subaltern mentalities—simultaneous in the text of the poem—*Nirat Nongkhai* is a crosshatch of discourses, the one displaying and celebrating the benefits of benevolent authority, the other demonstrating and criticizing despotic decisions. In performing this latter function, the poem signals human volition and human action that is not simply resentful but potentially destructive of authority, be it benign or despotic. In other words, *Nirat Nongkhai* carried a mutinous message. The poem's critics early in Chulalongkorn's reign chose to acknowledge that message and interpreted Nai Thim's poem as an act of resistance to authority (Chakrabarty 1987: 33).

The Poem's Critics and the Charge of Sedition

When the poem was published in 1878 at a foreign press, the Bangkok general, Chuang Bunnag, offended by Nai Thim's pointed remarks about the military judgment that had misguided the expedition, petitioned the king on 9 August 1878. He called for the poet's execution, citing cases earlier in the nineteenth century of minor officials who had offended military authority and had been executed (Jit 1980: 182, 203–4; Natthawut 1977: 429–30). These cases deserve to be unearthed and discussed, as does a case during the second Bangkok reign (1809–24) when one of the king's half brothers circulated a versified "anonymous letter" (*bat sonthe*) defending his teacher, a high-ranking monk who had been charged and convicted of sexual misbehavior. The prince, flogged until he confessed his authorship of the poem, died as a result of the interrogation, and courtiers found to be involved in the poem's production and distribution were executed (Terwiel 1983: 108; Thiphakorawong 1961: 80–82).

Poetry, even distributed anonymously, could be transgressive. Nai Thim belonged to a class of authors whose material was sufficiently defamatory as to merit punishment by death. Chuang accused the poet of criticizing him for dispatching the troops in the wrong season and not showing compassion for the troops, of altering the king's name, of setting one faction against another, and of using extremely vulgar language (Chulalongkorn 1934: 257–58; Jit 1980: 182–88; Natthawut: 1977: 430–33). The sections of the poem cited by Chuang were presumably those censored in the 1955 edition, although Jit Poumisak decided that what remained provided clear enough indications of what Nai Thim had actually written (Jit 1980: 189). While the king agreed Nai Thim had committed an offense, he desisted from executing him, largely because of the identity of his patron, Pheng Phenkun, who had served Chulalongkorn's father so loyally and who had doubtless played a part in the poem's publication. Instead, the king ordered that the poet be given fifty strokes of the lash and imprisoned (Chulalongkorn 1934: 260). Four manuscript copies as well as 305 bound and 100 unbound copies of the poem were confiscated and presumably destroyed as ordered in a royal decree issued on 20 August 1878 and published in the *Royal Thai Government Gazette* (Chulalongkorn 1934: 311, 314–15; Jit 1980: 214–16; Natthawut 1977: 436–37; RKBS 1978). On the basis of a printrun of 500, Jit Poumisak surmised that very few copies had actually been sold and circulated.

After his release from eight months or so in prison, Nai Thim returned to the entourage of Pheng Phenkun and rewrote a number of Thai literary classics—*Rachathirat* and *Sam Kok* among others—as plays, which Pheng produced. He became controversial yet again in the early 1880s when he wrote an unauthorized drama about royal affairs, provoking Chulalongkorn, who was confined to his sickbed, to write a parody ridiculing the script (Chulalongkorn 1972). After Pheng died, Nai Thim served as a retainer looking after the financial affairs of Pheng's grandchildren (the king's children by Pheng's daughter), and he served in the Privy Purse. Toward the end of his life, when his literary abilities were in decline, he wrote for the marketplace to earn a living and educate his children (Damrong 1955).

While the narrative of *Nirat Nongkhai* is certainly interesting enough on its own, and fertile material for Thai social history, it is the terms in which the king and his officials judged Nai Thim of the crime of lese-majesty or *min pramat*, i.e., causing injury to the sovereign power, that deserve to be scrutinized. Lese-majesty literally means "injured greatness." *Lese* comes from "injury" in Latin, from which "lesion" is also derived, and while the Thai-Sanskrit hybrid *min pramat* does not explicitly refer to bodily injury, the language describing the court's reaction to Nai Thim's poem carries a definite sense of injury (*chamchok*) to the king and his ministers. There is an affiliation between the king's name and his person, between his reputation and his body. A slur on the former is an assault on the latter.

> Those who called in question the prince's judgement, or doubted the merit of such as he had chosen for a public office, should be prosecuted as guilty of sacrilege .... By another law, it was determined that whosoever made any attempt to injure the ministers and officers belonging to the sovereign should be deemed guilty of high treason, as if he had attempted to injure the sovereign himself.
>
> (Montesquieu 1914: 204–5)

In other words, a verbal attack on an officer or minister of the king is interpreted as an attack on the king himself. And this attack is tantamount to violation of the sacred. The law on lese-majesty is one of the ways the sacred qualities attributed to the king are defined and protected.

Article 7 in the criminal code of 1805, the Three Seals Law, lists eight kinds of punishment, including two kinds of execution, for persons convicted of lese-majesty (actually, *pramat min* in the 1805 code), although the documents on Nai Thim's case I have read do not refer explicitly to this law (Lingat 1962: IV, 11). But the term *min pramat* appears twice in the materials relating to the case: the king's diary and a proclamation of 1878 drafted by the king himself (Jit 1980: 182–84, 210–14; Natthawut 1977: 234, 236–37; *RKBS* 1878). The interesting question is why the poem should be deemed such a threat to the king and his ministers that Chuang Bunnag demanded punishment by death in his petition.

The proclamation of 1878 sets out the offenses with which Nai Thim was charged: altering the king's name; "upsetting" (*monmong*) the king; making comments in vulgar language (*yapkhai*) about those who administer the king's affairs; and exaggerating an event that had been troubling to the kingdom. The poem was said to be contemptuous of state affairs and military authority, and this behavior, should it be imitated, would prevent military officers from leading their troops. In other words, the poem came close to inciting mutiny. When a person of rank sees one of his commoners (*phrai*) speaking beyond his station (lit., "in excess"), says a document of 25 August 1878, he should take action to check the behavior so that it does not dishonor members of the elite (Natthawut 1977: 438–39). Elsewhere, in his diary, the king recorded his opinions about Nai Thim's verse as poetry. While the king exonerated Sunthorn Phu from damaging the monarchy's name in poetry, he claimed that Nai Thim's poem had exceeded its form, it had gone beyond the *nirat* genre: "This book is unlike all *nirat* in which the other poets pine for their wives and children and tell only about their travels. This *nirat* is, in many ways, excessive in what it says" (Jit 1980: 184; Natthawut 1977: 434).

Taken together, these remarks about the poem in the official documents suggest that Nai Thim had violated the cultural code, in this case a literary genre, and that there was something threatening about the poem. Moreover, the nineteenth-century accounts of the poem's suppression are of interest in my investigation of the linguistic dimension in seditious activity. There were two distinct levels of language use in Standard Thai in the middle of the nineteenth century, belonging to the elite and to the subaltern classes respectively, a linguistic situation that Anthony Diller has proposed may be described as a kind of diglossia.[5] Certain aspects of the high-low distinction meet the criteria for diglossia described some years ago by Ferguson. The high variety was certainly endowed with prestige, superiority, beauty, and rationality, though it remains for historians of Thai language to determine to what extent nineteenth-century Standard Thai can usefully be characterized as a genuinely split linguistic domain (Ferguson 1972). Such diglossia as existed was not simply a matter of convention but of enforcement as well, as may be seen from King Mongkut's numerous pronouncements on the "correct" forms of language use. These included the proper way to write the names of kings, warnings against the use of idiomatic or "low" speech, fines levied for using wrong language in royal petitions, proper spellings prescribed for monasteries and place names, insistence on using correct prepositions, and, significantly for Nai Thim and his poem, remarks about what little power the authorities had to control writing (Mongkut 1968, passim).

The court's concern for the corruption of "proper" speech by commoners intimates a more deep-seated concern that the vulgarization of high culture was but one weapon that might be arrayed against the ideology and institutions of the ruling elite (cf. Scott 1977: 11). One of *Nirat Nongkhai*'s common motifs is the shouting or murmuring of the mass of soldiers, surging backward and forward, the kinetic energy of the mass translated into onomatopoeic sound. What thin line separated the collective din of *phrai* speech from the assertion of *phrai* will, especially at a time when everything from modern weaponry to printing technology would become more freely available to a freer labor force?

The threat posed to the king's person by Nai Thim's poem never died. *Nirat Nongkhai* entered the official record again in 1926, in the second year of Prajadhipok's reign, when Prince Damrong received a request to republish the poem as a cremation volume. Damrong refused the request, standing firm on legalisms and saying that the government had no objection to reissuing the poem, as all the principals were deceased, but the decision of 1878 ordering the books destroyed still stood. The king did not intervene to say otherwise, and the poem went unpublished for another thirty years. It was not simply a slow-footed bureaucracy that was at work to prevent the poem's reissue. One official correspondent commented that "the advantage of printing the book does not offset the damage that will be done" (NA 1926). The monarchy's apprehensions manifested in the documents of the 1870s were still very much alive in 1926. *Nirat Nongkhai* was finally published again in 1955 only after certain offending but unspecified passages were removed, and it is this censored version, reprinted when Nai Thim and his poem were rediscovered in the mid-1970s and again in 1980, that I and, so far as I can determine, all other critics have read (Jit 1975, 1980). Until *Nirat Nongkhai* is found and published in unexpurgated form, a shadow of uncertainty falls over any analysis of the poem. Jit Poumisak interpreted the scandal caused by *Nirat Nongkhai* as resulting from conflicts within the ruling group between the field commander, Jaophraya Mahin, who was Nai Thim's lord and patron, and the Bangkok general, Chuang Bunnag (Jit 1980: 189).

Jit said that the poem was written very much within the feudal paradigm of the time. In a departure from the idealized convention that literature be free from political concerns, the poem's composition was motivated by the factional struggles within the ruling class; hence, it was political (Jit 1980: 178–79). In fact, the nineteenth-century court also saw the composition of *Nirat Nongkhai* as determined by these factional politics to the extent that Nai Thim's interrogators encouraged him to implicate his lord, Pheng Phenkun, as the real instigator of the versified critique of the military debacle. But Nai Thim firmly denied that Pheng had in any sense ghostwritten the poem. He himself had been the sole author (Damrong 1955). Jit Poumisak identified another ideological element in Nai Thim's thought, namely, the social consciousness, liberalism, and sense of justice that would be characteristic of the new bourgeoisie. For Jit, the poem was thus proven to be a weapon of this new class (Jit 1980: 217–18).

State Poetics

Jit Poumisak's explanation of the incident in terms of the factional politics of the period certainly grasps the specific historical conditions of this controversy over what constituted proper poetry. In the 1870s, the king was locked in struggle with the old guard. Chuang Bunnag was a kingmaker who now opposed the king's efforts to wrest power from him, and Nai Thim's lord and patron, Pheng Phenkun, was a kind of foster child of the Jakri royal family who was sympathetic to its long-term interests. *Nirat Nongkhai*, even in the censored edition we are allowed to read, communicates dissatisfaction with Chuang's obstructionist tactics in palace politics. But Jit's explanation, which emphasizes the limitations of Nai Thim's ideology rooted in a nascent middle class, bears all the hallmarks of an "unsophisticated Marxist teleology, assigning value and significance in the extent to which consciousnesses are more or less 'developed'" (O'Hanlon 1988: 207).

There are other issues raised by this incident in the light of a vast neo-Marxist literature to which Jit Poumisak and others of his generation did not have access. I am referring to the debate, generated by Gramsci, Foucault, and their commentators, on how power operates and produces effects, on hegemony, domination, and resistance, and on "that conventional division between politics and culture, the instrumental and the symbolic, which operates in society at large, and in elite historiography, to mask the real mobility of power" (O'Hanlon 1988: 216). Jit did not discuss the *raison d'état*, the exigencies facing the late nineteenth-century Thai state, which guided the course of events as Nai Thim was prosecuted and punished, preferring to see this as a mere instrument in the king's hands for settling the dispute between Chuang and Pheng. Nor did he really account for the character of the poem, which is at once loyal to authority and subversive of it. How did criticism of Chuang in the poem slide over into lese-majesty, in the court's eyes? Why was Nai Thim taken to task for violating the *nirat* genre? How did we move from the nature of poetry to the authority of the state?

One of the lines of inquiry to take in addressing these questions has to do with discourse, with how language has materiality and is invested by relations of power. Poetry, by its nature, thickens language. It draws attention to the formal properties of language, to imagery and to sound, and away from the referential function, though the referential function is always present to a greater or lesser degree. According to its ruling-class critics of the nineteenth century, Nai Thim's poem had moved away from the formal properties of language, and from its genre, and too close to the referential (Jakobson 1972). The referential function had been given more weight—the "excess," as the king put it—than the poetic as allowed by the genre, though this was a genre that such poets as Sunthorn Phu earlier in the century had already much altered. The referents in this case were not only the political factions of the 1870s but also the living social body, the subaltern world of the conscripts called up to march on an ill-conceived expedition, the wretched living conditions they endured because the rainy season was no time to transport an army, and the probable death of I-Phum, the falsely accused Khorat servant woman.

It would seem from the ill-fated march and the literary criticism it has spawned that if the boundaries separating elite and subaltern domains are determined in part by the definition of what literature is acceptable to the elite, then we can speak of "state poetics." By poetics I mean commentary on what poetry should be, how it should be read, and what social purposes it should serve. In late-nineteenth-century Thailand, the place where high literature was produced, read, and discussed was the court and the residences of the aristocracy. The elite, centered around the court, prescribed and reproduced the conventions for poetry as well as for the dramatic and visual arts. The discourse that created these cultural products is what I am calling "state poetics." The way in which the nineteenth-century Thai state framed, articulated, and enforced a poetics became an issue that animated Thai literary studies in 1973–76, when critics began to argue about literature as a cultural product rather than as a repository of beauty, truth, rationality, and the sacred. This literary criticism of the 1970s, inspired by work that had been done in the 1950s, enunciated a theory of reading, a poetics, that challenged the state poetics made visible in the suppression of Nai Thim's poem, a poem that in turn became an emblem of the struggle for a new poetics.

As is the case elsewhere in Southeast Asia where the "theater state" flourishes (cf. Geertz 1980), there is much in the semiotics of Thai power relations that makes power attractive. In fact, there is much in *Nirat Nongkhai*, especially the poet's praise of his lord, which embraces the attractiveness of power and marks the poem as an elite document. Adopted by power and beneficiary of its patronage, Nai Thim, with his literary skills, became a medium for its representation in language. But the poem is a complex of discourses; what I suggested earlier was a crosshatch of discourses. It subverts the social order even as it upholds it. Two points may be made about this crosshatch of discourses: at the level of the subject-agent, Nai Thim; and at the more theoretical level of domains of discourse. For the first, Nai Thim is a figure of real ambiguity and contingency. He is not a fixed identity. He can celebrate power in one breath and hold it in contempt in the next. He can sing hymns of praise to his lord in one verse and etch in fine detail the distress, disease, and death of the troops—the results of decisions made by power—in the next. In this second voice, he speaks for the mute foot soldiers whom elite historiography has silenced. Nai Thim himself is no subaltern, but he has chosen in *Nirat Nongkhai* to be the subaltern's historian.

Domination, cultural or otherwise, can never be total. The dominant discourse never reaches everywhere; it never occupies all the space within its gaze (Turton 1984: 62). It follows from this insight, originally Gramsci's, that the world of the subaltern is only partially controlled and ordered by power. This line of thinking brings me to the second, more theoretical, point about the crosshatch of discourses. Quite apart from any role the poem played in factional politics at the elite level, it contested the elite's philosophy and conception of the world. More to the point, the elite read the poem as a challenge to its philosophy and thereby made it into a chronicle of resistance. It is this contestation that Chuang and the king had to respond to and neutralize. I think this aspect of the incident can be seen not only in the charge of lese-majesty (*min pramat*) but also, and most particularly, in the language used to censor Nai Thim in Chulalongkorn's diaries, the proclamations, and other materials.

Several of these documents, beginning with Chuang's petition quoted in the king's diary and repeated in the decrees, accused Nai Thim of using vulgar language (*yapkhai*) and upsetting the king—in short, of failing to show deference to the highest authority in the land. The same set of sources also accused Nai Thim of being irrational or confused (*fungsan*)—there have been such people in every reign, reported Chuang, and all were punished—and said that his actions were disrespectful. This charge of "irrationality," as well as accusations of untruthfulness and the insistence that Nai Thim's lord was really behind the poem's composition, were ways of denying the logic of Nai Thim's action. They were ways of denying his existence as a subject-agent who could think and speak for the mute foot soldiers. And this denial recognized the composition of the poem as an act of resistance on the part of Nai Thim not just to the command of the overbearing Chuang but to power itself. The most extreme denial of Nai Thim's existence would have been punishment by death, which he would have faced if the law had been applied to its fullest.

Similar tensions and struggles are at work and life itself is at stake on another "battlefield of symbol manipulation and language interpretation" where the ruling ideas of the ruling class prevail. In the Thai tradition of king-trickster tales, the brains and powerlessness of the trickster are pitted against the brains and power of the king. The official, written versions always take care to kill the trickster in the end (Brun 1987: 89–91). The language used to censor Nai Thim could be displayed as a matrix of polar opposites, with the beautiful, the true, the rational, and the sacred on one pole, as against the ugly (the poem transgressed the genre), the false (the facts were wrong), the irrational (*fungsan*), and the profane (*yapkhai*) on the other. *Nirat Nongkhai* does not sit squarely at the "low" end of this matrix, however roundly Chuang, Chulalongkorn, and Damrong condemned it; some of its qualities clearly situate it at the "high" end. What we seem to be witnessing in the *Nirat Nongkhai* incident is a struggle over hierarchies and boundaries, a struggle for the terrain in some intermediary space between the court and the subaltern world (cf. Stallybrass and White 1986: 194). The monarchy, the elite, the court (the appropriate term depends on context) sought to establish protocols of language and conventions for genres as a way of coding its own social identity, an identity that was changing rapidly as each decade passed. In such incidents as the publication of Nai Thim's poem, the ruling class experienced the limits of its control. Indeed, the outer limits of its very identity were being tested.

Embedded in a notion of the beautiful is a moral code and a code of behavior that the ruling class needed to uphold if it was to continue in power. In the transgression of poetic conventions and in the rupture of the codes of deference, loyalty, and allegiance represented by Nai Thim's poem, conventions and codes through which the ruling class maintained its dominance, we can observe the part that language and literature play in determining elite/subaltern boundaries. It is no less dangerous to the state today to have writers tampering with the "proper meaning" of monarch (Reynolds 1994: 150–51). In prosecuting the case of *Nirat Nongkhai* and its poet for lese-majesty, Chulalongkorn recognized how precarious and limited his own hegemony really was. Although the monarchy had no difficulty in resolving the case and was never in any way physically threatened by the disgruntled troops and their poet, the charge of lese-majesty leveled against Nai Thim stemmed from an anxiety about upholding the social and political order in its existing form.

Notes

1. My phrasing here suggests Thai-language discourse, but even in English historiography the subject has been neglected. For an important exception, see Streckfuss 1995 and his edited collection (1996), possibly the only treatment of the topic published in Thailand. In his 1995 article and doctoral dissertation (1998), Streckfuss analyzed the crime of lese-majesty as part and parcel of the discourse of national security.
2. Natthawut and Jit both reproduce many of the primary materials, and these are of great advantage to any historian studying the incident today. Wherever possible, I have consulted the primary materials myself, in which case I have provided a citation.
3. Natthawut also here alludes to an unpublished study of Pheng Phenkun's involvement in the case that presumably explores the incident in greater detail (1962: 1349). I have not been able to determine if this study still exists.
4. *Wan* is the name for a variety of plants with tubers or rhizomes. Some are edible or medicinal, some are used for sorcery and supernatural purposes.
5. Anthony Diller, personal communication, 15 February 1988.

5

Feudalism as a Trope for the Past

The existence of terms for feudalism in Asian-language discourses about past and present society poses problems about what the writer in English—anthropologist, literary scholar, historian, linguist, whatever—is to do with these feudalisms. Why do native speakers of Asian languages term their own societies "feudal" (feudal = term in language X) and how do they come to employ this term? Western writers usually dismiss these Asian-language feudalisms as too culture-bound to be of use in writing objective history. Such usage, so the argument might run, is too embedded in internal debates within Asian societies about who should—or should not—hold power. That is, feudalism is a category of social evolution that serves revolutionary or official nationalist interests, and such interests so skew its usage that the term cannot tell the disinterested observer anything illuminating about the political economy of a particular society.

Western academic historians more or less agree that while Asian social systems functioned with ties of bondage, subordination, and even vassalage, the lack of parcellized sovereignty, the absence of a fief system, and various other elements deemed critical to European feudalism have all disqualified Asian societies from being knighted with this term so essential to the evolution of Western society and the emergence of capitalism. Moreover, use of the term feudal for Asian societies violates a principal of cultural relativism for most students of Asia, because it assimilates Asian societies to the Western evolutionary schema, thereby denying those societies uniqueness and autonomy. To put the matter slightly differently, I suspect that most supervisors of dissertations on Filipino, Thai, Chinese, Vietnamese, or Burmese history, written in Western universities, would want to scrub the term feudalism from early drafts. The term is too problematic and begs too many questions. Yet many Asian historians writing in the vernacular insist on using the term precisely because it does hook Asian development onto a historicist or universal evolutionary sequence.

There are exceptions to these generalizations, particularly Japan and India. Japanese society, it is argued, experienced a feudal period, meaning that Japanese society at one time bore resemblances to Western feudal society, resemblances strong enough to make the term illuminating as a category (Davis 1982). It is no coincidence that Japan is also the one case of an Asian society approaching "parity" with Western countries in terms of industrialization, economic growth, and the hegemony of its commercial and business organization. The parity even extends to such Westernisms as competence in playing Beethoven, making "Scotch" whiskey, and collecting Rembrandts. Indeed, the feudal element in the Japanese past is deemed to help account for Japan's economic, industrial, and cultural prowess and its successful modernization.

Feudalism in the historiography of India is a slightly different kind of exception, because so much Indian history is written in English, thus clouding the distinction between feudalism (in English) as applied to Indian history by Indian historians and feudalism (in English, French, Dutch, whatever) as applied to Europe in the Middle Ages. I would argue that the signifieds of these two feudalisms are quite distinct, and that the evidence for this may be found in the preference among Western historians and social scientists, who are not much enamored of the idea of an Indian feudal past, for other terms such as segmentary state to characterize premodern Indian society.[1] But it must also be recalled that for more than a half century after the Rebellion of 1857–58, feudalism played a part in constructing a theory of Indian society that the British in their colonial historiography used to answer the important question "How are we going to keep India?"(Cohn 1977: 105–9) The feudal theory of Indian society served the British as a sociology, a classificatory system in which the British monarch and the "natural leaders" of India were placed in relation to one another as the dominant and the subordinated. In this discourse, the feudal classification inscribed relations of domination in the legal language of "obligations," "rights," and "duties." Moreover, such a classification labeled local society and its power-holders as reactionary and passé, thus preparing the way for interference in the name of progress. Other Western colonial powers used the feudal classification in similar ways. As independence movements gained momentum, young nationalists picked up the classification as a convenient way of demoting old leaderships and high culture in favor of a modern outlook.

When it is found in the English-language historiography of India written by Indian historians today, the term feudalism is really quite close to the Asian vernacular feudalisms that concern me here: its usage is bound up in a debate about the colonial past as well as the nature and direction of present society. In this context, "feudal" refers to a specific social formation in a Marxist historicist schema (as in the work of R. S. Sharma) or, more generally, to relations of domination in the precolonial, colonial, and postcolonial periods (as in the work of Ranajit Guha and the Subaltern Studies Group) (Sharma 1965; Guha 1983).

Most, possibly all, Asian languages with historiographies linked to Western historiography have vernacular equivalents of European-language "feudalism": Bengali *samantatantra* alternating with *samantabad*; Burmese *padei-tha-ya-za* (current usage) and *ahmu-dan-so-myei* (in use from about 1940 to 1960); Thai *sakdina*; Indonesian *feodal*; Tagalog *piyudal*; Chinese *feng-chien*; Japanese *hoken*; Vietnamese *phong kien*. Far from being a construct that tyrannizes, Asian-vernacular feudalism is a construct that essentializes. It can be found as the name of a period or social formation prescribed by party thinkers in the centralist historiography of socialist states (China, Vietnam, Burma) and as the name for relations of domination in a seditious discourse propounded by radical, marginalized, or disenfranchised groups (in Indonesia, Malaysia, the Philippines, Thailand). The obverse of pronouncements on the term in party cant is its appearance in a discourse of subversion. Thus, a military elite (Burma) may seek to explain its role by objectifying past society as feudal and highlighting its own modernist, nonroyalist, anticolonial policies. At the same time, a radical urban intelligentsia (Malaysia) attacks as feudal the dominant ideology, which retains remnants of a monarchist political system by appealing for loyalty to the sultanate (Muzaffar 1979, chap. 1).

In many cases, the vernacular terms (Indonesian and Tagalog excepted, as they borrowed the European-language term) delve deep into the past by drawing on terms of great antiquity to translate European feudalism. Official Burmese histories after 1962, for example, retranslated the term, rooting feudalism more deeply in Burmese language and history. The impulse was to plant feudalism firmly in Asian soil. Yet the activity of analyzing Asian feudalism (Chinese, Vietnamese, Thai, Burmese, whatever) also involved an act of discovery, not simply translation. Feudalism was already "there" to be found, excavated, and inserted into contemporary language via ancient words. It is such an activity and act of discovery that I now want to discuss by means of Thai material.

Metaphor and Proper Meaning

Since the late 1940s, the Thai term for feudalism, śaktina, has come to be used in radical discourse to characterize past society and its present-day remnants, a radical discourse in which the Communist Party of Thailand (CPT) and the urban intelligentsia participates. A particularly interesting example of a noncommunist radical treatise appeared in 1982, the year of the Bangkok bicentennial celebrations, entitled *Nine Reigns of the Jakri Dynasty*. In its arrangement of events in regnal sequence from 1782 to the present day (the incumbent monarch is the ninth in the line), the format of this history was patterned after "proper" history, but in fact this book is a counter-history, and counter to the brouhaha over Jakri accomplishments celebrated during 1982.

The proper format is filled with refutations of Jakri claims and achievements, and it candidly discusses one of the tabooed subjects of modern Thai history, the 1946 regicide of the eighth king. This counter-history, which provoked the political police to arrest some people presumed to be involved in its publication on charges of lese-majesty, begins: "Thailand was ruled by the śaktina system for many centuries. The śaktina lord ruled the land, establishing himself as the owner of all land, though he himself had expended no labor to clear it" (Raktham n.d.: 7). This mention of śaktina did not itself provoke the arrests, but I raise the example to illustrate how the term śaktina now belongs to a discourse aimed at subverting the proper meanings of such legitimizing institutions as the monarchy and the Buddhist monkhood.

The front cover bears a stamp declaring the work to be approved for the study of Thai history by the Fine Arts Department's Division of Archaeology in the National Library (no such division exists), and printed on the inside back cover is what appears to be the official logo of the Bangkok bicentennial year. These attributions are fake. The signs thus undo the fixed, legitimate, proper meanings of absolute authority by stating that one thing (the irreverent, scandal-ridden history that follows) is something quite different (an officially approved text). As metaphors, these signs make an improper analogy and imply the possibility of transformation and change, questioning the absoluteness of legitimate authority and proper meaning and thus of law. In Michael Ryan's words, "Metaphors lead astray.... Metaphors arouse passion by inciting feelings that may not be compatible with a political institution whose laws require a rational acceptance of unequivocal definitions of words" (Ryan 1982: 4). There is a direct connection between the unsanctioned transfer of meaning and resistance to sovereign authority, and Ryan goes on to show how metaphor—characterized by transformation, alteration, relationality, displacement, substitution, errancy, equivocation, plurality, impropriety, or nonownership—and sedition are interrelated.

Improper meaning is a material force, says Ryan. Writers such as novelists, poets, and essayists are often in trouble with authoritarian governments because they play with the proper meanings: what is seditious is the meanings that writers construe in their figurations of the world. In the following discussion of why there should be contention over the proper meanings of śaktina, I want to trace the activity of translating European feudalism as Thai śaktina, particularly in a 1957 text. After 1958, there was a distinct reaction against the śaktina = feudalism equation, a reaction that signaled a conflict about the nature of political authority. In my reading of the evidence, this reaction constituted a "war of interpretations"—not an academic debate, but a political war whose stakes were the terms in which reality was to be defined and indeed constructed.

History of the Term Śaktina

The Thai term for feudalism, śaktina, has been used commonly in Thai historical studies and academic discourse for the past twenty years. But it is also found in the speech of educated people, not necessarily radical or anti-royalist. Convincing myself that I was engaging in harmless sociological observation, I eavesdropped on a conversation in the posh Erawan Hotel Café, now demolished for something much grander, in early 1982 and listened to a banker and his client discuss "the śaktina manner" of another person, a woman not present, who evidently had a haughty, aristocratic air. The semantic range in spoken and written Thai includes: old-fashioned ideas and reactionary thinking; archaic institutions that linger on (the monarchy, the Buddhist monkhood); the perquisites and corruptions of clientship; and corruption in the bureaucracy. If technological backwardness and landlordism are added to this list, with the necessary changes being made for diverse Asian societies, the terms for feudalism in other Asian languages share a similar semantic range.

For uneducated, low-income Thai speakers, śaktina might indicate a sense of class difference: they (the śaktina with wealth, power, rank) vs. us (poor, powerless, low status). The derogatory, pejorative connotation is no more than thirty or forty years old. Indeed, the term used to have auspicious connotations. A young Thai historian, born in 1954, whose father named him Sakdina out of the best of intentions, told me ruefully that he is probably the last person in Thailand so named. He is the butt of much teasing from his university friends who have grown up with the ironic usages of the term in their speech.

Sakdina rama, a witty novel published in 1980 by a doctor at Bangkok's Ramathibodi Hospital, pokes fun at the favoritism and status-climbing of staff and patients (Phunphit 1980). Even the name of the hospital in the novel, Ramathipatai (combining Rama with the term "sovereign" that occurs in the Thai word for democracy), is wordplay, tweaking the social pretensions of the novel's characters. An anesthetist sees his noble rank raised after he assists on the successful treatment of one of the royal white elephants, an auspicious beast that itself holds noble rank. If the anesthetist had demonstrated similar skills in healing a pauper, there would be no cause for celebration. Part of the joke here is that the monarch's power to confer noble ranks was abolished in the 1932 coup that ended the absolute monarchy. In the novel, the referents of śaktina/feudal are not only royal approval and prerogative but also the injustices and inequalities that derive from class differences.

In academic discourse today, śaktina refers to a social formation, the śaktina system: the political, economic, social, and cultural order that characterized Thai society for some five hundred years. By no means do all historians and social scientists use "the śaktina system" to signify past Thai society. Some emphasize patron-client relations, the corvée system, and the monarchy, and reserve śaktina for its ancient, technical meaning: rank quantified in terms of land or labor. But for historians who do use śaktina, it is part of a discourse about Thai society, past and present, a discourse that stands in critical relation to the present order and may even aim to displace it, particularly such śaktina remnants as the monarchy and the Buddhist monkhood.

The modern meanings for śaktina, as outlined above, arise out of the Old Thai term *sakdina,* found in the Thai civil and administrative code of the fifteenth century. There the term refers to levels in a sociopolitical hierarchy underpinned by economic relations. The levels were differentiated by amounts of land allocated, e.g., from one hundred thousand units for the highest-ranking prince, to ten thousand units for a noble, and down to twenty-five units for a commoner and five for a slave. The Old Thai term is a Sanskrit-Thai hybrid: Skt. *Śakti* (the power of the god) bound to Thai *na* (ricefield). The Sanskrit term *śakti* conveys the sense of "energy or active power of a deity, especially a female deity" (Keyes 1987: 29).[2] In the twentieth century, there has been an ongoing debate about whether the units refer to actual plots, rather like fiefs, or whether they refer to units of manpower (e.g., one unit = one person), with some historians arguing that the social system evolved from one in which power was quantified in terms of land to one in which power was quantified in terms of people. Although the two terms are written and pronounced the same in Thai language, I transcribe the Old Thai term as *sakdina* and the Modern Thai term as śaktina to distinguish them and to emphasize the new meanings created in the past half century.

There is no evidence to my knowledge that the social system of premodern Siam was called the feudal/śaktina system until the twentieth century, and in its earliest appearances, in 1935, for example, the trope was simply a loanword (*fiwdalit*), glossed something like "a system of dispersed centers of power" (Nakkharin 1982: 24). The objectification of past society as śaktina society or the śaktina system was a post–World War II development. As late as 1942–43, the Thai word proposed for feudal was a Sanskrit neologism, *phakdina,* and the author mulling over the problem of finding an equivalent term in Thai concluded that "we have never had feudalism as the Europeans understand it, so we do not have an exact word for it" (Wanwaithayakon 1951: 129–30).

The sentence might well be reversed: "Since we do not have a word for it, we have never experienced feudalism."

There is some evidence that the term śaktina with its modern, ironic meaning was spoken in leftist circles before the end of World War II. One of the early union organizers has left a vivid account of a conversation at lunch in the publishing house where he worked. Kulap Saipradit, a prominent socialist author of the time, leaned over the table and called Prince Sakon, the "Red Prince" in the royal family, a śaktina, and the prince took the opportunity to explain the term as a graded register of rights to exploit (Rawi 1982; Kasian 2001: 10, 57, 147, 156). Such exploitation as existed in the mid-1940s, the Red Prince argued, derived from the rights to exploit exercised by the śaktina of old.

In the decade or so following World War II, the Old Thai term *sakdina* became fixed as a translation for European "feudal." *Mahachon*, the newspaper of the CPT, contributed to the semantic shift by translating "feudalism" in the Marxist-Leninist corpus as śaktina; its articles in 1947–48 sought to educate Thai readers about Marxist social formations. In 1950, in a work that remained the centerpiece of CPT theory until the 1970s, Thailand's social formation was labeled "semicolonial, semifeudal" along the lines of Mao's "The Chinese Revolution and the Chinese Communist Party" of 1939 (Udom 1979).

But interest in Marxism—and the śaktina and semi-śaktina social formations—among Thai intellectuals in the postwar period cannot be tied only to CPT proselytizing. The 1947–58 decade was the first real heyday of Marxist study and writing, encouraged by the relatively open forums for thought and debate allowed by the political circumstances. The progressives of the time wanted to undermine the periodization of the Thai past according to conventional historiography, and they used the Marxist unilinear sequence of social formations— primitive commune, slave society, feudal/śaktina society, capitalism, socialism—to do so (Reynolds and Hong 1983: 80–81).

At this stage, Thai intellectuals interested in analyzing the political economy of their society did not have Marx's long-unpublished *Grundrisse* available to them, and, unlike Chinese historians several decades previously, they knew nothing of the Asiatic mode of production. Asian society had to fit into a feudal or a semifeudal category. The analysis of social formations that first emerged in the late 1940s and

early 1950s adhered to a rigidly unilinear schema that had its origins
in prevailing Sino-Soviet theory. In the Soviet Union, the Asiatic mode
had been written out of the Marxian sequence following a vigorous
debate in the late 1920s and early 1930s as Stalinist historiography
took hold. Whereas Thai political economists by the 1970s had begun
to free themselves from a theoretical straitjacket, the postwar writers
labored under an orthodoxy made all the more imposing by the fact
that China had not yet distanced itself from the Russian revolutionary
model. The Sino-Soviet dispute was to begin only toward the end of
the 1950s (Reynolds and Hong 1983: 79–80).

The Real Face of Thai Śaktina Today

However common the unlinear sequence of social formations may be
in a certain body of Thai writing after World War II, the formations
were rather like shells as yet unfilled with Thai content. As if to
take the incompleteness of the earlier analyses as a challenge,
Jit Poumisak wrote *The Real Face of Thai Saktina Today* in 1957,
toward the very end of the open postwar period (Jit 1957: 356–491).[3]
In the reprintings of this work since 1973, "today," which gave the
work a contemporary thrust, was dropped from the title, presumably
so that the work would not seem outdated. What remains today are
"śaktina remnants" in consciousness, namely, the monarchy and the
Buddhist religion deemed essential to Thai identity and indispensable
to proper government.

Since the mid-1970s, Thai political economists have gone far
beyond Jit's analysis in their investigations of Thailand's social
formations, but the 1957 work is still powerful because of the way
it configures śaktina in consciousness. More than any other text of
the period, it created new meanings for Old Thai *sakdina*, and the
activity of creating these meanings is visible in language. The text
demonstrates how and why the term comes to mean "backward
agrarian order," "authoritarian rule," and "exploitative relations of
production," transforming the Old Thai term into a trope. By a process
of substitution and displacement, Old Thai *sakdina* becomes Modern
Thai śaktina. This improper transfer of meaning had seditious
implications. The text was unavailable and unread from 1958 until
1973, it was banned by government decree in 1977, and its author

was a political prisoner from 1958 until 1964. Early in the text, the following definition is given for śaktina:

> "Śaktina" literally means "power in controlling the fields," and if we expand on this meaning to clarify the term we can say that śaktina means "power over the land which was the crucial factor in agriculture, and agriculture in that age was the principal livelihood of the People." By explaining the term in this way we are able to see roughly that the śaktina system was a system bound up with "land."

This definition occurs in the first third of the work, the section that sets out the universal evolutionary schema, the structure of the social order, and the socioeconomic transformations that propel society forward. In this early section, the term does not mean graded ranks (*sakdina*) in the hierarchy. It means power. Jit's words for power here are *amnat* or *kamlang,* i.e., physical strength, the power to command, a pushing, shoving kind of power that lies behind the light, heat, ceremony, ornate clothing, and Sanskrit mumbo-jumbo of royal rituals.

The text anchors the term in ancient texts and simultaneously shakes it loose from its moorings in them. A number of devices accomplish this liberation of the term, such as assertion of a backward agrarian order and the naming of this order the śaktina system, a social system that rests on landed power. The śaktina is a class of land-lords (*jaothidin*), lords of the land who wielded political, juridical, and cultural power and did not simply collect rents. The text juxtaposes features of this backward agrarian order against categories in the Marxian lexicon that are given in English, in roman typeface. These features are thus hooked onto Marxian correspondences, wrenching śaktina away from its Old Thai moorings.

The text subverts the Thai language by refusing to use royal language that Modern Thai (proper discourse) prescribes for the ruler and his immediate family. The requirement to use royal language with the names of kings is avoided by using shorthand forms and by using such generic terms as *kśatriya* (the warrior caste) or committee chairman. Proper royal language isolates the ruler and consigns him to the category of which there is (almost) only one, him. The ruler is not to be touched by ordinary language and is thereby made pure and sacred. By refusing to use royal language, Jit's text defies these linguistic conventions and recasts "king" as the "committee chairman" who safeguards the profits of the śaktina class.

The text mocks the behavior and habits of the śaktina class and attributes to this idle class the motivation not to create beauty or enhance culture but to satisfy its appetites self-indulgently. In proper discourse during modern times the appetites of Thai rulers for power, wealth, sex, or sensual pleasure should be modulated and suppressed in discourse. Here they are brought to the surface and exposed.

Finally—and this device is particularly important in the remaking of Old Thai *sakdina*—the śaktina system is hooked onto European FEUDALISM, as the term appears in the Thai text. The Old Thai term is taken from its ancient context and identified with European feudalism by a system of pairing: "The *sakdina* system (FEUDAL SYSTEM) was the system of production in society that succeeded the *that* system (SLAVE SYSTEM)." On the face of it, such an identification of Thai society and European or ancient or South American societies is preposterous. Yet it is by insisting throughout on a foreign signified that the text seeks to make *sakdina* identical to FEUDAL and attaches the evolution of Thai society to a sequence of social formations that transcends the individualized experience of any one society. The foreign signifiers paired with śaktina make śaktina an essential stage in the evolution of human society, not just Thai society.

The Thai terms and examples hook onto the foreign term FEUDAL and pull it into the language; simultaneously, the foreign term clasps the Thai term and pulls it away from its Old Thai moorings. This capacity of the foreign term to pull śaktina to itself is exemplified in the following statement: "Here is the origin of the word FEUDALISM, the term for the English śaktina system, or FEUDALISME [*sic*] in French." Note that this is the reverse of "śaktina is the term for the Thai feudal system," which is what we might expect. Here Europe is made "the other." The way Jit's sentence represents the issue, only language makes śaktina and FEUDALISM different. Yet far from eliding the differences between the two signs, the typography actually heightens the alienation inherent in the pairing of them.

The stuff of cultural borrowing is labeling, naming, and renaming, but, contrary to appearances, this labeling does not create semantic identity. Although such pairs as śaktina/feudalism are used interchangeably in the text to give the impression of identity, the real

Šakṭina &
Feudalism

relationship between śaktina and feudal is one of metaphor rather
than one of identity. With Thai signifieds constantly intruding and
driving a wedge between the Thai term and the European term, a space
is created for metaphor to play in and beget more metaphor.

By means of this metaphoric play, śaktina springs free of its
moorings in the ancient texts and is set in motion, acquiring a kind
of motility. Because the phonological container is the same for *sakdina*
and śaktina, the new meanings created are rooted deep in Thai history.
And Old Thai *sakdina* now becomes but an element, one of many
manifestations of Modern Thai śaktina, the backward agrarian-order
vestiges of which persist to the present day. In other words, the text
takes the supernatural stuff out of *śakti* and realizes the term's genuine
exploitative, economic content.

Jit Poumisak's 1957 text did not itself create the new sign *sakdina*;
any number of previous writers used the term to refer to premodern
Thai society. The mechanics of creating the new sign are observable
in the text: the play with the term, the toying with the rules of Thai
grammar and proper discourse, are visible. The high language appropriate to sacral kingship is subverted by folksy idioms and ironic
asides. The substitutions and displacements as well as the mocking
sarcastic wit all serve to push aside proper discourse.

The metaphoric use of śaktina marks an epistemological break and
a change in the semantic code. Jit and his confreres were constructing
a new sociology, a new classificatory knowledge against the sociology
upheld by such people as Luang Wichit Watthakan (1898–1962), for
many years director-general of the Fine Arts Department of Thailand
and a prolific essayist and historian. Luang Wichit was instrumental
in explaining the 1932 coup that ended the absolute monarchy. He
assigned the proper meanings to 1932 that are with us today by
braiding together the plot of dynasty and the plot of nation-state
(Reynolds 1992). Jit's *The Real Face* is a rewriting of the works of
Luang Wichit and others in terms of a different epistemology, a different
sociology, and a restructured historiography.

Jit's attack on proper meanings by means of metaphoric play had
internationalist and political meanings that were seditious. It is through
the assertion of proper meaning that absolute authority exerts itself,
and the assertion of improper meanings in such works as Jit's entered
into the raison d'etre of the 1958 coup of Field Marshal Sarit Thanarat.

Improper meaning—the displacement of proper meaning—is a material force, as Ryan says, and this force was met by material force, incarceration. Jit Poumisak and other writers who had toyed with the proper meanings and asserted an alternative sociology were jailed, and the pluralism of the 1950s came to an end.

The Dominant Paradigm

The publication of *The Real Face* in 1957 came at the end of a period in postwar history that I described earlier as open in relation to the period that followed. The American alliance that was building throughout the 1950s (American technical and economic aid began in 1950; the SEATO pact was signed in 1954) was inevitable only in hindsight; the Phibun governments of 1941–58 played both sides of the street, and Thai delegations of students and writers traveled to Russia and China as late as the end of the 1950s (Reynolds and Hong 1983: 78). Through the writings of Jit Poumisak and others in the literary-journalist world, an articulate element of the Thai intelligentsia was trying to forge an internationalism inspired by the Russian and Chinese revolutions, especially by the Chinese communist victory in 1949. The way that śaktina operates in Jit's text—the way that śaktina hooks onto FEUDAL—is a sign of these internationalist ambitions. Thus, I relate the śaktina = feudal equation to a movement, an ideology, and a cast of mind that had liberating and utopian aspirations.

When Sarit took power in 1958, he imposed a monolithic hold on the military and the bureaucracy and propounded a political philosophy emphasizing indigenous values and institutions at the expense of foreign models and ideologies (Thak 1979: 152–71). A paradigm congruent with Sarit's political philosophy came to dominate Thai studies, a paradigm that drew a sharp distinction between European feudalism and precapitalist, premodern Thai society. Emphasizing the control of manpower rather than land as the basis of political power, the paradigm saw patron-client relations rather than class as the determining factor in Thai social relations. Thailand was unique, so the argument went, and an historicist theory of development was not applicable to Thai society.

There are several key texts that exemplify this new paradigm in Thai studies. Of particular interest in relation to Jit's 1957 work is

Khukrit Pramote's *Farang sakdina*, which appeared serially in late 1957 and early 1958. This text mocked the characterization of Thai society as śaktina. The preface stated:

> I have titled this book *Farang sakdina* for the sake of having a convenient expression, not because the meanings of *farang fiwdalit* (European feudalism) and Thai śaktina are the same, or because they are the same phenomenon. They are comparable only insofar as they occur at the same time. The Thai social system in ancient times was Thai, the ancient European social system was European. They had no connection with each other whatsoever.
>
> (Khukrit 1961)

It is difficult to read these sentences without seeing Jit and the others behind every one, although Khukrit never lowers himself to identify his targets on the left. The book is filled with cartoons of knights jousting, coats of arms, and the medieval baron receiving his loyal retainers. The book ostensibly explains the terms that appear in roman typeface: VASSAL, EXCOMMUNICATION of WILLIAM THE CONQUEROR (these familiar to us all) plus a host of obscure terms from heraldry and Vulgar Latin. Written with Khukrit's customary verve and wit, the book obfuscates as much as it explains. What is a Thai reader to do with "QUAS VULGAS ELEGERITLES QUUIELS LA COMMUNAUTE DE VOSTRE ROIAUME"? Indeed, what is anyone! By consigning European feudalism to the exotic, by caricaturing it, by packing the lot off to Camelot and Hollywood, Khukrit alienated FEUDALISM from śaktina. He denied the sign that Jit's text helped to create. In so doing, he also denied that socioeconomic processes play a fundamental role in the evolution of human society, and this is why his thought is characteristic of the old sociology. On the heels of his satiric treatment in *Farang sakdina*, Khukrit wrote two "scientific" or "rationalist" refutations of the new sign (1964, 1975). Khukrit was a real śaktina intellectual.

Another text that speaks to Jit's analysis but keeps Jit offstage is Khachorn Sukkhapanij's *The Status of Phrai*, the first edition of which appeared in December 1959, just after the Sarit period began. This text argued that manpower, not land, lay at the base of Thai political power. There are passages in this text that seem to be explicit refutations of Jit's thesis, and Khachorn appends a note of his own historian's "proof" of the proper meaning of Old Thai *sakdina*.[4] The subtitle of the university text in which Khukrit and Khachorn's work was published is *A Reader on the Fundamentals of Thai Civilization*, in other words, how Thai society in the past *really* worked. Khachorn put Old Thai *sakdina* back where it belongs, so to speak, in the Old Thai law code, with the meaning of "ranks graded and quantified according to putative land allocations." He, too, denied the new sign śaktina.

The most comprehensive analysis in English of Thai society, Akin Rabibhadana's *The Organization of Thai Society in the Early Bangkok Period* (1969), also dates from the period after the 1958 Sarit coup. The period delineated by the title notwithstanding, Akin's representation of Thai society has been taken to cover the fourteenth through the first half of the nineteenth centuries. Akin assumed that premodern mainland Southeast Asian states were underpopulated, an assumption that is explicit but never really tested in his exposition. This demographic assumption had two significant implications for the nature of rule in premodern Thai society: (1) as there was an abundance of land and a shortage of population, the key to the ruler's power was his ability, by means of compulsion or incentives, to acquire manpower; power was manpower; (2) the shortage of manpower was a deterrence against tyranny, for any oppressed subject could always flee an unjust ruler, resettle on the unclaimed land that lay about in abundance, and start a new life.

Akin's understanding of Thai social organization may be traced to both Western and Thai antecedents. On the one hand was the social and cultural anthropology he studied at Cornell University, where he did his master's degree in the mid-1960s. His structuralist-functionalist and systems-maintenance model, never made explicit in the study itself, owes much to a course he took on African studies, where he found an emphasis on labor, patron-client ties, and segmentary kinship, and a debate among African scholars on the importance of land vs. people.[5] On the other hand, the Thai text at the core of Akin's work is Khachorn's study, which Akin rewrites and extends. Akin, too, denies the new sign śaktina and seeks to restore its proper meaning: "The *sakdina* (dignity marks) system was a device that served as the most accurate guide to the different statuses of the whole population" (Akin 1969: 98). In this assertion of the proper meaning of *sakdina*, Akin follows Khachorn and Khukrit. The dominant Thai historiography converged with

American anthropology in Akin's analysis of premodern Thai society. His paradigm is congruent with the historiographic mode of the Sarit era that had come to dominate Thai studies after 1958.

The very categories—religion, the state, law, custom, kin relations, values, and norms—that fill Akin's analysis as explanations for this patron-client system "enter into the constitutive structure of the mode of production in precapitalist social formations" (Anderson 1974: 403). These are the extra-economic sanctions by which the mode of production operates. Yet in Akin's analysis, these sanctions, which he has described in persuasive detail, remain unconnected to the productive base. What is missing in the study is the link between these sanctions and how the economy worked. Akin ignored the very thing Jit had focused on, labor power and the means of production, especially land. It is possible to read Akin's entire study without realizing that the majority of Thailand's population in premodern times was a rice-cultivating peasantry.

In its neglect of economic matters, Akin's study comes close to what one writer has termed the "religious-structural" approach to the economy (Hong 1984: 3–4). Scholars who adopt this approach do not pay attention in their studies to the economic aspects of society, because when the Thai monarch ruled virtuously, there would be a natural and smooth flow of resources from clients to patrons. Clients would willingly cooperate in bringing their society closer to the ideal Buddhist state. In such a picture, peasants are never disgruntled at the economic exactions made of them, and while Akin's study allowed for conflict and client discontent at corvée demands, the conflict was not economic. He stresses that the relationship between client and patron was voluntary, "dyadic and contractual" (Akin 1969: 89). In contrast to Jit and other writers of the 1947–58 decade, Akin as well as Khukrit and Khachorn deemphasize economics and highlight norms, values, and individual choice as checks on tyranny by the patron.

Furthermore, what underlines the differences between Jit et al. and Akin, Khukrit, and Khachorn after 1958 is a debate over the nature of political authority. For Jit, royal absolutism, the political system of the feudal/saktina period, was exploitative and created class antagonisms. For the latter writers, royal absolutism in premodern times made "the system" work. But I believe this post-1958 paradigm must be seen in relation to the way Sarit's military regime revived the monarchy from the low prestige that had been its fate since the 1932 coup. Sarit changed the monarchy in Thai politics from a passive object to the active subject that prevails today. The paradigm of a unique Thai social system with a monarch as head of state served to underpin the adjustments that were being made to the way the military legitimated its dominance.

In their writings, Khukrit, Khachorn, and Akin denied the new sign by denying the metaphoric relationship between śaktina and feudal. The terms could no longer stand for one another. As we saw, Khukrit stated that the terms were unrelated, though they were synchronous (they lay alongside each other in time), and he asserted the differences between śaktina and feudal over and against similarities and identity. He sought to deny the new sign and restore the proper meaning of Old Thai *sakdina* as a quantified, graded hierarchy of ranks. Modern Thai śaktina lost its motility and was stripped of its meanings, and the metaphoric potentialities of Old Thai *sakdina* were declared illegitimate. In Ryan's language, they constituted an unsanctioned transfer of meaning.

The Return of Śaktina   (*1973 – 1976*)

In the explosion of Thai-language historical studies touched off by the dramatic and sometimes violent events of 1973–76, Modern Thai śaktina returned as a configuration for premodern Thai society (Reynolds and Hong 1983: 86–90). After fourteen years of oblivion as a censored book, Jit's text was rediscovered along with the earlier studies of Thai political economy and social realist literature from the 1950s. Students and lecturers who read *The Real Face of Thai Saktina Today* for the first time in that three-year period found in it a discourse on past society that gave voice to the political consciousness awakened by the mass protests of October 1973. The naming of premodern society as śaktina was a way of leaving that society behind, of objectifying it and distancing it from present consciousness.

Today, śaktina is a term used by academics as well as political dissidents. With a more sophisticated understanding of Marxism, knowledge of the Asiatic mode of production, and availability of *Grundrisse*, Thai scholars tried to determine the special Thai characteristics of śaktina, which some writers now refer to as the Asiatic mode of production. Thus, the dilemma of Jit's analysis—śaktina is the same as feudal but something Thai makes it different—continued in Thai socioanalysis that sought to define the country's social formations. How was it possible to describe Thai social formations (past, present, future) in such a way that the Thai particulars are individualized and intact within a scheme of universal evolutionary change? In their endeavors, Thai university economists found themselves at odds with the CPT, which for years had insisted on a Marxist semicolonial, semifeudal formation. Yet the debate about the real nature of Thai social formations was a shared one: academics, urban thinkers, returnees from the jungle, and revolutionaries still in the jungle all participated in this debate.

Faced with the return after October 1973 of śaktina as a trope for premodern society, some writers continued to insist on the non-equivalence of śaktina and feudal, very much in the mode of Khachorn, Khukrit, and Akin. Writing in 1975, a prominent novelist and essayist reacted against the new political consciousness by arguing for the "proper" definition of śaktina: status as reflected in certain rights and duties. And she emphatically resisted the characterization of modern society after 1932 as partially śaktina or containing śaktina elements. These had all been eliminated by legislation, she argued (Bunlua 1975: 19–24). This prominent writer's defense of the proper meaning of śaktina was aroused by the attacks of students and young lecturers on classical Thai literature. It was, they said, śaktina literature.

An even more striking example of how the debate over śaktina/feudal continued to be polarized may be found in a thesis submitted to the Thai Army College in 1980, *"Śaktina" and Subversion by the Opposing Side* by Colonel Sihadet Bunnag. The author argues that the śaktina system faded away long ago, but "the opposing side," i.e., the CPT, uses the śaktina characterization to attack Thailand's legitimizing institutions: "*śaktina* retains great significance for the opposing side. The attack on śaktina has an impact on our highest institutions and the work of the contemporary state" (Sihadet 1980: iii). The military officer was concerned about the use of śaktina in the speech of students and in the lyrics of popular songs that found their way into the heads of youth and gave them distorted ideas about the history of their forefathers (Sihadet 1980: 56–57). He thought that the new sign, śaktina = feudal, was predominantly Marxist-Leninist and propagated by the CPT, and his thesis was basically a polemic against this new sign. He insisted on the proper meaning of *sakdina*, and he referred with approval to Khachorn and Khukrit and the interpretation of the Old Thai word in terms of rights and duties, while rejecting the emphasis in Jit's text on land as the basis of śaktina power (Sihadet 1980: 37–38). In view of the polarization and oppositions reflected in the debate over śaktina vs. feudal, it is of more than passing interest that Sihadet Bunnag was, when he was a student at Chulalongkorn University, instrumental in the 1953 incident that led to Jit Poumisak's suspension from the university (Reynolds and Hong 1983: 83).

As in the case of *Nine Reigns of the Jakri Dynasty*, the link between śaktina and sedition was direct. The new meanings for the Old Thai term entailed an improper transfer of meanings. The military author wanted to take steps to minimize the usage of this improper transfer of meaning, which he deemed to be a threat to the state's well-being.

Conclusion

There are scarcely any Western historians who find feudal or feudalism a useful category for analyzing Thai society.[6] Yet Thai scholars turned increasingly to the term to characterize the premodern social formation. In the decade following the October 1973 uprising, Thai thinkers— inside the universities and outside, in the world of journalism, and in the resistance movement in the jungle—debated the śaktina = feudal equation and the particularistic Thai elements that were manifested in "Thai feudalism." In Thai language, feudal along with such terms as semicolonial, semicolonial capitalist, dependent capitalist, and so forth, were crucial coordinates on a grid of contrasting positions, each standing in dialectical relation to one another.

By following this history of the debate about śaktina = feudal in the post–World War II period, we can see that while the new sign śaktina depends on the Old Thai term, it also represents a liberation and transformation of the ancient term. The 1958 coup of Field Marshal Sarit marked a sharp break in Thai consciousness as signaled by reactions after 1958 to the assertion of śaktina = feudal by Thai radical thinkers before 1958. Such thinkers after 1958 as Khukrit, Khachorn, and Akin rejected the feudal characterization of Thai society and proposed that śaktina and feudalism were unrelated. This view belonged to a historiography shaped by a monolithic, authoritarian regime that brought the Thai monarchy back to politics and asserted the uniqueness of Thai society. And the paradigm of uniqueness served as a foil against the internationalist aspirations of the progressive thinkers between 1947 and 1958.

In the Thai case, among the signifieds in the "vernacular term = feudal" sign are the monarchy and the Buddhist monkhood, which today are regarded in radical quarters as śaktina remnants. The debate about śaktina = feudal at some point touches these legitimizing institutions, as the Thai Army College thesis makes clear. In a state whose legitimacy continues to derive from the monarchy and the Buddhist monkhood, the śaktina = feudal sign can, under certain circumstances, be deemed a danger. The different positions that people take over the proper meaning of śaktina come from strong feelings about the nature of legitimate authority. To my knowledge, no one has ever been arrested for writing or speaking about śaktina, but the term has had subversive and seditious effects. The metaphor has material force.

Notes

1. To the immensely varied political order that was medieval South India, says Burton Stein, "the terms 'centralized,' or 'bureaucratized,' or 'feudal' are widely and inappropriately applied" (Stein 1977: 5).
2. Keyes (1987: 29–30) here discusses Western historical writing, which toyed with whether or not the Old Thai term should be understood as feudalism.
3. For a translation of this work, see Reynolds 1994, chap. 2.
4. Khachorn Sukkhapanij, "Thanandon phrai [The status of Phrai]" in Khukrit Pramote et al., op. cit., pp. 115–20. Note the subtitle of the university text in which Khukrit and Khachorn (but not Jit) were published: *A Reader on the Fundamentals of Thai Civilization*—in other words, how past Thai society *really* worked.
5. Conversation with Akin Rabibhadana, Bangkok, 27 January 1984.
6. An exception is Georges Condominas, who uses feudal in studying early Thai state formations (1978: 111).

6

Engendering Thai Historical Writing

With important exceptions, gender relations have been neglected in the study of the Thai past. Related to the history of gender relations is the history of sexuality, which is also a topic historians have long shied away from or not treated dialectically and discursively.[1] Calls are still being made to address the tacitly heteronormative, gender-blind interpretations of Thai history (Loos 2005).

Thai people are as lovestruck as any other people in the world, and a rich lore of love magic, including some earthy customs found to be effective in winning a lover, prevails all over the country. Rivals in the complicated tangles created by the taking of mistresses are some of the best customers of this magic (Somchintana 1979). But Thai sexuality is poorly studied by the social sciences. Understanding of the AIDS epidemic in Thailand has been hampered by the fact that research on sexuality in Thailand is so weak, partly because of cultural norms that inhibit disclosure of personal information (Jenkins and Kim 2004: 34). Motivated by concerns about population growth, research has concentrated on fertility and married females. Only recently have studies through focus groups on the sexual relations of unmarried males and females helped health workers understand how the epidemic is spreading.

In the past ten years there has been a great deal of new research on gender relations, and there is promising new work on the history of sexuality and gender relations. But if it is true, as Peter Jackson has persuasively argued, that in Thailand are to be found some of the largest, most visible, and most diverse sexual subcultures outside the West, why has historiography not engaged the questions (Jackson and Sullivan 1999: 3)? As with other parts of the world, the study of gender and sexuality has become a subfield in Thai historiography, a specialized area that still does not touch mainstream historiography. The history of the nation-state remains immune from the findings of this subfield.

Gender and Nationalism

Nationalism is a historical movement that cannot be studied without looking at gender relations. More than many other ideologies, nationalism has a vision that includes women, particularly as reproducers of the nation and the transmitters of culture (Enloe 1990: 61). The rhetoric of nationalism "frames women narrowly" out of its own limited ideological perspectives (Radhakrishnan 1992: 84) and, in some nationalisms, equates nation with woman as mother. This happens in India and Malaysia but not in Thailand, even though the nurturing woman is fundamental to the way Buddhism constructs gender ideologically and in social practice (Keyes 1984; Andaya 2002). Yet history has tended to write women and the family out of nationalist movements, and Thailand is no exception (Reynolds 1999; Yuval-Davis and Anthias 1989).

Nationalism is a set of ideas that sharpens distinctions, including gender distinctions, between "us" and "them." In the 1936 historical musical drama *The Blood of Suphan* [*Luat suphan*], women were inserted into the narrative of the Thai nationalist struggle. The heroine, Duangjan, was portrayed as a warrior rallying her fellow-villagers to battle with the Burmese invaders, who stand metonymically in the Thai nationalist narrative for the trespassing, colonizing Other. The author of *Luat suphan* made Duangjan a warrior as capable as any man of fighting the Burmese colonial invaders (Barmé 1993: 121–24). The drama of the *Luat suphan* story lies in the doubly determined "us" and "them" conflicts and tensions: race (the Burmese as the colonizing Other) and gender (Duangjan is treated badly by a male Burmese officer).

In the Thai case, the participation of women in the movement leading up to the overthrow of the absolute monarchy in 1932, which historical research is now showing to have been a nationalist movement that in some manifestations contested elite nationalism, has been suppressed by most of the elite-centered studies to date, which have concentrated on the revolution as an oligarchic seizure of power by one ruling group from another (Barmé 1999; Copeland 1993; Nakkharin 1992; Suwadee 1990). Central to the debate about the monarchy in the 1920s was a discussion about equality before the law, and marriage law, among many issues, related to egalitarian rights. The Western powers required that Siam reform its marriage law as a condition of renegotiating the extraterritorial treaties.

But the sixth Bangkok king, whose position on women's rights was confused and ambivalent, resisted the push for monogamy, using a nativist argument that polygamy was an essential feature of Thai culture and society and should not be outlawed (Suwadee 1990: 202–4). The argument that supports the taking of mistresses (*mia noi*), which is essentially an argument for male rights and sexual access, can still be heard today in Thailand. It is an argument that explicitly blames the contradictions of legal rights and social practice today with regard to the *mia noi* system on Western pressure earlier this century and an alien, Western value system (Thawit 1988).

In the decades leading up to the revolution of 1932, the romantic Thai novel emerged, which portrayed the characters in control of their own fate and their own choices in matters of the heart. Just as nationalists were arguing about self-rule in the public sphere, so the characters in the romantic novel sought self-rule in the private domain. Thus there developed a common acceptance and understanding among the literate bourgeoisie of the "national Thai woman," a sovereign person entitled to rights of choice.

But there is an underside to this image of the "national Thai woman" that develops as a counter-representation to the national ideal. For it is at this time—in the 1920s, when journalists and novelists were exploring and criticizing upper-class polygamy and lower-class prostitution—that the category "obscene" takes shape in Thai literature. A form of pornography, *nangsu lamok* (indecent novels), was readily available in Bangkok at the very moment that equality of women and the monogamous marriage were being enshrined in law.[2] Moreover, it is a myth that gender relations was an issue imposed by foreigners on Thai public life, for gender relations were debated in the Thai press before the revolution. It was not Orientalist or "farang" knowledge that determined how the debate unfolded. The Thai-language content of women's magazines bears witness to the debate that took place in the decades leading up to the overthrow of the absolute monarchy. This public debate came to an abrupt end after 1932 for political and economic reasons when the military regime from 1939 until the end of World War II did its utmost to exert control over the way social issues were discussed (Nanthira 1987; Phimruthai 1990, chap. 2).

The nationalist narrative, which is basically about modernity, has suppressed or subjugated other narratives in the space now occupied by the Thai state, and it is only from the perspectives of local histories that we can glimpse the alternatives. The central Thai modernizing elite selectively reinterpreted "Thai tradition" to emphasize those elements that were most congruent with the discourse of modernity, and this emphasis sometimes meant pushing aside local narratives that would not fit easily into the dominant one. In southern Thailand, for example, the origin or foundation myth of local communities centers around "Lady White Blood," or, as she is sometimes known in the south, Royal Mother White Blood (*mae jao yu luat khao*) (Gesick 1995). Earlier last century, the central Thai national narrative omitted this matriarchal origin myth, although Royal Mother White Blood is still the focus of local community identity in parts of the south through the vehicle of theatrical performance (*manora*).

Gendered Knowledge in the Social Sciences

I was initially led to the topic of gender relations in Thai historiography through *Why Gender Matters in South East Asian Politics*, which surveyed English-language writing on Southeast Asian politics (Stivens 1991). Most of the contributors were scholars of Indonesia and Malaysia, with some attention to Burma and Vietnam. In almost all cases, the authors discovered, there was a conspicuous blind spot when it came to women and politics. Women were invisible.

How have political scientists working on Thailand dealt with gender and the participation of women in politics? If we look at the most well-known books on Thai politics, and I think they are typical of book-length studies, we find a conspicuous absence of references to, and discussions about, women and politics. The Morell and Chai-anan book devotes no attention to women, with only one reference to women in a table in the appendix (1981). The Girling volume (1981) has three references to women workers—typically, as it turns out, for there is quite a lot of research done on women in the workforce in Thailand (e.g., Thorbek 1987). In their way, the Girling and Morell and Chai-anan books are also political histories of postwar Thailand and differ little in method and content from what a historian would produce.

The contributors to *Why Gender Matters* concluded that the explanation for the absence of women in political studies has something to do with the nature of the field in Southeast Asia generally. Political science on the region has been concerned mostly with government, administration, leaders, treaties, and public political institutions. The discipline of political science seems to have inherited "a sometimes subliminal division of civil society into public and private spheres," with men monopolizing the former and women relegated to the latter as biological reproducers and domestic laborers (Stivens 1991: 12). This dichotomy creates a gendered division of labor and a gendering of knowledge that feminist thinkers have identified elsewhere in the world: politics is presumed to be men's business; nurturing and caring is women's.

The discipline of economics has many of the same problems. At a conference on the Thai economy I attended, the first two days were all about finance, monetary policy, promoting economic development, and industrializing the service sector and agriculture. The themes were growth, increasing GDP, maximizing returns, and increasing economic development. All the paper presenters were men. On the afternoon of the second day, the themes changed. Suddenly there were problems with all this growth: environmental degradation, pollution, health risks, new causes of poverty, all the terrible costs and consequences of rapid growth. Of the six speakers dealing with the social and health effects of economic development, five were women.[3] In the ordering of the conference presentations, it looked very much as if men were responsible for the history and reasons for economic policies, while it was the duty of women to examine the disastrous consequences of policies that stressed growth and maximization of returns. A related blind spot in economics that shows up the gendered knowledge of the discipline is that in studies of the economic development of advanced industrialized countries, the focus is typically on the market and monetary measurement, thus minimizing the contribution of the nonwaged labor of women (Morris-Suzuki 1992: 68).

The role of Western social science in affecting the academic disciplines in Thailand deserves more attention than it has so far received. Euro-American perspectives exert a powerful hold on feminist theory through the paradigm of "the modern," as exemplified by a Thai book, *Feminism*, which is based on Western theoretical writing (Kanjana 1992). This version of feminist theory, much of it from the French poststructuralist school and translated without being assimilated, does not necessarily help solve the gender problems that face NGO and social-service workers on a daily basis.[4] In its applications, this Euro-American theory is little different from the imported theory that is intended to facilitate economic and administrative modernization. The ultimate test of such a theory is its usefulness rather than the intellectual ferment it provokes. If a theory does not find local uses in Thailand, it risks being summarily discarded.

In historical studies, there has been some recent work that might herald a shift in academic thinking. Dhiravat na Pompejra, one of the few Thai historians skilled at handling the records of the Dutch East India Company, has scraped together the meager materials on Mon and Siamese women living with Dutch traders at seventeenth-century Ayudhya to show how they and their offspring became entangled in court politics as points of access to powerful officials (Dhiravat 1992, 2000). The social historian Junko Koizumi has set aside the much-debated and now unfashionable subject concerning the "status" of women and looked at the definition and redefinition of conceptions of women and the family during the early and middle nineteenth century (Koizumi 2000). Understandably, the nineteenth century has received more attention than earlier periods because of the abundance of materials. A revisionist study by Saipin Kaew-ngarmprasert led to a national controversy over the politics surrounding a monument to a local woman who featured in the suppression of a northeastern revolt in 1827 (Keyes 2002). Nidhi Aeusrivongse, hugely productive in so-called retirement, has also weighed into this subject.[5] But there is still a blind spot. The historiography of Thailand is still far too elitist, with too much attention to Bangkok politics and political history, to elites and the politics of the court, to civilian and military leaderships, to regime changes, and to national sovereignty. Power exerts an irresistible pull, and the central place the monarchy still occupies in public life has a lot to do with fixing the historian's gaze on the center.

The glamor of royal power is irresistible, for the history of the monarchy has been patiently and methodically fused with the history of the capital, Bangkok, and the nation. Even attacks on the authenticity of the Ramkhamhaeng inscription in order to subvert the national narrative did little to move the focus off-center. It could even be said that the controversy over the first Thai inscription strengthened the focus on the center by drawing attention to the famed sequence of Thai capitals in statist and nationalist propaganda rather than away from the center (Chamberlain 1991). And Bangkok, as Ayutthaya before it, still dominates the hinterland.

Of all the disciplines, anthropology has done much better in putting gender relations on its agenda. This is the case with island as well as mainland Southeast Asia (Atkinson and Errington 1990). It is not because anthropologists are more enlightened or that they are not burdened by genteel language.[6] Rather, the social phenomena that they study bring gender issues into the open: linguistic categories and their social correlates; the all-male Buddhist monkhood and pious laywomen (*mae chi*); asymmetric social relations; purity versus pollution in ritual and social life; kinship and rules of descent; spirit mediums.

In the 1970s and through the mid-1980s, a debate flourished briefly about whether or not Buddhism favored men over women in the religious attainments available to each (Keyes 1984; Khin Thitsa 1980; Kirsch 1975; Van Esterik 1982). Did distinctly Buddhist attitudes disparage women and therefore serve as an ideology of oppression that encouraged and rationalized prostitution? As one anthropologist put it, there seemed to be a "discrepancy between, on the one hand, the relatively high level of influence, personal autonomy, and economic independence that is characteristic of women in these [Thai Buddhist] communities and, on the other hand, the general disparagement of women, as a group, in traditional Buddhist beliefs and practices" (Eberhardt 1988: 73). This debate over whether or not Buddhism devalued women eventually came to an impasse, because gender was not conceptualized as a discursive and changeable category that depends on context, institutional practice, and ritual.[7] In the rite of passage into the Buddhist monkhood for young men, the ordinand symbolically adopts an ambiguous sexuality that might be described as androgyny (Keyes 1986: 73–74). The debate about Buddhism devaluing women did not, however, address key social facts, namely, that the Buddhist monkhood is an all-male preserve, and that the monastery is a masculine stronghold of supernatural power.[8] What has this meant for gender relations in Thai history?

In the case of northern Thai society, a vigorous scholarship has grown up concerning matriliny and spirit cults, and here the all-male preserve of the Sangha may be seen to make a difference in the way gender is defined and redefined in ritual acts. In these spirit cults, women mediums "acquire for themselves many of the characteristics of mystical power which are normally the preserve of men," and "latent hostility" for the all-male monkhood comes to the surface (Cohen and Wijeyewardene 1984: 257). Female mediums who become possessed by the spirits of deceased male lords or *jao* (kings or famous monks) are empowered to the extent that monks may bow before them, possibly the only instance in Thai society where this happens. Walter Irvine described how this "allows for a hesitant, low-keyed, but nonetheless real incursion into the monastery-centered masculine stronghold of supernatural power" (Irvine 1984: 318). It would seem, moreover, that Buddhism is prejudiced against spirit mediumship that favors the empowerment of women and has pushed the cults to one side. The large matrilineal cults are rare in the northern courts of the ruling princes, from which Buddhism ostensibly expelled them over the course of time (Tanabe 1991: 194).

This vigorous scholarship on matriliny and spirit mediums in northern Thailand that shows gender to be a discursive category has not made any discernible impact on historians, despite the history of events and social relations embedded in the myth and ritual, possibly because it is knowledge labeled as anthropological. The fact that this knowledge is seen as "regional" (northern Thai) knowledge makes it easy to dismiss. Specialization in academic work now compartmentalizes knowledge as well as genders it, and a lot of effort must be made to cross over the disciplinary boundaries and categories to learn about neighboring fields. The net effect of terms such as "periphery" and "marginal" is that mainstream historiography can easily ignore the gender issues, because the scholarship has labeled itself peripheral and marginal.

Gender in Thai History

At first sight, it seems surprising that the study of gender relations has not become a growth industry in Thai studies in view of two things the country is most famous for around the world, despite efforts by the state's publicists to manipulate the images: the military, and the commercialization of Thai womanhood.[9]

Study of the Thai military has concentrated on leadership and interference and dominance in the political domain, and there has been some recent work on military thought. But the role of the family, kin ties, and marriage alliances within the military elite receive only cursory examination.[10] There is an important sense in which women are behind the scenes in these marriage alliances and may be important sources of information in power relations. The masculine values and male bonding typical of military establishments—and what these masculine values and male bonding are defining themselves against—have gone unexamined in the Thai case. In the early 1990s, "Bik Jort" (General Sunthorn Khonsomphong) was photographed with a champagne glass and naked above the waist, and in another photo, with a tight polo shirt through which he flexed his biceps. The Thai press enjoyed poking fun at Mr. Tight Shirt (*ai sua khap*) and Little Lizard (*jinjok*) and tried to make him into an object of ridicule. But what is this picture saying about power and authority? The male body is the symbol of power? Power is physically desirable? Erotic? Was there a trace of homoeroticism in Bik Jort's male torso?

In a similar vein, at the popular level of the daily news, one thinks of how Thai journalists in the late 1980s and until the tragedy of May 1992 seized on the male characters in the local version of the Chinese classic *Romance of the Three Kingdoms* and identified senior military men with the mythical Chinese warlords (Reynolds 1996b). These comparisons with *Romance*'s characters were intended to poke fun at the generals, teasing them about their cunning (*kalorn*) and strategic deception (*yutthasat*), but they also reinforced the public expectation that someone who is important (*yai*) in Thai politics is male. The Thai generals who attracted these appellations more or less enjoyed the exercise, as it made their exercise of power notorious in a vaguely pleasing way by giving it a certain grandeur. The fact that women would not enjoy such comparisons underscores the extent to which public political power in Thailand is masculinized.

The persistent frequency of military regimes in modern Thai history might have something to do with the way power is defined and expressed as masculine as well as with the macho social type or *nakleng*, whose reputation for living dangerously, womanizing, gambling, and drinking persists in rural Thailand.[11] The *nakleng* is a subordinate masculinity. More theoretically, perhaps the primary type is the *nakleng*, and military manliness builds on the *nakleng* model of rural manly behavior. Recruitment for the infantry is largely from the rural male population. The military, when it is in power, rules in part by cultural hegemony like any other regime, and this cultural hegemony is inflected by masculine, macho values of a distinctively Thai type that run fairly deep in the culture. It is military swagger, as much as the actual fact of military rule, that so offended the opponents of the military.

The second factor that makes the absence of gender surprising in Thai historical studies is the modern representation of women within Thai society and externally to the world. The marketing of the country both domestically and abroad for tourism (airline advertisements, for example, or beauty contests) has long involved women and has brought about the identification of Thai culture itself with certain images of Thai womanhood. As in other countries, capitalism has commercialized Thai motherhood, and state propaganda has exploited it for ease of social control. Thailand is famous internationally for its beauty contests, where they have been used for many decades to build national identity, constitutionalism, and national prestige (Callahan 1998; Supatra 1993). It is possible that Thailand has more contests than any other country in the world, featuring such beauties as Miss Lychee and Miss Mango.

The marketing of female Thai beauty in the global consumer culture has led to a new ideal of beauty, a paragon of regional and global personhood. Contestants in the beauty pageants often undergo cosmetic surgery to appear more Eurasian, and the Eurasian face is popular on Thai television. Advertisements in the glossy magazines show a distinct preference for male and female models who are light-skinned with Eurasian features, a kind of pan-Asian model of beauty that suits the exporters of Thai products to Asian markets.

A semiotic chain links the ideals of female beauty as promoted in the media to the commercialization of female sexuality (Mills 1992: 86).[12] Polygamy, debt bondage, and the social practice up to and including the present day of Thai men taking mistresses (*nang bamroe*) or minor wives (*mia not*) are the institutions that help account for the easy way Thai female sexuality has been commoditized. Curiously, mistresses and minor wives seems to be a topic for literary rather than historical treatment. We can see from the now-classic soap opera and historical novel *Four Reigns*, written in the 1950s by M. R. Khukrit Pramote, how the tensions and conflicts of the characters about the position of women helped to make the novel hugely popular. These were the themes that many Thai readers recognized in their own family dramas.

Considering the richness of the historical evidence, it is surprising that no historian has turned Anna Leonowens to positivist ends, so to speak, and fashioned a mini-history of the Inner Palace, where the most powerful and influential women in the kingdom lived, at the end of the nineteenth century.[13] There we find a female state within the male-dominated state, a highly ordered society of women with various ranks of officials (*thao*) who governed the Inner Palace (*fai nai*) and took responsibility for finance, education, security, the resolution of disputes, and provisioning. There is more than sufficient evidence from biographies, court documents, and literature (including *Four Reigns*) to begin to come to terms with how this exclusively female society functioned in relation to the male-dominated bureaucracy. This, the most obvious topic in women's history, has only just begun to receive the attention it deserves (Hong 1999).

There is also a deep historical dimension to prostitution. The Thai state licensed prostitution in premodern times (Reid 1988a: 633) and continued to earn revenue from it through the Fifth Reign. The political economy of prostitution in Thailand historically helps to explain some of the problems today. The practice of bonding women for sexual services, which is the gateway through which many rural women enter prostitution in Thailand, is a direct descendant of debt bondage for sexual services, which persisted even after the laws on slavery were rescinded at the end of the nineteenth century (Reynolds 1979b). The law now provides less protection for women obtained in such transactions than it did when the slave laws were in force in Old Siam (Turton 1980: 282). The double standard that applies to male versus female sexual behavior in urban and provincial Thailand contributed to the spread of AIDS.[14]

Siam's semicolonial history is one of the reasons gender relations has been neglected in historiography. Because Thailand was not colonized, relations between the rulers and the ruled were not polarized in the same way as they were in colonial Southeast Asia. There was no plantation agriculture, land alienation, and rural indebtedness. There was no European-staffed police force to highlight the racial differences between the ruler and ruled, although the employment of Indian police in Bangkok raised some of the racial issues found elsewhere in colonized Southeast Asia. In the 1970s, radical Thai historiography made a determined case for exploitative relationships between feudal lord and peasant, but this argument is now not taken very seriously by historians. Through the post–World War II period, the dominant Thai historiography took comfort in what Katherine Bowie has called an "elite mythology of rural abundance."[15] The eruptions that we find elsewhere in Southeast Asia during the late colonial period—strikes, revolts, violent mass action of various kinds—are absent from the historical record. The protest movements, millenarian revolts by *phu mi bun* or so-called holy men, that occurred in the late colonial period have been explained away as regionally specific and archaic, as historians have assigned value and significance to these revolts according to the extent that political consciousness of the leadership is more or less "developed." They have not been seen for what they were, namely, the effects of internal colonialism as the Siamese dynastic state pushed into the more remote parts of the kingdom.

Some of these statements may well be true. Relations between the rulers and the ruled were not polarized in quite the same way as they were in colonized Southeast Asia, and it may be difficult to find a strike or an urban protest to study. But Thai historiography is only slowly recognizing the extent to which the ruling order was jostled, pushed, held up to scrutiny, and, if we look at the deliciously wicked pens of the political cartoonists during the 1920s and 1930s, ridiculed. Historical research now being done will show that the 1932 overthrow of the absolute monarchy was not simply musical chairs at the elite level, the displacement of one oligarchy by another, but the effect of a widespread social movement in the literate classes that had been under way for three decades. The extraterritorial treaties were a major factor in shaping elite consciousness from the 1880s through the early 1930s (Nakkharin 1992). Extraterritoriality was the absolute monarchy's Achilles' heel, the semi-colonialism it negotiated thereby compromising its own sovereignty (Hong 2002, 2003, 2004).

One effect on Thai historiography of the muddled and inadequately theorized colonial issue is that social history and labor history are still neglected. For modern Thai social history there is no shortage of little pocketbooks by such authors as Thepchu Thapthong, Chali Iamkrasin, and Nawa-ek Sawat Janthani, but these are "popular" social historians. Academic history has been very slow to make social history a legitimate field of study. In the historiographies of other nation-states, it is in the fields of social and labor history that studies of gender and gender relations, the family, and feminist history have emerged.

The elite mythology of rural abundance has determined that historical narratives can pay scant attention to the peasantry, the urban and rural laboring classes, and the ethnicity and gendering of social relations.[16] It could be argued by way of explanation that the legacy of Marxist political economy in Thai studies has faded.[17] The vocabulary of historians that prevails is genteel, and this gentility, buttressed by a popular, media-savvy monarchy, has had something to do with creating the blind spot that makes it impossible to identify exploitation, oppression, and conflict in the history of Thai social relations. In the fields of sociology and labor economics, the descriptive language is not at all genteel (Thorbek 1987).

Another reason it might be surprising that the subject of gender relations has not received more treatment by historians is that the Thai Left, particularly the Old Left of the 1950s, dealt explicitly with gender in a historical perspective using the work of Engels and Henry Morgan (Kulap 1976 et al., 1978b, 1979). These studies by Kulap Saipradit, Atsani Phonlajan, and Jit Poumisak were republished after 14 October 1973 and encouraged the critical reexamination of social relations in Thailand that was characteristic of that tumultuous moment. But rediscovery and debate about this Old Left feminism did not create a need for feminist studies in universities and teachers' colleges, and the follow-on has been weak.[18] Broader studies of the family and domesticity have not boomed, and attention has focused on female-specific occupations and groups that construe a direct relationship between domesticity and work (prostitutes, nurses, pious Buddhist laywomen, mae chi, elite-female philanthropy).[19] Perhaps, with the decline of the

Communist Party of Thailand and Marxism since the early 1980s, the socialism in earlier studies discredited them.

More importantly, I think, the paradigm has changed. In 1993, these essays sound very dated. They depict women as victims (*yua*) and criticize the *sakdina* class for oppressing women. While feminist scholarship in the West during the 1960s and early 1970s also portrayed women as victims of patriarchal structures and values, there has been a shift toward studies of difference, the social and cultural construction of gender, and woman's agency that has eclipsed the woman-as-victim paradigm. Research now emphasizes that in some respects sex work for women is of the same order as working in the fields or in the marketplace, namely, it is in keeping with an ideal of woman as mother to serve and enhance the well-being of the family (Manderson 1992: 469). Remitting income from sex work to parents expresses filial piety and the Buddhist value of loving-kindness (*metta*). The transaction in debt bondage problematizes but does not negate woman's agency.

Legal cases in the Thai archives show the ambiguities and contradictions in the position of elite women during the nineteenth century and how Thai society circumscribed their behavior (Loos 1998). A resourceful woman could turn male expectations of her "helplessness" to advantage (Hong 1991). In premodern times, Dhiravat na Pombejra relates the example of the Mon woman, Suet, of lowly origin and raised partly by the Dutch, who used her wits to rise to a powerful position at court in the mid-seventeenth century. She had children by two Dutchmen, and through her connections with one of Prasatthong's queens and other court women, she became one of the most powerful and influential merchants in the kingdom (Dhiravat 1992: 10–11). Indeed, the practice in the region of local women traders sharing their bed with foreign traders has been discerned as a pattern throughout Southeast Asia, where women often dominated certain sectors of trade and marketing (Reid 1988a: 632, 1988b: 162). Thailand is not an unusual case in this regard.[20]

One might expect that the comparatively open way sexuality is dealt with in Thai society would have led historians to look at the history of sexuality. In Thailand today, there are no legal sanctions against homosexuality, for example, with homosexuality and transvestism discussed candidly in the daily press.[21] Yet evidence from the nineteenth-century Thai court of what we would now regard as scandals suggests that there were sanctions against homosexuality at the elite level. During the Third Reign (1824–51), charges of corruption and treasonable conduct were laid against Prince Rakronnaret (Mom Kraison). Despite the fact that he had been close to Prince Jetsadabodin, the future king, and had in fact been a patron and kingmaker at the beginning of the reign, Prince Rakronnaret was executed toward the end of the reign. One of his transgressions was homosexual relations with young members of a theater group. The details of these relations in the chronicle by Thiphakorawong are not very extraordinary, so what was all the fuss about? The chronicle says that the prince's crime was that he did not stay with his wife. In the aristocracy at that time, the family was a key political institution, and reproduction of the family was important to the maintenance of family power. Noble and royal families maintained and extended their dominance by marriage alliances. This small fragment in the Bangkok chronicles shows that homosexual behavior was seen as a threat to the political order of the time, based as it was on family ties.

That emblem of Thai Buddhist culture, the Vessantara Jataka, reifies the formal, patriarchal duties of the male head of the household. But the story of Prince Vessantara, the Bodhisattva in the last life before he became a Buddha, can also be read as the antithesis of a good family man, who, as the Mom Kraison case shows, does not separate himself from his family. Much pain results for the children of Prince Vessantara because of his action in relinquishing them from his protection. The story is supposed to highlight the value and the sacrifice of the ascetic life, but the emphasis is really on the importance of the family unit. The story shows that it is wrong for a man to abandon his family.

Films and novels in contemporary Thai popular culture are still overwhelmingly concerned with the family, especially in terms of threats from without and conflicts within. The complicated tangles of relationships in family life are what makes popular culture popular (Hamilton 1992a). All these are reasons to suggest that gender relations, sexuality, and the family deserve the attention of historians.

Conclusion

Conventional historiography takes as its vantage point a prescribed center and fashions its story around details deemed relevant to that focal point.[22] Everything else is relegated to secondary position, because everything else is subordinated to motivating the narrative of that center. The regional or local perspective that has been subordinated to the center's authority and self-assumed right to dominate, slips away and disappears. Yet the local perspective lives on in memory and oral culture or performance of ritual, as in the Royal Mother White Blood in the *manora* performance in the south, deferring to the written history of the center.

History in Thailand has been important in public culture for the purpose of making Thailand's people obedient and loyal citizens. From the nation-state's perspective, the history of the nation-state is the most significant of the grand narratives for those citizens. History and archaeology have been vital in constructing Thai identity and providing a narrative that makes Thailand's story distinctive and successful. This narrative begins in ancient times and evolves continuously to the present. It is epic history—heroic, majestic, impressively great. Increasingly, it is not the state but the Thai, sometimes even Tai, people who are the subject of this grand, epic narrative.

The discipline of history itself is designed for dealing with the grand narrative, the big picture, and the epic-making event, because history is typically invested with power. History yearns for the total picture, the general over the particular, the larger over the smaller, and the mainstream over the marginal. The methods and yearnings of the discipline make it easier and more exciting to observe the earthquake and volcanic explosion than to keep track of the little tremors, the false warnings, the almost imperceptible blips that are registered day after day on Clio's seismograph. The epic of the national narrative still predominates in Thai history and still commands the attention of most historians, an epic that tends to squeeze out the bits that do not fit very well, such as the history of a contested nationalism, or the history of violence, or regional foundation myths, or the history of gender relations. Anything that detracts from distinctiveness and success and continuity with the ancient past is suspect.

Thai historiography must now study these fragments that do not fit. As far as the history of gender relations is concerned, these fragments should not be merely assembled into yet another grand narrative such as "the history of Thai women" or "the history of Thai sexuality" or "the history of gender relations in Thailand," thus creating a new specialist field in Thai history. Rather, the fragments should be allowed to shake the dominant historical narrative and challenge it, and in doing so, expose the predicaments and politics of modern Thai history. Otherwise, the study of gender relations will remain a field for specialists, or worse, an academic ghetto within Thai studies.

Notes

1.   Peter Jackson argues that in the Thai language, sexuality and gender are not clearly differentiated but "are collectively labelled as different varieties of *phet*," an indigenous category within which there has been a proliferation of identities (Jackson and Sullivan 1999: 5–6; Jackson 2000: 411–14).

2.   I am indebted to Matthew Copeland for this point. See also Barmé 2002: 131n.36, 229. A direct connection between the nineteenth-century English novel and pornography was suggested by Marcus 1977.

3.   "The Making of a Fifth Tiger? Thailand's Industrialisation and Its Consequences," Research School of Pacific Studies, Australian National University, 7–9 December 1992 (Medhi 1995). The conference was organized by Dr. Medhi Krongkaew, and the women speakers were Pranee Tinakorn, Suntaree Komin, Helen Ross, Suwattana Thadinithi, and Sirilaksana Khoman.

4.   For an example of the literature that informs social practice, see the handbook for paralegals issued by Klum Phuan Phuying (1990), a publication sponsored by the Ford Foundation and the International Commission of Jurists.

5.   Nidhi 2002. Hong 1998 and Iijima and Koizumi 2000 are particularly useful for engaging recent work by Thai historians, including that of Nidhi.

6.   Indeed, Katherine Bowie's work on textile production in northern Thailand glosses over the gendered nature of the production and concentrates on class. Keyes (1986: 72) points out that weaving is a significant aspect of female identity as girls grow into women. For an extensive discussion on the gendered nature of weaving, see Gittinger and Lefferts 1992, chap. 2.

7.   Although there does seem to have been a hiatus in the debate, the discussions in Manderson 1992, Penny and John Van Esterik 1992, and Van Esterik 2000 indicate how the debate was rekindled; Tanabe (1991) insisted on conceptualizing gender as a discursive category.

8.   Darunee and Pandey 1987 is still one of the few studies to address this key social fact. It does this by explicitly linking the marginalization of the status and value of daughters to the Buddhist construction of gender (1987: 130), but I think the authors go too far in a culturalist direction by relying on Buddhism to explain Thai patriarchy and female "passivity" and "submissiveness." Their discussion of matrifocality and the distinctive gender roles in the aristocracy and the peasantry is a helpful contribution to the debate. See also Manderson (1992: 470), who suggests that both the monasteries and prostitution are "anti-structures" to marriage.

9. Cynthia Enloe would see these two as intimately related (1990). Many foreigners would know Thailand from the Broadway musical and Hollywood film *The King and I*, which Manderson (1997) has linked to a genealogy of travelers' tales and collections of exotic erotica, including the 1991 Australian film *The Good Woman of Bangkok*, which capture the European obsession with foreign sexuality.

10. I have in mind here such older well-known ties by marriage as Generals Praphat Jarusathian and Tanom Kittikajorn as well as Suchinda Kraprayoon and the Nunphakdi family, but there are many others of more recent vintage.

11. Thak (1979: 339) explicitly connected the behavior of Field Marshal Sarit Thanarat to the *nakleng* social type, but the larger issue of masculinity and militarism remains unexplored. See also Keyes (1986: 87), who contrasts the *nakleng* with the Buddhist monastic ideal. Johnston (1980) discusses the *nakleng* in the late nineteenth century, but the gender theme there is undeveloped, although his doctoral dissertation had more details on maleness in the rural underworld.

12. Some of the complexities and paradoxes of the issue are discussed in Van Esterik 2000.

13. Apart from Manderson 1997, see the introduction by Susan Morgan to a reprint of *The Romance of the Harem* (Leonowens 1991) on the thorny issue of the Siamese "harem."

14. For a survey of the historical links between prostitution and STDs in Thailand, see Bamber et al. 1993.

15. See Katherine Bowie's deconstruction of the paradigm of the subsistence economy in Thai history, showing that Thai Marxist and royalist historians alike, as well as mainstream American social and cultural anthropologists, have collaborated in perpetuating the paradigm (1992).

16. On this and other points in my discussion, I have glided over the differences between Western-language and Thai-language historical writing. The foreign thesis most often cited in Thai-language historiography is David Johnston's (1975), precisely because it deals with rural unrest and the social consequences of rapid economic change.

17. It may have faded, but it is by no means extinguished; see Ji 2003. For an essay drawing on the socialist literature that emphasizes development as essentially a patriarchal project, see Bell 1992. The framework of this analysis is decidedly economistic and self-limiting, however, when one looks at the way gender is now discussed in the field of cultural studies.

18. Research with strong historical perspectives by Thai leftists famous in the 1970s (Kasian Tejapira, Seksan Praseakun, Somsak Jeemthirasakun, and Thongchai Winichakul, all male) have neglected gender relations. An exception would be Cholthira (1991), a woman. Her thesis bears residual traces of the Old Left debates about the matriarchal origins of human society.

19. Cook (unpublished); Dararat 1984; Khin Thitsa 1983; Natthawadi 1986; Suwadee 1990.

20. Darunee and Pandey (1987), for example, miss the Southeast Asian regional dimension of the predominance of Thai women in economic affairs.

21. Jackson 1989. But it is clear that the situation is very complex. While sanctions concerning male and female homosexuality are "generally non-interventionist," there are cultural norms that determine appropriate and inappropriate behavior, and some images are offensive (Jackson 2002a; Jackson and Sullivan 1999: 3–4).
22. In this discussion, my debt to Pandey (1992) should be clear.

CULTURAL STUDIES

7

Religious Historical Writing in Early Bangkok

T he reign of Rama I (1782–1809), the founding king of the Jakri or Bangkok dynasty, has long been known for its voluminous literary output. Chronicles, epic poetry, legal codes, and religious texts all issued from the court during the reign, with the king himself credited as either the author or the one who commissioned the compilation of most of this literature. As far as the chronicles are concerned, the tasks of establishing firm chronology and gleaning facts for political or religious history have preoccupied most scholars, and such is the state of Thai historiography that historians are still sorting out the authorships of, and the relationships among, the various recensions of the Ayudhya chronicle that date from this reign. Indeed, students of Ayudhya history are much indebted to Rama I and his court for collecting and copying this material; without it, our understanding of Ayudhya's political and legal institutions would be all the more deficient.

But what would happen if we were to look at one of these chronicles not for its data but for its place in a social and political context, if we were to look at its form as well as its content? In what ways was the surge of textual compilation and revision that took place in this period not merely a matter of bookkeeping but actually a part of the political process, a stage in the growth of Rama I's hold on the affairs of state? We can confront these questions by looking at the *Chronicle of Buddhist Councils (Sangitiyavamsa)*, dated 1789 C.E. (hereafter, *1789 Chronicle*).

Rama I acceded to the throne as a warrior king preoccupied with the defense of the kingdom and with social, economic, and political instability. The wars with Burma that had devastated the capital of

Ayudhya in 1767 continued until 1802, when Thai armies finally drove the Burmese from the north; the first twenty years of the reign also saw the subjugation of tributary states to the northeast (Laos), to the east (Cambodia), and to the south (the Malay states) (Wenk 1968, chap. 4). The military achievement of restoring territorial integrity to the Thai state was not Rama I's own, however. His most able general was his brother, the Front Palace Prince, and the work of reestablishing Thai sovereignty and suzerainty had already begun in the reign of Rama I's predecessor, King Taksin.

Taksin was responsible for moving the capital from Ayudhya, which had been the royal base for four hundred years, to Thonburi, across the river from Bangkok. For both Taksin and Rama I, the shift of the capital southward and the task of building a new royal base are noteworthy for their symbolic significance no less than for the considerable logistical and physical problems they entailed (the resettlement of the population; the transport of building materials downriver from Ayudhya to Bangkok for new monasteries, palaces, and fortifications; canal construction; rechanneling of the river; and flood control). Both kings were separating themselves from a discredited dynasty and starting out afresh. Like a newly born Indra who cannot inherit the palaces, retinues, and concubines of a predecessor but must be endowed with these anew, both Taksin and Rama I had to build a wholly new capital, appoint new ministers, and develop a new network of marriage alliances with nobles and vassals to secure loyalties. At the same time, neither Taksin nor Rama I was a blood relative of the last Ayudhya dynasty, and one way to overcome this weakness of genealogy was to demonstrate faithfulness to tradition. One of the reasons the period is so interesting, then, is that the kings at Thonburi and early Bangkok offer us the circumstances for seeing how the myth of the fresh start and the myth of continuity combine in a ritual of renewal (Wyatt 1982). Can the *1789 Chronicle* tell us anything about how this ritual was enacted in the reign of Rama I?

The *1789 Chronicle* may also shed light on important changes in Buddhism and the Sangha, since Rama I saw his patronage of Buddhism as a corrective to Taksin's mysticism and abuse of the monkhood. Taksin had abdicated, his rule having collapsed after he evinced signs of madness, and this "madness" was clothed in certain religious behavior.[1] The king took an interest in Pali and Malay texts on meditation and received advice from a high-ranking monk on yoga technique (Royal Institute 1919: 179–80; Reynolds 1973, chap. 2). According to one European account, Taksin hoped that his ascetic practices would give him the white blood of the gods and the ability to fly (Koenig 1894: 164–65). Having heard the supreme patriarch of the *sangha* read out the thirty-two mahapurisa marks of the Buddha, he identified twelve of them on his own person and, in the most far-reaching ambition of all, he envisioned himself as a *sotapanna* (stream winner), a type of deity who had embarked on the first four stages to enlightenment: stream-winner, once-returner, never-returner, *arahat* (Iaming and Phitsanakaha 1956: 424).

This behavior, characteristic of Buddhist practice at a time when power was dispersed and rebellious monks claimed supernatural abilities, might not in itself have brought about his downfall, but Taksin, in pressing for confirmation of his exalted spiritual status, required high-ranking monks to prostrate themselves before him in recognition of this status. Those who refused were punished. The highest-ranking monks, including the supreme patriarch, were replaced, and more than five hundred monks who had taken a stand against Taksin were flogged and sentenced to menial labor at the monastery of the new supreme patriarch (Royal Institute 1919: 197–98). The schism in the *sangha* ostensibly created by this incident alone was, in fact, symptomatic of the disunity and institutional chaos that troubled the Buddhist monkhood in the years following the fall of Ayudhya in 1767. Even after Rama I came to the throne in 1782 and reinstated the supreme patriarch and others who had taken a stand against Taksin, the faction that formed around the now-demoted favorites of Taksin continued to cause dissension in the *sangha*, a dissension as bitter and disruptive as any in the annals of Thai history. The harsh language in the "laws" on the *sangha* used by Rama I to reprimand the offenders testifies to the strength of the conflict, and these "laws," as well as other documents, make clear that schism in the form of controversy over monastic discipline was rife at the time (Reynolds 1973, chap. 2). Again, we may ask of the *1789 Chronicle* if it can tell us how schism in the *sangha* affected, or was reflected in, the legitimizing process.

The event that the *Chronicle* commemorates and describes in its eighth chapter is commonly referred to as the "Tripitaka Revision and Council of 1788," during which monks and lay Buddhist scholars met in Bangkok to make an inventory of Pali texts and produce an authentic edition of the canon. In its selection of events to narrate, the arrangement of those events, the relationship between the monarchy and the *sangha* on which it dwells throughout, and its reliance on certain sources, it belongs to a genre of religious historical writing whose progenitor is the Great Chronicle of Sri Lanka, the *Mahavamsa*.[2] In Thailand, there are at least four representatives of this genre: the *Jinakalamali* (A.D. 1516/17); the *Mulasasana* (the main body of which is dated A.D. 1420s); the *Camadevivamsa* (mid-fifteenth century); and the *Ratanabimbavamsa* (possibly A.D. 1429), the chronicle of the Emerald Buddha.[3] So close is the relationship of the *1789 Chronicle* to these others that four of its nine chapters draw material from the *Anakalamali*, and numerous stanzas derive directly from the *Mahavamsa* and other Pali works. The Bangkok court, having produced its own version of this genre in the *1789 Chronicle*, shortly thereafter had the *Jinakalamali* and the *Mahavamsa* translated from Pali into Thai, in 1794 and 1797 respectively (Dhani 1969: 157; Rattanapanna Thera 1968: xxxv).

All the chronicles in this genre rely on the *Mahavamsa* as a model and, like the *Mahavamsa*, have as their theme one of two subjects: royal support for preserving the Buddha's teachings, especially by supporting the lineal succession of the *sangha*; or the history of a particular relic or image.[4] This chronicle tradition centered on the Buddha's life, the patronage of Buddhism exemplified by the third-century Mauryan monarch Asoka and the spread of Buddhism, especially to Sri Lanka in the mission of Mahinda (Perera 1961: 29). One of the fundamental presuppositions of the *Mahavamsa* chronicle tradition was that Sri Lanka was destined by the Buddha to be the repository of the true doctrine, thus binding the fate of the doctrine to the contingencies of the political history of the island (Perera 1961: 33).

As the introduction to the 1923 published edition of the *1789 Chronicle* says of that document, it is "a history of Buddhism combined with the history of the kingdom," a statement that would apply equally well to the other chronicles in the genre (Phonnarat 1923: 10; Mahanama 1920: ii–iii). Written by monks so that other monks would be cognizant of the vicissitudes of secular rulers in their support for the religion, these chronicles glorified kings for their meritorious works and religious patronage and set criteria by which kings knew they would be judged

(Perera 1961: 39; Gokhale 1965: 356). In Sri Lanka this tradition of religious historical writing ends with the British occupation of the Kandyan kingdom in 1815, and in Thailand the genre comes to an end at roughly the same time, with the *1789 Chronicle*; no more chronicles like this are forthcoming.

The temporal framework in this historiographical tradition was a finite span of five thousand years during which the Buddha's teachings would endure. Over this period, a brief moment "within the abstract infinitude of cosmic time in which there are earlier buddhas and buddhas-to-be" (Wyatt 1976: 115–16), the practice of Buddhism would suffer a gradual but inexorable deterioration.

The author of the *1789 Chronicle* was a participant in the Council of 1788 and headed one of the four divisions of scholars organized to work on the Bangkok court's edition of the Tripitaka. He was born in 1735 and, in middle age, found himself favored by Taksin in two respects.[5] Taksin sent him to Phitsanulok principality in the north to bring order to the *sangha* after 1767, and the king subsequently conferred on him the high ecclesiastical rank of Phra Phimonlatham and the abbotship of a small monastery on the Bangkok side of the river destined to become the Jetavana monastery under Rama I. It was at this monastery that he taught King Mongkut's uncle, Prince Paramanuchit, one of the most distinguished scholar-monks of the nineteenth century. But under Taksin, Phra Phimonlatham, along with other recalcitrant monks, lost his rank when he refused to prostrate himself and recognize Taksin's claims to exalted spiritual status. Rama I, upon his accession in 1782, reversed the punishments by reinstating Phra Phimonlatham and the others Taksin had discredited and by demoting Taksin's favorites. In 1794, the king made him *somdet* Phra Phonnarat, the name by which he is known as the author of several histories, including the "two-volume" recension of the Ayudhya annals (Tri 1962; Wyatt 1976: 121).

One incidental fact suggests a clue to the character of this monk, whose life, as far as we know it today, is otherwise lacking in human interest. All biographers of Phra Phonnarat mention that when Rama I was planning to build a bridge for elephants to cross one of the canals that ringed Bangkok, the scholarly monk advised the king against such a bridge on strategic grounds: the king's enemies would thus have easy access to the royal base. The king heeded this advice.

Trivial as the incident may seem, it suggests that this monk was a man of the world, and that he was as capable of offering military advice as of compiling Pali chronicles. This worldliness of monks seems to have been a sign of the times, when the exigencies of military defense called for the skills of everyone, even those of Buddhist monks. Phra Phonnarat's mirror opposite—a monk who had been Taksin's supreme patriarch, who also held for a time the position of Phonnarat, who also helped Taksin restore order in the northern *sangha,* and who also served on the Council of 1788 even after disciplinary violations— once negotiated with a rebel on Taksin's behalf, hardly behavior to be condoned by a strict interpretation of the *Vinaya* (Damrong and Sommot 1923: 74–75).

From this biographical sketch, three points germane to the argument of this essay emerge. First, Phra Phonnarat experienced on one side, and then the other, the schisms in the *sangha* that troubled the reigns of Taksin and Rama I. Second, he was not a recluse; rather, he was close to the court and to the administrative and political problems it faced in resettling the population in a new capital. Third, this monk's high status in the *sangha* as well as his numerous historical writings indicate that the king had chosen him not only to preserve the integrity of the Thai past but also to celebrate the Bangkok court's own accomplishments in government and its return to Theravada orthodoxy. His audience for a chronicle in Pali was the *sangha* and his purpose in compiling such a document was to reassure the monkhood that Rama I's generous patronage in sponsoring the Council of 1788 and his firm leadership in efforts to resolve conflict and restore discipline in the *sangha* would bring stability to the kingdom after a disorienting period.

Despite these recommendations that Phra Phonnarat's history of the 1788 Council might be a valuable document, historians have tended to pass over it for a variety of understandable reasons. Heavy reliance on a common core of Pali sources and the strict conventions of the *Mahavamsa* genre account, to some extent, for the scant attention paid to the work. Seven of the nine chapters add little that is fresh to our knowledge of Buddhism in South Asia or Thailand: chapter 1 narrates the life of the Buddha and the first three Councils, concluding with that of Asoka in the third century B.C.; chapter 2 tells of the coming of Buddhism to Sri Lanka and ends with material from the *Jinakalamali*; chapters 3 to 6 reproduce the last sections of that same chronicle; chapter 9 enumerates the merit resulting from various good works and ends with the five *antaradhana*, or stages, in the disappearance of the religion. Only chapters 7 and 8 promise the historian something unique.

Chapter 7 is a recension of the annals of Ayudhya, a recension hitherto neglected but now thought to form part of a chronicle tradition that dates to the first half of the seventeenth century.[6] Chapter 8 is the story of the 1788 Council, reckoned as the ninth in the lineage of Councils. But even chapters 7 and 8 offer little that cannot be found in other sources. Coedès, who seems to have covered every inch of the scholarly map in Southeast Asian classical studies, has been here as well, having transcribed and translated the annals of chapter 7, and although the French scholar said he was not going to pass judgment on the value of chapter 7 as a historical source, his remarks clearly indicate that he was not very impressed with the *1789 Chronicle* as a whole. It was not, he said, an original work, but a compilation of various parts and pieces arranged without much skill (Coedès 1914: 3). The passages compiled by Phra Phonnarat were maladroit in style and often incorrect. In all fairness to the *Chronicle*, however, its redundancies in the early chapters had led Coedès to concentrate on the annals only to translate them and to provide occasional notes on dating and comparative references to other recensions. It was not his task to inquire into the role the text might have played in the history of the time.

By looking more closely at the language used to describe the events between 1767 and 1788, we can begin to understand the relationship between the *Chronicle* and the founding of a new dynasty. In the space of these twenty years, according to the *Chronicle*, the kingdom underwent a profound transformation. The fall of Ayudhya in 1767 threw the Thai state into chaos, disrupting normal social life, causing economic and material deprivations, and dividing the population into factions that contended with each other for scarce resources (Phonnarat 1923: 408–12). The harsh conditions broke up families, and food was in short supply. Many Buddhist monks, finding that they could not survive in the ordained state, disrobed and went off into lay life to seek their own livelihoods. Buddhism suffered in other ways as well, as disrespectful people committed violence against Buddha images and scavenged libraries for the cloth and cords that bound the Pali scriptures, thus leaving them prey to insects. Enough pious people survived to keep the Buddha's religion alive; parts of the Tripitaka were collected for safekeeping, and monks eventually returned to their ruined monasteries to rebuild. But for most people, the age was a dark age—the *kali-yuga*—and the period following the fall of Ayudhya is so designated in the *1789 Chronicle* at the end of the annals in chapter 7. The *kali-yuga* was one of four ages determined by the king's adherence to *dharma* (Spellman 1964: 111, 212). In classical Indian society, a people without a king is like a river without water (Gonda 1966: 47); and so it is in central Siam at this time. Life without a king was intolerable and unthinkable. At the conclusion of chapter 7, the kingdom is split into four regions, each with its own regional overlord, and Taksin has begun to undermine the power of these regional overlords in his striving for a unified kingdom.

Chapter 8, which records the Tripitaka Council of 1788, begins with Taksin still the preeminent political and military figure, but his harsh exactions turn the people against him after fourteen years of rule. He destroys many towns and removes large numbers of people from the south to his capital at Thonburi. When he shows signs of madness in 1781, "the people" become angry, turn against him, and kill him (Phonnarat 1923: 423). Then come the Jakri brothers, who had resolved long before this date that they would deliver the people from suffering but who had to bide their time until the right moment. They were merit-filled and compassionate ("they loved Buddhism more than their own lives," Phonnarat 1923: 438) and saw that Buddhism was threatened; scriptures, *stupa*, relics, and monastery buildings had been destroyed. Their campaigns to restore order become, in the framework of the *1789 Chronicle*, a struggle against the enemies of Buddhism, those with *a-dhamma* (absence of *dhamma*—disorder, disharmony, unrighteousness). It is worth noting here that military regimes in Thailand remained in power after World War II by maintaining a siege or crisis mentality and, at times, a state of martial law in order to protect the kingdom against Communists who, as many Thais point out, are atheists and enemies of Buddhism. In other words, social conflict, or the mere threat of it, thus enjoins a religious battle. In the *1789 Chronicle*, the monarchy also protects the people against the enemies of religion, the lawless, the disrespectful, and in the narrative, this responsibility now requires the construction of a new city that will protect its residents just as a Buddhist amulet protects its possessor.

The description of the newly constructed city is, of course, laudatory, but it aims at a particular effect. The visual experience of seeing the city is sensual, and to gaze on the palaces and pavilions, their glittering tiles and pediments studded with crystal and mother-of-pearl catching the bright sunlight, is to be transported to the homes of the gods. The narrator makes comparisons with various heavenly palaces and shrines by the use of appropriate similes: a palanquin for a Buddha image "was covered with gold and silver as beautiful as the palace of a *brahma*" (Phonnarat 1923: 430). Brahma deities are meritorious creatures who exist above and beyond the world of sensation and desire. These similes were not just to call forth recognition of familiar architectural forms or set a standard of beauty. By likening the terrestrial to the celestial, they also blurred the distinction between the heavenly world and the world of man; in reading the text, one is not certain whether the Indra being described is in his heaven or on one of the pavilion tympana. The ambiguity thus created by matching microcosmos to macrocosmos was one way the principal resident of the city, the king, acquired divine attributes (Mabbett 1969: 217; Mabbett 1985: 78). The architecture, recreated here in a literary mode, was a metaphor that set the king apart in a sacred category.

To experience this heavenly city (*krung deva*—the city of the god or Indra) was not just to admire its visual beauty but to derive from it physical satisfaction: "It brought great pleasure and contentment" (Phonnarat 1923: 433). Just as King Ramkhamhaeng was proud of his thirteenth-century capital at Sukhothai, crowded "to the bursting point" with people merrily celebrating a Buddhist festival day, so the author of the *1789 Chronicle* describes Rama I's capital as a city where people may experience pleasure and contentment. The heavenly city would attract people to come and resettle in the Chaophraya River delta. It is a lure, a promise, for with its construction and the increasing dependence of the population on the two Jakri brothers, the people of Bangkok "were protected from their enemies, from the lawless, and from danger, and were allowed to pursue their livelihoods in happiness" (Phonnarat 1923: 434). Food became more abundant and monks returned to their monasteries to study and practice meditation, free from anxiety about finding their next meal. Moreover, the advent of a king meant that collective efforts on a large scale, heretofore beyond the capacities of individuals or small groups of people, were now possible. One such effort, mentioned in the *Chronicle* as "difficult for individuals to accomplish," was the damming and rechanneling of the river (Phonnarat 1923: 441). Here the achievements of a people governed by a king are no different from those in an eleventh-century Old Javanese inscription that records a flood-control project successfully accomplished after individual effort had failed and the people had appealed to the ruler (Van Naerssen 1963: 19n.5).

The rest of chapter 8 tells of the Tripitaka Council, which produced an intact and authentic edition of the canon, an event that restored the religion to good health after the depredations of earlier years. The transformation that occurs, then, from the anarchy and chaos of 1767 to the peaceful and orderly society of 1788, is complete. Abundance, prosperity, and contentment have replaced scarcity, deprivation, and misery. And these better conditions permit people to lead a better life, a morally better life. The historical cause of this transformation is royal virtue, and the interdependent nexus linking royal virtue with agricultural and economic prosperity, which in turn begets the morally good life, is as explicit in the *1789 Chronicle* as in any other "traditional" Southeast Asian text. The rule of a king fructifies the land and thus enhances the opportunities for merit-making.

In reading over this transformation of the kingdom from a kind of Hobbesian state of nature, in which man was set against man, to a state of harmony and utopian fulfillment, one cannot help but recall the legend of the first monarch in Buddhist tradition, Mahasammata or "the Great Elect," who was invited by a warring and impoverished population to eliminate discord and restore order and prosperity. This legend was common in the Theravada Buddhist world, coming as it did from the *Sutta* section of the Pali canon, in the "Book of Genesis" of the *Digha-Nikaya* (Rhys Davids 1971, pt. III, chap. 27; F. Reynolds 1972: 18–19). The legend has been interpreted as a social-contract theory of government. Although applicability to actual historical communities is difficult to determine, the theory went farther than similar references in Sanskrit texts in postulating a contract between a ruler and his subjects (Spellman 1964: 19–25). The Mahasammata story is a legend that gives to the first king the duty of bringing harmony to the kingdom, and Rama I's historian, in dramatizing this transformation in his Pali *Chronicle* and crediting Rama I for its success, was evoking this legendary first king.

In a sense, all kings were "first" kings, for the king "is the author of time, not of chronological time which is but an abstraction, but of the time which ripens the actions of men" (Lingat 1962b: 14). Nowhere does a king, especially a king who might found a dynasty, better reveal himself as the author of time which ripens the actions of men than when he lays down the rules of society, the law. Early Mon authors in the Southeast Asian Buddhist world, engaged in adapting the Hindu law code to their society, had endowed the legendary first king, Mahasammata, with a hermit-sage who recited from memory the text of the law, which he found inscribed on the wall surrounding the world (Lingat 1973: 267). The hermit-sage was Manu, transformed from the lawgiver of Hindu society to law-transmitter for a Buddhist society, and Rama I, in one of his many acts of "restoration" and "renewal," compiled and promulgated a law code in 1805 that began with one of the Mon *dharmasastra*. In issuing this law code, he gave to his kingdom the law of Manu, which governs laymen and promotes their welfare, a law that establishes harmony in the world just as the first king established harmony in the world. The conclusion one can draw from this constellation of evidence is that the turbulence following the fall of Ayudhya provided Rama I, who was trying to fortify and rejuvenate the kingdom, with ample opportunity to tap a deep reservoir of myth concerning the creation of culture and the genesis of the social order, and the *1789 Chronicle* has historical value for the way it makes connections between the Jakri brothers and this reservoir of myth. Not to read the *Chronicle* with these wider dimensions in mind is to miss its historical value.

The final chapter of the *Chronicle*, which relates the decline of the religion in one-thousand-year intervals leading to the extinction of the Buddha's teaching five thousand years after his *parinibbana*, can be reinterpreted in a similar light. At first, the power to acquire the degrees of sanctity will disappear, followed by observance of the precepts, knowledge of the scriptures, and the exterior signs of the Buddhist ascetic. Finally, the corporeal relics of the Buddha will be consumed in a holocaust (Coedès 1956: 98–99). This prophecy of the inevitable retrogression of the religion, which was given its definitive form by the Indian commentator Buddhaghosa, acted to inspire Buddhist monarchs to do everything in their power to retard the process or, at least, to make the most of the stages remaining. People were fortunate to be born in an age when a Buddha had appeared whose message offered a way to escape the endless round of deaths and rebirths. The fourteenth-century Thai monarch Lithai was conscious of the prophecy, gave an account of it, and exhorted his subjects in an inscription of A.D. 1357 to "make haste to perform meritorious actions [in accordance with] the Buddha's religion while it still survives" (Prasert and Griswold 1992: 452–56). This sense of urgency may have impelled the same king to compose the Three Worlds cosmology as the end of the second millennium approached (Coedès 1957: 349–50). But what are we to make of the five-thousand-year prophecy in the *1789 Chronicle*? In discussing the *Chronicle*, Coedès thought the inclusion of the prophecy added little to the work and bore almost no relationship to its main subject (Coedès 1914: 6).

Though it is true that this material adds nothing new to Buddhist history or historiography, the inclusion of the prophecy can be seen as a cosmological abstraction or recapitulation of the terrible conditions that beset the kingdom after 1767. In the last chapter, the *kali-yuga* or dark age is mentioned again, and the description of the terrible conditions is identical to the conditions described in the "historical" section of chapter 7:

> When study of the scriptures declines, when it slips away, there will occur an age of vice and misery (*kali-yuga*) of the unrighteous people. When the king is without *dhamma* the people—the ministers, for example—follow likewise and become without *dhamma* in the same way.
>
> (Phonnarat 1923: 554)

Further deterioration of society proceeds in a downward spiral. The inability to know and follow *dhamma* results in drought. When laypeople are poor, they cannot offer the monastic requisites and monks cannot look after their disciples. The passage mentioning the *kali-yuga* immediately precedes the *Chronicle*'s description of the disappearance of the knowledge of the scriptures, beginning with the *Abhidhamma* and continuing until even the *Vinaya* is lost. The last vestige of the Buddha's teaching disappears when there is no layperson who remembers a four-line verse of the Buddha's words. At the time Phra Phonnarat compiled his chronicle, the retrogression of the religion had reached its third one-thousand-year stage, during which the scriptures would gradually disappear, and Rama I, in sponsoring the Tripitaka Revision of 1788, was forestalling the inevitable outcome. In other words, the last chapter of the *1789 Chronicle* transposes the events of 1767, a dark age, and places them in relation to the five-thousand-year prophecy, a temporal plane that has special meaning in Buddhist time. The *Chronicle* tells how that dark age of 1767 is to be understood, as a hint of the terrible conditions that will occur when the Buddha's teachings expire.

The *Chronicle* also makes connections between Thai history and the specially charged period of the Buddha's teachings in the way it narrates the sequence of Buddhist Councils that gives the *Chronicle* its name. Phra Phonnarat reckoned the 1788 Council in Siam as the ninth in a lineage reaching back to the sixth century B.C.E., when the first Council was called following the Buddha's death. The *Mahavamsa* does not reckon Southeast Asian kings in the line of Buddhist kings who convened Councils, but Southeast Asian Theravada Buddhist courts grafted their Councils onto the broader tradition as they saw fit, feeling themselves a part of the Buddhist world. The Burmese, for example, calculate the Council in King Mindon's reign (1853–78) as the Fifth and that in the 1950s under U Nu as the Sixth, although international recognition of these Councils as orthodox is another matter entirely (Mendelson 1975, chaps. 2, 5). Phra Phonnarat places the first three Councils in India, the next four in Sri Lanka, the eighth in the northern Thai state with its capital at Chiangmai in the year 1483, and the ninth in Bangkok in 1788.[7] In fashioning this lineage of Councils with Rama I's as the most recent, the author assimilated the history of the Thai kingdoms to South Asian history.

It was not just Rama I's patronage of the Council, the provision of writing materials, and personal consideration for the monks' comfort (the king's brother cooked rice himself for the Pali scholars) that bespoke the king's virtue, but also the fact that he initiated the Council. All the sources agree that the idea for the Council came from the secular side—the king, the court—but at first no one saw the need. Extant texts of the Tripitaka had already been copied and distributed to monasteries when a relatively minor official informed the king that the texts were defective or incomplete (Thiphakorawong 1960: 183).

The king then addressed high-ranking monks with this news, and when it was confirmed, he convened the Council. This procedure conforms to the tenets of monastic discipline, which suggest that a monk should not request anything he requires; instead, a thoughtful layperson must anticipate his needs. At the same time, this secular initiative, as recorded in the *Chronicle* and other sources, attributed to Rama I and his court a concern for the health of the religion, a concern that he shared with other great Buddhist kings of the past.

One of these great kings was Asoka, who had convened the Third Council in the third century B.C.E. (Reynolds 1972; Smith 1972). The historicity of this and other Councils is beside the point here; what mattered was the tradition.[8] For Phra Phonnarat to reckon the 1788 Council in a lineage that included Asoka was to borrow the prestige of that famous king and drape it over Rama I's own achievement. It was to declaim that Rama I was Asoka's equal by associating Rama I with a genealogical line of Buddhist Councils that included Asoka's. Such associations made Indian, Sri Lankan, and Thai Buddhist history a single, seamless cloth that covered the entire period from the time of the Buddha to the present day. Moreover, the appropriateness of Asoka's model was taken for granted; the time in which he lived was not remote and alien but immediate and familiar.

To come to the final point about the relationship between the *1789 Chronicle* and the historical context that produced it, we might ask how the schisms in the *sangha* during the Taksin-Rama I years are reflected in this document. Though the *1789 Chronicle* records a dispute in the *sangha* of a ritualistic question of ablution (Phonnarat 1923: 449–53), it does not mention the schisms that can be documented from other sources. The inattention to these schisms on the part of an author who experienced them firsthand is, at first, daunting, but the strict conventions of the *Mahavamsa* genre, whose single objective was to glorify the religion and the kings who supported it, rendered the issue inappropriate for the genre. To dwell on the disunity in the *sangha* would have detracted from this objective and undermined it. Even so, the relationship between the schisms, the *1789 Chronicle*, and the process of securing and legitimizing the throne for Rama I ultimately proves more interesting than it first appears.

The First Council, in India, was convened to deal with one of the disciples who had criticized the Buddha; the Second was convened to resolve a dispute over ten disciplinary points; the Third was convened by Asoka to purge the *sangha* of non-Buddhist ascetics who had deceitfully been ordained. The consequence of this last Council was the disrobing of sixty thousand monks, and it may be at the same time as this Third Council of circa 250 B.C.E. that Asoka issued his Schism Edict:

> No one is to cause dissension in the Order. The Order of monks and nuns has been united, and this unity should last for as long as my sons and great grandsons, and the moon and the sun. Whoever creates a schism in the Order, whether monk or nun, is to be dressed in white garments, and to be put in a place not inhabited by monks or nuns. For it is my wish that the Order should remain united and endure for long.
>
> (Thapar 1961: 262)

The fact that the Pali canon, the authorized version of the schisms for the Theravada School, fails to include the Third Council demonstrates the sensitivity to the schisms in the historical record (Warder 1961: 48). The circumstances of the convening of this Third Council, and the others as well, suggest that, apart from the textual editing and copying needs that ostensibly brought the monks together in 1788, the Bangkok Council had a sociological dimension somewhat concealed in Phra Phonnarat's telling of it. Schism was to Buddhism what heresy was to Christianity; there was no greater threat to the monkhood than factions in the *sangha*, and the schisms of the years 1767 to 1788 were contentious and disruptive. In a sense, the editing and copying accomplished in the 1788 Council were surface events, and we must look beneath them to discover the more complex significance of the Council. In Burma, the program of textual comparison undertaken during U Nu's Sixth Council "was more ritual than real" (Mendelson 1975: 279), and while this judgement may not quite apply in the Thai case, it is true that Rama I shared with U Nu, and with Mindon too, an abiding concern for *sangha* unity.

The French scholar Andre Bareau has pointed out that the Pali word translated as "council" is composed of two terms, "to chant (*giti*) together (*sam*)." An accurate rendering of the Pali terms is closer to the French word *concert*—concord, harmony, unanimity—than to "council." The Councils reaffirmed the unity of the *sangha*, which was based on the unity of, and relative agreement on, the Doctrine. The Councils were, in fact, "the only way of assuring this unity, since the Community lacked any central authority charged with assuming this function" (Bareau 1955: 134). Certainly, a Thai prince-patriarch of more recent times understood the sociological function of the Councils in this way, as a means of contending with dissident groups in the *sangha* and preserving unity (Vajirananvarorasa 1971).

It would seem, then, that the Councils sought to resolve conflict in the *sangha* and to institutionalize it. Rama I was no less stern in demoting those monks who had accepted Taksin's claims to exalted spiritual status than Asoka had been in disrobing sixty thousand ascetics, but the most distinguished of the monks loyal to Taksin was ultimately allowed to participate as head of one of the four divisions (Thiphakorawong 1960: 193). His participation thus institutionalized a schism that had persisted for some years by bringing into the fold a senior monk whose dissidence obstructed Rama I's efforts at reunification.

Similarly, the northern Thai king in the fifteenth century who had convened the Eighth Council ruled at a time when more than one monastic order had established itself. The Sinhalese order, led by monks who had traveled to Sri Lanka for reordination, was expanding, and the king brought a degree of unity by encouraging the reordination of monks in the orthodox Sinhalese manner (Ratanapanna 1968: 133–38). A second comparison with the two Burmese Councils in the past one hundred years is also instructive. Both Mindon and U Nu struggled with sectarian controversy and attempted to unify the *sangha* through the sponsorship of Councils (Mendelson 1975: 294, 297). In this context, the Sixth Council, in Burma, has been termed "a disciplinary action" on the part of the Nu government (Mendelson 1975: 355). Seen in this light, the 1788 Council in Thailand and the 1789 *Chronicle*, which commemorates it, become a declaration that the schism has been healed, that conflict has been resolved.

In the years between his accession in 1782 and the Council in 1788, Rama I was still in the process of establishing his claim to the throne. Indeed, he was not formally crowned until 1785, three years after his accession. A claim to the throne such as his needed to be substantiated by more than brute force and military victory. Like the ancient Khmer kings Jayavarman II and Jayavarman IV, who had little hereditary right to the throne and who spent some years trying to prove that right before performing the *Devaraja* ceremony that formally consecrated their reigns, Rama I spent the early years of his reign reaffirming traditional modes of Thai government, promoting a sense of normality in social relations, and demonstrating political wisdom. The legitimizing process, which really continued throughout the reign, was especially critical in the first six years until the 1788 Council; only after this date do the major historical, legal, and literary textual revisions appear.

The discord in the *sangha* was symptomatic of the turmoil after the fall of Ayudhya, and if Rama I's state was to last, this problem had to be overcome. Between his accession in 1782 and his Brahmanical coronation in 1785, Rama I decreed no fewer than seven of his ten "laws" on the *sangha*, most of them covering schism and indiscipline. These laws cited cases of indiscipline and then exhorted both monks and laypeople to help the *sangha* maintain a high ascetic standard (Lingat 1962a: I, 164–228). The 1788 Council and the *1789 Chronicle* were tacit declarations that the schism, if not eliminated, was at least under control, and this attainment was crucial to buttressing Rama I's kingship. A divided *sangha* meant a divided people, an ungovernable people, for the monkhood "provided a tight binding between the government and the people" (Vajiranana 1979: 37). And could it not be that the *1789 Chronicle*, written by a high-ranking monk who had taken a stand in the schism and had been honored for his orthodoxy by his new patron, was an expression of the *sangha*'s confidence in the new king? The 1788 Council and the writing of its history crowned the legitimizing process in the first six years of the reign, especially as far as the *sangha* was concerned. In this sense, the *1789 Chronicle* helped to make history as well as record it.

Phra Phonnarat's *1789 Chronicle* gave Rama I's Buddhist Council of 1788 a history, thus making it an auspicious sign that Rama I had found ways to resolve *sangha* conflicts and that his reign would endure. What was at stake was the stability of the relationship between monarch and *sangha*, and it was this stable relationship that the king and the monks closest to him sought to attain. Such a lesson from history, a lesson derived from all the works in this Buddhist historiographical tradition, was subsumed under a larger purpose in remembering the past, namely, that history was a means of understanding the ultimate terms of man's existence, his place on earth, and what was in store for him in the afterlife (Wang 1968: 2).

This episode in Thai history resonates with similar situations elsewhere in Southeast Asia, when invasion or interdynastic warfare called forth reflection on the past. The *1789 Chronicle* was a history for an occasion, and the author found the Buddhist historiographical tradition utterly appropriate and necessary for his urgent concerns. The fusion of this transcultural tradition with an indigenous Southeast Asian historical continuum was so natural as to make a distinction between the two indiscernible.

Notes

1. The term "madness" has various renderings in Thai. See the language (e.g., *sanya wippalat*) used by two Jakri princes in Damrong and Sommot Ammoraphan 1923: 74 and Sommot 1965: 10.

2. I use the term *Mahavamsa* to embrace the three stages in the development of the Pali chronicle of Sri Lanka: the *Dipavamsa*, the *Mahavamsa*, and the *Culavamsa*. See Perera 1961.

3. See Anan 1976. The arrival of the *Mahavamsa* in Thailand has not been dated exactly, but this group of chronicles strongly suggests a date in the fifteenth century. Also, a list of texts presented to a Burmese monastery in an inscription of A.D. 1442 includes the *Mahavamsa* (Bode 1966, chap. 3, appendix).

4. *Jinakalamali, Mulasasana*, and the *1789 Chronicle* belong to the former category; *Camadevivamsa* and *Ratanabimbavamsa* to the latter. All are in Pali with the exception of *Mulasasana*, which is in the northern Thai language Tai Yuan.

5. Biographical data in this paragraph come from Damrong and Sommot 1923.

6. M. Vickery in his review of the van Vliet recension of the Ayudhya chronicle proposes that van Vliet's source and the annals in the *1789 Chronicle* share a common parentage (1976).

7. The Eighth Council (Phonnarat 1923: 340–42) receives only glancing mention in the *Jinakalamali*, but it is presumed that a leaf from the original manuscript is missing (Ratanapanna 1968: 140 n.1, 164). Another chronicle that records the history of the north dates the Eighth Council in 1477 C.E. (Khurusapha Press 1963: 255–56).

8. Most scholars agree, for example, that the First Council was not a historical event (Prebish 1974: 241).

8

Buddhist Cosmography in Thai Intellectual History

I n Thai studies, what Western historiography would call intellectual history is still to be fathomed. The reasons for the scant attention paid to this topic are various, having as much to do with continued emphasis on political and economic history as with the lack of speculative literature (in Siamese) that would attract the curiosity of intellectual historians. For example, we hardly know what books—especially what Western books—were read by the nineteenth-century Siamese elite, let alone how such books shaped its outlook and its perceptions of change. Because Siam has been a predominantly Buddhist state, it would be useful to begin with Buddhist materials, in particular with Buddhist cosmography and the Siamese reassessment of it that has taken place since the encounter with the West in the middle of the nineteenth century.

Buddhist cosmography stood at the core of Siamese Buddhist belief for centuries, serving as an all-embracing statement of the world as seen through Siamese Buddhist eyes, as well as a primary instrument for educating subjects of the Siamese kings in Buddhist values. But as Siamese society changed, the function of the cosmography in that society changed also. At what point and to what extent did Buddhist cosmography come into conflict with newly acquired knowledge about the way the world worked? The nature of the available Siamese sources suggests a methodology by which the historian may pursue Buddhist cosmography through time, and chart the changing attitudes of the Siamese elite toward the cosmography's utility. When placed in relation to one another, such diverse sources as a nineteenth-century critique of the cosmography and remarks by various kings, monks, and scholars on the cosmography's significance form a relatively continuous sequence of critical appraisals.

The fullest details of Siamese Buddhist cosmography are contained in several recensions that date from the late eighteenth and early nineteenth centuries; one of these, the *Traibhumi of Phra Ruang* (Three worlds cosmography of Phra Ruang), was reputedly first compiled in Siamese prose from the Pali canon and commentaries as far back as 1345 C.E., which makes the original compilation nearly as old as the Siamese state.

Recopied and doubtless amended as the centuries passed, it continues to fulfill certain functions in modern Siamese Buddhism. At least three kings since the early nineteenth century had reason to refer to it; and in present-day Thailand, many elements of Buddhist cosmography offer points of reference in Buddhist sermons, in common parlance, and in debates about the strength of the Buddha's teachings today (Jackson 2002b). Cosmographical data has also proved of value to anthropologists studying contemporary life (Hanks 1963; Kirsch 1967; Tambiah 1970, chap. 3). But in the middle of the nineteenth century, the cosmography came under attack as certain cultural changes undermined its prestige; and no king after Rama I (1782–1806) commissioned a recension. It is the process by which the *Traibhumi* lost its prestige that is my subject.

The structure of the *Traibhumi* cosmography, and the relationship between merit and power implied by this structure, suggest why it endured for so long. Beginning with the hells and ending with the heavens, the cosmography ranks all beings from demons to deities in a hierarchy of merit that accrues according to *karma*—the physical, cognitive, and verbal actions of past lives. The Buddhist cosmic structure thus recalls Dante and the Great Chain of Being, a theme in European literature, philosophy, and theology from Aristotle and the neo-Platonists to the late eighteenth and early nineteenth centuries. In the European medieval cosmic hierarchy, rank indicated difference in kind, and therefore in excellence (Lovejoy 1973, chap. 2). By the grossest calculation, the merit gradings in the Buddhist chain number three, the "three worlds" to which the title of the text refers; but the three worlds are further subdivided into thirty-one levels. The highest world contains four levels of *brahma* deities—formless, insensate beings who have no needs and no wants. The beings inhabiting the sixteen levels of the middle world are also *brahma* deities; but here they are conditioned by form, though they have accumulated sufficient merit to free themselves from sensation and desire. The lowest world contains eleven levels of beings conditioned by sensation and desire as well as by form. It is in this lowest world that mankind dwells, six levels of deities above it and four levels of less meritorious creatures below it.

For each of the thirty-one levels, several properties combine to define the beings on any particular level. Many of these properties fall under a category of "corporeality." If one selects examples from the extreme ends of the cosmic hierarchy, the properties take the form of oppositions: form vs. formless, sense perception vs. no sense perception, sexuality vs. asexuality. Even the space occupied by the *brahma* deities and the damned offers evidence for this contrast in corporeality. Whereas the formless *brahma* deities exist in an almost limitless space with no perimeters, the damned in the hells are pressed tightly into cubes (Lithai 1982: 67–68, 259). A specific biology and physiology apply to each of these creatures. The *brahma* deities are either asexual or masculine, and are created by spontaneous generation. Since the meditation (*jhana*) practiced in previous lives nourishes and sustains them, they require no food or water and expel no wastes (Lithai 1982: 251). Beings at the lower end of the cosmic hierarchy are created by omnivorous, viviparous, or moisture-sprung generation. They are ever reminded of their corporeality. The damned in one of the hells, former nobles and officials who overtaxed and oppressed the king's subjects, flounder in a river of excrement and, in a phantasmagoric food cycle, are forced to find nourishment from their own wastes (Lithai 1982: 77). Vivid details of the horrible and unspeakable punishments inflicted on the damned were a great aid to the artists who illustrated the manuscripts and portrayed the cosmography on monastery walls (Wenk 1965, plate VII).

Another property that defines the levels—or discs, as one writer has termed them—is longevity (Hanks 1963: 107). The duration of an existence lengthens as one proceeds away from the center with the *brahma* deities and the damned destined to live for eons—the former in a state of tranquility, the latter in a state of torment and suffering. If one could propel oneself through this cosmos from the terrestrial level, one would find that distance, as well as time, telescopes. The levels nearest to that of mankind are measurable in comprehensible numbers; the farthest distances are incalculable. The stone-month, a Theravada Buddhist equivalent of the light-year, is employed in the text at one point to illustrate the vast distance to the *brahma* heavens (Lithai 1982: 245). The numerical designations in terms of time and distance for each level have another dimension. Carried over into the Siamese social system, quantifications of merit are expressed in the conferring of "dignity marks" (*sakdina*) on those in official service, a practice that is documented from the mid-fifteenth century (Akin 1969: 21–22). Status positions in society, like merit gradings in the cosmography, are quantifiable.

The text actually reads in reverse order, from hell to heaven. Having traversed the hells and lower worlds of subhuman life and been exposed to the sermon by the Universal Monarch in the middle of the text, the reader—or, if the text is illustrated, the viewer—is persuaded of the value of the Buddha's precepts. Once taken, they will lead one above the world of sensation and desire, on to the more rarefied levels occupied by the *brahma* deities.

Ascent in the cosmic hierarchy brings increasing self-reliance and self-sufficiency. As corporeality recedes below, basic needs diminish and whatever is required can be self-generated. The *preta*, the departed dead or "suffering ghosts" (the *phi* of popular Siamese Buddhism), are dependent on the offerings of relatives living above them on the terrestrial level; but they are perpetually frustrated from ever satisfying their hunger and thirst (Lithai 1982: 95–105). Above the *preta* lives mankind, which can satisfy itself, but only temporarily. Next, the *deva*, who exist above the terrestrial level at the top of the world of sensation and desire, and can create food for each other at will; other objects of their desires are self-produced (Lithai 1982: 240). Then come the *brahma* deities, who have no desires. Thus one's merit level is an index of one's self-reliance and freedom from the earthly world and its social and spiritual corruptions. Above and beyond self-reliance is nonreliance.

It is this convergence of merit and self-reliance that helps explain the relationship between merit and wealth in Theravada Buddhist societies (Hanks 1962). The wealthy person's self-reliance, based on material resources, is an analogue of the *deva*'s self-reliance; the best way to demonstrate the merit implied by self-reliance is to make merit with those resources.[1] Another of the many social analogies lies with the young man who becomes a monk. Although some contact with the laity is necessary for survival (food, robes, shelter), ordination is really a rite that promotes self-reliance. Furthermore, in the most extreme forms of Buddhist asceticism practiced by forest dwellers, the monks—like the *brahma* deities—rely almost entirely on their own resources. Denial and renunciation are ways of declaring self-sufficiency (Mendelson 1965: 217).

These details are drawn from the earliest complete copy of the text, an eighteenth-century recension that states that King Lithai (Mahadharmaraja)—a monarch now known for his political skills, as well as for his piety and religious patronage—compiled the cosmography from Pali sources in a year reckoned as A.D. 1345 (Andaya 1971; Coedès 1957). From at least the time of King Ramkhamhaeng, whose inscription of 1292 C.E. marks the beginning of Siamese orthography, Siamese monarchs of the Sukhodaya kingdom had encouraged the growth of Theravada Buddhism by sponsoring religious missions to Ceylon and by constructing monasteries for the Mon monks who returned with relics or fragments of the Pali canon. Some of these fragments would have been the sources listed in the text as the basis for Lithai's compilation.

All Theravada Buddhist peoples shared the same cosmography, as it was inherent in the Pali scriptural tradition (Gombrich 1971, chap. 4; Law 1925; Masson 1942), although not every Buddhist kingdom had the comprehensive synthesis in a single text that was Lithai's achievement. Fragments of the Pali canon and commentaries also reached Burmese, Lao, Mon, and Khmer courts; and through the centuries, the cosmography penetrated deeper and deeper into mainland Buddhist belief.[2] Even in non-Theravada Southeast Asia, artists portrayed aspects of the cosmography in Buddhist monuments. The bas reliefs on the Mahayana Buddhist Borobudur Temple in central Java depicting sinners being punished in the hells have their origins in a Nepalese text. The cosmography was not, in fact, exclusively Theravada but was part of a larger Hindu-Buddhist tradition.

One of the reasons Buddhist cosmography fitted so well into mainland Southeast Asian societies is that it included a place for the creatures of animism. One kind of spirit (Pali *peta*; Sanskrit *preta*) that dwells below the terrestrial level between the demons (*asura*) and the animals is none other than the *phi*, or ghosts, of the departed dead in popular Siamese Buddhism. The merit-maker dedicated the merit accruing from his donation to the comfort and betterment of his or her deceased relatives. Inclusion in Buddhist cosmography, originally a concession to popular belief in India and Ceylon, thereby "upgraded" what can be presumed to be indigenous Southeast Asian belief into the universal moral order of an Indian religious system. At the same time, a reverse process took place. Most of the sources listed in the *Traibhumi* come from the Pali commentaries; because Lithai's text was composed in Siamese, the Pali scripture containing the ghost stories was domesticated in a Southeast Asian society.[3]

People in the countryside were not the only ones apprehensive about disgruntled *peta*. It would seem, in the Siamese case at least, that these beliefs were at home in the court as well as in the villages. High-ranking monks reminded King Rama I (1782–1809) of the Buddha's suggestion to King Bimbisara that the ghosts of his departed relatives would not interrupt his sleep if he made merit for them.[4] Royal obligation is here projected onto a humble plane. Kings, no less than villagers, had responsibilities to ancestors.

In order to uphold the *Traibhumi* cosmography as containing the core of Siamese Buddhist belief since the fourteenth century, one must be confident that the Sukhodayan court actually had possession of the cosmography in some form. This point is moot because recently the 1345 C.E. date for Lithai's compilation has been called into question (Vickery 1974). The dating formula in the exordium and colophon of the *Traibhumi of Phra Ruang* cannot easily be reconciled with the calendrical systems in use during the Sukhodaya period; and the fact that the earliest extant recension of the complete text comes from 1778 casts doubt on 1345 as the date of the original compilation. After more than four hundred years, the text must be corrupt,[5] but is there any other evidence, aside from the dating formula, that might anchor the *Traibhumi* in the Sukhodaya period? In particular, does Sukhodaya epigraphy support a date in the fourteenth century?

No inscription mentions Lithai's cosmography by name or refers directly to it, although an unusual term for the Jatakas, one of the sources listed in the *Traibhumi*, appears in Lithai's inscription of 1357 (Griswold and Prasert 1992: 453). In fact, certain phrases from the *Traibhumi* seem so similar to passages in this inscription that they have been used to reconstruct lacunae (Griswold and Prasert 1992: 463 n.135, 136); but such stock phrases describing ideal kingship might have been common in Siamese parlance. There is no way of ascertaining if these phrases dated from Lithai's reign. Mention in Lithai's inscription of 1361 of the Universal Monarch's (Chakravartin) jeweled disk, described at some length in the *Traibhumi*, is another example of suggestive but inconclusive evidence (Griswold and Prasert 1992: 521). It is worthy of note, however, that these attributes typical of the Universal Monarch should appear in the epigraphy of the putative author of a manuscript (the *Traibhumi*) that describes that kingly ideal in such detail and, furthermore, that these attributes are not discernible in Sukhodaya epigraphy before 1345.

The most convincing external evidence that the *Traibhumi* cosmography dates in some form from the fourteenth century comes not from Lithai's reign but from that of his son and successor, Mahadharmaraja II. In a passage that is almost a recitation of the principal places and deities of Hindu-Buddhist cosmography, an inscription of 1393 C.E. names several of the beasts found in the *Traibhumi*, as well as the six heavens in the world of sensation and desire and the four levels of formless *brahma* deities (Griswold and Prasert 1992: 91–93). The sixteen levels of the *brahma* deities of form, the divinities of the nine planets, and the twelve signs of the zodiac are acknowledged. The list also includes the four continents and the chief mountains of cosmic geography. Elsewhere in the inscription, the Avici hell is mentioned (Griswold and Prasert 1992: 88). Although the purpose of this part of the inscription is unclear, the same cannot be said of an earlier section that lists different kinds of spirits. There, the ancestor spirits; guardians of mountains, rivers, and streams; and forest sprites are invoked as witnesses to the pact between Sukhodaya and its ally, the state of Nan, the proclamation of which is the purpose of the inscription (Griswold and Prasert 1992: 84–87). The sections listing the spirits and celestial levels stand on either side of a passage that apparently describes the ideal conditions pledged for Sukhodaya and Nan, a rhetorical structure which parallels and evokes the structure of the *Traibhumi*.

The mere listing of terms in the fourteenth-century epigraphy is insufficient evidence to place the entire text attributed to Lithai in that period. But the epigraphy does confirm that the bare outline of the cosmography was present, and there is no doubt that fourteenth-century Siamese religious practice was consistent with this view of the world. Lithai's daughter founded a monastery in 1399 C.E. and dedicated the merit to her deceased father and mother, her husband (and halfbrother), and father-in-law, expressing at the same time the hope that she be reborn as a man (Griswold and Prasert 1992: 58–59, 65). Here in the epigraphy, as in the cosmography text, gender is conditioned by *karma*.

The *Traibhumi* and the epigraphy both present spirits and *deva* in the same moral continuum. Though we sometimes think of animism as a religious system separable from Buddhism, it is clear that, from the Sukhodaya period, the Siamese elite (nobility, royalty, the Sangha) unselfconsciously included spirit cults within the religious practice suggested by Pali scripture. The fact that the cosmography found such fertile ground in Siam and the other Indianized states is perhaps evidence of the affinities the Southeast Asian cultural complex had with Indian civilization. In an article arguing for a common substratum in monsoon Asia, G. Coedès listed animism and ancestor worship as two such affinities (Coedès 1953). Because of these affinities, moreover, the integration of "animistic elements" in the Pali commentarial literature suggests that Buddhism arrived in Southeast Asia with the mechanism for its own propagation.

Grading of spirits, *deva*, and other sentient beings in the universal moral continuum was a way of classifying them; just as the Western sciences of botany and zoology are systems of classification, the *Traibhumi* too was a classificatory system, a taxonomy of all animate existence. The parallel with Western science is close in other areas, too. *Karma* so conditions the creatures within this system that one might usefully refer to laws of motion that prescribe the mobility of each creature as well as the rebirth possibilities (Lithai 1982: 91, 271). *Karma* thus gives order and regularity to the universe much as the Newtonian laws of Western science give order and regularity to the physical universe. In its own way, the cosmography was a scientific textbook—explaining planetary motion and the recurrence of the seasons, and covering such subjects as geography, biology, and meteorology (Lithai 1982: 88, 118–19, 284).

From the putative origins of the *Traibhumi* in the Sukhodaya period until the late eighteenth century, little is known of the history of Lithai's cosmography. For the Ayudhya period, we have only two fragments of illustrated manuscript from the first half of the sixteenth and seventeenth centuries and a northern Siamese version of 1689 (Wenk 1965: 20; Vickery 1974: 284n.27). The next important stage of the text's history occurred after the fall of Ayudhya in 1767; King Taksin, who reassembled the Siamese state at Thonburi, in 1776 commissioned a new illustrated copy and in 1778 a more extensive copy without illustrations.[6] These revisions, as well as a new edition of the *Tripitaka* commissioned in 1769 and Taksin's invitation to an orthodox monk from the south to be his supreme patriarch, mean that the reputation of this king as "unorthodox" requires qualification. Certainly these were commendable acts expected of a monarch at any period in Siamese history.

Taksin's successor, Rama I (r. 1782–1809), the founder of the Bangkok dynasty, also made merit by commissioning a recension of the *Traibhumi*, attending to this task even before his more well-known revision of the *Tripitaka* in 1788 (Wenk 1968: 38–42). In 1783, barely one year after he acceded to the throne, Rama I invited his ministers and the highest-ranking members of the Sangha, headed by the supreme patriarch, to the throne hall and queried them on a wide range of matters including ways of reckoning time, miracles performed by the Buddha, and the destruction and recreation of the world. When he discovered inadequacies in the monks' mastery of these subjects, he ordered a group of scribes and monks under the supervision of the supreme patriarch to compile an edition of the *Traibhumi*, using the Pali canon and commentaries as sources.[7] Work on the compilation lasted some nineteen years, no doubt interrupted by the revision of the *Tripitaka*, to which the scholars could refer. Presumably, as in the reign of Taksin, this revision relied to some extent on fragments of the *Traibhumi* that had survived the destruction of Ayudhya. In 1802–3, the king reviewed the work to date, only to find the language uneven and not in accord with the canon and the commentaries. He requested another draft and, to supervise the work, appointed the head of the Department of Royal Pundits, a man who had been a high-ranking monk under King Taksin.[8]

This was the last time the Siamese court produced a complete edition of the *Traibhumi*; and it was characteristic of this first king of the Bangkok period that the work should have been accomplished in his reign. Rama I, both a warrior and an administrator, left a sizeable cultural, literary, and political legacy to his successors (Dhani 1969). When he assumed the throne in 1782, he moved the capital to the east bank of the Chaophraya River and continued the process begun by his predecessor of neutralizing external military threats. The order he restored gave the Siamese elite time to reflect on the past, to take stock of the present, to identify the kingdom's strengths, and to search for new solutions to government and administrative weakness that had led to the fall of Ayudhya in 1767. This restoration process took place in an entirely indigenous context, free from the comparison with Western cultural models that was to follow several decades later. There was as yet no reason to scrutinize the system of thought represented by the *Traibhumi*.

The recensions of major literary and historical works produced in the reign were a form of reassurance, and an invitation to both Siamese and non-Siamese within the kingdom to place their confidence in the new dynasty. Such a work as the cosmography cast a net over such Buddhist subjects as the Mon and the Lao; indeed, one document suggests that the Siamese court obtained Mon and Lao versions of the texts being revised (Thiphakorawong 1960: 183). Military campaigns into Laos and Cambodia brought a fresh influx of non-Siamese ethnic groups, as captive populations were removed and resettled closer to the capital. Once the kingdom recovered, the reign became expansionist and integrative, much like the reign of King Lithai, who also had sought to recover the losses of a predecessor and to reassemble a polyethnic state (Wenk 1968, chap. 4). In these two cases, at least, kings who manifested a special interest in the *Traibhumi* were restoring territorial integrity to their kingdoms. Thai social scientists have exploited this issue to show that the cosmography is a political text embedded in relations of power (Cholthira 1974).

Was the *Traibhumi* cosmography a relic, preserved to evoke nostalgic memory of Sukhodaya society? The fact that Rama I ordered his compilation in 1783, before his official coronation, indicates that he felt it deserved his immediate attention. The king would not have been collecting museum pieces while he was still appointing his ministers. The status of the monks assigned to the compilation also indicates that the text had practical value. No less a figure than the supreme patriarch advised the work; since high-ranking monks were responsible for its contents, the cosmography must have formed an essential part of what every properly educated monk should know.

Dramatic visual portrayal of the cosmography in Bangkok monastery art at this time provides further evidence of the text's vitality. When Wat Phrachettuphon in Bangkok was restored and expanded in Rama I's reign, paintings of the *Traibhumi* adorned the walls of the northern *vihara*; and this monastery was not unique (Thiphakorawong 1960: 271–72; Damrong and Naritsaranuwattiwong 1961: XI, 320). In the words of a European visitor to the capital in the early Bangkok period, the walls of one of the monasteries:

> were completely covered with representations of heaven, earth, hell, and one of the stars of which their books speak. There were angels, men, and monkeys, foreigners, or caricatures of white men, and dignified natives—scenes of gaiety and sadness—by land and sea—of war and peace—temples and brothels, with almost every sketch which could be framed from their sacred books, or conceived by their versatile limners.... My informant, the prince, remarked that the object of these paintings was to instruct the illiterate, through the medium of their senses.
>
> (Abeel 1934: 258)

Visual representations had a didactic function. Such richly colored and animated paintings persuaded the monastery visitor of the moral consequences of his acts, and, in an age of limited literacy, endowed the text's contents with more vivid realism than did the literary versions. It was by means of these visual portrayals, as well as the teachings of monks, that most Siamese learned how they fitted into the Buddhist cosmos. Paintings of the Hindu-Buddhist heavens also covered walls within the Grand Palace compound (Dhani 1963: 13). Though these paintings would have been accessible to few of the king's subjects, the Grand Palace was at the symbolic center of the Siamese state; and whatever was portrayed there received the patronage of the royal family and the court.

Until the early nineteenth century, the written and illustrated versions of Buddhist cosmography served as a textbook of Siamese Buddhism and Buddhist kingship. The unquestioned use of the *Traibhumi* to express Buddhist principles and to explain natural phenomena soon came to an end, however, as the Siamese state entered a new era in which the *Traibhumi* had to compete with other systems of thought. The consequence was not a complete dismissal of Buddhist cosmography, but a redefinition of the "moral" or "religious" world in the face of the greater explanatory power of Western science.

By the 1830s and 1840s, the isolation from the West that characterized the first Bangkok reign had given way to a more cosmopolitan environment. European and American missionaries and travelers arrived to proselytize and to trade, their numbers swelling in the 1850s, when the Siamese court concluded commercial treaties with several Western nations. Whatever their business in Siam, these Westerners soon found that Bangkok Siamese, whose world was suddenly expanded, made teachers of them. They were quizzed on everything from steamboat construction to Christianity, as growing numbers of Siamese sought out their company to discuss technology and comparative culture. Most of the Siamese intrigued by the Westerners and their culture were members of the nobility and royalty, whose official duties brought them into contact with foreigners; but as early as 1831, monks, some of them commoners, were visiting the missionaries (Abeel 1934: 237–39).

Coincident with the arrival of the first Westerners was reform of the Buddhist monkhood, an insistence on strict ritual, canonical fundamentalism, and purity of ordination (Reynolds 1973, chap. 3). At least some members of the lay elite most willing to engage the Westerners shared with the reform monks their desire to strip away the accretions of superstition and mythology; the cosmography became a focus for their efforts. The intellectual dimensions of the reform thus extended outside the Sangha itself. These two circumstances—the presence of Westerners willing to discuss comparative culture, and a reform monastic order critical of monastic conduct—combined to force on more and more Siamese a new awareness of themselves and their past.

The most influential figure among those Siamese with an avid interest in Western culture was Mongkut, a prince and heir to the throne who spent the years between 1824 and 1851 in the Sangha. During his twenty-seven years as a monk, he met such men as Jesse Caswell, an American missionary, and Bishop Pallegoix, acquiring from them knowledge of English, French, and Latin. Mongkut's leadership of the reform movement made it a success; without someone of his status, it would have faltered. In the same way, his curiosity about the West helped to induce curiosity in others. He was an excellent linguist and a persistent student. Caswell, in correspondence, wrote that Mongkut "never misses a lesson and plies me with so many questions that I commonly have to tear myself away from him" (Bradley 1966: 36). With the missionaries, Mongkut also discussed Christian doctrine and whether the earth was flat or spherical, insisting, by one account, that he had accepted the earth's sphericity fifteen years before the missionaries' arrival (Bradley 1966: 38). In these conversations, Mongkut demonstrated the skepticism characteristic of the reform-minded monks, or, as Caswell termed them, the "liberal school." Mongkut and his followers denied the existence of heaven and hell, and rejected "everything in religion which claims a supernatural origin" (Bradley 1966: 39).

The kinds of exchanges recorded in Caswell's letters continued after Mongkut became king in 1851, though Mongkut—as monarch— was no longer so free to participate in them. One well-documented conversation between Europeans and Siamese officials took place in 1863 when Adolf Bastian, a German visitor in Bangkok, and Henry Alabaster, later to become British consul, met with the Siamese minister of foreign affairs, Jaophraya Thiphakorawong (Kham Bunnag), at the latter's home (Feer 1879). This minister, an historian who compiled chronicles of the first four Bangkok reigns, had been hospitable to such missionaries as the American D. B. Bradley, offering Siamese boats for use in missionary activities. He was quick to grasp the practical benefits of Western technology, and adopted such techniques as homeopathy and Western obstetrics for his wives (Lord 1969: 106–7). When failing eyesight drove him from public service in 1867, he summoned a Dutch physician from Java to remove cataracts. On that evening in 1863, Bastian, Alabaster, and Thiphakorawong discussed the origin of suffering, the plausibility of the Questions of King Milinda, and the authenticity of parts of the Pali canon. The skeptical Thiphakorawong concluded that the Jatakas were only fables, and that Nagasena could certainly not have descended from the *brahma* heavens (Feer 1879: 152). On another occasion, Mongkut told Bastian that the Nepalese doctrine of the Adi Buddha of Nepal was the Buddhist belief closest to the idea of the Christian God (Feer 1879: 159).

Conversation in a comparative framework was not the only means by which Siamese came to know of things Western. By midcentury, the "snort of the engine" and the "shrill of the whistle" pierced the calm of Bangkok (Lingat 1935: 208). The machine had arrived, and such machines as the steam engine and the printing press immediately found acceptance by commoners and officials alike. Astronomy, often a pivot point for this kind of culture-change in Asia, intrigued Mongkut, who used astronomical instruments in his studies of planetary motion (Nakayama 1969: 2). Mongkut's brother, the Front Palace Prince or Second King, collected clocks, which he cleaned and repaired himself; understood the use of the sextant and chronometer; and was anxious for the latest nautical almanac (Bacon 1892: 86–87). He studied mathematics, fortification, and gunnery, and was interested in experimental electrical apparatus (Neale 1852: 88). Among the gifts presented to him by Townsend Harris, the American envoy of the 1850s, were Leyden jars, pith balls, "the quadrant electrometer for showing the intensity of the electricity by the raising of the ball," and "electric mortar," which would explode hydrogen gas by an electrical spark (Harris 1959: 158, 568–70). Galvanism was a relatively new science, dating from the late eighteenth century. Articles on other sciences such as physics, physiology, chemistry, and medicine appeared in the *Bangkok Recorder* (Lingat 1935: 204).

Another student of science, a commoner, made percussion caps for the king. This man, who spoke only Siamese,

> had arranged himself quite a laboratory and makes many chemicals—distills alcohol—nitric acid. I happened to complain of the annoyance of my lucifer matches, that in this damp weather scarce one would light. "If they were prepared from the 'chloras potassa' you would not have so much trouble," was his reply.
>
> (Wood 1859: 256)

The Siamese, almost certainly Mot Amatyakul, who became head of the Royal Mint in Mongkut's reign and printed an edition of the laws in 1849, also made batteries and possessed an electro-galvanic apparatus "far superior" to that of the American visitor. One Westerner also reported on a visit to a monastery where he found a monk-alchemist "distilling" mercury from lead (Bastian 1867: 127).

The Siamese who engaged in these investigations were not searching for new scientific laws. Behind this curiosity about electrical and optical instruments, chemical activity, and the workings of machines lay a love of gadgetry. An element of pragmatism, as well as of novelty, recommended these machines. To be able to operate them and put them to use was the ambition of the men who possessed them. Yet the control over natural forces demonstrated by even the simplest of these machines could not fail to have some impact on the Siamese imagination. The empirical mind that ventured to try out these Western gadgets was the same skeptical mind that scrutinized Buddhism and debated religion with Westerners. These qualities of mind reinforced one another.

One product of the encounter with Western machines and Western arguments was a critique of the *Traibhumi* cosmography that, in the minds of skeptical Siamese, represented an obstacle to coming to terms with empirically derived knowledge of the world. Last revised more than sixty years previous, the cosmography was now under attack as a comprehensive statement of Siamese religion, the authority of this work now "frequently denied by many of the shrewder Buddhists in Siam," in the words of one Western observer in 1851 (Jones 1851: 539). No longer was it an unquestioned instrument for communicating Buddhist values and Buddhist culture. The explanations in the *Traibhumi* for natural phenomena—planetary movements, weather, biological processes—were shaken by explanations offered by Western science.

Implicit in the earliest documented conversations with Westerners, the critique was systematically and formally articulated in a book published in 1867. *Kitjanukit* [A book explaining various things], the first Siamese printed book issued entirely under Siamese sponsorship, belongs in the context of those conversations and debates on comparative religions and Western science that led to its composition.[9] In fact, the author of the book was Mongkut's minister of foreign affairs, Jaophraya Thiphakorawong, the same man who had been host to Bastian and Alabaster in the soiree of 1863. He was among those members of the lay elite sympathetic to Mongkut's reform of the Sangha; indeed, one could regard the views expressed in *Kitjanukit* as those of Mongkut, who, as monarch, could not address the public directly on such matters. Although the language of the book would seem to be too sophisticated for the use of schoolchildren, the work clearly had a pedagogical intention, the author stating on the first page his dissatisfaction with the old-fashioned texts then in use. The structural device for conveying the critique consisted of an imaginary pupil questioning his master.

Some questions received precise answers, some did not. If the master could not summon evidence sufficient to substantiate a point, he would say so. Aside from communicating new knowledge obtained by the empirical method, the master was also teaching the method itself, a method of universal utility. Altering the Siamese Buddhist view of reality required altering the method of investigating reality as much as altering generalizations about the world in the face of newly perceived relationships.

The relationships newly perceived by Thiphakorawong, Mongkut, and others of like mind were summed up in the observation that "worldly matters and religious matters are not the same" (Thiphakorawong 1965: 173). With this distinction, *Kitjanukit* divided the *Traibhumi* cosmography in two, the natural world and religion, each category of phenomena having a set of "laws" that guided its workings. The book presented examples from the *Traibhumi* cosmography, referring to it by name, and then countered the *Traibhumi*'s explanations with alternative ones drawn from meteorology, geology, and astronomy. In Thiphakorawong's view, rain falls not because the rain-making deities venture forth from their abodes or because a great serpent thrashes its tail but because of winds that suck water out of the clouds (Thiphakorawong 1965: 14–16). The author treated a host of other natural phenomena—diseases, earthquakes, comets, eclipses—in similar ways. Illness, for example, was caused not by a god punishing evil deeds but by air currents (Thiphakorawong 1965: 35–37). The explanation Thiphakorawong favored was still misplaced, but the etiology of disease was now environmental and devoid of moral content.[10]

Approximately halfway through the book, the author, through his imaginary master and pupil, addressed himself to religion, specifically to such fundamentals of Theravada Buddhism as *karma*, merit, rebirth, giving, and the precepts. The dialectical exchanges with the Westerners, which we know took place in Bangkok at midcentury, resounds in these pages, with Thiphakorawong's work providing another example that the framework for discussion was comparative religion. Indeed, the book might be seen as reflections on the outcome of those discussions. In replying to a question about the existence of heaven and hell, for example, the master examined Christianity, Islam, Hinduism/Brahmanism, and Buddhism and concluded that all religions have heaven to entice and hell to threaten (Thiphakorawong 1965: 158–61). Since the idea of *karma* was taken as a basic premise, it followed that heaven and hell must exist as destinations for the consequences of good and bad deeds.

Religion in Thiphakorawong's eyes was not so much philosophy and theology as social ethics; and Buddhist social ethics were realizable through Siamese institutions. In discussing the precept concerning sexual misconduct, the author took the occasion to explain and defend the institution of polygamy, a subject doubtless raised by puritanical missionaries (Thiphakorawong 1965: 153–58). The Buddha did not condemn polygamy, but he did not commend it either, so Thiphakorawong was left to rely on assumptions about masculine and feminine nature in order to defend the institution. Here, too, he drew on Islamic and Christian societies for comparison and contrast.

In this comparative framework, Thiphakorawong took every opportunity to extend the fundamentals of Buddhism to universal application. He evaluated giving and the precepts, for example, by the criterion of universal applicability and found that other religions shared some of the tenets of Buddhism. Though the tone of the work is not overtly defensive, it would seem that the author was striving to demonstrate that Buddhism had a status of universality comparable to that of Islam, Hinduism/Brahmanism, and Christianity.

The voice of the knowing master on these pages is that of a rationalist, logically pursuing his ideas from basic premises. Thiphakorawong retained the idea of *karma*/merit as an explanation for human difference, for with it he could account for the myriad gradations and variations of status, health, wealth, intelligence, physical type, and longevity found in human societies:

> If one reflects on the evidence one concludes that men are born unequal, differing from one another.
>
> (Thiphakorawong 1965: 110)

Thus, *karma*/merit accounts for human difference and hierarchy in a kind of Buddhist sociology.[11]

Karma even conditions gender, an idea that recalls the view of gender found in the *Traibhumi* hierarchy of animate existence. A "bundle of form qualities" (*rupa kulapa*) arises and then breaks into female, male, and neuter according to merit previously accumulated (Thiphakorawong 1965: 161). The Western science of genetics would be another way of accounting for this phenomenon, as well as for other kinds of human difference. Redrawing the line that demarcated the natural world and the moral or religious world permitted

Thiphakorawong to use the physical sciences to explain some natural phenomena, while leaving others determined by moral actions. Illness was now a "natural" phenomenon; gender was not.

One can carry the comparison with the *Traibhumi* one step further. Just as a sermon by the Universal Monarch lay at the heart of the cosmography text, so Thiphakorawong's exposition of Buddhist fundamentals had didactic intent. As a lay sermon on Buddhism, *Kitjanukit* reaffirmed Buddhist values, and reassured those insecure in their acceptance of the Buddhist outlook that they could resolve their doubts by using their rational faculties.

> My purpose is to make those of you who have doubts about Buddhism open your eyes and ears and think about the religion and the teachings of one who is a Buddhist.... There is no undertaking which has a higher calling than to endeavor to weigh and choose calmly in order to verify what is true and what is false.
>
> (Thiphakorawong 1965: 173)

With this theme in the final pages came the caveat that while misperceptions of the natural world could only "shame" one in the eyes of those who perceived accurately, misperceptions of religious matters obstructed the accumulation of merit and led to misfortune. The *Traibhumi* cosmography emerged from Thiphakorawong's analysis as useful for indicating the consequences of immoral acts but inadequate for describing the workings of the natural world, now defined in a distinctly mid-nineteenth-century Siamese Buddhist way.

Kitjanukit can be seen as a successor or "replacement" of the *Traibhumi*, which by midcentury could no longer stand as an unchallenged interpretation of the Siamese Buddhist world. One might go so far as to say that the publication of *Kitjanukit* in 1867 encapsulates the ending of one world and the beginning of another one. The book's dialectical exchanges represent the product of changes that had already taken place in Siamese society, changes that were part of a larger process that would involve every institution as the century progressed. It is perhaps not overemphasizing the Western element in Thai history to say that many of these changes involved adjustments on the part of the elite to cultural, economic, and political differences it perceived between its own and Western societies; the power of the West was manifest not only through the power of Western machines.

The linking of these changes to form a larger process has many illustrations. The demythologizing of the monarchy, for example, which was underway by Mongkut's reign and which accelerated during the reign of his son Chulalongkorn (r. 1868–1910), was connected to the discrediting of the *Traibhumi*. Could such an exemplar of kingly conduct as the Universal Monarch, with his shimmering jeweled disk, celebrated in such detail in the cosmography, find realization in the world of 1885, in which princes and officials could criticize absolute kingship in their petition to Chulalongkorn for a constitutional monarchy (Chai-anan 1970)?

Yet shifts in worldview usually occur at a glacial pace. If the cosmography had really been such a crucial interpretive vehicle, the society could not summarily abandon it after five hundred years' use. Tempered with a critical view of its contents, and a sense that it belongs to the Siam of the past, there has been since the mid-nineteenth century an enduring respect for the functions it fulfilled, and an unsurprising willingness to turn to it for its literary and mythological treasures. In the first decade of the twentieth century, King Chulalongkorn, informing himself for a book he was writing, addressed a series of questions to learned officials and high-ranking monks concerning the creatures in the heavens and hells, Yama (the deity ruling the underworld), the "geography" of the cosmos (the four continents, the concentric rings of mountain ranges), and the Culamani Cetiya in the Tavatimsa heaven of Indra (Fine Arts Dept. 1971). Among the sources the monks and officials used to research their replies were the various versions of the *Traibhumi* (Fine Arts Dept. 1971: 38, 43–44, 60–61). The king even expected the deputy head of the reform order to be in possession of some of this information, and was disappointed when he was not (Fine Arts Dept. 1971: 8–10). Such knowledge still constituted part of what every properly educated monk should know. In Thailand until very recently, the curriculum of Pali study for monks included a book of parables that retains the *Traibhumi*'s cosmographical structure; and a sermon by the charismatic monk *somdet* Phra Phutthachan (To) (1788–1872) on cosmographical matters has been reprinted many times (Siripanyamuni 1968; Phutthachan 1967).

But an era had really passed; the mold had been broken. The elite now placed itself at some distance from a literal understanding of the *Traibhumi*'s world. At the same time that he insisted on thoroughness in the replies to his questions, Chulalongkorn observed that these matters were "acts of the imagination," thereby making abstractions of them (Fine Arts Dept. 1971: 10). Within a decade, the idea that the *Traibhumi* belonged to a past age was sharply expressed, in a preface to the first printed edition (1912). Prince Damrong, explaining why he was making the text available to a wider audience, said it was an old book, difficult to obtain. If it were not published, it would soon be lost; and since no one was willing to publish it commercially, the Vajiranana Library was issuing it as a cremation volume (Lithai 1972: vi–vii). And when Rama I's edition of the *Traibhumi* was first published a year later, the preface included the following statement:

> When the *Traibhumi*, composed by sages in ancient times more than one thousand years ago, is compared with the writings of geography of today, [we can see that] investigations made in the arts and other branches of knowledge have progressed much farther. For these reasons some statements in the *Traibhumi* tend to be not quite correct.
>
> (Rama I 1913: iii)

This comment is close to Thiphakorawong's view of some fifty years previous—namely, that Buddhist cosmography must give way in the face of new knowledge that contradicts it. But here the conclusion is stated as a matter of fact, whereas the author of *Kitjanukit* was in the process of arguing for this conclusion. The argument grew stronger over time, divorcing the cosmography from contemporary monarchical symbolism and releasing it for new literary purposes. King Vajiravudh (r. 1910–25) used the *Traibhumi*'s idyllic northern country, an "Asiatic Wonderland" of eternal youth and communal property, to satirize socialist utopias (Kasian 2001: 13–18).

The theme expressed in the prefaces to the first printed editions, that the *Traibhumi* belonged to the past but deserved to be known in the present, has been reinforced in recent Siamese writing. In 1954, the scholar Phya Anuman Rajadhon published a synopsis of the *Traibhumi*'s contents, explaining that although these were the beliefs of yesteryear, they had inspired artists in sculpture, painting, and literature, and must be understood if modern readers were to come to terms with the classical arts of Siam (Anuman 1970b). Phya Anuman saw his book, which condensed and simplified into modern parlance the archaic language of the older texts, as an aid to understanding the Indic references in Siamese poetry, among other things. Of particular interest is his distinction that the cosmography's emphasis on heaven and hell was typical of Mahayana rather than Theravada tradition, a fundamentalist distinction reminiscent of the mid-nineteenth-century reforms in the monkhood that had drawn attention to the fact that much of the mythology in Buddhism was extraneous to the Buddha's teaching and was traceable to postcanonical accretions. An even more recent statement of the Thai Fine Arts Department reminds us that "these matters cannot really be regarded as basically Dharma" (Fine Arts Dept. 1971a: vi–vii). Mongkut and Thiphakorawong could not have agreed more.

Still another distinction by Phya Anuman raises the question of whether or not his attitude toward the *Traibhumi* indicates a growing separation between elite and popular culture since the nineteenth century. In introducing his modernized version, he argued that the possibility of pleasurable rebirth as portrayed in the *Traibhumi* had more appeal and made more sense to the "common man" (*khon chan saman*) than the idea of Nirvana. The cosmography's metaphorical way of explaining the rewards of merit-making had more didactic effect in communicating the teachings of the Buddha to the "common man" (Anuman 1970b: 7). This view echoes the remark by the Siamese prince, recorded by Abeel in 1834 and quoted above, that the object of paintings of the cosmography "was to instruct the illiterate through the medium of their senses." Certainly, aspects of the cosmography continue to be meaningful for people in the countryside. In one case, the episode in which the demon Rahu swallows the moon seems to be retained not so much as a pre-Western explanation of eclipses but as a moral lesson for the sibling hierarchy (Turton 1972: 239).

Both the remark of the Siamese prince early in the nineteenth century and the view of Phya Anuman in the mid-twentieth century suggest that the elite always saw the *Traibhumi* as belonging to popular culture; but this attitude may date only from the beginning of the Bangkok period. Nowadays, the Westernizing elite has a more "sophisticated" view of the cosmography than does the mass of Siamese in the countryside, though this distinction is only a matter of the degree to which each takes the cosmography for granted. In the language of Berger and Luckmann, it is possible to draw a line between a sophisticated and a naïve view of the cosmography, "naïve" here meaning unexamined (1967: 105).

Irrespective of class, cosmographical terminology is still in contemporary Siamese speech and is thus used to construct everyday reality. To the extent that many of Phya Anuman's readers would be university students, it would seem that his function in summarizing the *Traibhumi* was to explain and legitimate the cosmography's symbolic universe for a younger generation (Berger and Luckmann 1967: 93). The twentieth-century evidence presented here suggests that the decline in prestige of the *Traibhumi* cosmography text, initiated most dramatically by Thiphakorawong's critique in *Kitjanukit*, has not left Buddhist cosmography without social function. Even though the text itself was discredited, aspects of Buddhist cosmography continue to have social use. Thiphakorawong, one of the leading historians of his time, had, after all, written his critique of the *Traibhumi* in order to bring the cosmography up to date, to dismiss its irrelevancies, and to save and reassert the Buddhist principles imbedded within it.

The task of rethinking Buddhist cosmography in Siam was accomplished smoothly compared with a similar process underway in Japan, where Buddhists were sometimes hostile to the propositions of Western science. For Siamese Buddhists, the centering of the universe around Mt. Meru never assumed the importance it did for Japanese Buddhists, some of whom defended Buddhist cosmography as late as 1880, fearing that Christianity would undermine Buddhist teaching (Nakayama 1969: 211–13). Furthermore, the Japanese religious community was more complex than the Siamese; and the Japanese Confucians, Shintoists, as well as the Buddhists who wrote defenses or criticisms of Western science, were not members of the political elite. They were specialists, often speaking for their own constituencies. In the Siamese case, Buddhism was more closely linked to dominant values and to the social order than in Japan. The men most engaged in coming to terms with Western science, men like Thiphakorawong and Mongkut, who were well-read in Buddhist literature, were members of the political elite and were in a position to ensure by their example that the changes required by the new Western presence were under control, their own control. In the end, the Siamese accommodated Western astronomical theory as swiftly as they did, not so much because of the arguments and persuasions of Mongkut and

Thiphakorawong as because these men held positions of power and status in the court.

A final comparison throws other aspects of the Siamese experience into high relief. The kinds of intellectual adjustments made by the Siamese were of an entirely different nature from those required by the new cosmological systems introduced in Europe three hundred years before. In sixteenth- and seventeenth-century Europe, as in nineteenth-century Japan, theories on the centrism of the universe posed problems difficult of resolution for some, and arguments about these theories occupied generations of philosophers and speculative thinkers. In reaction to the Copernican system, for example, thinkers had to adjust to the fact that man would now assume a more elevated position in the universe compared to his lowly position in medieval cosmology, whereas in the nineteenth-century Siamese reevaluation of Buddhist cosmography, man's position in the universal hierarchy of animate existence (and therefore his position in the universe) remained the same.

The European revolution in cosmological thinking also had to fit such central elements of Christian dogma as the Ascension, the Incarnation, and Redemption, which had seemed to presuppose a single inhabited world, into a new cosmological system that assumed a plurality of worlds (Lovejoy 1973: 107–8). In Siam, the central premises of Buddhist thought (*karma*, merit, giving, the precepts) and important events in the life of the Buddha were not so closely tied to the cosmographical structure, at least in the Pali canon. The possibility of other inhabited worlds implied by the new Copernican cosmology was especially problematic for Europeans, since it challenged the uniqueness of man. Buddhist cosmography, on the other hand, had always assumed a multiplicity of other worlds. These few points of comparison with a corresponding period in the history of Western thought suggest not that religion was more or less of an impediment to change in the West, but that the philosophical and theological adjustments in European thought were more profound and far-ranging than was the case in Siamese Buddhist thought.

Siamese Buddhist cosmography was not dismantled; it was trimmed and refined. The Buddhist structure on which it was built remained intact and preserved the essence of Theravada Buddhism. But the text that conveyed that structure, the *Traibhumi* cosmography attributed to King Lithai in the Sukhodaya period, has had a varied history since its last recension in the eighteenth century. Now the text is finally a kind of relic, although its contents continue to exert a residual hold on the Siamese imagination. If Buddhist cosmography ever did once stand as the only symbolic universe for Siamese Buddhists, it must now coexist with other constructions of reality.

Notes

1. Rama III (1824–51) had asked high-ranking monks if a man with one coin could make as much merit as a man with one hundred or one thousand coins. He was told, "Men with little devotion and little wealth cannot make a great deal of merit…. Men with much devotion and much wealth are capable of making much merit." Question 8, dated 2 Dec 1838, in *Prachum phraratchaputcha phak thi 4* [Collected royal questions, part 4] (Bangkok, 1922), p. 91.
2. The Burmese version of the cosmography is summarized in Sangermano 1966, chaps. 1–5 and recapitulated in Yule 1968: 235–88; see also Ba Han 1965. Mon and Northern Siamese versions are cited in Damrong and Naritsaranuwattiwong 1961: XI, 320. The Khmer version may have derived from the Siamese; see Roeské 1914 and Feer 1877.
3. A number of these stories, some of which are found in the *Traibhumi*, are related in Law 1936.
4. *Prachum phraratchaputcha phak 2 pen phraratchaputcha nai ratchakan thi i* [Collected royal questions, part 2, the royal questions of the first reign] (Bangkok, 1923), pp. 7–8. This episode is also discussed in Law 1936: 47–49.
5. See Prince Damrong's introduction to Lithai, *Traiphum phraruang*, i–ii; Prince Naris is more specific in his correspondence with Prince Damrong (Damrong and Naritsaranuwattiwong, vol. XIII).
6. It is a copy of the illustrated 1776 recension that Wenk published. Could this copy, now in Berlin, be the same one taken to Germany in the nineteenth century, as reported by Prince Damrong (1966: 156)?
7. Rama I 1913: 2. Gerini 1895: 95–109 provides a detailed summary of this version, a sketch of the cosmic geography, a comparison with the Hindu scheme, and credits King Taksin as the author.
8. The appointment of this ex-monk illustrates how the new dynastic administration accommodated personnel favored by Taksin. For biographical information on this ex-monk, see Schweisguth 1951: 199.
9. Thiphakorawong 1965. The first section of Alabaster 1871 is based on this work.
10. It is interesting to note in this connection that the last time the court sponsored the Buddhist ceremony for countering epidemics was in 1820; see Fine Arts Dept. 1964: 387–88.
11. In sixteenth-century England, astrology could account for differences between human beings (Thomas 1971: 324).

9

A Thai-Buddhist Defense of Polygamy

R ama I's Three Seals Law Code of 1805, which recognized polygamy, was replaced on 1 October 1935 by the Civil and Commercial Code, whose volume 5 on family law recognized monogamy as the only legal union of wife and husband. By this later date, the goal of becoming a modern, Westernized nation had discredited polygamy in favor of monogamy as a model for the marriage relationship in Siam (Landon 1968: 156–66). Legal scholars have studied some aspects of the position of women under the old law code, including the property rights of women, and the arguments in favor of monogamy along feminist lines are well documented (Landon 1968: Appendix II G; Chamroon and Adul 1968). What is missing from the legal studies is the sense in which attitudes, religious values, custom, and the law jostled against each other even in the nineteenth century, sometimes encouraging the change from polygamy to monogamy, sometimes impeding it. From a Thai book published in 1867 comes a passage that I have translated and titled "A Nineteenth-Century Thai Buddhist Defense of Polygamy." I propose that the passage from this book, standing almost midway between the two law codes—sixty-two years after the Three Seals Code and sixty-eight years before the Civil and Commercial Code—offers an opportunity to study shifts in values and attitudes at a time when Western example had just begun to challenge Siamese marriage custom at the elite level.

This discussion is essentially an elucidation of the text, not only in terms of its argument and internal consistency but also in terms of the cultural, political, and social circumstances that created it. I begin with a brief discussion of the position of women in traditional Siamese society in the light of certain religious ideas and according to legal provisions in force until the early nineteenth century. Then I set the institution of polygamy in a cultural, political, and social context as a way of introducing changes in the status of women that took place in the middle of the nineteenth century. The Siamese monarch at the time, King Mongkut, revealed his sensitivity to Western missionary criticism of the institution in his public statements, and his royal decrees affecting the position of women are related to this criticism. One of Mongkut's most loyal and able ministers wrote a book from which the "Defense of Polygamy" comes, a book that had its origins in Siamese contact with Westerners in Bangkok.

The Position of Women in Traditional Thai Society

In most respects, women in traditional Siamese society were subordinate to men. "Traditional" in reference to Siamese society generally means before the middle of the nineteenth century. There must have been changes in the legal and social position of women through the centuries, but the documentary sources on this subject are too meager to perceive much of this change, and historians tend to fall back on the expedient of considering premodern society as a static society.

The subordination of women comes through the epigraphic and documentary sources, and this subordination was sanctioned by religion. Buddhism structured the world in such a way that *karma*—the physical, verbal, and cognitive actions of past lives—and the accrual or loss of merit in consequence of those actions conditioned the differences between any two individuals in social status, talent, wealth, and power. *Karma* also conditioned gender. To be a woman and not a man meant that a woman had an inadequate store of merit, and the only way to remedy this situation was for a woman to make merit through acts of religious devotion. Thus, in A.D. 1399, at the end of the Sukhodaya period, the Queen Mother founded a monastery and commemorated the event in an inscription in which she requested, "By the power of my merit, may I be reborn as a male ..." (Griswold and Prasert 1992: 65). In this worldview, differences in gender reflected inequalities of accumulated merit, and Buddhism, by explaining differences in this way, thereby ratified them as inequalities.

The cosmography from the fourteenth century discussed in the previous chapter sets out the Buddhist worldview in its most systematic form and reinforces inequality between the genders in a number of ways. The Buddhist cosmic order arranges all living beings in a moral continuum that ranges from the most horrifying hell to the most rarefied heaven; women are placed toward the more worldly, corporeal end of the scale. In the upper realms of animate life, the twenty levels where the *brahma* deities dwell, "there is not a single female, there is not a single *brahma* that resembles a female. None of the *brahma* deities feels the least desire for women" (Lithai 1982: 251). The *brahma* deities have accumulated such a store of merit that they have lifted themselves above sensation and desire; their senses do not require gratification, and hence they have no need of women. Earlier in the cosmography, when the ideal Buddhist king, the Universal Monarch, exhorts his subjects to observe the five precepts, he warns that any subject who violates the precept on sexual misconduct by committing adultery with another's spouse will be reborn in a fiery hell and will endure unspeakably painful punishment.

> When he is released from hell he will ascend and become a hermaphrodite for a thousand lives, and there will generally be many additional lives before he can be born as a male.
>
> (Lithai 1982: 150)

The implication, then, is that the female gender expresses something less meritorious, possibly something more carnal and corrupting, than the male gender. Certain anthropological data fits into this worldview. Vaginal excretion as it is used in Siamese love magic falls into the category of aggressive and dangerous substances; such data helps to explain why women are viewed as antithetical to the beneficial powers of monks (Terwiel 1975: 96, 144–46, 257). A. Thomas Kirsch made a similar point about ritual sex differentiation when he said, "Women are deemed to be more firmly rooted in their worldly attachments than are men: men are thought to be more ready to give up such attachments" (Kirsch 1975a: 185).

The Buddhist cosmography offers additional insight into the position of women in traditional society when it describes the ideal marriage relationship between the Universal Monarch and his queen. The queen is one of the seven gems, the possession of which designate the ruler as a Universal Monarch. The merit she has accumulated from previous existences brings her birth in a royal family, a necessary qualification for the wife of a Universal Monarch, and her beauty draws together all who live in the terrestrial realm (Lithai 1982: 166). She complements her husband: when his body is cool, hers is warm; when his body is warm, hers is cool. Their coexistence represents a completeness without extreme. And she waits on her husband:

> When the king comes and pays a visit to the gem woman in her dwelling place, she does not remain seated, but generally gets up to greet the king; she then brings her golden pillow and sits, attending and fanning the king; and she massages his feet and hands, and sits in a lower place. The gem woman never at any time goes to lie on the gem bed before the great Cakkavatti king; nor does the gem woman ever at any time leave the gem bed after he does. Whatever kind of work she is going to do, she first of all respectfully informs the king so that he will know. When the king orders her to do it, she does it; she never at any time disobeys the one who is her husband. Whatever she does, all of it satisfies her husband; and whatever she says, all of it pleases her husband. Only a Cakkavatti king and he alone can be her husband; as for other men, they cannot be her husband; and as for the gem woman, she is never the least bit unfaithful to this king.

(Lithai 1982: 167)

It is impossible to say what social reality lies behind this description, but it is reasonable to think that the relationship described here was the exemplar of the wife-husband relationship that reflected, and was projected back onto, Siamese domestic relations at the elite level.[1]

Furthermore, familial metaphors of political utility also appear in another Sukhodaya source half a century earlier, Ramkhamhaeng's inscription of A.D. 1292. There the metaphor of filial and fraternal service rendered by Ramkhamhaeng to his father and elder brother, who were kings before him, leading to a regular, uncontested succession to the Sukhodaya throne, converts a kin tie (that between son-brother and father and elder brother) into a political tie (that between subject and ruler) (Griswold and Prasert 1992: 265–67). It is from this inscription that modern Siamese derive the patriarchal notion that Ramkhamhaeng was the "father" of his people. In other words, it is not simply that harmonious political relations are analogous to harmonious domestic relations but that the political relationship itself was transmuted into a familial one (the king was not a ruler but a benign patriarch), thereby modulating or softening the punitive and instrumental rights exercised by legitimate authority. This transmutation was easier to accomplish at Sukhodaya, whose small scale permitted the king a visibility and approachability that the later, larger kingdoms could not match. The hierarchy of the family, with the wife dutifully serving the husband, thus expressed ideas of loyalty, obligation, service, and deference that had political implications in traditional society.

The Siamese monarchy was not unique in drawing the family into an ideology of authority. In the case of the Vietnamese monarchy, which leaned heavily on Confucian ethics, the connection between authority relationships in the family and the polity was explicit and outright prescriptive. Among the ten maxims Emperor Minh Mang issued in 1834 was one exhorting all Vietnamese subjects to "esteem the human relationships," the hierarchically determined proprieties of behavior between sovereign and minister, father and son, husband and wife, and older brother and younger brother (Woodside 1971: 189).

The family hierarchy, as it expressed differences between the spouses, was fixed in Siamese law. The law reinforced the subordinate position of women in the way it allocated property rights in the event of the death of a spouse or the dissolution of the marriage. Fundamental to the family law in the 1805 code was the conjugal power of the husband, which meant that he managed the property held jointly by the spouses, that he could sell his wife or give her away, and that he could administer bodily punishment to her, provided the degree of punishment was in proportion to the misdeed (Chamroon and Adul 1968: 91–92; Lingat 1952–55: 151). Before marriage, the affianced man presented his future parents-in-law with a sum of silver deemed to be compensation for the expenses they incurred in raising their daughter. By this exchange, in which the marriage resembled a purchase, the parents transferred the custody of their daughter to the man. Until 1900, if a childless marriage was dissolved by mutual consent, the wife was required to reimburse the husband for this sum as well as the value of any engagement gifts (Lingat 1953–55: 151). A woman was not a free agent and had to be placed under someone else's protection (Chamroon and Adul 1968: 91). Bondage may be too strong a word to describe this dependency, but as late as 1857 a royal decree gave husbands above a certain noble rank (*sakdina* 3000) the right to government assistance in pursuing a wife who had fled the household (Mongkut 1968: I, 205–6). A woman was also obliged to obtain the consent of her parents to marry, though her parents could not compel her to marry.

For the purposes of allocating property and inheritance rights, the law distinguished between prenuptial and postnuptial property, depending on whether the property had been acquired before or in the course of the marriage. Prenuptial property was the property each spouse contributed when the marriage took place. Under the 1805 code, the husband managed the conjugal property, but in the event of divorce by mutual consent, each spouse was compensated for prenuptial property disposed of in the course of the marriage (Lingat 1953–55: 157). As for postnuptial property, the husband received two-thirds and the wife one-third (Lingat 1953–55: 158). An adulterous wife lost all right to prenuptial *and* postnuptial property, though if a marriage was dissolved because of the husband's fault, the wife received some compensation from the postnuptial property (Lingat 1953–55: 160). If a husband abandoned a wife, he could recover his prenuptial property as well as his share of the postnuptial property. In sum, the law was more considerate of men even if the husband was at fault in a dissolved marriage.

In this discussion of family law, I have used the term "wife," but I must clarify that I am referring here only to the principal wife in the marriage. The Three Seals Code of 1805 reissued a law of 1361 C.E. that divided wives into three categories: the principal wife (*mia klang muang*), whose parents consented to her marriage; the secondary wife (*mia klang nok*); and the slave wife (*mia klang thasi*), who was acquired through purchase (i.e., by a man redeeming a woman from debt-bondage) (Chamroon and Adul 1968: 91; Lingat 1962: I, 210). Only a principal wife brought property into the marriage. Indeed, the propertyless condition of the secondary wife rendered her acquisition tantamount to a purchase, too.

This ranking of wives determined the "worth" of a woman in a number of ways. First of all, the law of 1361 mentioned above stated that a man seducing a secondary wife or a slave wife was subject to a fine in proportion to the rank of the woman (four-fifths and three-fifths, respectively, of what the fine would have been had the principal wife been involved) (Lingat 1962: II, 206). The lower the rank of the wife, the less consequential her seduction was thought to be. With respect to property rights, the slave wife had no claim on any part of her husband's estate, but the secondary wife had some inheritance rights (Lingat 1953–55: 152–53). As the position of women began to improve somewhat during the nineteenth century, the courts under certain circumstances allowed the secondary wife to receive one-third of the postnuptial property if, for example, she had contributed to it through inheritance or her own business ventures (Lingat 1953–55: 159). This ranking of wives with property rights apportioned according to rank was to be found in Burma as well (Tambiah 1973: 146).

In a book of essays and lectures from the 1950s reprinted in 1976, *A History of Thai Women*, several authors cast the condition of women in the highly charged language of radical politics and Marxian analysis: traditional society is referred to as feudal society in which women were regarded as sex objects and in which class differences swayed the law in favor of elite men (Kulap 1976). The fact that a man could sell his wife without her consent under the old law made a woman an item of commercial exchange no better than chattel (the Thai word here is *khwai*, "water buffalo"). Since education in Buddhist monasteries was available to men only, women were deprived of opportunity to develop their intelligence and talents (Kulap 1976: 125–26). These assertions, strident and radically rhetorical as they may be, have force because the authors use the very same sources that any legal scholar of Siamese family relations must use: the Three Seals Code of 1805 and the decrees of the mid-nineteenth century, which first began to loosen the strictures and confinements of the past.[2]

There is no question that women were disadvantaged under the law, but we should bear in mind several factors that alleviated the position of women. Under the older code, women could initiate divorce proceedings on very little evidence, which gave them the means to escape the tyranny of an abusive husband. The 1805 code required more substantial grounds for divorce (Lingat 1953–55: 151–52; Kulap 1976: 110). Moreover, jurisprudence or case law began to relieve women of the harsher prescriptions of the law, for example, by interpreting liberally what could be construed as prenuptial property held by a secondary wife. Under the inheritance laws, daughters had the same rights as sons in inheriting property from their parents. It should also be said that Siam, along with Ceylon and Burma, contrasts with India in terms of inheritance customs, the secular nature of marriage, and the permissibility of divorce. Women have greater property rights and enjoy bilateral inheritance in the Theravada societies (Tambiah 1973: 138).

Against the evidence of the subordination of women, one must also place evidence of women's attainments. The subordinate position of women in traditional society did not mean that all women found themselves as wives and mothers, their role in society defined by their relationships to men. In recent years, women have established themselves in business and commerce. Kirsch's hypothesis that women are disproportionately involved in entrepreneurial or commercial activity has much support in Siamese economic history since the 1855 Bowring Treaty, and there is some suggestion that this was the case in the Ayudhya period as well (Kirsch 1975a: 174). One can also find exceptional accomplishment among the princesses of the blood. This may seem an irony, but then they were *nang ham*, who were forbidden from marrying, and thus they were deprived of self-fulfilling roles as wives and mothers. I can only offer one example, admittedly from the second half of the nineteenth century, but I do so to provoke further inquiry. A daughter of Rama III (r. 1824–51), Princess Varasethasuta (1828–1907), enjoyed a considerable literary reputation and tutored both King Chulalongkorn (1868–1910) and Prince-Patriarch Vajiranana (1860–1921) early in their education. She eschewed the feminine domestic arts of sewing, embroidery, braiding, stringing flowers, cooking, and preparing betel. Rather, she preferred religious books, histories, and the works of poets, interests regarded as male pursuits (Vajiranana 1979: 11–12). We can surmise that there were accomplished women such as Princess Varasethasuta in earlier reigns in earlier centuries and that occasionally a woman could break away from the prevailing expectations of her sex, though opportunity to do so would only have come to members of a privileged class.

Polygamy in Its Cultural, Political, and Social Context

Siamese law, however illuminating on the legal status of polygamy and on the rights allocated to primary and secondary wives, in no sense explains why members of the Siamese elite, and kings in particular, were polygamous. The complex of economic factors and ideas about power and authority that supported the institution lie outside the law, and it is important to discuss these before moving on to the changes in the nineteenth century, because the "Defense of Polygamy" fails to mention polygamy in any but a moral context.

In premodern Siam, "the prestige of a man was measured by the number of wives and women who served him" (Kulap 1976: 91). The anthropologist E. R. Leach refers to the exaggerated polygamy practiced by Shan and Burmese rulers, and the numbers are indeed of a superlative magnitude (Leach 1965: 216). By one account, King Mongkut had six hundred wives and concubines.[3] The Buddhist cosmography text inflates these numbers even further when it attributes twenty-four million wives to the god Indra, whose counterpart on earth the Siamese king was (Lithai 1982: 231–32). This seemingly limitless number of wives and concubines was an index of self-sufficiency and, consequently, a check on greed and craving. Indra would have no cause to abduct another man's wife. The wealth of women was also a measure of the king's reproductive capacities. Kings were responsible for assuring the productivity of the land, and multiple wives and concubines contributed to the mythology of the monarch as a source of prosperity, abundance, and fecundity. This line of thinking is not far from the complex of ideas behind the royal linga cults in early Southeast Asia, which brought together sex and power in the worship of Siva's phallus. Within this nexus of myth and symbol, it was important for the king to be able to demonstrate his vitality. King Mongkut made this point in arguing for the right of a provincial nobleman to present the king with three young women. Mongkut said he was delighted to receive the women, since they added to his esteem. His subjects would know that he had not yet declined into old age (Mongkut 1968: I, 322).

But there were hard political realities behind this symbolism, too, as any student of Siamese history knows. Marriage and concubinage were ways of balancing power at the court and of securing the kingdom's perimeters. Vassal rulers seeking the protection of Siam would offer their female relatives to the monarch as tribute to pledge their loyalty. It was in this spirit that the Lao ruler of Vientiane offered his daughter to King Taksin in the 1770s at a time when the Siamese kingdom was aggressively pushing itself to the limits of its empire (Wyatt 1994: 191). Closer to the capital, provincial lords also constructed diplomatic marriage links. In another example from the late eighteenth century,

King Taksin received two daughters of the lord of a southern province, fathered a child by one of them, and returned the mother to the south where the male offspring founded a powerful provincial dynasty (Fine Arts Dept. 1962: 67n.1). This union of court and province, ideal as it seems, carried the usual risk of indirect rule: a provincial lord, especially one fortified with royal blood, could cultivate ambition and come to challenge the throne or at least, as was the case here, defy its directives. Nevertheless, kings persisted in forging marriage alliances in the hopes of building up a network of loyal vassals, for only with such a network would expansion of the kingdom protect the center. In ancient India, which shared its cultural heritage with Southeast Asia, the idea that possession of women can lead to sovereignty and the domination of the earth is found in certain Sanskrit passages in which the word for "hand" of the bride is the same word as "tribute" (Hara 1973: 102–3).

Between the nobility and royalty in the capital, women were exchanged to check the ambition of claimants or to further the careers of men loyal to the king. The rise to power of the Bunnag family in the late Ayutthaya and early Bangkok periods is the best known instance of this. The Bunnag nobles provided concubines for the king as well as wives for the princes born of the unions (Wyatt 1994: 118). Two of the nineteenth-century Bunnags, Dit and That, were particularly astute at concentrating their influence by placing their daughters in royal service or by seeing that their daughters married first cousins (Wyatt 1994: 220). The author of the "Defense of Polygamy" was a son of Dit and was thus a product of this latticework of political unions. By offering daughters to the Siamese king, chiefs of ethnic minorities such as the Mons and the Chinese pledged their loyalties and began the process of assimilation.

Not all the women of the Inner Palace were well-born and well-chosen women from the families of the nobility and regional elites. Some were ordinary women from peasant backgrounds whose striking beauty had caught the eye of officials seeking favor with the king. If the woman was of low status and deemed unfit to bear a child by the king, she entered royal service in the Inner Palace to take up any of a number of vocations and duties. This highly complex city within a city had, in addition to wives and concubines, women officials, ladies-in-waiting, and even a squad of female palace guards. The women were differentiated in status according to their duties and seniority.[4] A talented woman, freed from the backbreaking work of rice farming, had the leisure to cultivate the arts, to train herself in dancing and music, and to acquire respect for her accomplishments (Mongkut 1968: I, 321–22; Leonowens 1953: 91). Concubinage offered to a low-born woman the prospect of a step up on the social scale for both herself and her parents.

Polygamy, then, fit into a cultural system that encouraged the king to exhibit his own and the kingdom's reproductive capacities. In political terms, the institution of polygamy established relationships of influence, obligation, and access between the monarch and other power centers in the kingdom. Finally, the socioeconomic stratification of Siamese society made it advantageous for women to accept placement in the Inner Palace, where royal service brought social refinement and social advancement.

Siam at Midcentury: Mongkut and the West

King Chulalongkorn, who died in 1910, was the last polygamous king, but polygamy did not disappear formally until the promulgation of the Civil Code in 1935. To understand why this institution, so vital to the kingdom's cultural and political life, lost the sanction of law, we must go back to the reign of Mongkut, his father, who came to the throne in 1851. Sir John Bowring, the British envoy who negotiated the first trade treaty in 1855 that opened Siam to trade with the West, reported Mongkut's views on the subject as follows:

> On more than one occasion the King has written and spoken to me on the subject of polygamy, wishing I should explain to those who might be disposed to censure him, that the habit was Oriental, that it was sanctioned by Siamese laws and usages, and by the Buddhist religion.
>
> (Bowring 1969: I, 444)

Why was Mongkut sensitive about the institution and what did his reaction mean both for the position of women in Siam and for the future of polygamy as an institution protected by law and wide social acceptance? Mongkut defended the institution in word and deed, but it was in his reign that the position of women in Siamese society began to change. The exposure of the elite to Western custom and Western comment as well as the social and economic change stimulated by the trade treaties at midcentury cast the institution of polygamy in a new light.

Lying behind Mongkut's communications with Bowring was Western criticism, especially missionary criticism, of what Westerners saw as an exotic, self-indulgent, and uncivilized institution. In 1863, Mongkut authorized a published statement about the number of wives and children belonging to himself and his brother, the Second King. The statement appeared in the *Bangkok Calendar*, published and edited by the American missionary physician D. B. Bradley, and drew a comment about the "pernicious custom of polygamy." "Virtue can never have much sway in Siam, nor any true prosperity," said the editor, "until polygamy is made a crime by the Government" (Moffat 1961: 135). Mongkut was not offended by such criticism, however. On the contrary, he seemed to take it to heart, at least for the sake of the foreign community in Bangkok, and shortly after the article appeared, he published a correction to the effect that he had fewer wives than his brother, a claim that earned him restrained praise from the missionary editor (Moffat 1961: 136). An even more extraordinary example of Mongkut's efforts to reassure Bangkok's European community on this issue was the possibility that monogamy for the monarch would be written into the 1856 trade treaty with America. One of Mongkut's ministers summoned Bradley and two other missionaries to ask if it would be well "to have an article stating that the King of Siam should hereafter be allowed to have only one wife" (Moffat 1961: 165).

The reasons for Mongkut's sensitivity to this issue are complex, but it is well to recall a few things that bear on his response to what Westerners thought of polygamy. Before his accession in 1851, Mongkut had spent twenty-seven years as a monk. During this time, he had more freedom than a king to converse with Westerners, to question them about their custom, and to debate religion with them. American missionaries and a French bishop tutored him in English and French, and he developed an informed knowledge of astronomy from these contacts and the books he read. As an avid student of the West, he respected its representatives in Siam, many of whom, like himself, were religious men. He was receptive to Western suggestion and responsive to Western criticism.

Yet he was also of the princely class, a man born to be king, thoroughly trained to take the prerogative and power of his class for granted. Before he entered the monkhood in 1824, he had had two children, and by the end of 1855, after four years on the throne, he had nineteen more.[5] The institution of polygamy still balanced power in the kingdom and contributed to the monarch's prestige. If Western criticism of his polygamous ways disposed Mongkut toward even token reform, the princely example and prerogative that were his birthright bound him to the mores of the elite class. More than the Emperor Minh Mang (r. 1820–41), his Vietnamese contemporary, Mongkut was torn between the two poles of what he regarded as Western progress and Siamese custom. This tension may be the source of the picturesque popular image of him in the West that sometimes spills over into caricature. He had not begun to master the biculturalism that the next generation of Thai elite attained with such ease.

Mongkut's pronouncements on polygamy extended beyond the fairly small European community in Bangkok. In 1854, he issued a Siamese-language decree that loosened the restriction on women of the Inner Palace to make their tenure less captive (Mongkut 1968: I, 88–91; Moffat 1961: 150–51). Palace women of all ranks—concubines, women attendants, dancers—were permitted to resign from royal service if they were dissatisfied with their lot, provided they informed the king. In some circumstances, they would continue to receive a royal annual allowance for their upkeep. With the exception of royal mothers, including mothers of royal children from previous reigns, they could marry, an exclusion designed to protect the status of the royal children.

On 7 November 1858, just after the Bowring Treaty, Mongkut reissued the decree, and followed it a month later with a decree in which he announced that twelve palace women had resigned (Mongkut 1968: I, 295–301; Moffat 1961: 151–53). He gave their ages, their duties, the ranks of their fathers, and, in most cases, the reasons for their departure. Four of the women had entered royal service in the previous reign (1824–51), but for these women, he gave no reasons. Of the eight others, one had a nervous breakdown, two had entered the palace merely to take advantage of inheritance laws after their fathers died, the fourth and the fifth were asked to leave by their mothers outside (though their fathers wanted them to stay), the sixth had a troublesome personality, the seventh had pretentious airs and was "overly educated," and the eighth had a "quick hand" and was expelled by palace officials for petty theft. These last five women were all gifted dancers. We can detect some resentment on Mongkut's part in his account. None of the portraits are very flattering to the women, and in the last case the resignation was hardly voluntary. But at several points, the language of the decree reveals that Mongkut fully acknowledged the heretofore captive conditions of royal service in the Inner Palace. He uses the verb "to confine or detain" to describe those conditions, and he specifically states that the women did not have to ransom themselves to obtain their freedom: "Women who resign need not pay anything" (Mongkut 1968: I, 301). He fully appreciated that his gesture was unprecedented: "It is my wish that this new royal custom will continue in the future."

This "new royal custom" affected only women in royal service at the palace. Another of Mongkut's decrees, issued about six months before he died, reached further into Siamese society and affected all women, especially those at the bottom of the social hierarchy. Early in 1868, when a woman whose husband had sold her without her consent petitioned the throne, Mongkut consulted the old law and declared that since the provision in question regarded women as chattel (again, the word for water buffalo is used) and men as human beings, the law was unjust (*ha pen yuttitham mai*) (Mongkut 1968: II, 277–80). On 21 March 1868, Mongkut decreed that henceforth a wife could no longer be sold by her husband, parents, or guarantor without her consent, though the new measure still permitted wives to sell themselves into debt-bondage voluntarily. Unless a wife affixed her signature or mark in the presence of a government official or other witness, the sale was not valid. The March 1868 decree also addressed itself to the sale of children. Limited as it was, the decree heralded the more comprehensive emancipation decrees issued in Chulalongkorn's reign beginning in 1874 (Lingat 1931: 96–101).

These decrees of Mongkut improving the rights of women reflected the king's awareness of Western custom as much as they reflected the social and economic changes fostered by the Western trade treaties. Prolific in wives, concubines, and children, Mongkut nevertheless adjusted the rights of women under the law on what can only be described, according to the language of his decrees, as moral grounds. He left us very little evidence with which to read his mind, but the circumstantial evidence suggests that his sense of what was right on this issue derived from his own innate sense of justice informed by the increasingly powerful example of Western custom. The power of the West expressed in Western machines—the steam engine, the printing press, and Western weapons—helped to make Western custom compelling. Mongkut's magnanimity in realizing his discontented concubines arose from his concern for stature as an international (if not universal) monarch as much as it did from a concern for the rights of women. The subtle interplay between the Western example of "civilization" and the morality of polygamy is evident in the "Defense."

The Defense of Polygymy and Its Defender

Jaophraya Thiphakorawong (Kham Bunnag), the author of the "Defense of Polygamy," was born on 1 October 1813.[6] In the nineteenth century, Siamese men entered government service by apprenticing themselves to relatives and friends of relatives who already held official positions, and Kham owed his first offices to his membership in the Bunnag family, whose astute politics and intermarriage with the Jakris acquired for it a power which rivaled that of the royal family. Kham's father was Jaophraya Borommahaprayurawong (Dit Bunnag), supreme minister for military affairs at his death, in 1855; his uncle was Jaophraya Phichaiyat (That Bunnag), who at his death, in 1858, was supreme minister for civil affairs. The mother of Dit and That was a younger sister of the first Bangkok king's chief queen, one example among many of the intermarriage that bound the Bunnags to the monarchy.

Dit and That together dominated state affairs in the Third Reign from 1824 to 1851 and the early years of the Fourth Reign and were instrumental in enthroning the Fourth King, Mongkut, in 1851. The father, Dit, was known to Western visitors during the Third Reign as the Phra Khlang, minister of the royal treasury. Since much of the king's revenue derived from port duties and charges, Dit was also in charge of the Harbor Department; his brother, That, was deputy. Only in the latter part of the fourth reign (1851–68) were the treasury and harbor offices separated administratively. In the way Siamese government worked at the time, the first two strands of this influential position implied the third. Bangkok was the only significant port of entry to the central plains, and whoever commanded the treasury and harbor offices was one of the first officials to greet foreigners. Thus, the Phra Khlang was the de facto minister of foreign affairs (a Siamese equivalent of this English term was not in general use until later in the century), and it was with the Bunnags that Western envoys had to conduct their business. Of the five men appointed to negotiate the landmark trade treaty of 1855 with Sir John Bowring, four were Bunnags: Dit, That Kham, and Kham's half brother, Chuang (Sisuriyawong), two generations of Bunnags represented by two pairs of brothers.

Kham began his official career in Rama III's reign, during which he held two noble titles in succession, the second of these making him a deputy in charge of police affairs. In 1834, he constructed fortifications at Chanthaburi, a province on the southeast coast, and at Paknam along the Chaophraya River, which guarded access to the capital. In the 1830s and 1840s, he was credited with apprehending dacoits, cleaning up opium rings near Bangkok, and rounding up Chinese secret-society pirates who had been terrorizing areas of south Thailand. The campaign against opium was inspired by the king, whose vigilance in trying to suppress the opium traffic was religious at base. In 1839, the same year he issued a law on opium, Rama III had a metal opium container melted down and cast as a Buddha image to earn merit.

Along with the other powerful Bunnags, Kham helped place Prince Mongkut on the throne in 1851. While Mongkut was a monk during the Third Reign, the younger Bunnags, Kham and Chuang, befriended him and restored a monastery near their home for the reform-order monks led by Mongkut. Both Kham and Mongkut shared an avid interest in Western culture and religion that dates back to this period. The close association of the two men was good politics as much as a meeting of minds, and when the ministerial council convened to select an heir at the death of Rama III, it asked Kham to invite the prince to accede. The troops that surrounded the monastery to guard the prince before his coronation were Bunnag loyalists from the delta fortifications. Throughout his reign, Mongkut rewarded this Bunnag loyalty; in 1853, he raised Kham to the highest noble rank of Jaophraya and, in 1865, conferred the title of Thiphakorawong, by which Kham is best known.

These titles and ranks were rewards for royal service in the construction of public works as well as in the administration of the traditional Bunnag offices of treasury, foreign affairs, and the port of Bangkok. Thiphakorawong was also put in charge of building and supervising the repair of a number of reliquaries and monasteries, the most famous of which was the gleaming Phra Pathom *jedi* at Nakhon Pathom. For the labor and resources to complete the *jedi*, Mongkut placed the principality of Nakhon Chaisi at Thiphakorawong's disposal as an appanage.

Thiphakorawong, already experienced in harbor administration and foreign affairs under the tutelage of his father, rose higher in the Harbor Department when Mongkut became king in 1851. When the elder Bunnag died in 1855 shortly after Sir John Bowring left Siam, Thiphakorawong became minister of the royal treasury, or Phra Khlang, the position his father had held. It was in this capacity that he became acquainted with Western envoys, travelers, and missionaries, who came to Siam in increasing numbers during and after the 1855 treaties: Henry Alabaster, the British representative in Siam; William Maxwell Wood, an American ship captain who contributed to the burgeoning travel literature of Asian voyages; and Adolf Bastian, a German Orientalist who visited Bangkok in 1863, to name but a few. Of the missionaries, Dr. D. B. Bradley, an American resident since the Third Reign, was perhaps the most prominent, owing to his printing activities and to his attendance at court as a physician.

Both the Siamese and Western sources indicate that the relationship between Thiphakorawong and the Westerners in Siam was filled with warmth and mutual respect. The minister offered missionaries the use of some of his boats and made available his house in Chonburi for Europeans to convalesce. The missionaries found that he "was extremely fond of debating religion" and that he "was remarkably fair and gentlemanly in all his religious discussion whether written or oral." One Westerner called attention to "the courteous urbanity of his demeanour"; another referred to it as "easy and dignified." He was also praised for the modest way he lived and for his generosity in contributing personal funds to religious construction when government resources fell short. Despite the number of Western accounts of meeting the man, few of them provide us with much more than a hint of his appearance. William Maxwell Wood found him a "heavy, solid, sober-faced man," an impression confirmed by the one nineteenth-century photograph that survives in the Thai printed literature.

In the late 1860s, as the Fourth Reign drew to a close and the Fifth Reign began, Thiphakorawong's health failed and his active career as a minister came to an end. Growing blindness from cataracts caused him to retire from official service on 29 January 1867. At great personal expense, he brought a Dutch doctor from Java to treat his eyes. He continued to serve the monarchy, and at King Chulalongkorn's coronation in 1868, he offered thirty-five points of advice to the young king on such matters as justice, revenue, and crime prevention. He admonished King Chulalongkorn to be cool-headed, to command fear and respect, to take advantage of members of the royal family with talent, and to beware of those who would take advantage of the king's youth. All this advice was apposite to the Siamese monarchy in any period and especially prescient on certain points for the reign of King Chulalongkorn. The new king raised Thiphakorawong's status and made him head of foreign affairs and the Harbor Department, though these positions were only honorary because of the minister's ill health. Suffering from diabetes, Thiphakorawong died on 12 June 1870 of painful complications from kidney stones. He was survived by his wife; he had no children.

Jaophraya Thiphakorawong is best known in Thailand today as the author of chronicles of the first four reigns of the Bangkok dynasty commissioned by King Chulalongkorn. In the Siam of his day, only a government official would be privy to the chronicles, to royal correspondence and decrees, to decisions at court, and to the web of contact among kings, officials, and foreign envoys, all of which were necessary to authenticate an historical account. This intimacy with the official record and official life is both an indispensable asset, a sine qua non for a historian of his time, and an inescapable limitation for any historian nowadays seeking to write critical history of nineteenth-century Siam from the chronicles.

Kham Bunnag's reputation as an historian derives from posthumous consideration of his work, because most of his historical writing was completed at the end of his life after ill health had forced his retirement from government service. For most of his life, he was not a man of letters but a man immersed in affairs of state, to which the great variety of his official positions testifies. His interest in history, especially Chinese dynastic history, can be dated to an earlier period, however. In 1855 he commissioned a translation into Siamese of the Sui-T'ang dynastic history, one of a number of projects in Chinese history undertaken by Siamese noblemen in the nineteenth century.

Out of conversations with Westerners and other Siamese officials came Thiphakorawong's book, *Kitjanukit* (A book explaining various things), whose publication in 1867 makes it the first book printed entirely under Siamese sponsorship. A summary of *Kitjanukit* in English with the title *The Modern Buddhist* constitutes one-third of Henry Alabaster's study of Siamese Buddhism published in London in 1871 (Alabaster 1971). Alabaster, one of those Europeans who had vigorous conversations with Thiphakorawong about Western culture and religion, expressed his regard for the Siamese minister's outlook in the term "the modern Buddhist" because of the minister's curiosity about the West and his ability to debate without xenophobic defensiveness, qualities amply documented by nineteenth-century European sources (Feer 1879).

Thiphakorawong was critical of Siamese belief, particularly Buddhist belief, where it was contradicted by observation or empirical testing and where it did not have canonical justification. Along with Mongkut and the reform monks he led, Thiphakorawong sought to strip away accretions of superstitious belief and lay bare the fundamentals of Buddhist belief as revealed in the Pali canon. The focus for this effort in *Kitjanukit* was an attack on the Three Worlds cosmography that had served as an interpretive vehicle for Siamese Buddhism for five centuries. Mythological explanations for natural phenomena were now dismissed in favor of new explanations in terms of the workings of nature. With a constructive skepticism and an insistence on empirical proof, Thiphakorawong separated the natural world from religion, asserting that each had a set of laws that explained its own phenomena. The minister shared this skepticism with Mongkut and others of like mind. *Kitjanukit*, then, is both cause and product of a configuration of attitudes, perceptions, and responses that characterize the mind of the Siamese elite in the middle of the nineteenth century.

The "Defense of Polygamy"

When we confront the passage in *Kitjanukit* on polygamy, we find ourselves considering not legal clauses, customs, or politically advantageous marriage alliances but attitudes and opinions, informed to some degree by religious tenets and an awareness of ethics in Muslim and

Christian societies. It is as if the author had asked two general questions: (1) Why do we have polygamy? and (2) Is it acceptable? And he proceeds to answer these questions by asking three additional questions: (1) Is the nature of man and woman the same or different? (2) How does Siamese Buddhist marriage custom compare with marriage custom in other (Muslim, Christian) cultures? (3) What did the Buddha teach about polygamy? The passage is a working out of the answers to these questions. In keeping with the catechetical method throughout *Kitjanukit*, a pupil poses questions at the outset (para. 1) and the teacher answers in a reasoned argument with assumptions, propositions, and rebuttals. The passage is deceptively systematic and leads not to a conclusion but to an impression. Although the argument appears to be accumulating pluses and minuses (for and against polygamy), the reader comes to the end of the piece without knowing the sum.

What are the differences between men and women? The picture of women that emerges from the passage is sharper and more focused than that for men. Yet the picture consists of two contradictory images. On the one hand, women are passive and submissive; the woman yields to the man in sexual relations (para. 2). On the other hand, women are jealously possessive, ambitious, and ruthless, capable of murdering their own husbands in pursuit of ambition (paras. 3 and 4). The first image permits the author to declare the subordination of women to men (para. 3) and to speak of wives as acquisitions, almost a form of property (para. 9). Since more thought is given to the sexual convenience of the husband and since he is the active partner, polygamy reduces misconduct or demerit because it prevents the husband from forcing a wife against her will (para. 8). The second image, of the jealously possessive and ruthless woman, explains why a woman cannot have many husbands, for she would kill those she grew not to love (para. 3). While polygamy follows from the first image, an equitable polyandry is precluded by the second. The assumption that men and women are different leads to different (and unequal) social relations to accommodate the difference. The author ignores the possibility that jealousy and ruthlessness would presumably lead a wife or concubine to kill other women belonging to the husband she shared with them.

There is no evidence in the passage for a comparable picture of man's nature. Consideration is given for a husband's sexual convenience and for his need to make merit. A man must have many wives so that he can alternate among them and not force any one against her will, thus losing merit. A wife is the passive partner, and her sexual convenience is as immaterial as her need to make merit.[7]

In keeping with the international world in which Siam found itself in the middle of the nineteenth century, the passage considers Muslim and Christian practice and, in doing so, tests polygamy with the criterion of universality. Polygamy is found in the early histories of both Muslim and Christian cultures, and this universality and antiquity help to legitimate its practice in Siam. The sexual convenience of men explains the Muslim practice. If a wife is pregnant or menstruating, the husband may turn to another wife, and Muhammadan law stipulates four as the maximum number of wives to provide for a man's needs (para. 6). The European Christian example, already introduced at the outset, is more critical to the argument, because the European practice of monogamy raises the question of equality between the sexes. As the author says,

> Europeans say that woman's nature and man's nature are the same, since both men and women are humankind. Neither should have more advantage than the other (para. 7).

Furthermore, the author understands monogamy to be not a religious precept but a secular principle on which all members of the social hierarchy agreed:

> Monogamy is not based on religious teaching but is the commandment of sages seeking justice and the elimination of man's greed. The intention is merely that the state should progress (para. 7).

Thus the author sees marriage custom divorced from religion in European culture, but he stops short of recommending European marriage custom. The example of the evolution of European monogamy is simply there to be noted.

He then turns to consider what the Buddha taught with regard to marriage custom, and there, too, he finds marriage custom divorced from religion. The Buddha neither condemned polygamy nor did he commend it, though he did say that the practice was a root cause of greed and illusion (para. 9). The Buddha did not forbid polygamy in the precept concerning sexual misconduct, however. It is possible for a Buddhist to practice polygamy just as it is possible for a Buddhist not to practice polygamy. Unlike Mormonism in nineteenth-century America, which encouraged polygamy as a commitment to the new religious sect, marriage custom for the Siamese Buddhist hangs free of religion.[8]

To this last statement, one must add a qualification. While it is true that the Buddha made no prescription or proscription concerning the practice, the Buddhist idea of merit is bound up with the author's argument that a husband must have more than one wife at his disposal in order to avoid losing merit. The hierarchy of relations between the sexes implicit in this argument recalls the fact noted earlier that Buddhism explains the hierarchical precedence of male over female. The justification for polygamy is not entirely free from the tenets of Buddhism; the institution of polygamy still fits into the cosmic moral framework that Buddhism constructs. Social relations and religion are still wed to one another.

The answers to the two general questions, then, are that, first of all, we have polygamy because it accommodates the differences in man's and woman's nature. Indeed, it contributes to social harmony by reducing antagonism and conflict between the sexes. Second, it is acceptable because other societies practice it for understandable reasons and because it is not disallowed by Buddhist precept. Along the path to these answers lies the persistent assertion of male prerogative, which, as we have seen, is consistent with the provisions of Siamese law and the marriage practices of the noble and royal families. The juxtaposition in the passage of European Christian monogamous marriage against Siamese Buddhist polygamous marriage does not make an invidious comparison between the two, though such a comparison would be made in later years when reformers argued for a family law permitting monogamy only. Nevertheless, Thiphakorawong points the way to change by saying that if one assumes, as Europeans do, that men's and women's natures are the same, a different marriage custom (monogamy) will result.

Conclusion

Thiphakorawong was not himself a reformer, but he set as one of the terms of reference for reform of marriage law in later years the Western or European example of monogamous marriage. By simply noting European marriage custom and the equality between the sexes that it assumes, Thiphakorawong employs the comparative method and invokes the principle of cultural relativism. This cultural relativism is by no means scientific, however. When Thiphakorawong says that the European intention "is merely that the state should progress," his comparison carries the same loading of the West's advancement and its superior position on the evolutionary scale implicit in the comparative method as it was expounded by social evolutionists and developmental theorists in the West during the nineteenth century (Nisbet 1969, chap. 6). At the same time, the author yields nothing in his defense of the practice of polygamy. The psychological undercurrents at work here are identical to those at work in the kingdom's sovereign, who clearly relished the institution while permitting dissatisfied women to resign from it.

I see in this passage on polygamy (and in the book *Kitjanukit* as a whole) the germ of the idea that Siam would have to be attentive to Western morality because that was what the West wanted. From the middle of the nineteenth century on, Siam's elite demonstrated a willingness to be pushed by the West diplomatically, commercially, and legally (the extraterritorial provisions of the trade treaties). From the passage on polygamy, we can see that the morality of marriage custom, too, was a question of realpolitik. The family law promulgated in 1935 adopted monogamy as the only legal marriage contract, but it countenanced polygamy by recognizing all children conceived by a man, irrespective of the mother, if he chooses to register them. In a strict reading of the Thai law, there are no illegitimate children in Thailand (Smith 1973: 294). The 1935 law defers to Siam's need for status as a modern nation, but its loose enforcement suggests that the authority ideology that created and maintained the institution of polygamy is very much alive.

The passage draws no conclusion and leaves us only with a refracted impression of the mind behind this piece of writing. The wealth, social position, and political power of its author gave him an immense security, a psychological security as well as a social security. In the light of this immense security, the relativism and open-mindedness revealed in parts of this passage are deceptive. The overall impression is that of a sensibility unshakable in its moorings. This sensibility, which would not conceive of certain moral questions independent of Western pressure, dominated Siamese political life into the twentieth century.[9]

The "Defense of Polygamy" is a label I have given to Thiphakora-wong's discussion of the precept on sexual misconduct. In the first five precepts, a Buddhist undertakes to refrain from killing, stealing, sexual misconduct, telling falsehoods, and taking intoxicants; the "Defense of Polygamy" addresses the precept on sexual misconduct. I have broken the Thai text into paragraphs and numbered them for ease of reference.[10]

1. The question. Is the precept concerning sexual misconduct, that is, adultery with another man's daughter or wife, considered as misconduct in every religion and speech group? The only people who would say it is not misconduct are the ignorant; they would claim that he who seduces another man's daughter or wife is free of misconduct so long as the husband does not know about it. If one is confident that a couple gets along well together without rancor or quarreling, then one does not consider such an act misconduct. In Buddhism, both men and women take the precept concerning sexual misconduct, but adherence to this precept in practice is not the same for both. Men can have many wives, however many they want; women cannot have many husbands—in fact, are limited to one. Why is this so? Do men not have an advantage over women? Europeans have only one husband and one wife. Is that not much better? After all, man's nature and woman's nature are equally capable of love on the one hand, and possessive jealousy on the other.

2. The reply. It is true that both (men and women) take the precept concerning sexual misconduct but do not adhere to it equally, and it is necessary first of all to explain this precept. The Buddha forbade wrongful sexual conduct; one should abstain from it. (In order to do this) there is the precept and the vow to take the precept. When men take the precept in a certain way, the precept effectively becomes two precepts—one for women, one for men. If a man and woman have a sexual relationship that is acceptable according to the precept, the precept concerning sexual misconduct has been kept. The learned authors of the (Pali) commentaries explain that the man has the prerogative in sexual relations, while the woman only acquiesces. This is fitting if one thinks about it.

If the man pays no attention to the woman, she can do nothing and must silently accept the situation. So we see that men have the prerogative in sexual relations. As for men having many wives, this works only if the women do not already have someone possessive of them. The wives come willingly of their own accord or their families offer them if not disallowed by taboo. Ten categories of women are excluded. For example, if a man has relations with a woman who already belongs to a man or who is engaged to be married, both parties in the relationship are at fault. A man who seduces a woman raised by her family in one of the taboo categories violates the precept; the woman, however, does not violate the precept, because she does not have the prerogative in sexual relations. The family merely raised her in a protective way, hoping to get her a husband. Because they did not forbid her from having sexual relations, there is no misconduct and no violation of the precept concerning sexual misconduct.

3. As for saying that women cannot have many husbands, it is because women are subordinate to men. If women *were* to have many husbands just as men have many wives, the children would not know who their father was. Having been separated from their father, they might vilify and attack a man, possibly committing patricide. Another point is that male and female natures are different. No matter how many wives a man has and whether he loves them or detests them, he would never think of killing them. If a woman has many husbands, she is likely to kill those whom she does not love. Women are usually this way.

4. There are many fables (to illustrate these matters), and I shall relate one of them briefly. There was a man who made a daily blessing for the king with the intention of making the king as nimble as a crow, as ruthless as a woman, as forbearing as a vulture, and as strong as an ant. The king wondered about this and asked, "How is a vulture forbearing?" The man replied, "Let Your Majesty cage a vulture and then cage some birds and other animals. None of the animals is to have any food. The other animals are sure to die before the vulture." The king tried the experiment and obtained the result as claimed. The phrase "as strong as an ant" was explained as follows. Ants have more strength than man or any other animal in the world. To prove this, take an iron or copper filing the length

of an ant and coat it with sugar. The ant will be able to carry it off. Neither a man nor any other animal would be able to lift its size in copper or iron. Now for the phrase "as nimble as a crow." However long one were to keep a caged crow, it would never become tame. When set free, it would be as nimble as before. As for "as ruthless as a woman," Your Majesty should order a royal servant to find a newly married couple. In the first month or so, they are very much in love. Summon the husband and command him to murder his wife and bring the head to you. If he does so, you undertake to give him half your kingdom and appoint him as your successor. If the husband will not do this, summon the wife and command her to murder her husband and bring the head to you. If she does so, you undertake to make her chief queen and supervisor of the royal concubines. The king then ordered a royal servant to find a newly married couple who loved each other very much and did not quarrel. Once the couple had been found, the husband would appear before the king. The royal servant located a newly married couple who fit the requirements and brought the husband before the king. The king issued his command as described above, and the husband hid a knife in his belt and set off to kill his wife. When he arrived home, he and his wife went to bed together as usual, and when the husband saw that his wife was asleep, he got up to kill her. Then he began thinking how he would acquire half the kingdom and how wonderful it would be to become heir to the throne. But his wife had done nothing wrong; he ought not murder her. He felt compassion for her and would not murder her. Thus he forfeited the property he would have acquired. The following morning, he went to the king, explained that he could not kill his wife, and returned the knife. Then he returned home. The king ordered the royal servant to go stealthily and bring the man's wife for an audience, whereupon the king spoke to her with soothing words. The wife concealed the knife and went home. She waited until her husband was fast asleep, then plunged the knife into his throat, cutting off the head, which she brought to the king. Thus we see that women are more ruthless than men. If someone comes along with soothing words to charm her, she becomes capable of killing her husband. For this reason, women should not have many husbands.

5. As for a woman taking a husband who already has a wife jealously possessive of him, does that new wife who takes the husband not violate the precept concerning sexual misconduct? The answer is no, she does not, because the woman is not the instigator in sexual relations. (For the other woman) to be so jealously possessive is to have carnal desire, and this is not good. For this reason, the new wife is not at fault.

6. A man seduces a wife whose husband does not know about it. Only an ignorant person would say that the man is not at fault, and one should not say such a thing. We need not bother with this point. If a man sometimes seduces another man's wife, what should be said about it? Europeans hold that to have only one husband and only one wife is a good thing. Does this mean that what their religion teaches is the truth? This point can be explained by referring to the religious beliefs of former times. At the time of the birth of Jesus Christ and, subsequently, of Muhammad, there was no law prescribing monogamy. In those days, men could have many wives. Later on, Muhammadan law set a limit of four wives, because it was felt that this number was sufficient for a husband. That is, if one wife is pregnant, one can turn to the second wife. If the second wife is pregnant, one can turn to the third wife. If the third wife is pregnant, one can turn to the fourth wife. If the fourth wife is pregnant, one can turn to the first wife, who has probably given birth by then.

7. Another point is that if a wife is menstruating, it is unlikely that all four wives are menstruating at the same time, so there would be at least one wife not menstruating. Muslims thought along these lines and, accordingly, decreed a limit of four wives. Many years later, Europeans saw that having many wives or only four wives was not moral and just, because women were jealous and capable of killing each other or their husbands. There are many instances of this. This is why Europeans say that woman's nature and man's nature are the same, since both men and women are humankind. Neither should have more advantage than the other. Thus members of the community agreed together that a single wife was the best thing. Royalty and nobility, members of the elite and commoners, all consented, and the agreement was given the sanction of law for the entire state. If a man violated (this agreement) and took two

wives, he was subject to arrest and punishment. This tradition has continued to the present day. Monogamy is not based on religious teaching but is the commandmant of sages seeking justice and the elimination of man's greed. The intention is merely that the state should progress.

8.   To reflect a bit further on monogamy, if the wife is ill or pregnant or menstruating, a man filled with desire is going to miss out every month. He is not going to approve of the idea of having only one wife. He will think that to force a woman against her will is misconduct. If there are a number of wives, he can alternate among them.

9.   Buddhism teaches that to conduct oneself in a Brahmic way (i.e., ascetically) and to keep the most rigorous monastic discipline is of the highest calling. If a man cannot endure the ordained state, disrobes, and is content to live with one wife, the Buddha praised this as one form of Brahmic conduct termed "being faithful to one woman." As for having many wives, the Buddha did not commend it at all, criticizing it as a root cause of greed and illusion. But it was not possible to forbid men to have many wives, because wives that one acquires rightfully as a matter of course belong to one. The Buddha, therefore, did not include this prohibition as one of his precepts. The Buddha merely offered his praise and criticism. The precepts concerning falsehoods and theft are not necessary to explain and reinterpret, since these precepts are followed (by religions) throughout the world.

Notes

1.   For a discussion of the relationship of the cosmography text to Sukhodaya society, see Cholthira 1974.
2.   Three works published between 1973 and 1976 contain little Siamese historical data but discuss prostitution and rape and universalize the issue of women's rights in the context of feminist and socialist history (biographies of Angela Davis, Rosa Luxumberg, Clara Setkin, et al.); Klum phuying thammasat 1974; Jiranan 1975; Klum phuying sip sathaban 1976.
3.   Bowring 1969: I, 411, but this figure is surely exaggerated. In 1863, Mongkut himself claimed there were only twenty-seven royal mothers, thirty-four concubines, and seventy-four daughters of noblemen presented to serve as attendants; Moffat 1961: 134–35.

4. Anna Leonowens, a source to be used with great care, captures something of life in the Inner Palace. "This woman's city is as self-supporting as any other in the world: it has its own laws, its judges, police, guards, prisons, and executioners, its markets, merchants, brokers, teachers, and mechanics of every kind and degree; and every function of every nature is exercised by women, and by them only" (1953: 10–11). There were no eunuchs in the Inner Palace. One of Anna's young pupils rose to a high rank in the Inner Palace hierarchy, and her grandson has written her biography; Phitthayalapphruttiyakon 1964.

5. Bowring, cited in Moffat 1961: 134, reports Mongkut as saying he had twelve children before he was king and eleven since his coronation. The total figure of twenty-one, including two before his coronation, comes from the official genealogy of the royal family; Fine Arts Dept. 1969a: 44–49.

6. Biographical details are based on the following Western and Thai sources: Damrong 1969; Natthawut 1963; Thiphakorawong 1961, 1965–74; Wood 1859; Bradley 1871; Flood 1965–74.

7. A wife, however passive she might be according to this account, was not exempt from punishment if she committed adultery. New laws issued by Rama I in 1782 and 1798 made this clear; *Kotmai tra sam duang*, Volume V, Phraratchakamnot mai, nos. 14 and 37, pp. 250 and 345 in the Khurusapha edition.

8. Brigham Young referred to plural marriage as "celestial marriage." In Mormonism, "women entered heaven only when married to someone endowed with the priesthood, and a man arrived at perfection in the next world only with several wives;" Hirshson 1969: 121. Polygamy became illegal in the United States only in 1869 upon passage of the Cullom Bill; de Riencourt 1974: 325.

9. Aspects of the argument here have been taken up in Thongchai 2000c. The issue of polygamy in the context of Thai gender behavior was contentious some forty years after *Kitjanukit*; see Barmé 1999.

10. Translated from Thiphakorawong 1965: 153–58.

10

Thai Manual Knowledge:
Theory and Practice

Manual knowledge I understand to be knowledge that is self-consciously organized for preservation, retrieval, transmission, and consumption. To use fashionable cybernetic language, we could say that manual knowledge is formatted or encoded in particular ways to facilitate its practical use. Grammars, cosmologies, medical and astrology manuals, manuals on the art and science of warfare, and manuals on how to behave properly and how to be modern are all examples of formatted knowledge, but the list, of course, is not exhaustive. In premodern Siam, much of this knowledge was transmitted orally, and much of it was accessible to people of all classes. There were "low" as well as "high" versions of this manual knowledge. While it was asymmetrically distributed, it was not the preserve of the elite alone.

Knowledge is a form of cultural capital, a resource that enables people in a society to make sense of the world and to live safely, in good health, and with dignity. Study of knowledge as cultural capital is topical in the present historical moment as international financial institutions and donor governments seek to maximize the effectiveness of aid programs in the developing world. Aid programs have more impact if they mesh with local knowledge, so local knowledge becomes an important vehicle for aid even as local knowledge is held up as an instrument for local people to resist incursions from the outside. In view of the heated debates about biotechnology, intellectual copyright, and imbalances in the distribution of technology and expertise, the study of culturally specific knowledge has become a matter of national concern for many developing countries.

Anthropologists and development practitioners have long been interested in indigenous knowledge broadly in terms of ethnoscience, human ecology, farming systems, and participatory development (Sillitoe 1998: 224). For example, Roy Ellen glosses indigenous knowledge as "local, orally transmitted, a consequence of practical engagement reinforced by experience, empirical rather than theoretical, repetitive, fluid and negotiable, shared but asymmetrically distributed, largely functional, and embedded in a more encompassing cultural matrix" (Sillitoe 1998: 238). Some forms of manual knowledge that I examine in this essay look a lot like indigenous knowledge, according to Ellen's gloss.

The imminent extinction of plant and animal species, human languages, and population groups tied to particular ecosystems has drawn attention to indigenous knowledge. One of my aims here is to address what I see as the shallow historical base in studies of indigenous knowledge, sometimes called local knowledge, a term that came into fashion only a little more than twenty years ago (Sillitoe 1998: 244). Studies of indigenous knowledge appear to be almost exclusively in the domain of anthropology and ethnoscience, the genealogy of these studies reaching back to Malinowski's efforts to distinguish magic, science, and religion from each other (Nader 1996: 259–60). "Indigenous" or "traditional" knowledge does not seem to include the knowledge accumulated or cultivated in premodern Southeast Asian societies where historians have given very little attention to its study. Exploring the character of this manual knowledge may help us come to terms with "science" in premodern society (Soraj 2002b: 103–4). The tendency to compare indigenous knowledge with Western scientific knowledge is understandable, but the comparison is problematic, in that it makes Western science a benchmark and implicitly superior (Ellen et al. 2000: 14).

The approach I take is not always strictly historical. This is partly because it is difficult to date some of the source material, and partly because if we relax the rules for strict chronological accountability, we may learn a little more about the social meaning of manual knowledge. Owing to uncertain chronology, historians tend to shy away from manual knowledge, although students of language and medical anthropology, at least in the field of Thai studies, have been more alert to the importance of formatting knowledge in this way.

The mythical progenitor-teacher of some of the manuals—the Buddha's physician, for example, or the Hindu god Vishnu—and the omission of specific events and toponyms located in the "real" world strengthens the impression of the divine origins or transcendent quality of this knowledge. It seems timeless and thus defies the insistent demand that useful knowledge be situated in a particular time and place.

One of the questions I want to take up about knowledge formatted in manuals is whether or not it encourages orthodoxy and authoritarianism. It may be that the role of manuals in maintaining the social order discouraged knowledge-seeking activities as compared with societies whose social epistemologies were different (Soraj 2002a: 85). Some examples in the genre I am calling manual knowledge are filled with norms, with explicit obligations or duties, and with rules and regulations. Is the society in which such knowledge is highly valued predisposed to authoritarianism? Moral codes have religious sanctions but do not necessarily carry political sanctions. Texts that instruct readers/listeners on what they should or should not do are didactic but do not have to be authoritarian unless one regards all such didactic instruction as authoritarian. A more nuanced answer to the question would have to address the discursive practices that accompany the rules and regulations and the institutions that reproduce and enforce them. In other words, it is not so much the manual itself but the social and institutional setting in which it is used that determines whether the knowledge contributed to orthodoxy and authoritarianism.

Another question has to do with whether or not manuals facilitate the incorporation of knowledge from "the outside," i.e., foreign knowledge. Or do they impede the incorporation of foreign knowledge? It is possible, for example, that one of the names given to manual knowledge in Thailand, the Indic term *sastra*, implies codification of knowledge whose purpose is to limit incorporation of material from the outside, to seal off the corpus of knowledge from outside influences. Thus, the format itself might act as an inoculation against foreign material. We may discover that only some types of manual knowledge, such as religious scripture, are inhospitable to foreign material. Still another question has to do with the relationship between manuals used by Thai governments in the twentieth century and the previous "tradition" of manual knowledge. Is the modern manual derivative of the premodern manual tradition, or is it an entirely new genre that must be explained by the particular needs of governing the nation-state in the twentieth century?

Manual knowledge is found throughout the region. The *Serat Centhini*, a Javanese encyclopedia in the form of a meandering, dense, and at times bizarre narrative poem, has received extensive study by Indonesian cultural historians (Day 2002: 122–25; Day and Derks 1999). The Buginese *La Galigo* from Makasar is another example of a cultural encyclopedia in story form. Northrop Frye is usually invoked in discussions of cultural grammars such as *Serat Centhini* and *La Galigo* for suggesting that these works contain "essential stories" telling a society what it needs to know about itself, particularly in the form of ethical and religious knowledge that helps people to be competent members of society (1982). Astrological manuals have been important in Southeast Asia for centuries, surviving today in such books as *primbon*, Javanese manuals of prayers, divination, and spells. One such *primbon* has been termed the Javanese science of burglary, as popular with thieves planning a heist as with the police wanting to catch them (Quinn 1975). A historian of modern Malaya once extracted important information about the Malay court from a manual of Malay custom and behavior, the *Hikayat Deli*, that appears to reflect conditions in the Malay world of the late eighteenth or early nineteenth centuries (Milner 1982, chap. 5)

In the central Thai world, the diverse and flexible formats for storing and transmitting knowledge are called most generally "handbooks" or "manuals" (*tamra*), a word that has its origins in ancient Khmer (Uraisi 1984: 158, 319). An alliterative, doubled form, *tamrap tamra*, can be found in eighteenth- and nineteenth-century Thai materials and may still be encountered in printed books. All sorts of information, schema, procedures, and rules may be called *tamra*. Nowadays, the *tamra* label is used as a clever marketing ploy to sell "how to" manuals and pop-psychology books. Determining just what is and is not a *tamra* might be a valuable exercise, but use of other terms for knowledge in the manual format, such as *sat* (Skt. *sastra*), *khu my* (handbook), and *khamphi* (religious treatise, canon), suggests that the terms do not have discrete meanings but are often used interchangeably. Although some scholars would insist on distinguishing between manuals (*tamra*) and handbooks (*khu my*), in practical usage their semantic ranges overlap. A book on magic (*tamra saiyasat*), reprinted many times over the past three decades, also identifies itself as a handbook (*ku my*) and a treatise (*khamphi*) (Turton 1991: 165).

Knowledge encoded in the manual format was dignified by the Sanskrit term for "science" or "corpus of knowledge," *sastra* (*sat* in phonemic transcription), to the extent that *tamra* and *sastra* in many instances are used synonymously. The royal wordsmith of the twentieth century, Prince Wan, gave *tamra* as a translation of *sastra*, and *tamra* continued to be used until a few generations ago to mean "authoritative text" (Narathip-praphanphong 2001: 289).[1] In Indian history, *sastra* were the paradigmatic formats for "a verbal codification of rules, whether of divine or human provenance" put to the service of regulating certain human practices (Pollock 1985: 501). In Modern Thai, the neologisms coined for Western disciplinary knowledge all end with the *sastra* suffix: *prawattisat*—history; *manutsayasat*—the humanities; *phumisat*—geography; *ratthasat*—political science; *witthayasat*—science; and so on. An eighty-page sex manual published in 1908 was the work of two Thai princes who allegedly went to India to study the "science"—was the word *sastra*?—of physiognomy (Barmé 2002: 187).

Grammars of language are perhaps paradigmatic of the type of formatted knowledge we are talking about, whether or not they are called *sastra*. A grammar is a corpus of knowledge that is rule-based and normative. In other words, while allowing for language's infiniteness (the grammar cannot circumscribe all the utterances possible in a language), a grammar accounts for those utterances in the rules and the hierarchy of rules it lays down. The "science" of the famous Sanskrit grammar of Panini had its origins in the codification of Vedic sacrifices. Some of the technical concepts of grammatical description and the style of analysis in Panini's grammar may be found in "the methods developed for codifying complex Vedic sacrifices" (Staal 1994: 2918). One of the three main sections of the *Tripitaka*, the "Abhidharma"—the "higher" or "further" Dharma—has been described as a grammar because it lays out the underlying structure of the Dharma as found in the discourses of the Buddha.[2]

In the courts of Thai kings and the petty princes in the tributary states, great value was placed on the possession of knowledge in the form of *sastra*, knowledge that had to do with acquiring and exercising power, with waging war, with managing the constantly shifting balances of allies and enemies, with the art and science of governing. The relative advantage that had to be calculated in the politics of any relationship—rivals within the court, enemies without— did not fail to make use of spells, curses, incantations, and auspicious omens. Brahmans knowledgeable in the *sastra* and adept at providing these aids had been retained in the Thai courts since the Sukhodaya period. Knowledge of spells, incantations, and the manipulation of cabalistic signs was a secret knowledge and jealously guarded lest it fall into the hands of rivals or enemies. Practitioners—teachers, astrologers, magicians—knew certain tricks to make their spells, incantations, forecasts, or prescriptions more effective than those of their rivals (Brun 1990: 50). Theravada Buddhist monks also came into possession of these *sastra*, although such knowledge is sometimes regarded by devout Thai Buddhists as the dark side of the religion. The occult has always been a barely suppressed discourse in Theravada Buddhism, much sought after by those in need of protection or good fortune, but frowned upon by educated, elite, urban Buddhists (Terweil 1975: 279). For all of these reasons, some kinds of manual knowledge held a sacred, almost a magical, value. Handwritten medical texts, for example, were thought to confer "power" on their owner or on the household where they were kept.[3]

In Thailand, the elite cachet of the Indic term should not obscure the fact that possession of *sastra* was not the preserve of the elite alone. There was, and is, a popular dimension to this knowledge that has been overlooked in the historiography of premodern times. It has been suggested, for example, that with the close genetic relationship between chief and shaman, curing practices, which are typically encoded in the oral and oral-written manual format, played an important role in harnessing the Indic (Golomb 1985: 50–56). Medical therapies, sorcery, and maybe even early forms of astrology were not "foreign" or "introduced" but indigenous knowledges. They latched on to the Indic linguistic and numerological systems and their associated practices that circulated with Brahmans and Buddhist monks. In the countryside, practices codified in the manual tradition helped the Indic to take root.

The Danish anthropologist Viggo Brun, who undertook an extensive study of the formal, semiotic, and pedagogical properties of manual knowledge, suggests that the Theravada Buddhist canon, the *Tripitaka*, is the paragon of the manual format.[4] We can appreciate the value of Brun's insight if we remember that the monastic or lay religious specialist is someone who offers exegeses of the Buddhist canon. The teacher explains words by finding recognizable contexts in which to locate the Buddha's teachings. The ability to gloss the canon, written originally in Pali, a language that required arduous study, placed the religious specialist in an influential social position. An essential and early element in the education of monks is the ability to translate Pali into Thai. Thus, translation is the first step to be taken in learning the skill of glossing, and glossing is vital in the dissemination of knowledge coded in the manual format. The religious teacher mediates between the master manual (religious scripture, the canon) and practice (how Buddhists should behave).[5]

A distinction needs to be made between the oral and the written-oral traditions of transmitting knowledge. Many types of written manuals have ancestors in oral form. The repetitiousness of manuals may very well derive from earlier orality, which demands repetition as an aid to memory and reception (Maier 1988: 82–84). Although many manuals have been printed, they still make up only a small proportion of the manuscripts in the manual tradition (Brun 1990: 63). It may be that in Thailand and other societies where the manual tradition flourishes, writing does not command the status and respect it does in societies with character-based orthographies such as Chinese and Japanese.

Brun calls the manual format the "guru tradition," after the Thai word for teacher, *khru*, which entered the language long ago in its early contact with Indic culture. By themselves, manuals may not seem useful at all. They are schematic in form and look arcane, even baffling, to the uninitiated: verbal formulas; numerical tables and diagrams; cabalistic signs; calendrical charts; figures of lotuses, relic monuments, and other graphics filled with numbers. A teacher is required to elucidate the classifications and their relationships, because the rationale behind the arrangements of the taxa is not obvious. The teacher makes the knowledge effective or "enables" it (Turton 1991: 159–61). Those wishing to partake of the knowledge passed down through a line of teachers entered into a formal teacher-pupil relationship (*khun khru*). As the medium of this knowledge, some of it dealing explicitly with the acquisition and maintenance of power, the teacher possessed an authority that was spiritual. Periodically, pupils pay homage to this line of teachers, which stretches back infinitely into the past. The power of ancestral teachers invoked in the initiation, practice, and transmission of the knowledge contained in the manuals "surrounds the tradition like a magnetic field," in Brun's memorable phrase (1990: 46).

Brun distinguishes the "traditional" manual from the textbook, or *tamra rian*, which has become the word in Modern Thai for "school text." The form and function of the older manual and the modern school textbook are very similar, but there are significant differences, if for no other reason than because the institutions in which these texts were produced and circulated were very dissimilar. Schools came to occupy a social space very different from the entourages around teachers in which secular and religious learning took place before the advent of mass education for secondary and, later, primary education early in the twentieth century. The older Thai term for "school" (*samnak*) as an entourage of students originated in the religious setting of the monastery, where young men received their basic education in literacy and morality. In premodern times, "school" was not a particular site of learning so much as a relationship between teacher and pupil, a relationship that lingers today as one of the key relationships that inflects contemporary Thai society, for example, in the networking that goes on in the civil service, in politics, in business, and in the Buddhist monkhood.

Cosmologies

Pollock attributes to the Indian *sastra* literature a "massive authority, ensuring what in many cases seems to have been a nearly unchallengeable claim to normative control of cultural practices" (1985: 500). An example of a Thai *sastra* that could be characterized in this way is the Three Worlds cosmology, a treatise attributed controversially to 1345 C.E., when the Siamese king Lu Tai was serving as the Front Palace prince and presumptive heir to the throne (Lithai 1982). As explained in chapter 8, the Three Worlds cosmology contains no historical information, apart from some details in the prologue and colophon. In the sense that it classified and ranked all animate existence on the basis of merit, it established "rules" for the social hierarchy in premodern Siam. It offered aesthetic and emotional reasons for social difference through its semiotic capacity to make inequality enchant, to use Clifford

Geertz's famous phrase about the theater state. Those who ranked higher in the hierarchy were more wealthy and more powerful. What was more beautiful was also more desirable and "better" in a moral sense. The cosmology articulates the aesthetics of what is morally superior and socially dominant in such a way that its norms and idealizations might be described as a "theory" of premodern Siamese society.

Sustained engagement and criticism of the Three Worlds cosmology over the past thirty years or so is a measure of the hegemonic role it continues to exert. A spirited debate took place in the mid-1980s over whether the Three Worlds cosmology could continue to serve the needs of a rapidly changing society. Some participants in the debate held up the cosmology as the revelation of religious truth, while others engaged it as the product of a particular historical moment and saw its limitations (Jackson 2002b: 175–83). One of the reformist monks in the debate, Phra Thepwethi—or Phrayut Payuttho, as she prefers to be called, who was then known as Phra Ratchaworamuni—argued that the Three Worlds was still important for its ethical and spiritual content. The fact that the text served as a lightning rod for these vigorous exchanges underscored its near-canonical status, which it had attained as a locally made compilation of exegetic Buddhist literature. To the extent that they found the cosmology outdated, the Buddhist reformers in this debate were searching for a new master manual to replace the Three Worlds cosmology.

Along with other key documents and historical episodes in the Thai canon, this indigenous manual of religious knowledge was opened up to scrutiny in the years following the democratic uprising of October 1973 and the collapse of military rule. Cholthira Kalatyu Satyawadhna, one of the key figures in the rediscovery and promotion of Jit Poumisak as a revolutionary hero, published a book of essays on the first anniversary of the October uprising. She called the text Thailand's "first dissertation," because the knowledge it purveyed was for practical use, and she surmised that its royal author might be seen as Thailand's first academic (Cholthira 1974: 3, 17, 37). She relativized the text's knowledge of nature as scientific in the context of its time and credited it with offering practical lessons in reproduction and obstetrics. But Cholthira also saw the Three Worlds as rationalizing Buddhist imperial rule and dynastic succession (Cholthira 1974: 46–47). Contrary to the comforting picture of the early kingdom of Sukhothai in the thirteenth and fourteenth centuries as a land of bliss and plenty and beneficent patriarchal rule, she read the text as a vital prop to absolute monarchism (Cholthira 1974: 44).

Half a decade later, in their study of Thai political thought from ancient times to the present, two political scientists, Sombat Chanthornvong and Chai-anan Samudavanija, also identified a political agenda in the text, which was compiled at a time when the nearby Siamese kingdom of Ayudhya was increasing its economic and political power at the expense of Sukhothai (Sombat and Chai-anan 1980: 91–92). They argued that the Three Worlds cosmology assisted the kings of Sukhothai in using Buddhism as a form of "indirect" rule, an argument about religion as a political instrument that continued in the debates about the Three Worlds during the mid-1980s (Somkiat 1983). In modern Thai language, the term for "wheel-turning monarch" had come to mean "emperor" and "imperialist/imperialism," terms that became popular in the politically charged 1970s, with American troops on Thai soil until 1974. Sombat and Chai-anan published their study of Thai political thought after the bloody coup of 6 October 1976, the political fallout from which discredited state institutions, including the monarchy, which was implicated by many in the return of the military in 1976.

In her 1974 essay, Cholthira acknowledged that the author of the Three Worlds cosmology was knowledgeable in the *sastra* (Cholthira 1974: 17). In view of the "massive authority" invested in the Three Worlds through the royal patronage it received over the centuries, it is not difficult to see the work as a *sastra*. But with the cachet of being locally produced knowledge, it is challengeable in a way that the Buddhist *Tripitaka* is not.

Astrology

The world in which human beings live is part of a cosmic order that can be understood only imperfectly, but in the movement of the planets and stars, for example, there are signs of this cosmic order that can be deciphered. Astrology was the science of reading these signs, a science of divination. Astrologers were the specialists who divined propitious moments to take action, using calculations from their manuals to determine auspicious times and to neutralize unwelcome occurrences.

Astrology required accurate time-keeping and calendars, and for that reason was a science indispensable to maintaining historical records. In China during the Han dynasty, the Prefect Grand Astrologer drew up calendars and identified auspicious days for imperial activities (Bielenstein 1980: 19). The father of the great Han historian Sima Qian was Grand Astrologer and on his deathbed charged his son with the ambition of succeeding to the position (Durrant 1995: 5). Indeed, one of Sima Qian's first achievements was to collaborate with other court officials in drawing up a new calendar to replace the defective one the Han had inherited (Watson 1958: 50). The tasks of keeping records of the correlations between celestial and terrestrial phenomena and records of important human events were conjoined in an official who was both astrologer and historian.

In Siam, the first dynastic chronicle was written in the late seventeenth century by an astrologer specifically instructed by his patron, the king, to assemble the history from the records of the court astrologers (Hodges 1999: 33–34). At that time, observatories had been built in Ayudhya and Lopburi to assist visiting French astronomers in their observations of the heavens, and it is possible that the presence of the French spurred the compilation of the dynastic history (Hodges 1998: 89). As servants of the crown, astrologers in Siam possessed knowledge vital to making decisions about when to go to war and when to meet foreign envoys to achieve the most favorable outcome. In the reign of the late-sixteenth-century king Naresuan, astrologers were asked on numerous occasions to decide most propitious moments to prepare the Siamese army for battle against the Mon ruler at Pegu in lower Burma (Cushman 2000: 125, 169, 173). They also interpreted the king's dreams. Astrologers were close to power and, because of their expertise, provided advice as valuable as that of a minister of state. In Thailand today, the Thai nation and the country's capital each have horoscopes, their respective futures readable in the conjunction of heavenly bodies distinctive to the nation and the city.[6] Astrological information in manual form is intimate knowledge that even today tracks the links between the cosmos and the terrestrial world, vital for understanding the past as a guide to the future.

A third element, writing, links divination and astrological knowledge. The first glimpses of Chinese language and Chinese characters are found on oracle bones used for divination (Wilkinson

2000, chap. 15). Similarly, in early Mesopotamian civilization, the invention of writing in the form of pictographs gave the gods the power of communication with their subjects through the medium of diviners (Ginzburg 1980: 13–14). In this context, it is not surprising that the divining class of court officials, Brahman astrologers, were involved in the production of early Thai manuals of literacy.

Grammars and Manuals of Prosody

Siam in the late seventeenth century not only produced its first dynastic history but also its first manual for teaching literacy, called the *Jindamani*, sometimes translated as *Gems of Thought* (Wyatt 1969: 21–22). *Gems of Thought*, which set out the principles of the Thai writing system as well as of metrics, versification, and different poetic genres, was a classic example of knowledge in the form of *sastra*.

Codifying prosody in a manual format emphasized the textuality of Thai literature, but much of Thai poetry was performative in "sung" verse. Poets acquired their reputations not only for their ability to recite long poems, sometimes for hours, but also for their ability to improvise on topical themes. Orality, not written text, was the means by which this literature was enjoyed and reproduced. The vitality of this performed poetry is quite a different matter from literacy in the narrow sense in which we usually use the term.[7]

In the early nineteenth century, many editions of *Gems of Thought* flourished before the printing press had arrived with the Western missionaries, as famous teachers adapted the principles of language usage to suit their own tastes and talents. The means of production made it easy to insert material. The manuscripts were copied on accordion-pleated paper, and blank space was an invitation to supplement the text or simply to practice by copying out verse forms and rhymes. If a page was torn, additional pages could be affixed to create more space in which to write. In this way, the text became amended and extended, thus accounting for the repetitious and tangled character of the copies that survived. When *Gems of Thought* was revised in 1849, the compiler, Prince Wongsathiratsanit, "supplemented" the copy he inherited. The manual was printed for the first time in 1870. A subsequent edition, printed by the American missionary Dr. D. B. Bradley, classified the alphabet for the convenience of

foreign students of Thai (*Jindamani* 1971b: 149–52). Yet, at the beginning of the twentieth century, there were still so many manuscript
copies in circulation that an authoritative family tree of the manual
was difficult to construct.

As printing technology made the text more widely available, the
tenability of *Gems of Thought*—in its countless versions—as the master
text for teaching literacy was undermined by new handbooks, such as
the *Rapid Reader* compiled by Phraya Sisunthornwohan in the 1870s
at the beginning of the Fifth Bangkok Reign. The usefulness of *Gems
of Thought* gradually faded as the education system expanded and the
new texts became more widespread. The anthropologist-sage Phya
Anuman (1888–1969) inherited from his father the version printed by
Dr. Bradley and kept it in his library for many years. He remembered
flipping through the pages as a child, although he had already learned
his Thai alphabet from another text. He never consciously discarded
the book but simply lost track of his dog-eared copy as it ceased to
be of practical value and disappeared into the mists of time (Anuman
1969: 27).

When Thai poetry and song began to contend with print and the
Thai language became a subject in secondary school and university
courses, a recodification of the principles of Thai language was required
for the curricula. The principles of language (*lak phasa*) are rules for
the language preserved as a set of paradigms in four textbooks or
manuals that have been called the *janthalak* tradition after the title of
the fourth volume, which means "versification." The manuals, the best
of which were written by Phya Uppakit Silpasarn (1879–1941), who
taught Thai language at Chulalongkorn University and whose authority
stands behind the books to the present day, set out Thai phonology and
orthography, the parts of speech, syntax, and versification (Uppakit
Silpasarn 1979). The principles of language in the *janthalak* tradition
convey a sense of prescriptive authority, which inevitably poses problems
for students of the Thai language both within Thailand and abroad
when they encounter forms that deviate from the paradigms. The
eminent American linguist William Gedney, who among his many
talents understood the history of Thai poetry, felt that the *janthalak*
textbooks did not pay sufficient attention to historical context and
gave the impression that the verse forms were coeval and eternal
(Gedney 1989: 490–92).

One way to interpret the so-called *janthalak* tradition is to see it as an updated version of the core manual science found in *Gems of Thought* in all its multiple versions, the master manual or *sastra* for teaching literacy in premodern Siam. Phya Uppakit was very conscious of Thai as an Eastern language, and when he updated the volume on syntax in 1937, originally prepared for school teachers by the Ministry of Education following the structure of the English language, he saw himself as editing and "correcting" the principles to accord more closely with the structure of the Thai language (Uppakit 1979: vii). This was in the decade of Thai hypernationalism, when the governments of the day were simultaneously celebrating the essential features of Thai civilization and devising ways to remake and reform Thai practices in terms of international models.

Medical Knowledge

Siamese medical knowledge allows us to track a history that also had a complex genealogy in the manual tradition. In its written form, much of this knowledge was preserved by court physicians who guarded it jealously to keep it from other practitioners. But medical knowledge preserved at the court paralleled and mutually informed a body of knowledge transmitted primarily in oral or oral-written form in the countryside. This medical knowledge is not, and never was, a uniform system of medicine, although the cultural dominance of the court and the practice of writing it down and making it known to Western visitors might lead historians to think otherwise. Regional differences in history, language, culture, and environment meant that there were marked variations in the way illnesses and their treatments were classified in different parts of what is now known as Thailand. One may even speak of intra-regional diversity. Some of these regional variants have been obscured or lost with the passage of time.[8]

The seventeenth-century visitor to Ayudhya, Simon de la Loubère, was scathing about medical practice in Siam, complaining that "medicine cannot merit the name of a science among the Siamese," although he had to admit that it did not fail to cure a great many diseases. He referred to the manual format of medical knowledge as "recipes" (lit., *receipts*), "which they have learnt from their ancestors, and in which they never alter anything" (Bamber 1989: 28). He might have observed that the static, schematic knowledge in the manuals required the skill of teachers and doctors to activate it in order to bring it alive. It was this body of medical knowledge that was codified several times during the nineteenth century, beginning in the early decades and continuing through to the end. In 1832, the third Bangkok king had hundreds of medical texts inscribed on stone together with diagrams of Thai massage practices and statues of yogins installed at the Jetavana monastery, popularly known as Wat Pho (Brun and Schumacher 1987: 10–11; Mulholland 1987: 13). The royal texts in the manual format were compiled for the first time in 1871 at the beginning of the Fifth Bangkok Reign, a multi-stranded compilation that is characteristic of the manual format. It was better to be inclusive than systemic, which has left the scholar of today plenty of work to do in trying to assemble logical sequences.

Like grammars, medical manuals gradually grew to be baggy monsters, owing to the reluctance of compilers to discard anything that might be important. They had lost touch with the criteria used for the selection of ingredients in earlier stages and preferred to leave the texts unrevised (Bamber 1998: 352). This reluctance to interfere with the contents made the texts increasingly unwieldy and illogical in their classifications. One of the characteristics of popular belief is its contradictoriness, fragmentation, dispersal, multiplicity, and difference. The general messiness of the manuals is not a sign of lazy editing but an index of the "unsystematicness" of this knowledge as well as a tribute to all teachers who have contributed to the corpus.[9]

In 1895, King Chulalongkorn intended to make the royal texts on Western medicine available to the general public, but the project of publishing the medical texts ceased shortly after it began. A royal edition eventually appeared in 1908. From the middle of the nineteenth century, Christian missionaries had been introducing Western medical research, which almost immediately reached the court through the *Bangkok Recorder*, published by the missionaries. Articles appeared on the circulatory system, fever, and diseases such as malaria and smallpox (Davisakd 2002, chap. 1). Fifty years later, at the end of the nineteenth century, the uphill battle to publish texts on "traditional" Thai medicine make it clear that Western medicine was displacing "traditional" medicine, at least in the capital's medical schools. Eventually, many decades later, the court-based knowledge of medicine and pharmacy was given a new lease on life in 1957 when the Ministry of Education permitted the Wat Pho traditional medical college to open (Mulholland 1987: 14–18). In recent years, schools that teach traditional medicine at Wat Mahathat and other places in the provinces have opened as traditional medicine has become more marketable.

One way to understand what happened to Thai manual knowledge in medicine over the half century is to see it as undergoing a reclassification in the central Thai "library" of knowledge, similar to the fate of the Jatakas, the birth stories of the Buddha allegedly narrated by the Buddha himself. Confronted with new historical knowledge about Buddhism from Western scholars such as T. W. Rhys Davids and E. B. Cowell, the court removed the Jatakas from their status as religious teachings and reclassified them as pre-Buddhist folklore, a genre of literature (Jory 2002). They continued to be respected, but ceased to have value as orthodoxy. In the case of the medical manuals, they were consigned to the category of "indigenous" medical knowledge until holistic medicine was revalued and appreciated again later in the twentieth century. The medical manuals were not malleable enough to absorb the new medical knowledge from the West. In fact, however widely used and respected in the countryside, they became for the court and the Westernizing elite a trope of "tradition" and "Thai-ness" in contrast to the "modern" and "scientific" valuations carried by Western medicine. Research on the ensuing political use of Western medicine in the decades following the change of government in 1932 has only begun to probe what this meant for the relationship between knowledge and power in twentieth-century Thailand (Davisakd 2002).

Manuals on Warfare and the Arts of Strategy

Treatises on warfare were reproduced at the Burmese as well as at the Thai courts, and it would not be surprising if historians found similar treatises in the Cambodian and Laotian courts. Thai historians date the original version of the *Treatise on War* (*tamra pichai songkhram*) to the late fifteenth century in the reign of a king known to have conducted trade with the ruler of Benares and the Coromandel Coast. These trading relations via Muslim merchants led to the court's importation of Brahmans, with their knowledge of *sastra*. The manual on warfare was later revised in the late sixteenth century by King Naresuan, whose feats on the battlefield against the Burmese have earned him a place in the Thai pantheon of hero-kings.

War strategies in the manual format were very schematic. The manuscript copies of the Burmese and Thai treatises on warfare contain illustrations of battle formations in the shape of a crab, dragon, lotus, garuda, and other figures, but there is virtually no sense of temporal change. Possibly the formations were mnemonic devices for keeping in mind troop positions taken from the most potent mythopoeic symbols of Indic lore. The Thai treatise also discusses trickery, that vital item in the arsenal of any military force. Outsmarting the enemy by stealth and cunning was as important to victory as weapons or numbers, so an itemized list of tricks is proffered to the military commander.

In 1825, at the beginning of the Third Bangkok Reign, the Front Palace prince, who was the younger brother of the king, sponsored a new edition of the *Treatise on War*. According to the prince, the *Manual of War* was in short supply; the texts were hand-copied rather than printed, and there were few such copies by this time. Revising and reissuing the manual would ensure the defense of Buddhism, the stability of the kingdom, and the longevity of the dynasty (Damrong 1969: 3–4). By its very nature, the manual contained secret knowledge, supposedly accessible only to those qualified to use it, such as military commanders, so copies were limited. Damrong says, though this does not appear in the Front Palace prince's preface to the manuscript, that the manuals on warfare composed or commonly utilized during the late Ayutthaya period were overwhelmingly in the nature of Vedas, mantras and spells and incantations (*khongkraphanchatri*). Thus the study of manuals that actually concerned strategies and methods of war had declined. This, surely, was at least one cause of Ayutthaya's loss to the Burmese army" (Damrong 1969: [3]). That is to say, this knowledge amounted to superstition and demonstrated the enfeeblement of military prowess that ultimately resulted in Ayudhya's defeat.

About fifteen years later, a very different military manual came into the Thai court. In 1841, Prince Chutamani translated an English work into Thai that was given the name *Artillery Manual* (*tamra pun yai*) and published for the first time in 1923 (Phrapinklao 1970). Reprinted in 1970 at a royally sponsored cremation of a major general who had worked his way up through the ranks of the artillery division,

Artillery Manual represents an early episode in the modernization narrative of the Thai army. Part 1 might be described as a history of European artillery, from medieval military engines to flintlock pieces that came into use in the middle of the eighteenth century. Part 2 of the treatise contained instructions on drill formation and included commands printed in English. Part 3 was concerned with warship cannons and fixed artillery for fortifications, of no small interest to a harbor-based state fated a decade later to be confronted by European gunboat diplomacy. It was later recalled that the Front Palace Prince was frequently away down river maintaining his cannons and fortifications. In the 1840s, the court was worried that Britain would use force to revise its treaties as had been the case in China, and indeed, this is exactly what happened. Did the Westerners who watched with bemusement as Prince Chutamani drilled his troops in the 1840s and 1850s have any idea that he had extracted the commands "Quick march!" and "Inward, about face!" from *Artillery Manual* translated from English?

In the twentieth century, discourses of security and self-protection that meant something other than armed conflict became important. The key word here is *yutthasat* (Skt. *yuddha sastra*)—literally, "the arts of war," but often translated as "strategies" or "strategies and tactics." This translation is not quite acceptable, because it misses out on root meanings of *yudha*, a term of Vedic origins that has connotations of armed might, warfare, fighting. In fact, the name of the kingdom that precedes Bangkok on the central plains, Ayudhya, incorporates this same morpheme, a fitting name given that the thirty-three kings of Ayutthaya are said to have fought seventy wars in 417 years, or about one war every six years (Battye 1974: 1).

In the last twenty-five years or so, the arts of strategy (*yutthasat*) have acquired new meanings to do with the tactics people can use on a personal level in managing their lives, whether it is jostling with competitors in the business world or with rivals in the civil service. One has to be able to maneuver, and thus *yutthasat* might be defined as strategies of maneuverability in a world filled with competition and conflict. The economic boom in Thailand in the late 1980s and early 1990s created a huge market for business manuals, whether translated from English, as were some of Lee Iacocca's marketing manuals, or from Japanese, of particular interest for insights into corporate strategies.

The manuals translated from Chinese via Taiwan or Hong Kong exploited the many versions of *Romance of the Three Kingdoms*, which had long been popular for dealing with everyday problems on a personal as well as on a business or professional level (Reynolds 1996b, 1997). Earlier this century, when one of Thailand's most prolific authors wrote his own version of *Romance of the Three Kingdoms*, he proposed that the *Romance* itself was a kind of *sastra*, because knowledge of its contents yields knowledge of the self as well as of others (Yakhop 1992, preface).

In the wake of the 1997 financial crash, we now have a multitude of "strategies" (*yutthasat*) for dealing with the crisis, which is seen to be one of culture, the environment, and health as much as it is economic. The long military history of this term for "strategy" recommends *yutthasat* as efficacious for all sorts of nonmilitary purposes. The recommended methods include tricks, strategems, and "amoral" techniques for solving problems and getting the better of one's rival. These methods have nothing ostensibly to do with the state's institutions for defense and maintenance of public order, yet they, in my view, are linked to the way the Thai state has contributed to a public discourse of strategy and tactics. If we think of the pocketbooks on the arts of strategy as self-help manuals to parry the blows of modern life in business and the bureaucracy, we can identify some very Buddhist themes in them about the "underlying assumption of perfectibility, or at least the potential for self-development of any who would learn and practice" (Turton 1991: 172). Knowledge that leads to this self-improvement, which is a knowledge that challenges notions of fixed social hierarchies, is available to everyone, irrespective of class. One of the mantras of modernity is that everyone has the potential to develop (Turton 1991: 168).

The place of incantations, curses, mantras, "magic," and discourses of invulnerability in the panoply of military practices, the so-called arts of war, is worth further consideration, because in the Thai countryside today, these practices have not yet been consigned to the dustbin of history. Prince Damrong commented that the prevalence of these practices and the absence of freshly edited copies of the *Treatise on War* combined to enfeeble the Siamese rulers at Ayudhya. Yet we find in popular usage, in the countryside, in the hands of those very same men whom the kings and their commander-nobles levied to defend the

Buddhist realm, practices that might be called "incantations, curses, mantras, and 'magic.'" These practices helped the foot soldier to face up to his fate, for "there was no legally sanctioned way to remain a lay member of Siamese society without participating in its wars" (Battye 1974: 7). The poor foot soldier had recourse to evasion by flight or debt-bondage, but if forced into the field despite the cunning measures he might take to avoid conscription, he would come prepared with all the defenses he could muster.

This manual knowledge of invulnerability can make a man feared and attractive, perhaps attractive because feared, and it offers insights into a neglected aspect of Southeast Asian warfare, namely, masculinity and warfare. "It could be argued," says Andrew Turton, that "if 'intimidation' and 'surveillance' are major and related means of the exercise of power then popular ideas of 'invulnerability' and 'invisibility' are among their opposites, in thought certainly, but also occasionally in political practice" (Turton 1991: 176). These manuals of invulnerability constitute a type of local knowledge (science, art, technique) that codifies phenomena in a way that is pervasive, deep-rooted, and connected. Transmitted in the form of verbal formulas (*katha*), the most powerful knowledge comes from teachers who store it partly in written books (Turton 1991: 156, 160).

The knowledge is proof against weapons (swords, spears, axes, clubs, guns), but also against other modes of human attack (fists, and magic, too), against superhuman attack by spirits, and against natural dangers (fire, tigers, bears, poisonous snakes, insects). Some formulas are dedicated to forms of social confinement (escape from the prisoner's yoke, ropes, going without food), and some formulas are said to be proof against fear. By far, most formulas are designed to protect the body from penetration (bullets, spears) and to ensure that if the skin *is* broken, the wound will not be fatal (Turton 1991: 159). These discourses of invulnerability must be understood in terms of ideas and practices about the body and the self. They have to do with "endurance, pain, confidence, courage, and risk-taking," and with "individual potentiality and capacity for self-improvement," and thus they are a sort of rural variant of what the business tycoons think they are getting from Lee Iacocca's marketing maxims, or the advice from *The Romance of the Three Kingdoms* on how to be more cunning in the business world.

At the popular level in rural Thailand, we find a "focus on memory for all sorts of accumulated knowledge: the characteristics of weapons, animals, other people, assessment of odds, and of appropriate physical and social skills and behaviours in risky and often solitary situations" (Turton 1991: 163). In younger men, there is boastful competitiveness and bravado, or "fairground virtuosity"; in older men, one finds quiet confidence in this accumulated knowledge. These older men with special powers, who are teachers, village abbots, headmen, irrigation chiefs, and so on, develop social followings and entourages. They teach and share their knowledge, and they are talented in mobilizing others (Turton 1991: 171). Turton does not mention the "man of prowess" paradigm. He simply delivers an impressive accumulation of detail about what being a "man of prowess" entails. In the process, he glosses what manliness might mean in the northern Thai countryside.

One of the central Thai terms for invulnerability knowledge includes a word (*chatri*) that is a variant of *ksatriya*, a metaphor and metonym for male bravery and fighting skill. *Ksatriya*—the warrior caste and all it stands for—has here been pulled into the rural domain and re-formed into something related but distinct from the elite manifestations of "warrior" (*ksatriya*). The question that arises here is of the degree of ambiguity and subversion at work in this appropriation of "warrior." A northern peasant leader exhorts his followers to "fight like *chai chatri* (warriors)," appropriating the elite ideology of *ksatriya*, of which *chatri* is the popular variant. At the same time, the peasant leader's call to fight may be read as the ennoblement of Thai popular notions of masculinity (Turton 1991: 158–59). This line of thinking raises questions about the larger connections between popular, masculine notions of invulnerability, which we can associate with rural life, and defense of the Buddhist realm, which we have seen was the preoccupation of the king, aided by senior monks and the *Treatise on War*.

Turton, who is a cautious anthropologist, declines to experiment with the possibilities. He does not mention "soldier" or "army," preferring instead to take the reader in the other direction, away from elite and statist phenomena. But I find it difficult to avoid the conclusion that the manuals of war periodically updated by the court were intended to systematize military knowledge and, in doing so, subordinate the heterodox and potentially threatening discourses of invulnerability available to everyone. "Systematize" means that the elite sought to discipline these discourses/practices of invulnerability but also exploit them at the same time. Thai commanders needed to draw on the bravado and the "fairground virtuosity" of rural men and the ennoblement of popular masculinity of those who practiced these discourses of invulnerability. There is a strong case here for the connectedness of elite and popular levels in matters of war and security rather than their bifurcation.

Manuals on How to Behave, How to Be Modern

Manuals of etiquette might be described as cultural grammars of behavior telling people what they should and should not do. The Three Worlds cosmology contains instruction of this kind. It itemizes the consequences of improper conduct, the bad *karma* that comes from failure to respect elders or teachers, or from acting without loving-kindness and compassion. A Khmer manual (*tamra*) of behavior, the *Gatilok*, composed in the early twentieth century, was a similar compendium of ethical knowledge, promulgating Khmer Buddhist ethics for monks, officials, and ordinary folk.[10]

In 1913, Jaophraya Phra Sadet (Pia Malakun), a Thai nobleman, produced a manual of manners, *Characteristics of a Properly Behaved Person*, which became a fundamental text of the national curriculum in a subject known as "Public Manners/Behavior" (Phra Sadet 1987, 1999). In the late 1980s, Thai people of forty to fifty years of age could still remember the ten principles of *Characteristics of a Properly Behaved Person*: neatness; do not act indecently (includes table manners, how to dress); show respect; behavior should inspire affection; be dignified; deportment that is pleasing to the eye; be good-natured; do not think only of yourself; act honestly and be trustworthy; do not behave badly (i.e., stay away from alcohol, opium, hemp, gambling). Most of these principles are very bourgeois and very Buddhist.

Born in 1867, Pia Malakun played important roles in Chulalong-korn's reform program, particularly in the Department of Education, where he worked for Chulalongkorn's brother, Prince Damrong, and later as private secretary to Damrong when the latter became Minister of Interior in 1892. He acquired a pedigree education, having been one of the first students at Suan Kulap School, established for the aristocracy and headed by Damrong, and he was ordained at Wat

Bowonniwet, the monastery favored by the royal family to the present day. He also helped establish the system of craft schools as well as an organization that grew into the mass-based Teachers Association of Thailand (Khurusapha). He believed that behavior was as important in learning as physical education, Buddhist studies, and arts and crafts. When Prince Vajiravudh went abroad to further his education in England, Jaophraya Phra Sadet accompanied him as his personal attendant. In Vajiravudh's reign, he became head of the civil-service school, which had evolved from the elite cadet corps for royal service (the Royal Pages Bodyguard Regiment), and when he died, in 1916 at the rather young age of forty-nine, he was Minister of Education.

The system of mass secondary education introduced as part of King Chulalongkorn's reform program at the end of the nineteenth century was still evolving in schools often situated in the monasteries that had been the kingdom's institutions of learning in premodern times. The graduates of these schools went on to serve in the burgeoning bureaucracy, and some of them had come from families in which their parents had almost certainly been uneducated—hawkers, petty traders, perhaps even peasants and market gardeners. In the two decades from 1900 to 1919, the Thai bureaucracy more than tripled, to eighty thousand people. *Characteristics of a Properly Behaved Person* was a manual designed to teach them how to behave in Siamese "polite company," in the office, and in their public duties. There is no doubt that the reformers wanted to preserve the high moral content that had distinguished the curriculum in the monastery, which had been the education institution in premodern times. Learning to read and write had always entailed learning how to behave correctly, and *Characteristics of a Properly Behaved Person* continued that practice, albeit in a new institutional setting.[11]

To explain the appearance of *Characteristics of a Properly Behaved Person*, we need to go beyond the needs of the new system of mass education, however. In the 1830s, when Western imperialism was yet having only an indirect effect on the way the Siamese elite saw itself, two poets wrote verses offering instructions on deportment. One of these, by a high-ranking prince-monk and court poet, was inscribed on a wall in a Bangkok monastery sometime before 1834. The other, *Proverbs for the Edification of Women*, was an extensive list of dos and don'ts for commoner wives written by Sunthorn Phu, a male poet.

These versified manuals of deportment were steeped in the hierarchy of the time: the wife must defer to the husband; she must not dress in an alluring manner so as to attract the attention of other men; she must take care to reflect well on her husband's reputation; and so forth.

There is a lot about *Characteristics of a Properly Behaved Person* that is Buddhist, and not simply because early-twentieth-century Siam was largely a Buddhist society. I am thinking particularly of a manual of behavior that every young man who had been a monk had been exposed to—the Vinaya, the book of monastic discipline. A new edition of the Vinaya was produced in 1916, an edition we might call the reformers' edition, because it was edited by Chulalongkorn's younger half brother, Prince Vajiranana Varorosa, who would spend his entire adult life as a monk. The Vinaya sets out hundreds of rules. Many of these are about ascetic-specific behavior: how to wear the monastic robe; what material goods can be legitimately possessed by the monk; how to spend the day. But there are also rules about personal grooming, how to conduct oneself when eating (who to eat with, when, and what). These rules are remarkably detailed—how to take up a mouthful of food with the fingers, when to open the mouth (not before the mouthful is brought to the mouth). And don't speak with your mouth full! The monk is instructed in how to walk, and it is said even today that new ordinands, especially the short-timers who ordain for only a few weeks, are conspicuous in the clumsiness of their gait. There are many rules about association with women. A monk is allowed to cross a river in a boat with a nun but is not allowed to travel up- and downstream in the boat with her. The monk should not go off to observe armies in battle dress, although he may visit a soldier-relative if it is an emergency. Anything that looks like fun is out of the question, such as gambling, children's games, and playing that produces a loud noise, or tumbling, wrestling, boxing, and racing like elephants or horses, and no throwing (baseball and cricket are out). "Animal-like knowledge," such as love magic, is forbidden, and the monk should avoid making garlands and latticeworks of flowers, which have to do with courting. The words "not" and "should not" and "the bhikkhu shall not" appear very often.

A high percentage of Thai Buddhist men had endured this regimen for the three months of their monkhood, and their families, who had visited them and received them at home after their disrobing, had witnessed the effects on the behavior of their sons, nephews, and brothers. Although from hindsight *Characteristics of a Properly Behaved Person* looks very bourgeois, very middle class, it is not difficult to see this manual of behavior as having been partially determined by a centuries-old adherence to "proper behavior" and no more or less class-based than the monastic code of discipline that was one of its precursors.

By the time the absolute monarchy was removed in 1932, a project of populist self-making was already underway at the hands of the new civilian-military elites that Chulalongkorn's reforms and civilizing mission had produced. The author that usually commands most attention for this topic is Luang Wichit Watakarn, a Sino-Thai whose early education had taken place in a monastery and who had worked his way up the bureaucratic ladder by putting his many talents in the service of several Thai governments, most of them military, from the early 1930s until his death in 1962. With a distinguished diplomatic career already behind him, Luang Wichit made his own contribution to the Thai public sphere through his historical and biographical writings, his plays, and his essays on personal and national self-making. He was put in charge of the Fine Arts Department from 1933 until 1937, when he was made Minister of Education, in which capacity he presided over the refashioning and promotion of Thai culture.

Several of his "how-to" books celebrate personal achievement and offer a step-by-step plan to personal growth and success. These include works written before World War II, such as *Brain*, first published in 1928, as well as similar publications that preoccupied him after the war, such as *The Power of Thought* and *The Power of Determination* (Wichit 1998, 1999, 2001). These are manuals for everyman and everywoman on how to cope with the pressures and setbacks as well as the opportunities and potentialities of everyday life. These "how-to" books, which he never stopped writing, were cobbled together from Western readings and movements he had encountered during his diplomatic career overseas and from Buddhist precepts and homilies that came naturally to him from his early education. They instruct the reader in how to be modern, how to be a productive worker, how to cultivate the self to achieve self-control as well as one's personal ambition. Every activity, including recreation, should be purposeful, and the day's routine was set out for readers in a timetable of duties and tasks. *Brain* even contains blank charts and schedules that the willing reader is invited to complete according to his or her own needs. There are regimens for knowledge, observation, good judgment, argument, self-control, clear thinking, and right reasoning.

After World War II, Luang Wichit published *Success in Life*, which contained brief biographies of international figures who had made an impact on their countries and on world history: Eamon DeValera, Stalin, Mussolini, Hitler, Gandhi, Nehru, Chiang Kai-shek, Mao Zedong, Zhou Enlai, and with passing mention of other American and European leaders. The political proclivities of these men—republican, fascist, communist, pacifist—mattered little to Luang Wichit. For him what was important was that these were all "event-making men," in Sydney Hook's words, who wielded power effortlessly and turned it to their own ends and who could inspire lesser mortals to great feats (Hook 1945). The qualities that distinguished these men—strength of mind, powers of concentration, self-confidence, and willpower—were outlined in a 1928 work, *Great Men*, which was reprinted four times by 1932 (Wichit 1970).

These "how-to" manuals belong in the genealogy of premodern manuals of behavior and deportment such as the Vinaya as well as its modern variants, but in their advice on self-making, they also have affinity with the homegrown success literature of the "Sino-Thai migrant makes good" variety and with the arts-of-strategy pop-psychology manuals. The public self was also the object of official attention in various other ways in the decades after 1932. In 1936, and again in 1948, the government produced manuals of citizenship to advise the Thai people on how to observe their duties and realize their rights as citizens in the new era (Connors 2003: 45).

Conclusion

It seems clear, looking across the decades from the early nineteenth century to today, that some kinds of manual knowledge were discredited by encroachments, challenges, threats, and desires thrown up by the encounter with the West. Certain kinds of manual knowledge—military and medical, for example—were disparaged in favor of something that looked more efficacious, fashionable, or "modern," as defined at each historical juncture. In almost every case, this attitude served to disparage the local in favor of something foreign. In the past twenty years, as globalization has reigned supreme, things have swung around in the other direction: small is beautiful; low-level technology has cachet; and local knowledge is superior to high-tech, more costly knowledge; rural know-how, or what is construed as indigenous knowledge, has become privileged and highly valued, even as it must be supplemented by appropriate technology from abroad (Reynolds 2002: 328–33).

I do not think there is anything inherent in manual knowledge that excludes or resists the foreign. On the contrary, it would seem from several of these examples that manual knowledge facilitated the incorporation of foreign material and served as a medium for domesticating it and making it look ordinary, practical. This is particularly the case with technology or science, which is domesticated by packaging it in the manual format. In the massive changes to medical education during the half century from the 1880s, the content of the pharmacological textbooks (*tamra*) became almost completely based on Western medicines, thus devaluing the indigenous medicinal plants that had been used for centuries (Prathip 1998). Manual knowledge "captured" foreign material; it was a mechanism for adopting and adapting foreign material.

What was the role of printing? At first, one would think that printing freezes this type of knowledge and makes it less malleable. But printing also facilitates the circulation of manual knowledge by making it more accessible. At the same time, printing also encourages self-instruction and eliminates the need of the teacher. If you can get your hands on a manual, you can teach yourself. Of course, this contradicts the notion that manual knowledge requires a guru—a teacher or an instructor—to enable it. The proliferation of self-help manuals that do not require teachers is a distinctively modern transformation of the genre, as the author (or publisher) of the manual becomes the teacher. Printing also increases competition by multiplying strands of this knowledge, which in turn creates new markets. Printing technology has changed the market.

The historian is better off thinking of manual knowledge not as the preserve of a particular class but rather as belonging on a continuum up and down the social, political, and religious hierarchy. This is clear, for example, with the treatises on war, which were closely guarded at court, and with the manuals of invulnerability. The court treatises and the rural man's manual must be understood dialectically, as mutually defining, rather than as separate and distinct traditions of knowledge. The late-nineteenth-century aristocratic reformers regarded the early-nineteenth-century *Treatise on War* as both "out-of-date" (i.e., backward) and "lower" and "less developed" because of its magic, spells, and incantations. Yet, in earlier centuries, magic, spells, and incantations were valued sections in court treatises on warfare. And magic, spells, and incantations belong in the arsenal of the strutting young man in the countryside who seeks to prove his prowess and protect himself against his enemies.

Manuals in themselves are not orthodox or authoritarian. They are polysemic, amoral, apolitical. If a teacher, or institution, or powerful or socially influential individual insists on using manual knowledge in a particular way, then the knowledge in the manual is bent for certain purposes. Institutions, as we saw in the case of the Sangha's book of discipline, the Vinaya, are inclined to format knowledge as an aid to standardization and reproducibility. But we cannot look to knowledge formatted in this way for insights into a particular politics.

Finally, how a society keeps its knowledge, reproduces it, or circulates it, helps us understand that society. The social meaning of the manuals—who uses them, how, and in what conditions— helps us map out a typology of knowledge as practiced at both the elite and popular levels and everything in between. What happened to the older forms of this manual knowledge as they passed through the transformative half century from about 1880 through 1930 is of interest especially in comparison with what is happening to local knowledge today, when its popularity and prestige has never been greater.

Manuals facilitate teaching and learning. They facilitate the exercise of power and of authority, and yet they are also empowering. They are aids for living, and for helping people take care of the body, the soul, and the mind.

Notes

1.   Thus an astrology manual was called *tamra horasat*; a medical manual was called *tamra phettayasat*; a manual of magic/sorcery was *saysasat*.
2.   Gethin 1998: 208. I am indebted to Jason Carbine for this insightful reference.

3. Bamber (1998: 341) is not explicit, but I expect that the Thai term *saksit* is behind his term "power."

4. Brun 1990: 44. It is along these lines that Pollock suggests that *sastra* has the double meaning of "rule" or "book of rules," on the one hand, and "revelation," on the other (1985: 502).

5. Cf. Pollock (1985: 504), who frames this issue slightly differently for the Indic *sastra* literature.

6. For a circumspect discussion of the political, social, psychological, and religious importance of astrology in Thailand, see Nerida Cook's chapter 8 in Reynolds 2002, especially pp. 192–96.

7. See Chetana Nagavajara 1994: 32–46 for a discussion of orality and memory.

8. Successive studies by Western scholars of Thai medical practice increasingly emphasise the diversity of these traditions, with Bamber (1989: 14) being gently critical of Brun and Schumacher (1987) for regarding the northern medical tradition as a variant of the central tradition rather than one that stands on its own.

9. On the "unsystematicness" of popular knowledge, an insight of Antonio Gramsci's, see Andrew Turton 1991.

10. Hansen 2003: 817–21. I am indebted to Penny Edwards for this insightful reference.

11. Wyatt 1969, chap. 5, is still a very eloquent statement of the relationship between monastic education and the larger society.

THE DIALECTICS OF
GLOBALIZATION

11

National Identity and Cultural Nationalism

I n 1989, the fiftieth anniversary of the name-change to Thailand
of the country then known as Siam was a nonevent. The 1980s
marked many important anniversaries in the history of Thai
nationhood: the golden jubilee of the "revolutionary coup" of 1932
and the Bangkok bicentennial in 1982; seven centuries of the Thai
writing system in 1983; the fifth-cycle birthday of the Thai king in
1987; and commemoration of the longest reign in Thai history in
July 1988. Yet, while all of these were significant public events in the
Thai calendar, the fiftieth anniversary of the country's name-change
came and went in Thailand with little interest shown by the government,
the media, or the public, despite the fact that the 1939 name-change
has always been controversial because of the ethnic chauvinism it
reflected and fostered.[1] Precisely because the name-change marks a
discontinuity in modern Thai history, it presents an opportunity to
explore Thai identity, a concept promoted by many Thai governments
since 1932 as integral to Thai nation-building.

It must be said that Thailand is not the only country in the
region to change its name either to capture and channel ethnic loyalties or to adjust to international realities. An extensive search was
launched for a name for Taiwan, for example, when its position in the
international community was radically altered in the early 1970s
following the normalization of relations between the People's Republic
of China and the United States of America. The new international
alignment was an opportunity for China, which had claimed Taiwan
as part of China since 1949, to assert its claim linguistically. In
1986, when Taiwan was joining the Asian Development Bank, as
many as sixteen names came under consideration, some of which were

unacceptable either to China or Taiwan. Even the punctuation carried semiotic force and became a point of contention. The names with parentheses, such as "China (Taiwan)," were favorable to the island's government, because the emphasis was on China, while the titles with commas, such as "Taiwan, China," were not, because they suggested that the island belonged to "the other" China, precisely the claim that China wished to assert (*AWSJ* 1986). The name of the island state would be an emblem of its sovereignty no less than of its relationship to China.

Elsewhere in Asia, Cambodia, Sri Lanka, and Myanmar have all changed their names in recent years. In the case of Cambodia, the country's name has changed four times—in 1970, 1975, 1979, and 1990—as different regimes have sought to signal particular leadership styles and international alignments or to disassociate themselves from deposed predecessors. Ironically, given the importance Cambodian governments have attached to the different terms, Cambodia and Kampuchea both derive from the same Sanskrit name of a tribe in northern India, the Kambuja, reputedly ruled by a monarch. The different transcriptions are for foreign as much as for domestic consumption. As with important toponyms in Thai history, such as Ayudhya, Sukhodaya, and many others, the Indic name Kambuja, incorporated into the Cambodian origin myth, echoed ancient Indian history. Wordplay in the naming of principalities was a time-honored way of conferring status and pedigree on Southeast Asian namesakes.

"Ceylon" and "Burma" were legacies of the colonial period. They were favored by the English-speaking, British-educated elites that came to power with independence essentially because Westerners were used to these names, and they were easy for foreigners, particularly English speakers, to pronounce. But, in fact, Ceylon was always called Lanka by its Sinhalese majority ("Sri" is a Sanskritic honorific), and "Myanmar" is a closer rendering than "Burma" of how Burmese speakers pronounce the name of their country. The decisions to adopt "Sri Lanka" and "Myanmar" represent a late phase in the continuing process of decolonization as former colonies of the Western imperial powers further authenticate their separation from colonial masters. Such decisions also signal internal power struggles as the dominant ethnic groups have laid claim to national symbols, the country's name being one such symbol with a high profile in the arena of international affairs and diplomacy.

Thus, a country's name is relational not only to its past and the ethnicity of its inhabitants but also to the names of its neighbors, allies, and enemies. In an important way, names of countries, like the composition of national flags and anthems or the location of boundaries, are indicators of sovereignty. They denote a particular space on the earth's surface and the collectivity of peoples living in that space. National identity is a relational category brought into existence by comparison and contrast, and a country's name serves a vital differentiating function in that existential process.

Yet, identity is an amorphous concept, confused with self, essence, and uniqueness. Ross Poole rightly traces popularity of identity to the psychoanalyst Erik H. Eriksen, who proposed the term to link social life and self-conception (Poole 1999: 44). Of all the disciplines, anthropology, sociology and developmental psychology have been the most methodical in developing analytical procedures for studying identity. In understanding how notions of authority develop in the Thai family, for example, personhood takes shape against the backdrop of peoplehood in the national community but is seen to be a more ambiguous and conflictual category than national identity (Reynolds 2002, chap. 10). Poole's confident statement that national identity is "the primary form of identity," because it underlies and informs all other identities, is more contentious, however, because not all nation-states have managed to fuse language, culture, and polity so successfully that "who we are" stems in some fundamental way from national identity (Poole 1999: 67–69).

Official promotion of Thai identity within the country through the schools and the media has tied the notion of identity so closely to government policy and the marketing of the country domestically and abroad that its use as a category for analysis is questionable. At first sight, Thai identity seems too ubiquitous, too naive, and too vulnerable to official propagandizing to warrant serious study. On closer inspection, however, the articulation and promotion of Thai identity by state institutions raises a number of interesting issues. The notion of Thai identity can be interrogated for its history, its presumed content, and its deployment in fashioning cultural, ethnic, and linguistic policy at the national level.

Culture Policy

"Siam" had been a term used from ancient times by other countries such as Champa, China, Cambodia, and Vietnam to designate the kingdom dominated by the Thai-speaking peoples of the Chaophraya River valley.[2] The kings, until the end of the absolute monarchy, encouraged the use of Siam and prided themselves on being rulers of a diverse ethnic population. When the cabinet of the government under Field Marshal Plaek Phibun Songkhram decided in 1939 to change the name to Thailand, it was responding to nationalistic aspirations elsewhere in Asia and to concepts of nationhood that were already in international circulation. By monopolizing the nation semantically for Central Thai speakers, the ruling elite sought to instill pride and equality with the West in the country's citizenry (Anderson 1978: 212). "Thai" also had the advantage, significant in that era of high colonialism, of meaning "free." Through the decades, Thai prose writers, poets, and orators, whether they be royalists or socialists, have delighted in the wordplay of *thai/that* as it rolls off the tongue, the term "free" being a near-homophone of the term "slave."

The name-change in 1939 was but one manifestation of culture policy during the first Phibun government from late 1938 until 1944. In a series of edicts that had a bearing on the national culture fostered by the government of the day and all governments since then, the Phibun regime sought to motivate the country's citizens to pursue national goals and to inculcate in them a sense of collective selfhood. The edicts, called *ratthaniyom* or Cultural Mandates, followed a practice under the absolute monarchy of issuing *phraratchaniyom* or "royal prescriptions."[3] In fact, the impulse of the ruling elite to prescribe cultural norms and to set guidelines, if not fix the conventions, for artistic creation was a deep-seated one during the absolute monarchy, especially during the four decades or so preceding 1932, when printing technology encouraged cultural production outside of the court's auspices, thus enabling commoners to challenge the court's prerogative to validate that production.[4] As the power of the center grew and expanded, the Thai state encountered regional and minority cultures different from its own. These encounters engendered reflection on what the dominant, national culture should be, and by the 1930s, the government was undertaking strenuous efforts to codify and promote a national culture.

The name-change from Siam to Thailand was promulgated in the first Cultural Mandate, issued on 24 June 1939, the seventh anniversary of the coup that overthrew the absolute monarchy. A second Mandate, of ten days later, set out in the most general terms what would constitute treasonous activity—for example, revealing to foreigners information that might be damaging to the nation or acting against the national interest as agents or spokespersons for foreign governments. This edict helped to foster the belief in the ruling elite and the population at large, a belief later translated into legislation, that certain political groups and political activity—most notably, communist—were "un-Thai" or even "anti-Thai" and thus dangerous, subversive, and destabilizing. By this Mandate, Thai identity and national security were forever joined.

The fourth Cultural Mandate, of 2 August 1939, discouraged use of the terms "northern Thais," "northeastern Thais," "southern Thais," and "Islamic Thais" in favor of "the Thais." The fourth, sixth, and eighth Mandates, of 1939–40, were designed to channel loyalties towards national symbols such as the flag, the national anthem, and the royal anthem, and to encourage the prosperity and well-being of Thai as against Chinese or ethnic minorities. The words of the national anthem had to be approved by the army, another instance of the way identity was to be framed in terms of national security. With economic nationalism one of the hallmarks of the first Phibun regime, the fifth Mandate, issued in December 1939, exhorted Thais to support the indigenous economy and to practice economic self-reliance. Others of the Mandates issued until early 1942 were aimed at building national growth and unity through hard work; encouraging people to use and respect the national language; prescribing proper dress, both Western and Thai; motivating people to engage in healthy, productive activities in their daily lives; and nurturing the protection and care of the young, the old, and the infirm.

The Cultural Mandates were foreshadowed in the House of Representatives under the previous government in 1937 and later realized in two royal decrees of 1940 and 1941 that gave legal force to the more detailed and specific measures affecting the country's citizens. The first decree, entitled the National Cultural Maintenance Act, defined culture as "qualities which indicated and promoted social prosperity, orderliness, national unity and development, and morality of the people" (Thak 1978: 256). The second decree, Prescribing Customs for the Thai People, defined decorum and improper dress. Certain kinds of clothing, such as sarongs, sleeping garments, "only underpants," or, for women, undershirts or wrap-arounds worn in public places, were deemed to be damaging to the prestige of the country (Thak 1978: 257). So common was some of this clothing, even in the capital, so appropriate was it in a tropical climate, and so long had it been worn, as one may see from Thai mural painting through the centuries, that it took more than a pronouncement by the state to prohibit people from wearing it. The much-ridiculed orders cited by Likhit (1988: 94) that husbands should kiss their wives before going to work and that women should wear hats and gloves in the Western manner were refinements of the Cultural Mandates. During the war years, the wearing of hats became a particularly contentious issue, with those refusing to observe the custom subject to official investigation and reprimand. The old custom of chewing betel was also officially discouraged, along with spitting on roads and sidewalks (Thamsook 1977: 33). Through such measures, old Siam was to be transformed into new Thailand.

In her accounts of the first Phibun period, Thamsook Numnonda emphasizes how the Cultural Mandates sought to create in Thai citizens a sense that their country had entered a new epoch. In this new society, the citizenry would cultivate the values of enterprise, propriety, decorum, self-reliance, valor, purity, and a sense of what the military regime deemed to be "civilized." The regime utilized print and broadcast media to promulgate these values, and thus the Cultural Mandates and the numerous supplementary orders, decrees, and acts that followed penetrated that part of Thai society exposed to such media in a way unprecedented in Thai history. Everyone who could read a newspaper or listen to a radio was aware of what the government wanted of its citizenry. The Department of Public Information (called the Department of Publicity in some English accounts) was the key bureau for disseminating the new culture policy, and its publications have left historians with a wealth of source material. The Great Communicator himself, Prime Minister Phibun, had a hand in producing some of the cultural programs. Annette Hamilton has shown how Thai adeptness at using new media technology—print, radio, film, and video—has given a particular and peculiar shape to national identity in Thailand by spawning lurid and violent images that defy what the national identity managers, beginning with King Vajiravudh, have sought to forbid and repress (Reynolds 2002, chap. 12).

With the elite and the tiny urban bourgeoisie striving to align themselves with imagined international norms, the cultural pronouncements by the new military government finessed an ambiguity. While the intent of some pronouncements was to preserve a genuine and unique Thai culture, the intent of others was to override some cultural practices—so-called improper dress, for example, or betel-chewing—in order to save embarrassment in the eyes of Westerners, who might regard such practices as uncivilized (Thamsook 1978: 238). Parity with the West was a preoccupation of the Thai elite at this time, and parity applied to dress and deportment as well as to sovereignty. Being a pure and genuine Thai, however that was to be defined, had to be balanced against behaving in a way deemed acceptable to Westerners. In fact, this Western standard was as much a construction, an imagining in the minds of the ministers, officials, and bureaucrats who conceived and implemented the culture policy, as the "Thai culture" being put forward as authentic and innate. Where, for example, did the culture managers acquire the idea that husbands should kiss their wives before going to work? From Western films and photographs? The pathways by which the ruling elite of the country, which had never been a colony, came to insist on Western—mostly British?—tastes, fashion, and deportment have only recently received the serious study they deserve (Peleggi 2002a; Thongchai 2000c).

The edicts advanced the interests of the dominant ethnic group, the Thai-speaking people of the central plains, as against the interests of other Thai-speaking populations and the ethnic Chinese. The concept of Thai culture as the national culture masked cultural and ethnic heterogeneity in the name of national uniformity, but it was a contrived uniformity. In matters of language policy, for example, the promotion of Central Thai as the national language in the ninth edict involved a certain amount of artistry, since a large majority of people considered and still consider their mother tongue to be other than Central Thai.[5] The ban on use of the region-based nomenclature for Thai groupings—northern, northeastern, and southern—in favor of "Thai" assumed that language and ethnic differences could be eradicated, or at least reduced, merely by outlawing the common names for those groupings.

Central Thai, especially in its written form, has been perhaps the preeminent component of identity for those seeking to define and promote a national culture, as Tony Diller has argued (Reynolds 2002, chap. 4). In any taxonomy of culture, Thai language inevitably ranks first (e.g., Samnakngan khanakammakan 1988: 38). Seminars are convened to discuss "Thai linguistic culture," whose advocates understand that a national language is not naturally present but is something that the education system must nurture (e.g., Khana anukammakan 1983: 95). Moreover, keeping Central Thai in its preeminent place has involved considerations of national security, as we shall see shortly.

Another dimension of cultural production in the new Thailand was artistic expression in addition to the populist drama, music, and literature fostered by the Office of the Prime Minister and the Department of Public Information (Charnvit 1974: 39–40). Government patronage of the arts under the new post-1932 leadership intensified through the work of the Italian sculptor Corrado Feroci (Silpa Bhirasri) (1883–1962), who had been in Siam since 1923 and who was instrumental in establishing the Academy of Fine Arts in the Department of Fine Arts (Peleggi 2002a: 194n.58). The use of a foreigner in such a position signaled a commitment to modern forms of expression, which really meant Western art forms (Michaelsen 1993: 64). Phibun's eleventh Cultural Mandate was designed to encourage art appreciation by decreeing that Thai citizens should attend art exhibits (Michaelsen 1990: 35). On the production side, the government sponsored art competitions, such as the one included in the annual Constitution Fair established in 1938.

The robust bronze sculpture "Farmer Sowing Rice" (ca. 1940), a work by Sitthidet Saenghiran, was a product of these prewar years.[6] As manifest in the numerous sculptures and paintings of Feroci's students, government patronage of the arts during the first Phibun period put the stamp of heroic realism on art production that is still visible to drivers suffering through Bangkok traffic as they slowly circle the Democracy and Victory monuments built in this period. Sculpture and monuments were particularly important, not only because Feroci himself was a sculptor but also because their public exposure gave expressive force to the state ideology being fashioned.[7]

Another general point to make is that the claim inherent in the Cultural Mandates, i.e., that they were shaping a national community, is a debatable one. Chai-anan Samudavanija has argued that the Mandates strengthened the state to the detriment of the nation by forging an ideology for the state (Reynolds 2002, chap. 3). In giving that ideology a specifically Thai character, the ruling group was not only endeavoring to rationalize and legitimize its accession to power but also to undermine the influence of the Chinese bourgeoisie that had supported the change of government in 1932. Moreover, the Cultural Mandates had the effect of subordinating local or folk cultures, which had enjoyed more freedom of expression under the pluralistic name of "Siam," by placing them in a hierarchy of importance with the state-defined "national" culture at its apex. Thus, what is at stake in the Mandates is the creation of a state identity separate from, and in large part hostile to, society, an identity that the ruling group could mobilize against those social forces that might undermine its power base. In Chai-anan's analysis, promotion of state identity stunted the growth of civil society and thus of Thai constitutionalism by placing severe constraints on cultural expression (Reynolds 2002, chap.3).

Finally, one may ask if the prescriptions initiated new culture policy or simply consolidated and codified notions of identity and ethnic Thai preeminence that had been aired in the Thai media during the previous two decades. B. J. Terwiel's reading of tracts of the 1930s suggests that the Phibun government's Cultural Mandates embodied what popular writers had been saying for some time (Reynolds 2002, chap. 5). These writers with a populist touch, the most famous of whom was Luang Wichit Watthakan (1898–1962), serve as a bridge between the royalist nationalism of King Vajiravudh (r. 1910–25) and the nationalism of the military and civilian regime of the late 1930s. Chamrat Sarawisut, for example, sought guidance from Luang Wichit on nationalism and took for granted that intrusions on personal behavior, such as prescriptions in the eleventh Cultural Mandate on how Thai citizens should ration their working day and spend their spare time, were justified if they served the well-being of the nation.

Also manifest in this writing are totalitarian tendencies that shaped allegiances between the Thai people and their military rulers. Already in the early 1930s, the Ministry of Defense was publishing in its house magazine articles by Phibun himself on the world crisis that called forth a strong leader as much as "an animal herd needs its leader" (Charnvit 1974: 35, quoting a Thai source). In the mass media were certain predisposing sentiments and attitudes that help account for the ease with which the coup group translated ethnic Thai chauvinism into public policy.

Some of the measures that flowed from the Cultural Mandates were certainly popular; others were regarded as silly and laughable. But the nationalistic culture programs did not thrive simply because they were conceived and promoted in an ingenious, persuasive way. To the extent that it was successful, the cultural engineering struck a chord in the mentality of the day. It remains for other researchers to explore the question of the national culture programs in this crucial period as an instrument of rule by the Phibun regime, sometimes nurtured, more often imposed, by government ideologues. At the same time, the national culture, as an elemental expression of individual and collective selfhood, was something that many citizens of Thailand recognized in their individual lives. Thai culture and its twin, Thai identity, cannot be explained away simply as concepts stage-managed by the state.

The National Cultural Maintenance Act of 1940 was followed by the National Culture Acts of 1942 and 1943, which established the National Culture Council, a body that enjoyed ministerial status and was headed by the prime minister himself.[8] In the 1950s, Phibun, by then prime minister for the second time, established a Ministry of Culture (Barmé 1993: 147), and there has been a stream of commissions, councils, boards, and bureaus charged with national culture policy since then. Sometimes responsibility for the promotion of national culture has rested with the Office of the Prime Minister, an indication that the highest authorities in the land view Thai culture with grave concern, sometimes it has rested with the Ministry of Education, sometimes with both, and sometimes with other ministries such as Interior and Health. There is much bureaucratic competition for patronage of the national culture of Thailand, not least because the monarchy is one of Thai culture's most visible, most generous, and most grateful icons.

Thai Culture Magazine (*warasan watthanatham thai*) began publishing in the early 1960s under the auspices of the Ministry of Education. By the late 1970s, the journal's advisory body was headed by the director-general of the Department of Religious Affairs and his deputy, a sign of the role Buddhism plays in defining the national culture in Thailand. The journal's contents are typical of the several journals devoted to celebrating and promoting Thai national culture. Everything from food to folk culture, Thai martial arts, national holidays, and regional languages and rituals are presented in an unscholarly style for a popular readership. Very occasionally an article on Muslim culture in the south slips into the magazine.

Falling within the ambit of national culture policy, the term for Thai identity (*ekkalak thai*), with its connotations of uniqueness, is a comparatively recent coinage from English, dating back only to the 1950s. The term does not appear in the 1950 edition of the *Dictionary of the Royal Institute* reprinted through 1968, but it does appear in a dictionary by Charoen Chaichana of 1958 with a gloss explaining its precise equivalence to English "identity."[9] This midcentury concept of Thai identity had a progenitor, however. Long before this time, in the twilight years of the absolute monarchy, the aristocracy had scanned the colonized horizons of its kingdom and effected a taxonomy of the "national character of the Thai people" (*uppanisai khong chonchat that*). In 1927, in a much-quoted speech about the Siamese political system and what Western social science now calls political culture, Prince Damrong Rajanubhab invoked history to aid in this enterprise, proposing that what distinguished the Thai people from Burmese, Vietnamese, Cambodians, and Malays was (in his English usage) "love of national independence, toleration, and power of assimilation" (Damrong 1975: 6).

What gave bureaucratic if not linguistic life to the concept of Thai identity was the violent coup of 6 October 1976 and the return to power of right-wing soldiers and politicians. In January 1977, the same month as the marriage of the Thai crown prince, an event that might have been timed to help restore some much-needed shine to the monarchy after the events of the previous months, the Office of the Prime Minister began issuing a monthly magazine, *Thai Identity* (*ekkalak that*). In style and content, *Thai Identity* articulated the now-familiar shibboleth that a strong national Thai culture was vital to the country's independence and sovereignty. Articles on Thai music, social values, maps, the writing system, kites, customs, popular Buddhist texts, and, in the manner of *Thai Culture Magazine*, a token piece on southern

Thai Muslims, found their way into its pages. In the magazine's self-conception, *Thai Identity* was a kind of cultural soldier in the battle to defend Thailand as it tried to hold its own against the pressures of Western culture.

The prestige of state institutions had been badly damaged by the way the military had returned to power after the violence of 6 October 1976, and the magazines reflected a campaign to restore some of the lost prestige. Nineteen seventy-seven was also the year that national identity made it into the National Education Plan (Connors 2003: 14). Something more sinister had been at work, however. Right-wing ideologues who backed the coup had portrayed elements of the left through the 1973–76 period as un-Thai, even anti-Thai, and in some cases as less than human. Government patronage of Thai national culture now served the cause of social order and stability by demonstrating the state's commitment to what every Thai citizen was deemed to hold dear, namely, Thai identity. Thus, the concept of Thai identity, with its disarming ring of transcendence and permanence, has a specific history and conditions of existence.

A royal decree of 25 February 1979 established the National Culture Commission, the body charged with coordinating the work of the numerous bureaucratic units responsible for national culture.[10] The commission's charter laid down ten functions it was to perform in the preservation and promotion of Thai culture, stating that culture, "a distinctive characteristic of nationhood," was essential in maintaining the stability and integrity of the nation (Khanakammakan 1982: 721–24). It must have been about this time, but possibly as late as 1980 or 1981, that the government established the National Identity Board (*khanakammakan soemsang ekkalak khong chat*), which was responsible to the Office of the Prime Minister.[11] Many of the activities and programs involved with promoting national culture have since come within the board's purview. Each year, it publishes a long list of books and pamphlets in Thai and English on such topics as festivals, royal coronations, the ordination ceremony for Buddhist monks, and biographies of prominent figures in the royal family. Under the auspices of its Subcommittee for the Propagation of Thai Identity (*khana-anukammakanphoephrae ekkalak khong thai*), the board has since 1977 also produced radio and TV programs. In the published transcripts, the programs are classified under the rubric of Nation,

Religion, and Monarchy (*chat satsana mahakasat*), the three pillars of nation-state ideology in Thailand.

The publication of English books and pamphlets, the first of which, *Thai Life*, came out in October 1981, for the consumption of foreign visitors, suggests something else about the government's promotion of Thai culture, namely, the connection between Thai culture and tourism. The marketing of Thai culture domestically and to foreign visitors subsidizes or underwrites the cost of efforts to preserve Thai culture, which is seen to be under threat by Western ways. Like many developing countries with monuments and ruins, Thailand sells itself abroad by commodifying its culture and tradition.[12] In the historical moment in which this is taking place, the assimilation of non-Thai groups—as well as the exclusion or subordination that flows from a policy of assimilation—may be held in check, as it is disadvantageous to tourism to conceal ethnic differences. In the promotion of the country for foreigners, it is important to go so far as to dramatize *some* ethnic differences, because they enrich the tourist adventure by making it more diverse and attractive. Thus, the packaged tourist jaunt to northern Thailand includes the villages of ethnic minorities in the hills, despite the fact that highland-lowland relations have historically not been particularly harmonious. Some of the most bitter conflicts in the country over management of the ecosystem are occurring in the highlands.

In January 1981, the National Identity Board began to publish *Thai Magazine* (*warasan thai*), a glossy collection of essays distributed, at least initially, without cost. As with *Thai Identity*, respected academics are persuaded from time to time to write an article for *Thai Magazine*. The contents are decidedly royalist, with articles on past and present monarchical accomplishments, but the coverage also includes, at the opposite end of the socioeconomic spectrum, "The Peasant: Backbone of the Nation" (October–December 1981). The current official formulations of what is quintessentially Thai never fail to include the peasant. And, as Philip Hirsch has pointed out, the village is deployed discursively as the irreducible "natural" community for governing the rural population and for managing rural development (Reynolds 2002, chap. 11).

Culture has a very broad definition in the mission of *Thai Magazine*. More than customs, rituals, and traditions, culture encompasses Thai ingenuity and enthusiasm, which in the 1980s was supposed to lead to economic progress and NICdom, Thailand's place among the New Industrialized Countries of the region. "Technology and Thai Products" was the title of an article published in 1988 (April–June). Thus, it is not surprising to find "the culture of work," a domain in which the social scientist prescribes the interrelations of human resources, Thai social values, and the requirements of the modern economy that will maximize productivity (Samnakngan khanakammakan 1988: 89–102). In this vein, the Ministry of Education in December 1989 sponsored a "Festival of Arts, Crafts, and Vocational Studies" under the theme "Education for NICdom" (*kansuksa su khwampennik*) and produced thousands of bumper stickers for the occasion, an example of the way the education bureaucracy could mobilize culture for national economic goals. NICdom itself, with its complex strands of bourgeois consumption, economic performance, and global personhood, was thus being stamped onto Thai identity. At the same time, Thai identity has shown a great capacity to resist and modify the global products favored by multinational enterprises.[13] The path from kingdom to NICdom is not without pain, however, as news from Thailand of lethal toxic spills and environmental degradation makes headlines in the international media.

In the fourth issue of *Thai Magazine* (October–December 1981), the editors, seeing that the public was confused about the concept, addressed the question of the meaning of Thai identity by providing a brief etymology of *ekkalak*, an etymology I found notably inadequate for researching this essay, and a concise schema of the concept's constituent parts. After due deliberation, the National Identity Board took the foundation for Thai identity to be nationalism (*chat*), whose six components include (1) territory, (2) people, (3) independence and sovereignty, (4) government and administration, (5) culture, and (6) pride. It is not clear whether the six components are listed in an order of priority, but there must be some rationale or sequence, for the arithmetic procedure of adding two more components—religion and monarchy—between numbers 4 and 5 yields a new result, the eight-fold schema labeled "Thai identity." Other taxonomies of Thai identity—or "Thai-ness"—are even more elaborate after culture has been added to the nation-religion-monarchy trinity of Thai nationalism (e.g., Wira 1981, chap. 4).

Ethnicity

Thailand is hardly unique in being a country where the boundaries of the nation-state do not coincide with the extent of an ethnic population or a single speech group. The first two components listed in the national-identity construct are territory and people, and in virtually all discourses of nationhood, there is a tension between ethnicity and territory. In trying to manage this difficult problem, Thai government policies of the late 1930s and many times since then have sought to favor ethnic Thai and to exclude or subordinate other ethnic groups. It could be argued that this favored treatment of the dominant ethnic group creates barriers internally that mirror the boundaries or fences that demarcate the perimeter of the nation-state (Thongchai 1994: 170).

It is no coincidence that the Phibun government from the late 1930s was as active in dealing with the Chinese "problem" as it was in making claims on territories of its former empire that now belonged to French Indochina. The Phibun regime's assertion of Thai-ness in the circumstances of the late 1930s was translated into efforts internally to give preferential treatment to ethnic Thai as against ethnic Chinese. The Chinese as an alien economic force, held responsible for backward conditions, especially in the peasantry, was a construct to that historical moment and reached its apogee on the eve of the Pacific war (Seksan 1989, chaps. 4–5). This construction of Chineseness had begun in the reign of King Vajiravudh and derived from the hardening of the nation-state's borders, events in China becoming politically important to the overseas Chinese as well as to the Thai ruling class, and the concept of citizenry that went hand-in-hand with the nation-state.

A "pure" Thai-Buddhist society, uncontaminated by foreign elements, sat at the opposite end of this ethnic pole. Luang Wichit's historical works grounded this pure Thai-Buddhist society in the nation's life-history at Sukhodaya, thus demonstrating that an ethno-religious character specific to the Thai people had temporal priority (Reynolds 1991). Peter Jackson has followed debates in the 1980s over the Buddhist cosmography text that dates from the Sukhodaya period that suggest the pure Thai-Buddhist legacy of Sukhodaya is still very much contested terrain (Reynolds 2002, chap. 7). It is in this context of the modern, nationalistic meanings attributed to the early state of Sukhodaya that recent attacks on the authenticity of the putative first Thai inscription (e.g., Sujit 1988) have caused consternation among the official custodians of the nation's biography (Chamberlain 1991).

In the critical period of Thai national-identity formation, the Phibun regime had laid claim to territory in Laos and Cambodia as Thailand's own. To make its case, the military government issued a directive declaring that Vietnamese, Laotians, and Khmers who were Thai shared the same bloodlines (*yat phinong ruam sai lohit*). In a revealing document of late 1940, just after the Thai invasion of disputed Lao territories and western Cambodia, the Department of Defense asserted that these Vietnamese, Laotians, and Khmers were of the "same nationality" as the Thai, "as if they were of the same blood," and should be referred to as "our Thai brothers and sisters in Vietnam, Laos, and Cambodia."[14]

In some circumstances, this notion of "the same blood" has been stretched even further, and by no means are the proponents of the notion always from the armed forces. Sujit Wongthes, a prominent Thai writer and intellectual who helped to champion the return of the purloined Cambodian lintel in his publications, argues that Siamese (a term which he prefers to Thai) ancestry includes the Mon-Khmer peoples who preceded the Thai in the lower mainland. Sujit's "the Thais were always here" is a sarcastic riposte to claims over Khmer monuments in Thai territory as if they had actually been built by ethnic Thai (Sujit 1986).

Thai irredentism at the level of government policy thus has intriguing echoes in sentiments and yearnings for Tai affiliation among ordinary, if educated, Thai people. These yearnings quickly surfaced after diplomatic relations with China resumed in the 1970s, paving the way for visits to Tai "brothers and sisters" in the Sipsongpanna area of Yunnan, but they were also prominent in the 1920s and 1930s. In July 1940, the noted Thai ethnographer and autodidact Phya Anuman Rajadhon recalled how he had stood with a tour group at the confluence of the Mekhong and Ruak Rivers where the borders of Burma, Laos, and Thailand intersect. There he looked over to the opposite bank of the Mekhong and around him at the ancestral settlement areas of Thais now in the central plains, musing how the scattered Tai speech groups had come to be so different. In his epistolary account appended to the studies of Tai speech groups that resulted from this visit to the northern homeland, Phya Anuman remembers the moment with great affection and nostalgia, contributing with his words to the race memory that has entered the Thai discourse of nationhood (Anuman 1970a).

On 7 September 1945, at the conclusion of the Pacific war, the government of Pridi Phanomyong (1945–47) changed "Thailand" back to "Siam" in an effort to counter the semantic monopoly of Thai over other ethnic groups, thus asserting a more genuine national consciousness that would include all peoples within the country's borders, whatever their ethnicity (Anderson 1978: 213). At a time when England was pressing the Thai for heavy war reparations, the name-change might have been intended to signal to the British that the new government, in contrast to its predecessor, which had declared war on England under the name of "Thailand," was nonexpansionist and nonchauvinist (Preecha 1988: 17). After Phibun returned to office, "Siam" again became "Thailand" once and for all in 1948. On three occasions since then, however, the "Thai" vs. "Siam" issue has been debated during the drafting of new constitutions (1949, 1961, and 1974). As the extensive debates of 1961 indicate, what was at stake was the kind of national community the central government saw itself as fostering, with figures such as Luang Wichit defending the policies he embraced some twenty years previously (Suphot 1985). The persistence of the "Thai" vs. "Siam" issue also suggests that while alternative nationalisms have been marginalized, they are not dead and buried.

Just how and in what way military governments have been expansionist and chauvinist is open to question. It has been argued that Thai governments have not pursued irredentist policies in the manner portrayed by many historians. The primary aim of border security has been to remove grounds of conflict rather than to extend the country's perimeters at the same time that government strategies have sought to create "Thai" out of other ethnicities, as the late Gehan Wijeyewardene has argued (Reynolds 2002, chap. 6; Wijeyewardene 1990: 49).

Such strategies create resistance, as calls for ethnic autonomy by minority peoples vie with state demands for national integrity. Both the strategies and the resistance can take violent forms, as the case of the Lua in Cholthira Satyawadhna's pioneering study demonstrates (Cholthira 1991). The most populous highland group in Nan Province, with a history of rebellion against lowland encroachments, the Lua was a showcase for the Communist Party of Thailand (CPT) before its demise in the early 1980s, thus confirming simultaneously the long-standing government prejudice that non-Thai populations were subversive and that Communism was fundamentally non-Thai. Government policies in the 1980s to integrate the Lua into the nation-state have erected the kind of ethnic fences alluded to above and reversed the CPT policies that tolerated Lua cultural differences.

Anthony Smith has distinguished between two trajectories in the formation of nations, which he schematically associates with Western and Eastern nationalism (Smith 1986, chap. 6). His formulation builds on a dichotomy proposed several decades ago by Hans Kohn and holds that the Western concept of nation is territorial, whereas the Eastern concept tends to be ethnic. According to Smith's typology, ethnic nationalism is characterized by the successful transformation of ethnic into national ties. Smith thus sees the Western concept of nation as constructed whereas the Eastern type is "natural." But the very notion of ethnicity is a modern, Western concept, a product of the territorially bounded states in which elites have been obliged by the nature of the bounded unit to rule over diverse peoples. Smith's typology externalizes ethnicity, whereas it is in fact part and parcel of nationalist discourse everywhere. The modern national community, both Western and Eastern, was imagined as a new sense of ethnos, a kind of super-ethnicity (McVey 1984: 12). This new sense of ethnicity was to be inclusive, but it perforce rendered some population groups anomalous and thus laid the foundations for separatist movements.

Though never forced to cede all its sovereign powers, the Thai ruling elite bears many scars of struggle over territory, in part because it had to learn this kind of territorial nationalism during boundary disputes and conflicts over territory with the Western imperialist powers (Thongchai 1994). These disputes and conflicts have given it a sense of territorial selfhood, its geo-body. It is difficult to imagine how the ethnic nation could ever come into its own in Thailand, however significant Smith's criteria of "genealogy, populism, customs and dialects, and nativism" may seem in the Thai case (Smith 1986: 137). But the performance of classical and folk dances on the national stage, cherishing the supposed origins of the nation in the ancient kingdom of Nanchao in northern Southeast Asia, and the cultural populism sponsored by Thai governments over the past half century have all reinforced the "national imaginaire," in which the Thai national community evolved "according to its own inner rhythms" with "self-expressions and destinies [that] are radically different, even unique" (Smith 1986: 138).

The notion of a unique destiny for the dominant ethnic group enters into the nation's horoscope. Astrologers determined a horoscope for the new capital at Bangkok in the late eighteenth century, as Nerida Cook has pointed out, and this horoscope through the years has become the national horoscope conveniently binding together the destiny of Thailand's capital, its dominant ethnic group, the nation-state, and the present royal family whose ancestor founded the city and the present dynasty (Reynolds 2002, chap. 8). Nation-building is a process far from over, however, and debates about the national horoscope betray the extent to which the nation is a unified entity, especially in terms of its history. In spatial terms, moreover, such areas as the deep south of the country, with its Malay Muslim population, have a communal identity that continues to resist the guile and force employed by the Thai state to integrate them (Surin 1988).

Thus, there are still rifts and splits in *chat,* the Thai word for the shared linguistic and cultural traits that make up nationality. *Chat* derives from Sanskrit *jati,* whose root-meaning of "birth" has come into the Thai language carrying powerful resonances of bloodties and, most importantly of all, shared descent (Keyes 1976: 206). A study by the Malaysian scholar Tan Liok Ee has focused on corresponding terms in the Malaysian case in an effort to understand problems of legitimacy when the nation does not naturally coalesce with "ineluctable" communities. Her case study offers comparative perspective that may suggest a line for future inquiry with regard to *chat.*

In Malaysian nationalist discourse, two terms for nation/nationality vie with each other in dialectical conflict, underscoring the communal conflict between Chinese and Malays in modern Malaysian political life. Malay *bangsa* entered the Malay language early via Sanskrit and originally denoted legitimacy of royal descent. Later on, it came to mean "race" or "ethnic group." Thai language has the term *wong,* the same loanword from Sanskrit meaning "lineage," but *wong* was not destined to experience the same evolution in nationalist discourse as *bangsa.* Chinese *minzu,* a modern word not to be found in Classical Chinese, was coined via Japanese to evoke the concept of community held together by ties of descent, language, and culture that nineteenth-century Japanese and Chinese thinkers were confronting in the works of Western writers. Both Malay and Chinese have alternative terms for nation in the sense of an autonomous and sovereign political unit. These are *negara* in Malay and *guojia* in Chinese. In the Malaysian nationalist discourse, "the rhetoric of *bangsa* and *minzu* was consciously developed to assert (in the case of *bangsa*) or resist (in the case of *minzu*) dominance in the process of defining the claims of *negara/ guojia* on citizens and to claim a moral legitimacy for their respective positions" (Tan 1988: 45).

In the Thai case, there has been no overt contest for *chat*, which denotes the cultural community with its shared ties (*chat thai*). The nation-state ideology seeks to make this cultural community conterminous with the autonomous and sovereign political unit (*prathet thai* or *muang thai*), but the "fit" is not exact and requires constant tinkering and occasional coercion. As there is no explicit *bangsa-minzu* struggle in Thailand, we might then ask what the "other" is against which *chat* is mobilized. Is it the various minorities who straddle borders on the periphery and make it difficult for the nation-state to maintain its territorial integrity? Is it enemy *chat* on the other side of the borders, particularly the Vietnamese? Is it the ethnic Chinese within the nation-state? But what is "ethnic Chinese" when so many Thai citizens are Sino-Thai? Much has been written about the assimilation process in Thailand over the past two centuries, but little attention has been paid to assimilation's counterpart, namely, repression of Chinese identity and otherness, a psychic as much as a social and political repression. Some thoughtful research needs to be done on the psychological dynamics masked by the tiny hyphen in Sino-Thai.

Perhaps *chat* contains traces of all these "others" as well as any conceivable "other" that does not conform to the Thai-Buddhist-monarchical-territorial construct enshrined by the National Identity Board schema. In any case, *chat* is not a monolithic, self-evident entity that springs forth prefabricated to serve the cause of national unity and harmony. There would not be such a lively, well-funded, publicly patronized discourse about Thai identity if it were so self-evident.

Heritage

The reputation of Siam/Thailand in competition with other national cultures for civilizational status on the world stage has been complex in its creation. Along with many developing countries, Thailand has eagerly joined the memory boom by exploiting modern technologies of representing history and culture and by promoting and marketing heritage with a vengeance. The result is a distinctive "mythscape" known the world over (Bell 2003). The country is now known internationally as much for its appeal as a destination for cultural tourism as for its hedonism (Peleggi 1996: 433).

But long before international tourists attracted by historical parks and museums became vital to national economies everywhere for foreign exchange, heritage had figured in the Thai elite's conception of itself in relation to neighboring kingdoms and subordinate principalities. Among the duties of monarchs in the Indic world was the restoration of monasteries and other religious buildings as well as the upkeep and refurbishing of palaces and temples built by the ruler's ancestors. In the latter case, family pride was at stake, but in the imperative to preserve Buddhist buildings, sites, and images, there was a deeper, religious motive to make it possible for the radiant power of the Buddha to flow down through time (Byrne 1995: 271). In a religious world that recognized the impermanence of matter as a fundamental condition of existence, the monarch was obliged to conserve and restore Buddhist monuments in order to stave off the inexorable decay of the religion prophesied early in Buddhism's history.

Along with modern dress, a distinctive political system, and national culture, heritage was promoted as part of the nation-building project in the 1930s (Peleggi 2002, chap. 1). Much of this cultural heritage was created long before Tai peoples descended from the northern river valleys into the watershed of the Chaophraya River in Central Siam, however. From the ninth to the early fifteenth centuries, the Khmer empire held sway over much of Siam, particularly the northeast, where most of the older monuments were built in Khmer style. When the rising kingdom of Ayutthaya conquered Angkor in the fourteenth century, the victorious Siamese plundered the Khmer center for its artifacts and artisans. Sanskrit and Khmer loanwords entered the Thai language, and the styles of Buddha images and monastery architecture dating from this period manifest Khmer motifs and designs. From this date through French colonial control in the early twentieth century, after World War II, and through the period of the Khmer Rouge from 1975–79, Thai governments have expressed strong proprietary feelings, backed if necessary by the threat or use of force, about the western Cambodian provinces of Battambang as well as Siam Reap, in which Angkor is located.

Thus, what constitutes Thai historical heritage is problematic, as illustrated by the story told by Charles Keyes of a lintel stolen from a Cambodian monument at Phnom Rung now located in Thai territory (Reynolds 2002, chap. 9). The lintel was purchased by a private foundation and eventually ended up in the Art Institute of Chicago, where it was noticed by Prince Subhadradis Diskul, a distinguished art historian and a son of Prince Damrong Rajanubhab. In the ensuing uproar in the Thai media, the controversy over the lintel's cultural home—was it Thailand or Cambodia?—underscored how the historical record has become an emblem of national identity, just as the country's name, its monarchy, its language, and its territorial sovereignty have become emblems of nationhood. The case of the purloined lintel was assimilated to the history of Thai-Cambodian disputes so easily because of the lengthy history of the Thai court's proprietary interests toward Cambodia from the late eighteenth century (Peleggi 2001: 34).

Heritage for Thailand, especially in connection with the national imaginaire and as a focus for domestic and international consumption, was given its modern form during the reign of King Chulalongkorn (r. 1868–1910). By the last decades of the nineteenth century, the ruins at Ayutthaya, near the royal summer palaces at Bang Pa-in, were already a destination on sightseeing tours. The title of the provincial governor of Ayutthaya, "preserver of antiquities," pointed to his responsibilities as a de facto curator of the ancient site (Peleggi 2004: 141). In 1907, Chulalongkorn established the Antiquarian Society, whose avowed aim was to halt the loss of Siam's historical record in both its textual and monumental forms. While the king in his speech inaugurating the society blamed invading powers, particularly Burma, for destruction of the historical record, he spoke as a historian and curator who wanted to see history not only preserved but clarified and corrected (Chulalongkorn 2001). Actually, as Chulalongkorn's own reign has drifted further into past time, the material remains of the reign have acquired the patina of age worthy of ancient ruins. Wimanmaek, the king's teak mansion in Dusit Park, was rescued from its dilapidated state in the 1980s and transformed into a modern museum where "royalist mythology, nouveau riche aspirations, and historical nostalgia come literally under one roof" (Peleggi 2002a: 168).

During the reign of the fifth Jakri king's son, Vajiravudh (r. 1910–25), antiquarianism became a tool to foster the collective historical memory. Indeed, in the year after his father's speech establishing the Antiquarian Society, Vajiravudh had journeyed to Sukhothai and written a memoir in which he lamented the ruinous state of monuments bequeathed by the ancient Thais (Peleggi 2004: 142). It was in Vajiravudh's time on the throne that both the Fine Arts Department and, in one of the last official acts of the reign, the Archaeological Service were established (Peleggi 2004: 148). When the king's uncle, Prince Damrong, left the Ministry of Interior in 1915, he took charge of the Wachirayan Library and proceeded to collect chronicles from every corner of the kingdom and deposit them in the library, thereby making the capital at Bangkok the historical archive of the fledgling nation-state.

Over the past thirty years, Thailand has grown wealthier and more enmeshed in the international economy, thus equipping it to devote more resources in taking care of the heritage it has been cultivating since the late nineteenth century. In the late 1970s, the then-current national economic development plan declared that heritage conservation was of prominent concern. The aim was to prevent looting of sites and the illegal traffic in antiquities, while simultaneously stimulating tourism, a labour-intensive industry that would provide jobs for young, semi-skilled workers. One reason heritage has been such a success story in Thailand for governments, labor, and consumers is that heritage management has not been imposed as an "inappropriate ideology transfer," as has been the case elsewhere in the world (Byrne 1991: 273).

As a result of the economic policy decision of the late 1970s to make heritage a national resource, four sites—at Sukhothai, Ayutthaya, and the Khmer sites at Muang Singh and Phnom Rung—were developed as historical parks. Additional sites followed in the early 1980s. By the year 2000, the Office of Archaeology and National Museums maintained ten historical parks (Peleggi 2002b: 22, 27). By 1991, UNESCO's World Heritage List included the two most famous historical parks at Sukhothai and Ayutthaya, thereby enhancing Thailand's competitive position as a tourist destination. In addition to its strategic geopolitical location on international trade routes that stretch from eastern Asia to the Middle East and Europe, Ayutthaya is celebrated in its promotional literature as a royal center, one of many examples that could be cited of how the cultural capital of the incumbent monarchy is "borrowed" and invested in the creation and promotion of Thai national heritage. Curiously, the historical park in Thailand that commands most patronage from domestic Thai tourists is the Ancient City (Muang Boran) at Samut Prakan, thirty kilometers east of Bangkok. Established in 1972 by the Thai importer of Mercedes-Benz automobiles, the Ancient City is an agreeably contrived mini-Thailand containing hundreds of replicas in reduced size of historical monuments and buildings from all over the country arranged iconically in the form of a miniature map of the country that takes about three hours to walk through (Peleggi 2001: 78). Historical parks allow heritage to be performed in a vivid and tangible way.

Especially since the economic boom of the 1980s, and even through the economic gloom of the late 1990s, heritage in Thailand has become big business. Glossy magazines, commercial advertising, and tourism promotions market *moradok*—the Thai word originally meaning "inheritance" but decreed by officialdom to stand for the English word "heritage"—in the family, the village, the provincial center, and the nation (Askew 1996: 186). Inevitably, conflicts have arisen between the conservators and developers, on the one hand, and those wishing to preserve the community or the neighorhood, on the other. This has been the case particularly in Bangkok, the destination for many international visitors, where land prices are high and where the economic pressure is most intense to make property earn a profit.

In 1995, the Rattanakosin Committee proposed a plan for the development of Bangkok centering on the Old City on Rattanakosin Island where the Grand Palace, the Palace of the Front Palace Prince (now the National Museum), and various monasteries were built in the late eighteenth century (Askew 2002: 292–94). As is often the case with urban redevelopment in areas of dense population, the impetus was to "clean up" the Old City by removing the wooden buildings, deemed to be unsightly, and the hawkers who crowd the city pavements. Opposition to the plan began even before its unveiling, owing largely to the presence in the immediate vicinity of Thammasat and Silpakorn Universities. This opposition became deafening in 2001, when the council of Thammasat University decreed that the undergraduate programs would be relocated to another campus at Rangsit on the capital's northern outskirts (Askew 2002: 295). In effect, this was a conflict between Bangkok as an ancient site and a modern metropolis. As in many other examples of the creation of Thai national heritage, the royalist history of Rattanakosin Island was cultural capital that could be invested for private as well as public gain, even if it meant the destruction of neighborhoods, street life, and picturesque river frontage.

National Security

It is typical of the magazines devoted to culture discussed earlier that, apart from the traditional martial arts, topics even remotely associated with the military are absent. And the eight-fold schema that defines Thai national identity fails to mention the military explicitly. But it does not take much imagination to see why the military in the past saw itself as the guarantor of the robust health of the eight components. The integrity of the territorial self needs to be maintained, the people require protection, independence and sovereignty need to be defended, administration and government must be stable for efficient rule, and national pride as well as respect for religion need policing from time to time. Thai culture and its subtext, "the Thai way of life," has become as sacred an object as the monarchy. Armed force shields these objects, so vulnerable because so sacred, and ensures their survival. The preservation of Thai-ness (*kanraksa khwampenthai*) requires the defense of Thai-ness. Thus the Thai military is a trace, an absent presence, in each of the eight components.

The martial ethos infusing the eight components has a lengthy history, which would have to be told properly beginning with the reign of Vajiravudh if not before. Already in the 1930s, prior to the Phibun regime's Cultural Mandates, popular patriotic literature was drawing on the Japanese martial code of *bushido*. During the time Phibun was minister of defense, the military had staged dramas and films portraying the vital role soldiers were playing in the country's destiny. The irredentist movement, usually identified with Phibun's claims on French territories in the early 1940s, had begun to emerge some years previously, thereby framing the military's ambitions for permanent rule with motive and rationale (Barmé 1993: 108–14). The pervasive militarist imagery was too heavy-handed for Corrado Feroci, under whose direction the Victory Monument was designed and built after the war with France in the early 1940s. When forced to comply with the addition of soldiers to the base of the monument, Feroci referred to it as "the victory of embarrassment" (Michaelsen 1993: 69).

Thai identity in this formative period was thus already laden with notions of military valor and the ultimate sacrifice of life itself in the national interest. Luang Wichit's writings took episodes of national liberation from the historical record. Ayutthayan history in particular provided shining examples of warrior heroism in the person of King Naresuan and, at the end of the era, Taksin, both of whom were victorious over Burmese aggressors (Reynolds 1991). The proclamation on 12 May 1944 of a national code of valor must therefore be seen not so much as a strategic imitation of Japanese military values in order to ingratiate the Thai government with the Japanese occupation command as yet another codification of the militarized political culture already underway for at least two decades (Thamsook 1977: 36–37).

Another side to the new Thailand of the 1930s that bears on the issue of national security is the way opposition groups and movements, and specifically the Socialists and Communists, were characterized as alien to Thai society and culture. Anti-Communism was deeply embedded in the country's elite from the time of the absolute monarchy, so deeply that until recently studies of Thai Marxism, socialism, and Communism have typically been studies of anti-Communism (Kasian 2001). The Communist label made it easy for government authorities to attribute the activities of radical opposition groups to foreign powers. By shifting the inspiration of radical movements to an external, alien source, military governments were able to declare those movements to be non-Thai, "unnatural" to the Thai social fabric, and thus qualified for exclusion from the national community. This meant incarceration, of course, or, at the worst, death by execution. It helped such an enterprise to be able to define the content of "Thai," hence the codification of Thai identity by Field Marshal Phibun's Cultural Mandates and General Prem's National Identity Board.

One of the keywords in Thai military jargon as well as Thai nationalist discourse is stability (*mankhong*), as is evident in the semantic weight put on the term in the Thai name for the Internal

Security Operations Command (ISOC) (*kong amnuaykan raksa khwamnwnkhong phainai*). The term for national security is in fact *khwammankhong haeng chat*. Stability and security being near-synonyms in this discursive formation, the same term applies to the stability of the family as to the security of the monarchy (Wira 1983: 108–9). One of the early Phibun regime's greatest successes was a popular radio program in the 1940s in which two male characters, Nai Man Chuchat and Nai Khong Rakthai, engaged in a dialogue about what we might call national security for the masses.[15] The clever banter of Nai Man and Nai Khong covered all the pet topics of the era, everything from Chinese dress to nutrition and the right of the nation-state to self-defense. It is by such means as these programs that the spit-and-polish of military discipline has been fused with common Thai notions of tidiness, propriety, and orderliness (*khwamriaproi*).

Military order and bourgeois orderliness are amiable companions, a hint that what made military coups successful in Thailand was not merely control of the instruments of force and violence. When the coup group of 23 February 1991 named itself the National Peacekeeping Council, it used *khwamsangop riaproi* to reassure the public, a term that loses something in translation as "peacekeeping." The term signaled a return to what the military regarded as the status quo (i.e., to military rule before the elected Chartchai government came to office in 1988) and sought unsuccessfully to neutralize the force required for a military takeover.

Among the innumerable instances that illustrate the way the Thai military has nurtured national culture for reasons of national security, I would cite the attendance of the secretary-general of the National Security Council at a seminar in 1983 to celebrate the seventh-century anniversary of the putative invention of the Thai alphabet. Squadron Leader Prasong Sunsiri, who later became minister for foreign affairs in the government of Chuan Leepai in the early 1990s, was present as an active participant, presenting a paper on "Thai Language and National Security" (Prasong 1984). On that occasion, he made a number of pronouncements about the necessity of controlling as well as facilitating the study of foreign languages in Thailand, the need to monitor language study because incorrect usage is damaging to the social order, the fractious consequences to the Thai body politic of non-Thai language use, and the extent to which knowledge of Thai language is instrumental to the smooth functioning of government. Thus language, which falls under "Culture" in the National Identity Board's schema, was a matter of vital concern for the chief official of the National Security Council.

When it was in power, the Thai military was assiduous, aggressive even, in promoting Thai national culture and national identity in an effort to enshroud itself with the trappings of authenticity and legitimacy. The genius of the military and the state security organizations lay in having nurtured a mentality in the bureaucracy and social institutions that embraces the very values the military cherishes. National security, it might be said, was the tiered parasol that shades and protects the National Identity Board's eight-fold schema. Many of the values nourished by the culture bureaucracy through the education system and the mass media are equally at home in army camps and police barracks, in monasteries and schools.

This aspect of Thai identity—the way it has come to serve military ambitions—is inadequately theorized in Thai studies and thus deserves more thought, as does the political economy of Thai national culture programs, about which little has been said here. This is not to affirm that the way in which national security and identity connect is permanent or inevitable, but that it has been produced over many decades in distinct historical moments of great complexity. In an epoch when the middle class and the business tycoons insist on democratic institutions and a laissez-faire economy, the national-security–national-identity formation from time to time frustrated the institutions of parliamentary democracy, despite the fact that it was the military itself, rather than the radical movements portrayed as such, that was alien or "unnatural" to the Thai body politic. Was it not Bakunin who stressed how separate the military is from the people, having been transformed into enemies of civilian society by military education and set apart by the ridiculous embellishments of regiments and ranks, making all soldiers seem like clowns?[16] Though the agency and process of its complex creation are beyond discussion here, a discursive formation of security came into being in twentieth-century Thailand that permeates social and public life and embraces culture as well as defense and public order (Streckfuss 1998).

Many of the more than 65 million people living in Thailand have notions of Thai identity in their heads, and the last question we might raise here is how this notion came into consciousness. One theme evident from this discussion is that there is something hegemonic about Thai national identity. The meanings of Thai identity, in other words, are given to consciousness by those in power, by ruling elites, and by state managers, and much academic research by social scientists within Thailand over the past two decades has been devoted to exposing the character of hegemonic practices that have resulted. While there is plenty of evidence to show how the hegemony of Thai national identity has operated since the late 1930s, more attention might be paid to the implications of the proposition. To attribute the construction of Thai identity entirely to cultural programs of the Thai state is to subscribe to the theory of false consciousness. In other words, what Thai nationals believe about Thai identity, what they feel in their heart of hearts about their food, their language, their kinfolk, their religion, their monarchy, and so on, has been planted there by state institutions to cultivate a sense of belonging, thus making the governing of those 65 million people easier and more peaceable.

To put the inquiry into another register and meet this criticism of false consciousness, one would have to develop a concept of the speaking subject, while giving due regard to the institutional determinants of identity formation. Under what circumstances and at whose prompting do Thai speakers find Thai identity natural and meaningful in their personal experience? How do Thai speakers, however specified in terms of class, region, or gender, mediate Thai identity and its discursive practices? Subjectivity that may be called "Thai" is constituted by many discursive practices and not only the ones sanctioned by the National Identity Board and the National Culture Commission.

A related criticism of Thai identity as a hegemonic construct is that the instrumentalist intent assumed in such a construct is misleading. Society does not cohere simply because the nationalist ideology, fashioned by the ruling elite, strikes a responsive chord in the population. The concept of a dominant ideology assumes an over-integrated, overly systemic view of society. Dominant ideologies are not "clear, coherent and effective" but are fractured and contradictory in most historical periods (Abercrombie et al. 1980: 156–59). In the spaces between these fractures appears an anarchistic and disordered world, full of unscrupulous power-holders and unpredictable spiritual forces. The mass media in Thailand pictures this world as lurid and violent rather than as reassuring and serene, which is the way the colorful promotions of the culture bureaucracy would have it.

Another theme that needs to be developed more fully is resistance to the way identity of either the ethnic or national kind is promoted and internalized. How do people, particularly at the regional and local level, contest and struggle against the process? Or is Thai identity simply not an issue for them? We might better understand Thai identity as primarily a negative force, the name for that which resists the pressures and intrusiveness of what is foreign and alien. The power of Thai identity lies in its imagined capacity to differentiate inside from outside and, in the process of doing so, to hold the subversive Other at arm's length.

More research on this issue is in order along the lines of the reception of Pancasila rhetoric in Bali. The five principles of Pancasila formulated a pan-Indonesian nationalist ideology whose intent is to integrate the multi-ethnic, multi-religious polity. But local interpretations of this ideology often "belie the official image of an unenlightened floating mass." Using the theoretical insights of Gramsci and Bakhtin, Carol Warren has shown that the dominant ideology thesis presumes that subordinate classes are much more affected by hegemonic cultural production than is in fact the case. Precisely because the rhetoric that surrounds hegemonic cultural production has heavy symbolic loading and seeks consensual response, it is "particularly susceptible to subaltern reconstruction" and subversion (Warren 1990: 201).

Subordinate classes can respond creatively and constructively to the most hierarchical, repressive, and paternalistic dominant ideologies. Perhaps the way Thai national identity has been studied here and elsewhere has dwelt too much on hegemonic notions of Thai identity and thus has given them too much agency, even if these notions have often rather too ingeniously been reformulated by elites from folk and ethnic traditions that lie far from the center of power.

Notes

1. Preecha 1988 gives the most exhaustive account of "Thailand" vs. "Siam," including a history of usage and the way the two names serve as markers of different positions in contemporary Thai political debates.

2. It is commonly understood that *sayam* in Thai is a translation of "Siam" in English (or its equivalent in other foreign languages), but this may not be so. If the three

treaties made in 1855–56 with Great Britain, the United States, and France are compared, it is noticeable that *sayam* occurs only after the de Montigny Treaty of 1856. In the two earlier treaties, we find *krungthep* or *muang thai* rather than *sayam*. It is not unlikely that *sayam* was coined during Mongkut's reign and is thus as colored by political considerations as the country's naming in 1939 or 1948. I am grateful to Professor Yoneo Ishii of Sophia University for this suggestion (personal communication, 4 September 1991).

3. The edicts have been translated into English in Thak 1978: 243–54. The most comprehensive discussion of them is in the thinly disguised sardonic wit of Thamsook Numnonda (1977, chap. 3; 1978); see also Likhit 1988: 94–99 and Barmé 1993, chap 6. Likhit and the contributors to Thak 1978 translate *raithaniyom* as "state-ism," which is a literal rendering of the Thai term. In terming the edicts Cultural Mandates, I follow Charnvit 1974 and other historians (Thamsook 1977, 1978; Wyatt 1983), while recognizing that the Thai term makes no mention of culture.

4. Although the history of culture policy pursued by Thai ruling elites both during the absolute monarchy and after 1932 has yet to be researched comprehensively, many instances have already surfaced of how state norms and conventions were contested. See, for example, Reynolds 1994 and 1991b.

5. For additional examples of linguistic engineering during the first Phibun regime, see Thamsook 1977: 34 and 1978: 240–41.

6. See the frontispiece in Reynolds 2002; the work and its sculptor are discussed in Michaelsen 1993: 69–70.

7. See Michaelsen 1993, which provides an extensive account of Feroci's influence on That art and art education.

8. These acts are translated in Office of the National Culture Commission n. d. The 1942 act is also in Thak 1978: 258–60.

9. As explained in Charoen's *Standard Dictionary and Thai Congress* (*Pathanukrom kham mattrathan lae banyat sap phasa thai*), Kasem Bannakit Bookstore, 1958, *ekkalak* entered the Thai language at the instigation of the Coinage Committee (*Khana kammakan banyatsap*), chaired by Prince Wan Waithayakorn (Kasian 1991). The term commonly used for identity in Modern Thai today is *atthalak*.

10. Translated in Office of the National Culture Commission n.d.: 28–29. The Thai text is in Samnakngan khanakammakan 1988: 123–25.

11. For references in this section on the National Identity Board, I am indebted to Vacharin McFadden of the Australian National Library, Canberra. I have been unable to date the establishment of the board more precisely, but I suspect that the change of government under General Prem Tinsulanonda in early 1980 brought the National Identity Board to prominence.

12. There are a host of ways in which Thai women have come to exemplify Thai tradition, such as beauty contests, beginning with the Miss Siam Pageant inaugurated in 1934. Searching for beautiful women throughout the country was an official duty of government officials (Callahan 1998: 37–38). For general perspectives on the trade in female sexuality, see Heyzer 1986, chap. 4.

13. For an example of how these enterprises "think" about the internationalizing of local snack cultures, see the Spring 1989 issue of *Impact*, the in-house magazine of Pepsico Foods International, in which a Thai marketing manager says, "I believe in the concept of a global product, but our version may not be identical." I am grateful to Mr. Tim Hessell of Sydney for this material.

14. The document, dated 7 December 1940, was signed by the deputy minister of defense (Kasian 1991). On the annexation, see Wyatt 1984: 255–56.

15. A good selection of the radio programs has been translated in Thak 1978: 260–316. The Thai easily put Man and Khong together as *mankhong*. *Chuchat* means "uphold the nation"; *rakthai* means "love for Thailand/the Thai."

16. I owe this observation to Dr. Gill Burke of the Australian National University.

Epilogue

E arly in December 1993, a convoy of forty-six vehicles, containing fifty journalists and others, crossed the Thailand-Myanmar border as the first officially organized overland motor caravan from Thailand to China. Similar journeys were envisioned to take travelers to parts of northern Laos and to Beijing. Organizers of the motor caravan included the Tourism Authority of Thailand, with sponsorship from the Petroleum Authority of Thailand, and Thai Airways. The cooperation of the Myanmar Ministry of Hotels and Tourism, the China National Tourism Administration, and the Travel and Tourism Administration of Yunnan Province was also required to ensure the success of the expedition. At Kengtung in Myanmar's Shan State, an outdoor cultural show was performed to entertain the tourists.

In Jinghong, the capital of the Xishuangbanna region in Yunnan, live many Tai Lue people, whose culture resembles that of the Thai. The Tai Lue "kingdom" vanished after the Chinese communist victory in 1949, and the territory became an autonomous prefecture. Through it, from north to south, runs the Mekong River on its long journey to the Gulf of Thailand. One of the Thai journalists on the caravan commented that the traditional Tai songs and dances seemed to have been heavily influenced by the Chinese Cultural Revolution, and the folk dances "were more akin to Russian ballet than any Thai folk dance this writer has ever seen." The journalist pointed out somewhat ruefully that the Chinese have succeeded well in "assimilating" the Tai people of Sipsongpanna (Anussom 1994). The punctuation marks around "assimilated" in the original dispatch suggest that Tai Lue multiculturalism might have brought to the journalist's mind what Chinese "assimilation" has meant to Tibetan culture, namely, the displacement of local culture. For the Tai Lue living in Yunnan, the admixture of Russian motifs to the native cultural matrix raises a question about the integrity and durability of Tai Lue culture.

This brief account of the first officially organized caravan tour from Thailand to China serves as a point of departure for a discussion of the dialectics of globalization in modern Thai history. Despite the feel of newness and adventure in this account, older instincts were at work in the dispatch of a motor caravan through the Shan states into southern China. The gaze from Bangkok to the north, for reasons of business, politics, or recreation, is of long historical formation and constitutes a process of reclamation rather than of fresh discovery (Reynolds 1996a: 119). Not least of the deep structural factors at work was the instinct of the Thai states in the nineteenth century to invade the Shan State of Kengtung when the geopolitics of southern China-northern Southeast Asia deemed it advantageous for them to do so (Melchers 1986).

As Thailand's economic boom pushed Bangkok-based business to the far corners of the country beginning in the mid-1980s, it became increasingly difficult to speak of any part of the country as remote. Conventional infrastructure, such as roads, bridges, and rail links, as well as telecommunications via satellite dishes, cable television, and mobile telephones, transformed villages and provincial towns into places where a certain cosmopolitanism flourishes. While there are asymmetries to the cultural flows across borders, and the ownership of the technology that makes possible these flows rests in the hands of a few, it cannot be denied that the center-periphery framework that used to function in cultural analysis is less and less applicable to the globalizing process.

The forces that drove this development are complex and derive, in the Thai case, from business expansion, tourism, and government development strategies (Hewison 1992). The Sino-Thai merchant culture that was instrumental in founding the Bangkok kingdom more than two hundred years ago still dominates today and is responsible for the expansion of Bangkok business to neighboring regions.

When we speak of the porosity of borders, which is a distinctive feature of globalizing trends, the long-standing security interests of the Thai military must be taken into account. The Thai military has good reason to be vigilant on the borders, for it has economic interests there. Lucrative extraction of resources from less developed neighbours such as Myanmar and Cambodia by means of military-built infrastructure has brought wealth to tiny border locales. In the

Golden Triangle, the most wanted drug dealer in northern Southeast Asia, Khun Sa, cultivated international respectability by moving some of his capital into gem cutting rather than the production of heroin (Naowarat 1993).

Apart from the lucrative extraction of resources that has transformed humble hamlets into prospering markets for international products, the policies of the ASEAN countries to stimulate decentralization and to push development towards the periphery led to a proliferation of economic quadrangles, squares, and circles (Wrangel 1993). The Golden Triangle over which Khun Sa once presided was supposed to become the Golden Quadrangle, fulfilling the dream policy of former Thai Prime Minister Chatichai Choonhavan to turn the battlefields of Indochina into market-places. These macro-economic strategies had the blessing of national governments, but they may at the same time erode national loyalties. The new geometries of regional development raised the possibility that people who flourish in the border zones might not only develop economically but also culturally and politically "away" from the citizenship into which they were born (Cornish 1994). The loyalties on which independent central governments have relied since the end of World War II are changing.

The disintegrative and disruptive consequences of these complex transformations in political and economic terms have long been recognized. The cultural dimensions as well as the telecommunications technology that serves as the vehicle for cultural flows are less well understood, although novel interdisciplinary fields have emerged to study the emergent global forms of cosmopolitanism. In a race to keep up with what is happening, academic pursuit of the transformations has brought about a new vocabulary of analysis to account for the cultural processes under way. The "global ecumene," a region where cultural interaction and exchange takes place, is one such term (Hannerz 1989). Arjun Appadurai's much-quoted ethnoscapes, mediascapes, technoscapes, finanscapes, and ideoscapes are another set of terms that strive to make sense of the emergent global cosmopolitanism (Appadurai 1990).

This vocabulary has subverted an older terminology of "centerperiphery" asymmetries. Asymmetries structured by political and economic imbalances still exist, but advanced media technology also has the capacity to empower local cultural producers. In some of the prognoses being made for the post-nationalist period there is a sense not only of powerful new technologies of "invention" and "imagining," but also of transformations that may be integrative as much as disintegrative. Small language communities may be able to retain their linguistic identity and thus cohere, because desktop publishing can meet the literacy needs of speakers relatively inexpensively.

Protagonists in the Thai debate on globalization can choose to side with optimists, who see opportunity and maybe even liberation in what is happening, while pessimists have plenty of evidence to call attention to the damaging environmental, social, and cultural consequences of globalization. Developers who want to build golf courses on rice fields ally themselves with the multi-national tourist industry, for example. In terms of advertising and cable news networks, the metropolitan capitalist countries (USA, Britain, Germany, and increasingly Japan) possess global languages that are challenging Thai lifestyles and habits of consumption. International Madison Avenue-style advertising techniques have steadily encroached on local practices since the 1970s when big U.S.-based agencies arrived to take over the market. Many people associate the commercialization of sex and the commodification of charismatic monks with globalization and fear that cultural standards are being undermined (Fairclough 1994: 22; Jitraphorn 1993: 24). A survey of Thai teenagers showed that they feel an emphasis on using sex appeal in advertising is damaging to Thai culture (Chalinee 1994: 58, 61, 200, 203).

I would not want to trivialize these consequences, but it is important to realize that globalization is proving to be, as Foucault said of power/knowledge, "productive." As with other parts of Southeast Asia, the media are used by ordinary people in ingenious ways (Hamilton 1992: 85). Video, a media form that the state has found difficult to control, spews out images that can serve all sorts of purposes, to enchant as much as to subvert (Hamilton 1993, 2002). Another way of saying this more specifically with reference to the contemporary Thai social formation is that globalization is not inherently constructive or destructive. Local activists for improvement in human rights can turn to Amnesty International, just as environmentalists campaigning to protect the natural environment benefit from the international environmental movement such as Greenpeace or the World Wildlife Fund (Jitraphorn 1993: 25).

Globalization can be integrative and identity-forming on a personal level as well, for example, in the domain of sexuality. "Gayness" as a masculine model for Thai male homosexuality has emerged only since the 1960s, not as a breach of an indigenous sex/gender dichotomy but as a male identity that renders explicit what was previously implicit and transforms into an identity what was previously a behavior. In Peter Jackson's view, gay male sexual identities in Thailand have deep, local cultural roots and are not wholly shaped by contact with Western gay cultures (Jackson 1997, 1999).

Nineteen ninety-four was the "Year to Campaign for Thai Culture" and an opportunity to consider the dialectic that takes place between past and present. With globalization comes anxiety about the survival prospects of indigenous culture, anxiety that may be as old as human culture itself but that has been expressed most acutely and forcefully in the colonial and post-colonial periods. Underlying this anxiety, which seems to be characteristic of the globalizing process, is an instinctive worry about the authenticity of self, culture, community, and nation. As cultural flows import more and more material from "out there," whether "out there" be Hong Kong, Tokyo, Taiwan, or San Francisco, new regional and ethnic identities are being forged. But the question of what is *really* Thai is of growing concern to culture managers and even ordinary folk. At the same time, the modern techniques of cultural production enable the culture managers to fashion a virtual reality of Thai culture past and present that can be visited and, when converted to electronic bytes, exported.

Historical Precedent

Projecting globalization into the past in a search for the roots of Bangkok's astonishing cosmopolitanism is risky but may have its rewards. Cosmopolitanism here means encouraging an orientation to engage with the other, an activity that of necessity establishes a tension between the local and the global (Featherstone 1990: 9).

The Bangkok state was founded in 1782 as an ethnically plural entity, certainly more plural at its core than the contemporary Vietnamese court at Hue or the Burmese royal base at Mandalay (Kasian 1994: 59). Mon, Lao, and Karen war captives and refugees were settled as laborers and rice cultivators when the Siamese court moved south at the end of the eighteenth century. Later, in the wake of Siamese expeditions to re-establish control over tributary states in the Malay Peninsula, Muslims were uprooted from the south and resettled around Bangkok and the old center at Ayutthaya. The Marxist historian Jit Poumisak used the term *kwat torn*, which conveys the sense of cattle being herded, to describe the dispossession and resettlement of peoples. An eloquent account of the dispossession of the Phuan people from northern Laos, who were resettled in central Siam, paid homage to the sturdy determination of these peoples who have come to terms with but have not forgotten their deracinated history (Breazeale and Snit 1988).

While Siamese administrative mechanisms encouraged assimilation and identification as Siamese, the policies, at least in the nineteenth century, did not subjugate the minority cultures to the point where they were extinguished. After many decades, the Phuan people now living in the Central Plains still speak Phuan. A kind of hybridization was possible, and was even tolerated and encouraged, for those who wished to retain a semblance of the culture of their ancestors. The reform policies of the late nineteenth-century King Chulalongkorn sought to bring all indigenous peoples, that is, all the peoples who had been subjects, into the Thai state (Turton 2000: 71). Central Siam was accustomed to polyethnic populations long before the term "multiculturalism" was invented. Memory of this polyethnic past and awareness of polyethnic community, preserved in something as innocent as the endless conversations one hears in Thai about loanwords and etymologies that relate to this past, predisposes people to be cosmopolitan.

The massive numbers of Chinese who migrated to Siam, beginning in the eighteenth century via the junk trade, are a special case. Their semi-assimilation, by which they preserved a sense of lineage and affiliation with overseas Chinese elsewhere in the diaspora, has been a key to Thailand's post–World War II economic expansion. Despite racist policies of the state directed against the Chinese during the reign of the sixth Bangkok king, Vajiravudh (r. 1910–25), and during the military regime of Field Marshal Plaek Phibunsongkhram beginning in late 1938, these affiliations were not lost, a fact that lies buried in the history of the much-vaunted assimilationist policies that pushed and pulled the Chinese to speak Thai, dress Thai, and pledge their loyalty to the king and Buddhism (Kasian 1992; Skinner 1957). Given the importance of the overseas Chinese in the economies of Hong Kong, Singapore, Taiwan, Malaysia, Indonesia, these affiliations within the Asian Chinese diaspora have facilitated the expansion of Bangkok-based business in the region.

As Bangkok-based business led by the Sino-Thai elite expanded into northern Southeast Asia and identified markets in the socialist states, old proprietary interests in lands containing Tai peoples were awakened. In some of these lands, such as in Laos for instance, the Bangkok court had strategic and economic interests dating from the early nineteenth century. For one thing, nationalist myth-making in the 1920s and 1930s had placed Siamese-Thai origins in the kingdom of Nanchao in southern China. Many Sino-Thai have reconnected with relatives in the People's Republic of China (PRC) following resumption of diplomatic relations in the 1970s, so the rediscovery of the pan-Tai world in northern Southeast Asia has had important cultural as well as economic dimensions (Turton 2000; Reynolds 2003). The Tai brothers and sisters (*phinorngkan*) in Laos, Burma, Vietnam, and southern China are different in important ways from the Siamese-Tai of the central plains of today's Thailand.

There is now substantial Thai research interest in these differences on the part of anthropologists, historians, and archaeologists who discuss their findings in magazines and highly publicized seminars. The cultural and economic dimensions of the expanding Bangkok social formation suggest that the motivations for Thai "interest" in these regions are complex: to build on affiliations, which would be good for business, by identifying similarities; and, to enlarge the definition of Thai-ness by focusing on differences. A flexible approach to what defines Thai-ness that avoids essentializing differences and emphasizes a continually evolving Thai identity has been a feature of Thai cosmopolitanism since the mid-1970s.

Beyond the region, where Thai curiosity and willingness to engage with Tai peoples comes naturally because of linguistic and cultural affinities and leads to a kind of ethnochauvinism, a history of interaction with America since the end of World War II has shaped Thai consumer tastes as well as the political culture generally. As the Americans prosecuted the Cold War in Southeast Asia, the country remained relatively open to foreigners, and particularly open to

Americans. The Peace Corps sent hundreds of young Americans to Thai provincial and district schools, and large numbers of Thai civil servants, business people, and educators received their college education and advanced degrees from American institutions. Young Thais returning from their American education in the late 1960s and early 1970s brought back experiences in the anti-war movement on American campuses that played a part in the overthrow of the military dictatorship in October 1973.

This is not to explain the activism that led to the 1973 event as something imported from Berkeley or Columbia University but to acknowledge the internationalization of Bangkok urban cultural politics. The idea of periodizing Thai literature by labelling these years "the American era" seems calculated to touch sensitivities about autonomy, but the fact is that this periodization has not been challenged or set aside by Thai intellectuals (Anderson and Mendiones 1985). Strategic and economic ties between the United States and Thailand began to fray long ago, but with large numbers of American-educated Thais still in positions of responsibility in all sectors of the bureaucracy, business, and public life, it will be some time before the political culture breaks free from its American connections.

It may be a tautology to argue that the quick reception of modern communication in Thailand facilitated Thai cosmopolitanism, because the reason for that receptivity may lie in an openness and receptivity to the world generally. But it is a fact that, compared with other countries in mainland Southeast Asia, Thailand more readily accepted the printing press, cinema, radio, FM radio, and color and cable television. Long historical habits of developing the theatrics of power as well as a rich repertoire in the performing arts help explain the predisposition for modern technologies of representation, but the canniness and ambition to control these technologies is not well understood. This history of rapid appropriation of technologies of communication has proven decisive in establishing economic dominance in the region, because the televisual age privileges cultural producers, be they individuals, companies, or government departments, who can take advantage of these technologies.

The way knowledge was formatted and transmitted in the premodern period before Western science began to exert its pull on the Siamese elite also helps to account for Thai cosmopolitanism. As discussed in chapter ten, manuals on astrology, medicine, and grammar had a capacity to absorb new material while appearing to remain unchanged. Their fragmentation, repetition, and unsystematicness meant that the alienness of foreign cultural elements were easily stripped away and made non-threatening. In terms of architectural styles, the admixture of many different artistic traditions—Khmer, Mon, Burmese, Lao, Chinese, Western—meant that a new cultural motif was accepted into a building's design without in any way appearing to be odd or out of place. A Thai colleague, Dr. Thanet Aphornsuwan, once told me how he passed a Bangkok monastery on his way to school every day, never noticing that the gates were adapted from the European gothic cathedral. When he went to the West he discovered the origins of the style, and only then did he begin to think the gothic portals on the Thai Buddhist monastery were odd.

Public Intellectuals and Globalization

The Thai name given to the globalization process is the Pali-derived calque *lokanuwat/lokaphiwat,* although not all words that name epochs and international styles are translated into the language. Many remain loan-words with distinctive spellings and diacritics that mark them off as alien forms. But *lokanuwat* is now a buzzword in Thai, having made its way into the language at the end of the 1980s at a time when "internationalization" and "NIC" became emblems of Thailand's emerging role in regional and world economics. Like the word for "dynamism" (*phonlawat*) that also became popular at this time, globalization is a word that captures the boom times from the mid-1980s to the Asian financial crash in 1997.

Credit for coining the translation has been given to Chai-Anan Samudavanija, a political scientist at Chulalongkorn University, now president of the King's School, who had been an active public intellectual since his return in the early 1970s from graduate studies in America. In publications directed at the general public, Chai-Anan waxed lyrical about the transformations taking place, proclaiming that in the age of globalization "knowledge will no longer serve power but will be a power unto itself, autonomous" (Chai-anan 1994: 71). This futuristic and visionary outlook is typical of those public intellectuals who are confident of the capacity of telecommunications to be a liberating rather than a repressive influence in social, political, and economic life. The present Thai prime minister, Thaksin Shinnawatra, who made his fortune by importing and selling telecommunications technology, exemplifies this type of modern Thai visionary.

In the early 1990s, Chai-Anan held the position of senior academic advisor in the Chaiyong Limthongkul Foundation, an educational and philanthropic enterprise headed by Sondhi Limthongkul, the owner of Manager Group, a media conglomerate. Through its Thailand-Australia Foundation, Manager Group established a base in Australia, at the Asia and Pacific Studies Centre at the University of Central Queensland (Mackay Campus), where it intended to develop management training courses and cultural exchange. As one of the pioneers in the introduction of advanced telecommunications technology to Thai print media, Sondhi might be taken as a globalizer par excellence. Many of Thailand's leading public intellectuals were lured to write for the Manager Group's publications, and Chai-anan himself had a regular column in the Thai-language *Manager*. Attributing the loan-translation of *lokanuwat* to a single individual, Professor Chai-anan, might seem to contradict linguistic principles about how language changes (that is, not at the instigation of individual speakers), but the attribution underscores my thesis about the perceived role of public intellectuals in interpreting what is happening to the country.

Given the Thai propensity for word play, it is not surprising that writers take advantage of the *lokanuwat* currency by exploiting the word's resonances with similar-sounding coinages, *lokawibat*, for example, which means "global catastrophe," or *lokawiwat*, which has the tamer meaning of "global change." In October 1994, the Royal Institute of Thailand stepped into the debate and insisted that the term *lokaphiwat* be used on the grounds that *lokanuwat* carried a connotation of "worldliness," which is not at all what "globalization" should mean in the Thai language. By alliterative punning on *lokanuwat*, which sounds awkward to the Thai ear and is thus the cause of much humor, a single punchy word can call into question the benefits being touted for a globalized Thailand as well as the ethics of the globalizers. A couple of collections of short stories, for example, played on the greed (*lophanuwat*) and unbridled consumerism (*phokanuwat*) that turns rice fields into golf courses and bush land into monoculture eucalyptus farms for the Japanese woodchip industry (Suchat 1994a,

1994b). The first part of the latter term literally means "eat" as well as "consume" or "use up" and conveys the sense that human beings are engulfing the planet with their voracious appetites for resources. The moralizing message directed at the more rapacious and unscrupulous globalizers is clear.

In the noisy and bruising world of Thai political culture, the debate about the pros and cons of globalization has become more tense and urgent as the ecosystem has deteriorated and as development has radically altered social relations. Some of the arguments are familiar to comparable debates in other countries. Multinational enterprises and foreign investment are held accountable for overdevelopment and damage to the environment. Urbanization and industrialization have drawn people from the countryside, disrupting family and community life in the process. It is of interest that some of these points were made in early 1994 in an article in *Muang Boran*, an archaeology and heritage magazine, because there is a clear connection between heritage management and globalization as discussed in chapter ten. The article's Thai title, rendered rather weakly in the magazine as "Effects of Globalization on Thai Society," but best translated as "From 'Globalization' to 'Global Catastrophe' in Thai Society," is a punning indictment of the catastrophic consequences (*lokawibat*) of unbridled development hailed as globalization (*Muang Boran* 1994). A social scientist at Chiangmai University said emphatically, "Globalization has already taken place, and it is a very powerful force" (Jitraphorn 1993: 25).

Many, but by no means all, of the public intellectuals engaged in these debates have a history of leftist radicalism or activism. Some debaters come from the NGO (nongovernment organizations) movement where many veteran activists from the tumultuous 1970s found a place for themselves in the practical politics of grassroots development. They are advocates for the disenfranchised and the rural and urban poor. Among their number are former Marxists who fled Bangkok in the crackdown that accompanied the return of military power on 6 October 1976 and who then made their way to overseas universities where they acquired advanced degrees. Upon returning from abroad they took up teaching positions in the university system and began to write for the popular press. While Marxism as such no longer exerts a hold on the way development issues are framed, today's public intellectuals who lived through the 1970s, even as youngsters, developed analytical, organizational, and oratorical skills that they have brought to bear on current problems. The politics of culture, dependency theory, and economic determinism were vigorously debated in the 1970s, and with some modifications two decades hence, they are still worthy of scrutiny and argument. With his characteristic flair for a phrase, Kasian Tejapira has termed the protagonists of current debates "globalizers" versus "communitarians" (Kasian n.d.).

One such debate about globalization took place at Thammasat University at the end of 1993 in the heady days of the boom, when a historian, a freelance journalist, and a committed globalizer met to exchange views. The historian, Thawit Sukhapanich, performed the etymological duties required on these occasions and pointed out that the Thai term means literally "to adapt to the world" (*patibat tam lok*) (*Warasan thammasat* 1994: 106–7). It was necessary to spend time defining the term, he said, because although many Thai speakers used it, few knew what it meant. Of the three kinds of speakers Thawit identified in his unscientific survey, one group grasped the opportunities and processes, especially in terms of telecommunications, the second group criticized and resists globalization; and the third group, by far the largest and the one in which Thawit counted himself, was more or less confused, wondering what all the fuss is about.

Thawit, the historian, understandably took a long view and pointed out that Thais have been globalizing for centuries, from Ayutthayan times when there were sizeable Portuguese, Dutch, and Japanese settlements in the port polity, to the present, thus proving that Thai culture has long been capable of adapting to what the Western world had to offer in terms of values, knowledge, and abilities. The gist of Thawit's argument was that the Thai language was somewhat deficient in the vocabulary of globalization, because there had never been a time when Thai society was *not* globalizing. There was never a period before globalization, so there was no need for a term to describe what came naturally to the society (p. 108).

The second speaker, the freelance journalist Thianchai Wongchai-suwan, referred to Braudel and Wallerstein as thinkers who had pioneered the world-system theory that helps modern people understand the changes now taking place. Thianchai preferred "global evolution" (*lokawiwat*) for his gloss on globalization and asserted that modernization theory had failed to deliver the benefits it promised. Deforestation and AIDS are global phenomena that have penetrated everywhere. Thianchai warned that retreating into Eastern spiritualism was simply gross ignorance of the problems at hand. As described in the previous chapter, in the aftermath of the 1997 financial crisis Thianchai launched an ambitious publication series in which he and his collaborators tracked the deleterious effects of globalization and kept up a steady criticism of what the globalizers envisaged for the country.

Somchai Phakkhaphakwiwat gave possibly the most spirited presentation at the seminar. A lecturer in political science at Thammasat University who had done graduate work in Spain and studied both Spanish and Italian, he was a living advertisement for globalization. He was a specialist on the stock market, wrote a weekly column, and presented a two-minute television program on world financial trends. He too had been an adviser to Sondhi Limthongkul, whose Manager Group had successfully exploited the talents of many intellectuals in its publications. To conquer the problems of doing business in traffic-clogged Bangkok, Somchai had fitted out his van with electronic communications and entertainment equipment (computer, mobile telephone, cassette recorder, fax machine). To relax in the van he sang to the accompaniment of karaoke. Somchai's facility with languages, telecommunications, and international finance indicates why he might have an irrepressibly optimistic view of opportunities for Thai globalizers. As far as he was concerned, Thai culture was being internationalized, and global culture was being domesticated (*Warasan thammasat* 1994: 121). A more eloquent proselytizer for globalization, for whom the phenomenon was an ideology and way of life, could not be found.

Thirayut Bunmi was another public intellectual, "a social thinker" (*nak khit khong sangkhom*) as he called himself, who in his publications was striving to explain the meaning of the present globalizing epoch (Thirayut 1993). A student leader in the mass mobilization that brought down the military government in October 1973, Thirayut was an adviser to the Socialist Party of Thailand and coordinator of the Democratic People's group until the military coup in early October 1976. At that time he fled to the jungle with many other young intellectuals and for four years served in Nan province, one of the secure bases of the insurgency, as Secretary for the Co-ordinating

Committee of Patriotic and Democratic Peoples. There followed a period of graduate study in the Netherlands until his return to Bangkok in 1985. Since then he has been an active speaker and prolific author, his past as a Marxist intellectual being evident in his pamphlets and articles.

In his books Thirayut had been spelling out what he thought *lokanuwat* meant for Thai society. He ranked Thailand as a moderate-to-high "outward-oriented" society. Predictably enough, the societies at the top of his list are the "Little Dragons" of Asia—Singapore, South Korea, Hong Kong (Thirayut 1994: 52). Although he was wary of globalization, Thirayut was at the same time willing to see opportunities in the process, in the sense that the global culture penetrating Thai society was bringing ideas, doctrines, strategies, and movements that could be helpful to NGO workers and others fighting for the underdog. As the communications revolution broke down national boundaries and linked societies together, global culture introduced universal (*sakon*) standards in such matters as human rights, democratic institutions (elected parliaments, for example), conservation and environmentalism (Thirayut 1994: 40). He has since become more jaundiced about the globalizing-Westernizing-modernizing moment, and argues that Thailand must enter a post-Western phase in order to survive (Thirayut 2003).

Popular culture was also seen to be "standardized," "universalized," and "homogenized" (*an nung an diawkan*). In fact, multinational enterprises found that they had to develop sophisticated advertising campaigns to present their products in a way that would appeal to local (Thai) consumers (Chalinee 1994, chap. 6). In this context, local agency could be seen to have the power to bend and twist standards set elsewhere. The top executive of a Thai conglomerate who boldly declared "We want Thai people to eat mayonnaise" had his work cut out for him as far as marketing this most alien of products (Friedland 1989). Thirayut acknowledged that in reaction to the way global culture penetrates Thai society, local culture would assert itself to establish its uniqueness (*ekkalak*) (Thirayut 1994: 40). Although he recognized the damaging consequences of globalization for Thailand, Thirayut was, on the whole, a pragmatic optimist, looking for Thailand's economic development to give it the capacity to contend with the undesirable and hazardous effects of unplanned growth.

Criticisms of a homogenizing global culture take the form of a polemic, because increasingly the cultural forms are Asian, from Hong Kong or Japan, for example. Be that as it may, the polemic against the imposition of global culture from elsewhere touched a nerve in the sensibilities of Thai people in all classes. The polemic derives from earlier experiences when the Siamese élite was caught in the dilemmas of being a semi-colony, retaining sovereign powers yet limited in the changes it could advance. Thai sovereignty is the raw nerve that has been touched. Earlier this century the exemplar and procreator of high culture, King Rama VI (r. 1910–25), embroiled himself in the politics of defining Thai-ness at a time when the legitimacy of the absolute monarchy was being questioned. In order to protect the institution from republican challenges, the monarchy cloaked itself with Thai-ness by representing itself as a cultural artifact epitomizing what *thai* really meant, "free." Thai-ness became essentialized, palpable, something that could be codified in law and bureaucratic regulation. The legacy of this entanglement of culture and politics survives today. Imitation of something designated as non-Thai was thereby construed as a political crime.

The Cult of Imitation

The common theme in the pessimistic assessments of globalization among Thai public intellectuals of a homogenized universal culture raises the political issue of whether that universal culture will overwhelm and dominate local agency. Bio- and social diversity are diminishing, thus limiting the capacity of human society to confront in a creative way the vast and rapid changes taking place.

This line of argument was articulated forcefully in a speech at Mahidol University by the Chiangmai-based historian, Nidhi Aeusrivongse, who writes regularly for *Art and Culture,* a glossy monthly magazine known for its provocative and nationalistic editorializing. *Art and Culture* was one of the publications that campaigned in 1988 for the return to Thailand of the Cambodian lintel that had been spirited away through the antique-dealer network to the Chicago Art Institute. In the speech, Nidhi expressed alarm at the sway of global culture, which he identified as European, and which had three characteristics: its hegemony, which meant that no country or community of people could escape its influence; the dissolution of borders, which meant that local agencies had lost control over decisions that are now made elsewhere; and virtually instantaneous communications (Nidhi 1994: 92).

The polarization of "the local" (*thong thin*) and "the global" (*saphawa lokanuwat*), implicit in the point about the dissolution of borders, was crystalized towards the end of the speech in the following comment: "In the age of globalization there is more danger in imitating European models [*kanlork tamra farang*] than we have ever realized" (Nidhi 1994: 94). Such a formulation of the problem does not point to who is responsible for the threat to Thai society, the European (*farang*) or, as Nidhi also says, "the hegemony of capitalist society."

Here and elsewhere in the debate about globalization, the power of multinational enterprises to affect local conditions independent of local agency has been overstated (*Muang Boran* 1994: 7). In any case, the issue of imitation—"imitating foreign models," in Nidhi's words— is an old one in Thai cultural debates about whether foreign products, be they consumer products, political systems, health regulations, or even sexual identities are suitable to be copied. The concern being expressed today is reminiscent of similar concerns expressed at the beginning of the twentieth century. The difference in circumstances, in the terms of Nidhi's argument, is that local Thai agency is losing the power to choose, because the range of choices offered is decided in board-rooms in Hong Kong, Tokyo, London, and New York. This is why local knowledge, or *phum panya* in Thai, is seen to be the key to empowerment of the disenfranchised and dispossessed and as fundamental to proposals for alternative development (Reynolds 2002: 328–30).

Nearly ninety years ago the sixth Bangkok monarch argued defensively about the power of Western institutions and ideas in shaping cultural and political life. "The Cult of Imitation" was written in 1915 by King Vajiravudh and first published in the newspaper *Phim thai* of April that year (Copeland 1993, chap. 3). A longer series, *Mud on our Wheels,* later appeared which was originally published in English. The series dealt more extensively with the potential damage to the social fabric and the political institutions of foreign models. For these and other essays, the king used a penname, Asvabahu, one of the epithets of the Buddha ("a vehicle for men as a horse is a vehicle") that emphasized the role of the king as a teacher, and indeed the tone of these essays is didactic and moralizing (Vella 1978: 320). Adopting a penname also allowed the king to speak of the monarch in the third person, a rhetorical device that had many advantages in light of the polemic he was developing.

It is important to recall the historical moment when "The Cult of Imitation" was put forward by this most important public intellectual of the 1910s. It was not long after 1907 and 1909 when the Siamese had lost parts of their empire to France and Britain. Just after Vajiravudh's accession an attempted coup in 1912 resulted in the arrest of ninety-one persons, some of whom were imprisoned for a dozen years. Apart from personal dissatisfaction with the king and jealousy at his attempts to train a junior cadet corps of Wild Tigers, the more politically astute of the conspirators were critical of the monarchy as an "unprogressive and dying institution." The Young Turk movement, the democratic revolution in Portugal, and Japan's constitutional monarchy were "foreign models" that motivated at least some of the officers (Vella 1978: 53–60). The Bolshevik triumph a few years hence did not give the king any comfort either. Not least of these foreign models, because of proximity and the large number of Chinese immigrants in Siam, was the Kuomintang victory and the establishment of a republic in China in 1911–12. Vajiravudh in "The Cult of Imitation" referred scathingly to Sun Yat-sen's wearing of a "frock coat," seeing in this simple item of clothing a sign of a deviant and dangerous European political ideology (Vajiravudh 1951: 2). To dress as a European was to dress slavishly and therefore to follow inappropriate and disloyal political doctrines. It was a tumultuous time, and the inexperienced king was seeking to bring affairs of state under his control after being shaken by the coup attempt. The irony of the argument in "The Cult of Imitation" was that this king had spent his school years in England, had acted on the stage there, and was the most bicultural king of the dynasty.

"The Cult of Imitation" was a diatribe against slavish copying of the West. The targets were the visible signs of Westernization, such as clothes, manners, and customs. But by the end of the essay the political consequence of this slavish copying, if it was to continue, was clear: the destruction of the monarchy. He mocked those who thought that even a shabby Western garment would be sufficient to ingratiate themselves with Europeans. The god-like powers of this imitation were such that people who fell under their spell were contemptuous of their own abilities and mindlessly followed the lead of the West. The message was that self-reliance and autonomy were the values of "civilization" (*siwilai*) that should be cherished by all Siamese (Vajiravudh 1951: 6).

In making this argument, the king was perpetuating the equation of Thai, the speech and ethnic group, with *thai* meaning "free." His father, Chulalongkorn, had abolished debt slavery and his uncle, Prince Damrong Rajanubhab, in his histories had made the reform of labor relations into a doctrine of progress in the narrative of the Siamese-Tai people. So when Vajiravudh accused those who were worshipping "the cult of imitation" of being slaves he was trying to shame them by touching the sensitive nerve of Siam's semi-colonial status, which his ancestors in the dynasty had negotiated.

As explained earlier, this polemic against imitation cannot be read without acknowledging the political and social circumstances in which it was produced. It is also necessary to read the polemic not only as a case for preserving the monarchy but also as an insight into the psyche of the early twentieth-century élite. In this regard, the pessimism and caution expressed by Nidhi Aeusrivongse, the historian and public intellectual, have much in common with the sixth Bangkok king.

There is a major difference in the two epochs, however. The danger to the author of 1915 was that he might lose absolute authority, and seventeen years later his successor did indeed lose that authority. The danger of which Nidhi in 1994 warns is not that sovereignty will be lost, but rather that its late twentieth century equivalent, Thai-ness, what makes "us" different, will be lost. What is common to the two discourses is an "us" and "them" mentality. The hegemonic aspect of globalization has reawakened concern about the viability of the "us." It is to sketch the particular historical formation of the Siamese-Tai "us" in the present epoch that I now turn.

Cultural Nationalism and Authenticity

In the globalizing epoch of post-nationalism, when telecommunications are breaking down older forms of loyalty to national communities, it is culture, rather than sovereignty, that is increasingly one of the irreducible givens that identifies and differentiates a community. It is

not surprising that diasporas—Indian, Chinese, Vietnamese—are now
the topic of intensive scholarly work. They are archetypal post-nationalist
communities, collectivities that share language, history, and ethnicity
but not geo-body. With modern techniques of reproduction, fragments
of culture can be pried away from their native environs and then travel
by means of satellite communications.

The process by which "Thai-ness" was formed in twentieth-century
élite consciousness is well known. As explained in chapter eleven, this
"Thai-ness" was made concrete and bureaucratized at several specific
moments, its main features being disseminated through the media, the
schools, and other institutions. These moments included the late 1930s,
when the military regime, which was militantly anti-royalist, needed
to Thai-ify itself, and the period following the coup of 6 October 1976
when the prestige of state institutions, including the monarchy, were
seriously damaged by the violent methods used to reinstate military
rule. Throughout the early 1980s the character of Thai identity (*ekkalak
thai*) continued to be an occasional topic in public seminars (Sanga and
Athom 1981). During the economic boom from the mid-1980s through
the financially years of the late 1990s the extensive Tai diaspora in
northern Southeast Asia became of great interest to Bangkok-based
intellectuals and culture managers, because the Tai peoples scattered
throughout the region were drawn into the Thai/Tai orbit and made
it possible for the national imaginaire to remain rural and urban,
agricultural and hi-tech in the globalizing age.

The tourist industry, in collaboration with the government tourism
authority, is a willing agent in the development and marketing of Thai-
ness. In 1985, at the beginning of the economic boom the Tourism
Authority of Thailand conducted market research on how Thailand
was perceived in overseas markets. An international advertising agency
was hired to promote and aggressively sell Thailand's image abroad.
From 1986, there followed a series of campaigns unabashedly playing
on the Orientalist clichés about the exotic East: "Brilliant Thailand"
(1986); "Visit Thailand Year" (1987); "Exotic Thailand—Golden Places,
Smiling Faces" to promote "Thailand Arts and Crafts Year" (1989);
"I Love Thailand" (1990); "Exotic Thailand—See More of the Country,
See More of the People" (1991) (Chalinee 1994: 177–79). "Amazing
Thailand" was a campaign launched at the end of 1997 to reclaim the
tourist business that had been lost because of the bad publicity in the

wake of the financial crisis. The international tourism campaigns are often coupled with domestic cultural themes, so that a kind of feedback mechanism operates which confirms that local identity is shaped in part by how the country is being sold to foreigners. What has been commodified for the international tourist may be consumed by the Thai national, whether that something is a self-image or a handicraft.

Heritage is a particularly interesting way that national or community identity can be forged and reshaped in the globalizing epoch, because heritage is quintessentially local, with the material for its fabrication and validation belonging to *this* place. Yet it is more and more the case that the value and prestige of heritage sites increase as they are validated by the international heritage bureaucracy, particularly UNESCO through its International Council of Monuments and Sites (ICOMOS). World Heritage listing is much sought after for the international status and authenticity it gives to a particular site, no less than for the commercial gains through tourism. With tourism, one of the chief vehicles of globalization, the irony is that as the tourism industry develops standardized comforts for the international tourist, the past is iconicized to become a seemingly reliable source of national identity (Peleggi 2002b, chap. 1). The investment in heritage sites is such that they have become national icons on display for the citizenry to visit and admire. But so extensive is the renovation of some of them that their authenticity is often called into question. They are, in fact, sites at which authenticity has been "staged" (Cohen 1988: 374–75).

One such site in Thailand, which has conveyed important meanings to the Thai citizenry about benevolent government throughout the twentieth century, is the Sukhothai Historical Park in north-central Thailand, created in the 1980s with UNESCO assistance (Byrne 1993: 186–93; Peleggi 2002b: 37–43; Peleggi 1996). The restoration of the monuments in the park was criticized by a Thai historian, Professor Dhida Saraya, for "newly created environments stemming from historical fictions and myths . . . a park rich in fantastic structures and recreational sites reflecting no trace or shadow of the urban setting and planning of the past" (Peleggi 2002b: 42). In response to this criticism, the Fine Arts Department, which was overseeing the restoration, made important changes to the development plan, but the site was so highly charged with symbolism and tourist potential that it was impossible to resist inventing more tradition. A Loy Kratong festival is now held, bringing record numbers of Thai visitors to the Park in November. The historical legend of the festival is a fabrication, "entirely against history," in the emphatic words of an archaeologist and ethnohistorian, Srisakra Vallibhotama, who has been a persistent critic of such heritage projects (Peleggi 2002b: 67). Yet archaeology in Siam and elsewhere has been a key science in documenting the national community's history on a particular piece of geography (Peleggi 2004, passim). Archaeologists take sides either to defend projects of this kind or to contest the authenticity of the final result as a misrepresentation of the past.

Once it is accepted that traditions can be rediscovered and even created, it is very difficult for state culture managers to steer the process of fabricating tradition. The nation-state ceases to have absolute control over interpretations of the past. In this regard, heritage is an example of globalization having a liberating effect, for it has the capacity to pluralize the past. Private or semi-private interests can refurbish sites and present them for consumption by tourists, citizens, and young people, yet these sites may not have the sanction of education authorities or restoration specialists in the Fine Arts Department.

In the dialectic by which the globalizing process facilitates and sometimes forces local identity to establish itself, it is not surprising to find an "us" and "them" mentality. In Thailand this is expressed in different ways by different speakers and constituencies. As the debate among public intellectuals illustrates, there may be anxiety about the consequences, or there may be an expression of confidence that Thais are natural globalizers able to make the necessary adaptations. Media people generally fall into this latter category and can be astute in their understanding of what is happening. One communications lecturer, Bunrak Bunyakhetmala, who has been described as the Marshall McLuhan of Thailand, believes that the telecommunications revolution will bring into existence an "ersatz Thai" (*thai thiam*) culture, a transnational culture that might even be exported. This ersatz culture will coexist with "authentic Thai" (*thai thae*) culture, which is composed of the drama, music, and literature that has been handed down from the past (Bunrak 1994: 442). Thus Bunrak distinguished the two kinds of culture in an interview in English, taking pains to use the Thai terms and explain them. Kasian Tejapira puts the issue slightly differently in arguing for the liberation of identity from nationality, a kind of fragmented subjectivity or split personality (Kasian 2002).

When writing in Thai on transnational communications, Bunrak made a slightly different point, knowing that many public intellectuals, academics among them, are concerned about the important issue of local identity. "It is not possible to explain the phenomenon of 'inside' *(phai nai)* without making reference to what is produced on the 'outside' *(phai nork)*. This would seem to be the 'crisis' in Thai studies everywhere" (Bunrak 1994: 104). That is to say, Thai identity is relational and can only be visible against what is non-Thai. Thai studies, concentrating on Thai culture, history, politics, languages, and so forth, are manifestly concerned with what is inside the society, although as the overland caravan to Yunnan with which I began this discussion illustrates, what is defined as "inside" has rapidly expanded over the borders to the north.

The Siamese Thai gaze to the north and the current fashion to study the Sinified Tai in southern China and the rest of northern Southeast Asia must be understood as a kind of ethnic nostalgia, a reclamation of identity that resides in the yet-to-be-globalized Tai minority peoples in the region. Central Thai interest on the part of government culture managers as well as of public intellectuals trained as archaeologists and anthropologists in the Sinified Tai peoples of Yunnan in China or the Vietnamized Tai peoples in Vietnam is a sign that diversity within the borders of Thailand is diminishing. Or perhaps one should say "perceived" to be diminishing because of the homogenizing potential of globalization.

The gaze to the north is itself a globalizing phenomenon, because the popular and academic writing on the culture of the Tai peoples in neighboring countries emphasizes affinity and thus draws these people into a Siamese Thai orbit. It is now being claimed, for example, that the Zhuang people of Kwangsi province, with some 13 million speakers, are the "oldest" Tai group, their culture being a kind of relic of what Tai/Thai culture used to be before the more "advanced" civilizations of India and China affected it (Srisakr and Pranee 1993). The public intellectuals who write for the glossy monthly *Art and Culture* have been determinedly studying the Zhuang to document their contribution to Southeast Asian culture, and this has led to the revival of interest in the Dongson culture, significantly called "bronze drum culture" in Thai writing to avoid using a toponym from Vietnam (Aphisit 1994).

Apart from the investigation of Tai/Thai origins in the rest of Southeast Asia, other kinds of reactions to the globalizing trends illustrate how local culture is being attended to, even engineered. Public intellectuals have returned to the issue of culture, both on the national level and at the grassroots. Beginning in the early 1980s, for example, development workers, religious leaders (Christian as well as Buddhist), and health professionals involved in the work of NGOs began to campaign for the strengthening of village societies in order to help rural people contend with the more damaging effects of overdevelopment. The ideology that lies behind this campaign has been called "the community culture school of thought" by an economic historian, Chatthip Nartsupha, who himself has been an active public intellectual for the past two decades (Chatthip 1991a, 1991b).

As Chatthip advocated in the early 1990s, this particular reaction to globalization is characterized not by its collaboration with the globalizers but by resistance to them. Just as the Thai Buddhist monk-philosopher Buddhadasa sought to find the core of Buddhism by a radical critique of the Buddhist canon, so the "community culture" movement seeks to establish the core of Thai-ness by a radical critique of urban culture (Reynolds 2002, chap. 13). Citing the ideas of the eminent haematologist Prawet Wasi, who won the Magsaysay Award in 1981 for his work with NGOs and who has been a leader in AIDS prevention, Chatthip argued that the community culture ideology was anti-state (Chatthip 1991a: 124–25). It promoted local community values, and it believed that development must take into account the spiritual and environmental dimensions of human experience. Others who support the movement stress its mutuality, empathy, and egalitarianism (Jitraphorn 1993: 25). Chatthip used the term "anarchistic" to describe the movement's thrust. This odd term refers to the self-help, mutuality, and autonomy of village life which constitute "the fundamental discourse that has existed from the beginning." Moreover, in Chatthip's words, the values being advocated "are characteristics of Thai consciousness, which, from ancient times, has been inseparable from Thai communities" (Chatthip 1991a: 136). There is an explicit attempt in this formulation to distill the essentials of Thai-ness, albeit at the village level. In fact, the values advocated by the community culture school of thought in Chatthip's rendering of what it stands for bear a striking resemblance to what King Vajiravudh wrote in 1915 in his essay on "The Cult of Imitation."

Finally, there is the issue of local agency and how it is conceptualized and mobilized by activists and cultural conservationists alike. Coincidental with the discussion of "internationalization" and "globalization" in the late 1980s, the term *phum panya* made its appearance. Roughly translated as "native/local wisdom," the term for "native" is the Indic term *phum* (Pali, *bhumi*), the same term that appears in the Malay discourse of Malaysia-for-the-Malays, *bumiputra*. The business manuals that assume reader familiarity with *The Romance of the Three Kingdoms* trade on the cultural pride that "we" (in Asia) are more savvy than "them" (in the West). It is this notion of "native wisdom" that has been exploited in business manuals such as *Wisdom of the East: A Manual for Utilizing People* (Foeng Moeng Long 1991).

The idea of "native wisdom" is remarkably similar to the concept of "local genius," advocated in the 1950s by H. G. Quaritch Wales, an Englishman who published his own books and whom academics never took seriously (Wales 1951; 1957). As discussed in chapter one above, the concept enjoyed some vogue with Western historians of Southeast Asia after World War II as they attempted to displace colonial history with "autonomous" history (Sears 1993).

The difference between "native wisdom" and "local genius" is that the former is increasingly a weapon in the hands of both globalizers and their critics. "Native wisdom," almost certainly a calque of "local knowledge," is a powerful marketing tool, as transnational advertising agencies localize their advertising campaigns to sell their products. But at the same time, the notion of "native wisdom" lies behind the community culture ideology advocated by the NGO workers struggling to help villagers resist capitalists and state planners. In the words of one of these workers, "popular [native] wisdom is a whole body of knowledge presented holistically and representing the villagers' art of living" (Seri 1992: 140). "Native wisdom" thus expresses the irreducible "something" that stands for local agency. Significantly, the term for "wisdom" is one of the stalwart words for "intellect" in the Buddhist lexicon. The Thai Buddhist philosopher Buddhadasa used the term "native wisdom" to characterize the Thai faculty of reason that is as capable of contributing to the processes of globalization as the Western faculty of reason (Jackson 2003).

Conclusion

Like other discursive formations such as modernity, development, or democracy, the origins of globalization are alleged to lie somewhere else, "over there" in Europe or America, and therein lies its promise and its peril. But in fact, when placed in a longer historical trajectory, globalization appears less novel, less a distinctive historical moment, and also less threatening than both its critics and advocates claim. It is also less emancipatory than its advocates promise. It needs to be placed alongside other civilizational tropes that have dominated the thinking of the Thai elite and the middle classes for the past two centuries.

In the middle of the nineteenth century Siam was entering an unsettling and unpredictable epoch. The court, well aware of the conquests by the Western imperial powers already underway in Siam's neighbours, chose to make strategic compromises, beginning with the Bowring Treaty of 1855. The loss of income, because tariffs were forcibly lowered, and the loss of jurisdiction, because of the extraterritorial clauses stipulated by the Treaty, resulted in economic and political semi-colonialism. For the élite there was also a psychological dimension to this semi-colonialism, a desire to be "civilized" in terms of social mores, hygiene, technology, dress, and even deportment and dining habits. Initially the impulse was to be "civilized" to provide for the needs and comforts of Europeans and a few Americans. A prominent historian and nobleman of the period, who met with some of these Westerners and was the very same "Modern Buddhist" who wanted to reconfigure the Buddhist world-view to accommodate Western science, gave a hint of this semi-colonial mentality in his chronicle of Mongkut's reign. The larger roads, on which the Europeans expected to ride their horses and drive their carriages, were "filthy and unattractive, shaming us (*khaina*) in the eyes of foreigners" (Thiphakorawong 1961: 6)

Thongchai Winichakul has excavated the history of *siwilai* (civilized), one of the tropes of modernity that emerged in the middle of the nineteenth century in élite consciousness (Thongchai 2000b). This was one of the earliest words borrowed from English and one of the few to survive in transliterated form, as if leaving it as a loan word could bring into the Thai language its magical powers of civilizational

improvement. Combined with *jaroen,* an old Khmer word dating from
at least the fourteenth century that was refitted with new meanings of
secular development and material progress, *siwilai* became the trope
of transformation into the new age.

There were both spatial and temporal aspects to this semi-colonized
consciousness. Looking outwards at the declining fortunes of the royal
houses in the rest of Southeast Asia, the Siamese aristocracy took some
comfort from the fate it was escaping. Its consumption of European
products and its desires for the hospitals and railroads the king and
princes observed on visits to Europe imparted a keen sense of difference.
Siwilai, acquired from Old Europe, was a mark of this difference
spatially. When it looked downward in the local hierarchy at the rural
and aboriginal peoples who made up most of the population the
aristocracy was looking at its own past, what it had come from in its
scramble to be *siwilai.* This was the temporal dimension, the history
of its own backwardness (Thongchai 2000a). In these dynamics of
modernization "Thai" could easily come to mean "backward," and
this is what the aristocracy feared even as it created the conditions
that forced the issue.

It is anachronistic and misleading to jump across time and compare
siwilai with globalization, but similar dynamics are at work that raise
the specter of the loss of local identity and sovereignty. In the early
1990s Thai shoppers enjoyed buying the products with the "inter-"
(*intoe*) or international brands. Boutiques in foreign cities had to hire
Thai-speaking assistants to cater to Thai tourists eager to purchase
Benetton, Adidas, and Pierre Cardin (Kasian 2002; Reynolds 2002:
312–13). These were the privileged global travelers who could afford
to go abroad; the less affluent had to be content with buying the
(possibly counterfeit) international brands in sumptuous Bangkok
shopping malls. The cachet of owning these foreign-made products was
irresistible, even if the products were made in Thailand! This was
un-Thai, as Kasian Tejapira has said, but at the same time, oh, so Thai.

The tensions inherent in the dialectical relationship between
globalization and local identity today, or between *siwilai* and Thai
sovereignty in the late nineteenth century, are uncannily similar.
Globalization in its local, Thai manifestations is of long historical
formation and is not merely a product of World Bank policy or free
trade agreements. The Thai middle classes, the new rich, even the cash

croppers and tenant farmers want to make their own modernity instead of always feeling that they have to get it from somewhere else. This desire is leading to the search for new, authentic selves at the personal, community and national levels.

Bibliography

Abeel, David. 1934. *Journal of a Residence in China*. New York: Leavitt Lord.

Abercrombie, Nicholas, Stephen Hill, and Brian S. Turner. 1980. *The Dominant Ideology Thesis*. London and Sydney: George Allen & Unwin.

Acker, Robert. 1998. "New Geographical Tests of the Hydraulic Thesis at Angkor," *South East Asia Research* 6.1 (March), pp. 5–47.

Adas, Michael. 1981. "From Avoidance to Confrontation: Peasant Protest in Precolonial Southeast Asia," *Comparative Studies in Society and History* 23, pp. 217–47.

Airriess, Christopher A. 2003. "The Ecologies of *Kuala* and *Muara* Settlements in the Pre-Modern Malay Culture World," *Journal of the Malaysian Branch of the Royal Asiatic Society* 76.1 (June), pp. 81–98.

Akin Rabibhadana. 1969. *The Social Organization of Thai Society in the Early Bangkok Period, 1782–1873*. Ithaca: Cornell University, Department of Asian Studies. Southeast Asia Program Data Paper 74.

Alabaster, Henry. 1971. *The Wheel of the Law: Buddhism Illustrated from Siamese Sources*. Reprint edition. Farnborough: Gregg International.

Anan Ganjanapan. 1976. *Early Lan Na Thai Historiography: An Analysis of the Fifteenth- and Sixteenth-Century Chronicles*. M.A. thesis, Cornell University.

Andaya, Barbara Watson. 1971. "Statecraft in the Reign of Lu Tai of Sukhodaya," *The Cornell Journal of Social Relations* 6.1, pp. 61–83.

———. 2002. "Localising the Universal: Women, Motherhood and the Appeal of Early Theravada Buddhism," *Journal of Southeast Asian Studies* 33.1 (February), pp. 1–30.

Anderson, Benedict R. O'G. 1978. "Studies of the Thai State: The State of Thai Studies." In *The Study of Thailand. Analyses of Knowledge, Approaches, and Prospects in Anthropology, Art History, Economics, History and Political Science*, ed. Eliezer B. Ayal, pp. 193–247. Athens, Ohio: Center for International Studies.

———. 1990. *Language and Power: Exploring Political Cultures in Indonesia*. Ithaca and London: Cornell University Press.

Anderson, Benedict, and Ruchira Mendiones, eds. and trans. 1985. *In the Mirror: Literature and Politics in Siam in the American Era*. Bangkok: Editions Duang Kamol.

Anderson, Perry. 1974. *Lineages of the Absolutist State*. London: New Left Books.

Ankersmit, F. R. 1989. "Historiography and Postmodernism," *History and Theory* 28.2, pp. 137–53.

Anuman Rajadhon, Phya. 1969. *Atthachiwaprawat phraya anuman ratchathon* [The autobiography of Phya Anuman Rajadhon]. Cremation volume for Phya Anuman Rajadhon. Bangkok.

———. 1970a. *Ruang khong chat thai* [On Thai nationality]. Cremation volume for Chaliew Phumichit. Bangkok.

Anuman Rajadhon, Phya. 1970b. *Lao ruang nai traiphum phraruang* [A summary of the Traibhumi cosmography of Phraruang]. Bangkok.

Anussom Thavisin. 1994. "Pioneering a New Tourism Frontier," *Bangkok Post Weekly Review* 7 (January).

Aphisit Thirajaruwan. 1994. "Chonchat juang khrayat trakun thai thi kao kae lac yingyai thisut [The Zhuang: The oldest and the most numerous Tai]," *Sinlapa Watthanatham* 15.10 (August), p. 187.

Appadurai, Arjun. 1990. "Disjuncture and Difference in the Global Cultural Economy," *Public Culture* 2.2 (Spring), pp. 1–24.

Askew, Marc. 1996. "The Rise of *Moradok* and the Decline of the *Yarn*: Heritage and Cultural Construction in Urban Thailand," *Sojourn* 11.2, pp. 183–210.

———. 2002. *Bangkok: Place, Practice and Representation*. London and New York: Routledge.

Atkinson, J. M., and S. Errington. 1990. *Power and Difference: Gender in Island Southeast Asia*. Stanford: Stanford University Press.

Atwill, David G. 2003. "Blinkered Visions: Islamic Identity, Hui Ethnicity, and the Panthay Rebellion in Southwest China, 1856–1873," *Journal of Asian Studies* 62.4, pp. 1079–108.

Aung-Thwin, Michael. 1976. "Kingship, the Sangha, and Society in Pagan." In *Explorations in Early Southeast Asian History: The Origins of Southeast Asian Statecraft*, ed. Kenneth R. Hall and John K. Whitmore, pp. 205–56. Ann Arbor: Center for South and Southeast Asian Studies, University of Michigan, Papers on South and Southeast Asia no. 13.

———. 1979. "The Role of Sasana Reform in Burmese History: Economic Dimensions of a Religious Purification," *Journal of Asian Studies* 38.4 (August), pp. 1–88.

———. 1985. *Pagan: The Origins of Modern Burma*. Honolulu: University of Hawaii Press.

———. 1990. *Irrigation in the Heartland of Burma: Foundations of the Pre-colonial Burmese State*. DeKalb: Northern Illinois University, Center for Southeast Asian Studies Occasional Paper 15.

————. 1991. "Spirals in Early Southeast Asian and Burmese History," *Journal of Interdisciplinary History* 21.4 (Spring), pp. 575–602.

AWSJ. 1986. *Asian Wall Street Journal.* 21 January.

Ba Han. 1965. "Burmese Cosmogony and Cosmology," *Journal of the Burma Research Society* 48.1 (June), pp. 9–16.

Bacon, George B. 1892. *Siam, the Land of the White Elephant.* New York: C. Scribner's and Sons.

Bailey, Anne M., and Josep R. Llobera, eds. 1981. *The Asiatic Mode of Production: Science and Politics.* London, Boston and Henley: Routledge & Kegan Paul.

Bamber, Scott. 1989. *Trope and Taxonomy: An Examination of the Classification and Treatment of Illness in Traditional Thai Medicine.* Ph.D. dissertation, Australian National University.

————. 1998. "Medicine, Food, and Poison in Traditional Thai Healing," *Osiris* 13, pp. 339–53.

Bamber, S., Kevin J. Hewison, and Peer J. Underwood. 1993. "A History of Sexually Transmitted Diseases in Thailand: Policy and Politics," *Genito-Urinary Medicine* 69 (April), pp. 148–57.

Bamrung Suwannarat and Chusak Ekkaphet. 1980. *Wannakam sangkhom lae kanmuang* [Literature, society, and politics]. Bangkok: Klum khon mai.

Bareau, A. 1955. *Les premiers conciles bouddhiques.* Paris: Presses Universitaires de France.

Barmé, Scot. 1993. *Luang Wichit Wathakan and the Creation of a Thai Identity.* Singapore: Institute of Southeast Asian Studies.

————. 1999. "Proto-Feminist Discourses in Early Twentieth-Century Siam." In *Genders and Sexualities in Modern Thailand,* ed. Peter A. Jackson and Nerida M. Cook, pp. 134–53. Chiang Mai: Silkworm Books.

————. 2002. *Woman, Man, Bangkok: Love, Sex and Popular Culture in Thailand.* New York and Oxford: Roman & Littlefield Publishers, Inc.

Bastian, Adolf. 1867. *Reisen in Siam im Jahre 1863.* Jena.

Battye, Noel Alfred. 1974. *The Military, Government and Society in Siam, 1868–1910: Politics and Military Reform during the Reign of King Chulalongkorn.* Ph.D. dissertation, Cornell University.

Bell, Duncan S. A. 2003. "Mythscapes: Memory, Mythology and National Identity," *British Journal of Sociology* 54.1 (March), pp. 63–81.

Bell, P. 1992. "Gender and Economic Development in Thailand." In *Gender and Development in Southeast Asia,* ed. Penny and John Van Esterik, pp. 61–82. Montreal, McGill University, Canadian Asian Studies Association.

Bellah, Robert. 1985 [1957]. *Tokugawa Religion: The Cultural Roots of Modern Japan.* Revised edition. New York: The Free Press.

_____. 1965. *Religion and Progress in Modern Asia.* New York: The Free Press.

Bentley, G. Carter. 1986. "Indigenous States of Southeast Asia," *Annual Review of Anthropology* 15, pp. 275–305.

Berger, Mark T. 2003. "Decolonisation, Modernisation, and Nation-Building: Political Development Theory and the Appeal of Communism in Southeast Asia, 1945–1975," *Journal of Southeast Asian Studies* 34.3, pp. 421–48.

Berger, Peter L., and Thomas Luckmann. 1967. *The Social Construction of Reality: A Treatise in the Sociology of Knowledge.* Garden City, N.J.: Doubleday & Company.

Bielenstein, Hans. 1980. *The Bureaucracy of Han Times.* Cambridge and New York: Cambridge University Press.

Biros, Nicole. 1990. "Métamorphoses et polymorphismes en Asie du Sud-Est," *Equinoxe, revue romande de sciences humaines* 3 (Spring), pp. 55–77.

_____. 1992. *Srivijaya – empire ou emporium? Une étude de cas de l'orientalisme.* Ph.D. dissertation, L'Université de la Sorbonne Nouvelle, Paris III.

Black, C. E. 1966. *The Dynamics of Modernization: A Study in Comparative History.* New York: Harper & Row.

Bode, Mabel. 1966. *The Pali Literature of Burma.* Reprint edition. London: Luzac & Co. for the Royal Asiatic Society of Great Britain and Ireland.

Bowie, K. 1992. "Unraveling the Myth of the Subsistence Economy: Textile Production in Nineteenth-Century Northern Thailand," *Journal of Asian Studies* 51 (4), pp. 797–823.

Bowring, Sir John. 1969. *The Kingdom and People of Siam with a Narrative of the Mission to that Country in 1855.* 2 vols. Reprint edition. Kuala Lumpur: Oxford University Press.

Bradley, William L. 1966. "Prince Mongkut and Jesse Caswell," *Journal of the Siam Society* 54.1 (January), pp. 29–41.

Breazeale, Kennon. 1971. "A Transition in Historical Writing: The Works of Prince Damrong Rachanuphap," *Journal of the Siam Society* 59.2 (July), pp. 25–49.

Breazeale, Kennon, and Snit Smukarn. 1988. *A Culture in Search of Survival: The Phuan of Thailand and Laos.* New Haven: Yale University Southeast Asia Studies, Monograph Series 31.

Breman, Jan. 1988. *The Shattered Image: Construction and Deconstruction of the Village in Colonial Asia.* Dordrecht and Providence, R.I.: Foris Publications.

Bronson, Bennet. 1977. "Exchange at the Upstream and Downstream Ends: Notes toward a Functional Model of the Coastal State in Southeast Asia."

In *Economic Exchange and Social Interaction in Southeast Asia: Perspectives from Prehistory, History, and Ethnography*, ed. Karl Hutterer, pp. 39–71. Ann Arbor: University of Michigan, Center for South and Southeast Asian Studies, Papers on South and Southeast Asia 13.

Bronson, Bennet, and Jan Wisseman. 1976. "Palembang as Srivijaya: The Lateness of Early Cities in Southern Southeast Asia," *Asian Perspectives* 19.2, pp. 220–39.

Brun, Viggo. 1987. "The Trickster in Thai Folktales." In *Rural Transformation in Southeast Asia*, ed. Christer Gunnarsson, Mason C. Hoadley, and Peter Wad, pp. 77–93. Lund: Nordic Association for Southeast Asian Studies.

———. 1990. "Traditional Manuals and the Transmission of Knowledge in Thailand." In *The Master Said: To Study and ... to Soren Egerod on the Occasion of His Sixty-seventh Birthday*, ed. Birthe Arendrup et al., pp. 43–65. Copenhagen: University of Copenhagen, East Asian Institute Occasional Papers, no. 6.

Brun, Viggo, and Trond Schumacher. 1987. *Traditional Herbal Medicine in Northern Thailand*. Berkeley: University of California Press.

Bulbeck, F. D. 1992. *A Tale of Two Kingdoms: The Historical Archaeology of Gowa and Tallok, South Sulawesi, Indonesia*. Ph.D. dissertation, Australian National University.

Bunlua Theppayasuwan. 1975. "Śaktina kap khwammai khong kham nai phasathai [Saktina and the meaning of the word in Thai]." In *Chumgthang phasathai* [Thai language at the crossroads], pp. 19–24. Bangkok: Krungthep.

Bunrak Bunyakhetmala. 1994. *Thanandorn thi si jak rabop lok thung rat thai* [The fourth estate: From the world system to the Thai state]. Bangkok: Green Frog Press.

Burnay, J. 1930. "Inventaire dos manuscrits juridiques siamois," *Journal of the Siam Society* 23.3 (April 1930), pp. 135–203.

Butcher, John, and Howard Dick. 1993. *The Rise and Fall of Revenue Farming: Business Elites and the Emergence of the Modern State in Southeast Asia*. New York: St. Martin's Press.

Byrne, Denis. 1991. "Western Hegemony in Archaeological Heritage Management," *History and Anthropology* 5, pp. 269–76.

———. 1993. *The Past of Others: Archaeological Heritage Management in Thailand and Australia*. Ph.D. dissertation, Canberra: Australian National University.

———. 1995. "Buddhist *Stupa* and Thai Social Practice," *World Archaeology* 27.2, pp. 266–81.

Callahan, William A. 1998. "The Ideology of Miss Thailand in National, Consumerist, and Transnational Space," *Alternatives* 23.1 (January), pp. 29–62.

Chai-anan Samutthawanit. 1970. *Phaen phatthanakanmuang chabap raek khong thai: kham krap bangkhom thun khong chaonai lae kharatchakan hai plianplaeng kan pokkhrong, r. s. 103* [The first Thai plan for political development: The princes' and officials' petition in 1885 to the king for a change of government]. Bangkok.

———. 1972. "Thianwan," *Sangkhomsat parithat* [Social science review] 10.11 (November), pp. 64–72

———. 1979. *Chiwit lae ngan thianwan lae k. s. r. kulap* [The life and works of Thianwan and K. S. Kulap]. Bangkok: Thiranan Press.

———. 1994. *Kanplianplaeng kap khwamru nai yuk lokkanuwat* [Knowledge and change in the age of globalisation]. Bangkok: Manager Publications.

Chai Ruangsin. 1979. *Prawattisat thai samai pho so 2352–2453 dan setthakit* [Economic aspects of Thai history from 1809 to 1910]. Bangkok: Thai Watthanaphanit.

Chaiyan Rajchagool. 1994. *The Rise and Fall of the Thai Absolute Monarchy: Foundations of the Modern Thai State from Feudalism to Peripheral Capitalism*. Bangkok: White Lotus. Studies in Contemporary Thailand, vol. 2.

Chakrabarty, Dipesh. 1987. "Comment I (on 'The hidden transcript of subordinate groups')," *Asian Studies Association of Australia Review* 10, pp. 32–35.

Chalinee Atthakornkovit. 1994. *An Analysis of Marketing Communications Development and Practices in Thailand from 1987 to 1991*. M.A. dissertation, University of Canberra.

Chamberlain, James R., ed. 1991. *The Ram Khamhaeng Controversy: Collected Papers*. Bangkok: The Siam Society.

Chamroon Netisastr, Luang, and Adul Wichiencharoen. 1968. "Some Main Features of Modernization of Ancient Family Law in Thailand." In *Family Law and Customary Law in Asia: A Contemporary Legal Perspective*, ed. David C. Buxbaum, pp. 89–106. The Hague: Martinus Nijhoff.

Charnvit Kasetsiri. 1974. "The First Phibun Government and Its Involvement in World War II," *Journal of the Siam Society* 62.2 (July), pp. 25–88.

Chatthip Nartsupha. 1986. *Ban kap muang* [The village and the city]. Bangkok: Sangsan.

———. 1991a. "The 'Community Culture' School of Thought." In *Thai Constructions Knowledge*, ed. Manas Chitakasem and Andrew Turton, pp. 118–41. London: University of London, School of Oriental and African Studies.

————. 1991b. "Naew khit watthanatham chumchon [The community culture school of thought]." In *Watthanatham thai kap khabuan kanplianplaeng sangkhom* [Thai culture and movements for social change], ed. Chatthip Nartsupha. Bangkok: Chulalongkorn University.

————. 1999. *The Thai Village Economy in the Past*. Trans. Chris Baker and Pasuk Phongpaichit. Chiang Mai: Silkworm Books. (Originally published as *Setthakit muban thai nai adit* [The Thai village economy in past time]. Bangkok: Sangsan, 1984.)

Chetana Nagavajara. 1994. "Literature in Thai Life: Reflections of a Native," *South East Asia Research* 2.1 (March), pp. 12–52.

Cholthira Satyawadhna. 1991. *The Dispossessed: An Anthropological Reconstruction of Lawa Ethnohistory in the Light of Their Relationship with the Tai*. Ph.D. dissertation, Australian National University.

Cholthira Kalatyu. 1974. *Wannakhadi puanchon* [Literature of the people]. Bangkok: Aksonsat.

————. 1974. "Traiphum phraruang: rakthan khong udonkan kanmuang thai [The Traibhuimi of Phra Ruang: The foundation of Thai political ideology]," *Warasan thammasat* 6.1, pp. 106–21.

Christie, Jan Wisseman. 1983. "Raja and Rama: The Classical State in Early Java." In *Centers, Symbols, and Hierarchies: Essays on the Classical States of Southeast Asia*, ed. Lorraine Gesick, pp. 9–44. New Haven: Yale University, Southeast Asia Studies, Monograph Series 26.

————. 1986. "Negara, Mandala, and Despotic State: Images of Early Java." In *Southeast Asia in the Ninth to Fourteenth Centuries*, ed. David G. Marr and A. C. Milner, pp. 65–93. Singapore: Institute of Southeast Asian Studies; Canberra: Research School of Pacific Studies.

————. 1990. "Trade and State Formation in the Malay Peninsula and Sumatra, 300 B.C.–A.D. 700." In *The Southeast Asian Port and Polity: Rise and Demise*, ed. J. Kathirithamby-Wells and John Villiers, pp. 39–60. Singapore: Singapore University Press.

————. 1991. "States without Cities: Demographic Trends in Early Java," *Indonesia* 52 (October), pp. 23–40.

Chulalongkorn, King. 1934. *Jotmaihet phraratchakit raiwan phraratchaniphon phrabat somdet phrajunlajomklao jao yu hua phak thi 7* [The royal diaries of King Chulalongkorn, vol. 7]. Bangkok: Sophonphiphatthanakon.

————. 1939. *Phraratchawijan nai phrabatsomdet phrajunlajomklao jaoyuhua ruang jotmai khwamsongjam khong krommaluang narintharathewi* [A study by King Chulalongkorn of the memoirs of Princess Narintharathewi]. Bangkok.

———. 1963. *Phraratchaphithi sipsong duan* [Royal ceremonies of the twelve month]. 2 vols. Bangkok.

———. 1972. *Wong thewarat* [The Devaraja's lineage]. Bangkok: Khurusapha Press.

———. 2001. "The Antiquarian Society of Siam Speech of King Chulalongkorn," *Journal of the Siam Society* 89.1, 2, pp. 95–99. Translated by Chris Baker.

Chulalongkorn, King, and Prince Wachirayan Warorot. 1929. *Phraratchahatthalekha phrabatsomdet phrajunlajomklao jaoyuhua song mi pai ma kap somdet phramahasanajao kromphraya wachirayan warorot* [Correspondence between King Chulalongkorn and Prince-Patriarch Wachirayan Warorot]. Bangkok.

Coedès, George. 1914. "Une recension palie des annales d'Ayuthia," *Bulletin de l'École Française d'Extrême-Orient* 14.3.

———. 1953. "Le substrat autochtone et la superstructure indienne au Cambodge et à Java," *Cahiers d'histoire mondiale* I, 2 (October), pp. 368–77.

———. 1956. "The Twenty-five-hundredth Anniversary of the Buddha," *Diogenes* 15 (July), pp. 95–111.

———. 1957. "The Traibhumikatha Buddhist Cosmology and Treaty on Ethics," *East and West* 7.4, pp. 349–52.

———. 1968. *The Indianized States of Southeast Asia.* Trans. Susan Brown Cowing. Honolulu: East-West Center Press.

Coedès, G., and C. Archaimbault. 1973. *Les trois mondes (Traibhumi Brah Rvan).* Vol. 89 in Publications de L'École Française d'Extrême Orient. Paris.

Cohen, Erik. 1988. "Authenticity and Commoditization in Tourism," *Annals of Tourism Research* 15, pp. 371–86.

Cohn, Bernard S. 1977. "African Models and Indian Histories." In *Realm and Region in Traditional India*, ed. Richard G. Fox. New Delhi: Vikas Publishing House.

Cohen, P., and G. Wijeyewardene, eds. 1984. "Spirit cults and the position of women in northern Thailand," *Mankind* 14.4. Special issue 3.

Comaroff, John. 1982. "Dialectical Systems, History and Anthropology: Units of Study and Questions of Theory," *Journal of Southern African Studies* 8.2 (April), pp. 143–72.

Condominas, Georges. 1978. "A Few Remarks about Thai Political Systems." In *Natural Symbols in South East Asia*, ed. F. B. Milner. London: University of London, School of Oriental and African Studies.

Connors, Michael K. 2003. *Democracy and National Identity in Thailand.* New York and London: RoutledgeCurzon.

Cook, N. 1981. *The Position of Nuns in Thai Buddhism: The Parameters of Religious Recognition.* M.A. thesis, Australian National University.

Cooke, Nola. 1998. "Regionalism and the Nature of Nguyen Rule in Seventeenth-Century Dang Trong (Cochinchina)," *Journal of Southeast Asian Studies* 29.1 (March), pp. 122–61.

Copeland, Matthew. 1993. *Contested Nationalism and the Overthrow of the Absolute Monarchy in Siam.* Ph.D. dissertation, Australian National University.

Cornish, Andrew. 1994. "ASEAN and Its Fringe: Neo-Geometrics in Southeast Asia." *ASSESS Newsletter* (Centre for East and Southeast Asian Studies, James Cook University of North Queensland), 1, pp. 12–13.

Cowan, C. D., and O. W. Wolters, eds. 1976. *Southeast Asian History and Historiography: Essays Presented to D. G. E. Hall.* Ithaca and London: Cornell University Press.

Creese, Helen. 1993. "Love, Lust and Loyalty: Representations of Women in Traditional Javanese and Balinese Literature." Unpublished paper; Fourth Women in Asia Conference, University of Melbourne.

Cushman, Richard D., trans. 2000. *The Royal Chronicles of Ayutthaya.* Edited by David K. Wyatt. Bangkok: The Siam Society.

Damrong Rajanubhab, Prince. 1929a. *Jotmaihet ruang taisuan nai kulap sung taeng prawat somdet phrasangkharat khun thun klao thawai* [A record of the investigation of Mr. Kulap who wrote the biography of the supreme patriarch for presentation to the king]. Bangkok.

———. 1929b. *Rainam nangsuphim khao sung ok pen raya nai prathetsayam* [A bibliography of newspapers published in Siam]. Bangkok.

———. 1955. "Prawat luang phatthanaphongphakdi [The life of Luang Phatthanaphongphakdi]." In Luang Phatthanaphongphakdi, *Nirat Nongkhai.* Cremation volume for Khun Santhatwutthiwithi. Bangkok.

———. 1961. *Phraratchaprawat ratchakan thi 5 kon sawoei rat* [Biography of the fifth king before his accession]. Bangkok.

———. 1966. *Nithan Borannakhadi* [Tales of ancient times]. Bangkok.

———. 1969. *Ruang tang jaophraya krung rattanakosin* [On the appointments of Jaophraya in the Bangkok period]. Bangkok.

———. 1969. *Tamnan ho phrasamut* [History of the library]. Bangkok.

———. 1975. "Laksana kanpokkhrong prathet sayam tae boran [The nature of rule in Siam from ancient times]." In Kukrit Pramoj et al., *Prawattisat lae kanmuang nangsu an prakop wicha phunthan arayatham thai* [History and politics: A reader on the fundamentals of Thai civilization], pp. 3–29. Bangkok, Thammasat University.

Damrong Rajanubhab, Prince, ed. 1914. *Khamhaikan chaokrungkao* [The testimony of the Ayutthayans]. Bangkok.

_____. ed. 1968. *Phraratchaphongsawadan chabap phraratchahatthalekha* [The royal chronicle, royal autograph version]. Bangkok.

_____. ed. 1969. *Tamra phichai songkhram* [Treatise on war]. Cremation volume for Nang Sanit Noranat (Talap Bunrattaphan). Bangkok.

Damrong Rajanubhab, and Naritsaranuwattiwong. 1961. *San somdet* [Princes' letters]. Bangkok: Khurusapha Press.

Damrong Rajanubhab and Sommot Ammoraphan. 1923. *Ruang tang phrarachakhana phuyai nai krung rattanakosin* [On appointments of high ecclesiastical dignitaries in the Bangkok period]. Bangkok.

Dararat Mettarikanon. 1984. "Kotmai sopheni 'ti thabian' khrang raek nai prathetthai [The first proclamation of prostitution law in Thailand]," *Sinlapa watthanatham* 5.5, pp. 6–19.

Darunee Tantiwiramanond, and S. Pandey. 1987. "The Status and Role of Thai Women in the Pre-modern Period: A Historical and Cultural Perspective," *Sojourn* 2.1, pp. 125–49.

Davis, David L. 1982. "Hokensei and Feudalism." In *Austrina, Essays in Commemoration of the 25th Anniversary of the Founding of the Oriental Society of Australia,* ed. A. R. Davis and A. D. Stefanowska, pp. 383–400. Sydney: Oriental Society of Australia.

Davisakd Phuaksom. 2002. "Kanphaet samaimai nai sangkhom thai: chuarok rangkai lae rawetchakam" [Modern medicine in Thai society: Germs, the body, and the medicalized state]. Regional Studies Program, Division of the Arts, Walailak University. Project on the Indigenous Knowledge of Southern Thailand Focusing on the Human Arts and Behaviour, under the Directorship of Professor Sutthiwong Phongphaiboon, sponsored by the Thailand Research Fund. Unpublished mss.

Day, Tony. 1984. "Second Thoughts about a History of Batavia," *Indonesia* 38 (October), pp. 147–61.

_____. 1994. "'Landscape' in Early Java." In *Recovering the Orient: Artists, Scholars, Appropriations,* ed. Andrew Gerstle and Anthony Milner, pp. 175–203. Singapore: Harwood Academic Publishers GmbH.

_____. 2002. *Fluid Iron: State Formation in Southeast Asia.* Honolulu: University of Hawai'i Press.

Day, Tony, and Will Derks, eds. 1999. "Narrating Knowledge: Reflections on the Encylopedic Impulse in Literary Texts from Indonesian and Malay Worlds," *Bijdragen tot de taal-, Land- en Volkenkunde* 155, part 3, pp. 309–492.

De Casparis, J. G. 1986. "Some Notes on Relations between Central and Local Government in Ancient Java." In *Southeast Asia in the Ninth to Fourteenth Centuries,* ed. David G. Marr and A. C. Milner, pp. 49–63. Singapore: Institute of Southeast Asian Studies; Canberra: Research School of Pacific Studies.

De Konnick, Rodolphe. 1996. "The Peasantry as the Territorial Spearhead of the State in Southeast Asia: The Case of Vietnam," *Sojourn* 11.2, pp. 231–58.

De Silva, K. M., et al., eds. 1988. *Ethnic Conflicts in Buddhist Societies. Sri Lanka, Thailand, and Burma.* London: Pinter Publishers.

Dhani Nivat, Prince. 1963. *The Royal Palaces.* Thai Culture, n.s. no. 23. Bangkok: Fine Arts Department

———. 1969. "The Reconstruction of Rama I of the Chakri Dynasty." In *Collected Articles by H.H. Prince Dhani Nivat.* Bangkok. Siam Society; reprinted from the *Journal of the Siam Society* on the occasion of his eighty-fourth birthday.

Dhiravat na Pombejra. 1992. *Court, Company, and Cambong: Essays on the VOC Presence in Ayutthaya.* Ayutthaya: Ayutthaya Historical Study Centre.

———. 2000. "VOC Employees and Their Relationships with Mon and Siamese Women." In *Other Pasts: Women, Gender and History in Early Modern Southeast Asia,* ed. Barbara Watson Andaya, pp. 195–214. Honolulu: University of Hawai'i at Manoa, Center for Southeast Asian Studies

Dobbin, Christine. 1983. *Islamic Revivalism in a Changing Peasant Economy: Central Sumatra, 1784–1847.* London and Malmo: Curzon Press.

Dove, Michael. 1985. "The Agroecological Mythology of the Javanese and the Political Economy of Indonesia," *Indonesia* 39 (April), pp. 1–36.

Durrant, Stephen W. 1995. *The Cloudy Mirror: Tension and Conflict in the Writings of Sima Qian.* Albany: State University of New York Press.

Eberhardt, N. 1988. *Gender, Power and the Construction of the Moral Order: Studies from the Thai Periphery.* Madison: University of Wisconsin-Madison, Center for Southeast Asian Studies, Monograph 4.

Ellen, Roy, et al., eds. *Indigenous Environmental Knowledge and Its Transformations: Critical Anthropological Perspecives.* Amsterdam: Harwood Academic Publishers.

Elson, R. E. 1997. *The End of the Peasantry in Southeast Asia: A Social and Economic History of Peasant Livelihood, 1800–1900s.* Basingstoke: Macmillan Press Ltd.

Emmerson, Donald K. 1984. "'Southeast Asia': What's in a Name?" *Journal of Southeast Asian Studies* 15.1 (March), pp. 1–21.

Enloe, C. 1990. *Bananas, Beaches and Bases: Making Feminist Sense of International Politics.* Berkeley: University of California Press.

Evans, Grant. 2002. "Between the Global and the Local there are Regions, Culture Areas, and National States: A Review Article," *Journal of Southeast Asian Studies* 33.1, pp. 147–62.

Fairclough, Gordon. 1994. "Sacred and Profane: Monk Embroiled in Sex and Plagiarism Scandal," *Far Eastern Economic Review* 3 (March), pp. 22–23.

FCCT. 1988. *The King of Thailand in World Focus.* Bangkok: Foreign Correspondents Club of Thailand. "Power and Awe Surround Royal Family," reprinted from *Toledo Blade,* 6 September 1987.

Featherstone, M. 1990. *Global Culture: Nationalism, Globalization and Modernity. Theory Culture and Society* 7, nos. 2–3. Special issue: *Global Culture.* London: Sage Publications.

Feer, Léon. 1877. "Études cambodgiennes, la Collection Hennecart de la Bibilothèque Nationale," *Journal Asiatique* IX (7th series), pp. 161–234.

———. 1879. "Le bouddhisme à Siam, une soirée chez le Phra Klang en 1863, le dernier roi de Siam et ses projets de réforme religieuse," *Mémoires de la Socété académique indochinoise de France,* vol. I, pp. 146–62.

FEER. 1987. *Far Eastern Economic Review,* 24 December.

Ferguson, C. A. 1972. "Diglossia." In *Language and Social Context,* ed. Pier Paolo Giglioli, pp. 232–51. Harmondsworth, Penguin.

Fine Arts Department, comp. 1962. *Ruam ruang muang nakhon sithammarat* [A collection of pieces on Nakhon Sithammarat]. Bangkok.

———. 1964. *Latthi thamniam tangtang* [A miscellany of beliefs and customs]. Vol. I. Bangkok: Khlang Witthaya Press.

———. 1969a. *Ratchasakunlawong* [Royal genealogy]. Bangkok.

———. 1969b. *Ruang tang jaophraya krung rattanakosin* [On the appointment of Jaophraya Nobles in the Bangkok period]. Cremation volume for M. L. Chuchat Kamphu. Bangkok.

———. 1971a. *Chumnum ruang muang sawan muang narok lae muang samkhan nai samai phutthakan* [A collection of materials concerning heaven and hell and important principalities during the time of the Buddha]. Bangkok: Fine Arts Department.

———. 1971b. *Jindamani* [Gems of thought]. Bangkok: Bannakhan Press.

Foeng Moeng Long. 1991. *Phum panya tawanok khamphi kan chai khon* [Wisdom of the East: A manual for utilizing people]. Trans. Adun Ratanamankasem. Ed. Thorngthaem Natjamnong. Bangkok: Dokya Press.

Fox, James J. 1986. "The Ordering of Generations: Change and Continuity in Old Javanese Kinship." In *Southeast Asia in the Ninth to Fourteenth Centuries,* ed. David G. Marr and A. C. Milner, pp. 315–26. Singapore: Institute of Southeast Asian Studies; Canberra, Research School of Pacific Studies.

Friedland, Jonathan. 1989. "A Finger in Every Pie," *Far Eastern Economic Review,* 28 December, pp. 42–44.

Gedney, William. 1989. *Selected Papers on Comparative Tai Studies*. Edited by Robert J. Bickner et al. Ann Arbor: University of Michigan, Center for South and Southeast Asian Studies.

Geertz, Clifford. 1977. "Centers, Kings, and Charisma: Reflections on the Symbolics of Power." In *Culture and Its Creators: Essays in Honor of Edward Shils*, ed. Joseph Ben–David and Terry Nichols Clark, pp. 150–71. Chicago and London: University of Chicago Press. (Reprinted in Clifford Geertz, *Local Knowledge: Further Essays in Interpretive Anthropology*. London, Fontana, 1993.)

————. 1980. *Negara: The Theater State in Nineteenth-Century Bali*. Princeton: Princeton University Press.

Gerini, G. E. 1895. *Chulakantamangala, or the Tonsure Ceremony as Performed in Siam*. Bangkok.

Gerini, G. E., comp. 1912. *Siam and Its Productions, Arts and Manufactures*. Hertford, Eng.

Gesick, Lorraine. 1995. *In the Land of Lady White Blood: Southern Thailand and the Meaning of History*. Ithaca: Cornell University, Southeast Asia Program, Studies on Southeast Asia.

Gesick, Lorraine, ed. 1983. *Centers, Symbols, and Hierarchies: Essays on the Classical States of Southeast Asia*. New Haven: Yale University, Southeast Asian Studies.

Gethin, Rupert. 1998. *The Foundations of Buddhism*. Oxford: Oxford University Press.

Ginzburg, Carlo. 1980. "Morelli, Freud and Sherlock Holmes: Clues and Scientific Method," *History Workshop* 9 (Spring), pp. 5–36.

Girling, J. 1981. *Thailand: Society and Politics*. Ithaca: Cornell University Press.

Gittinger, M., and H. L. Leedom Lefferts Jr. 1992. *Textiles and the Tai Experience in Southeast Asia*. Washington, D.C.: Textile Museum.

Glover, Ian, et al., eds. 1992. *Early Metallurgy, Trade and Urban Centres in Thailand and Southeast Asia*. Bangkok: White Lotus.

Gokhale, B. G. 1965. "The Theravada Buddhist View of History," *Journal of the American Oriental Society* 85.3, pp. 354–60.

Golomb, Louis. 1985. *An Anthropology of Curing in Multiethnic Thailand*. Urbana and Chicago: University of Illinois Press, Illinois Studies in Anthropology 15.

Gombrich, R. F. 1971. *Precept and Practice: Traditional Buddhism in the Rural Highlands of Ceylon*. Oxford: Clarendon Press.

Gonda, J. 1966. *Ancient Indian Kingship from the Religious Point of View*. Leiden: E. J. Brill.

Griswold, A. B. 1961. *King Mongkut of Siam*. New York: Asia Society.

Griswold, A. B., and Prasert na Nagara. 1992. *Epigraphic and Historical Studies*. Bangkok: The Historical Society.

Guha, Ranajit. 1983. *Elementary Aspects of Peasant Insurgency in Colonial India*. Delhi: Oxford University Press.

Gullick, J. M. 1988. *Indigenous Political Systems of Western Malaya*. Revised edition. London: The Athlone Press.

Gutman, Pamela. 1976. *Ancient Arakan, with Special Reference to Its Cultural History between the Fifth and Eleventh Centuries*. Ph.D. dissertation, Australian National University.

Guy, John. 1986. "Vietnamese Ceramics and Cultural Identity: Evidence from the Ly and Tran Dynasties." In *Southeast Asia in the Ninth to Fourteenth Centuries*, ed. David G. Marr and A. C. Milner, pp. 255–69. Singapore: Institute of Southeast Asian Studies; Canberra, Research School of Pacific Studies.

Hagesteijn, Renée. 1989. *Circles of Kings: Political Dynamics in Early Continental Southeast Asia*. Dordrecht and Providence: Foris Publications.

Hall, Kenneth R. 1985. *Maritime Trade and State Development in Early Southeast Asia*. Sydney and Wellington: George Allen & Unwin.

Hall, Kenneth R, and John K. Whitmore, eds. 1976. *Explorations in Early Southeast Asian History: The Origins of Southeast Asian Statecraft*. Ann Arbor: University of Michigan, Center for South and Southeast Asian Studies, Papers on South and Southeast Asia 11.

Hamilton, Annette. 1992a. "Family Dramas: Film and Modernity in Thailand," *Screen* 33.3, pp. 259–73.

——. 1992b. "The Mediascape of Modern Southeast Asia," *Screen* 33.1, pp. 81–92.

——. 1993. "Video Crackdown, or The Sacrificial Pirate: Censorship and Cultural Consequences in Thailand," *Public Culture* 5, pp. 515–31.

Hanks, L. M. 1962. "Merit and Power in the Thai Social Order," *American Anthropologist* 64.6 (Dec. 1962), pp. 1247–61.

——. 1963. "The Cosmic View of Bang Chan Villagers, Central Thailand," *Proceedings,* Ninth Pacific Science Congress, 1957, vol. 3, pp. 107–13. Bangkok.

Hannerz, U. 1989. "Notes on the Global Ecumene," *Public Culture* 2, pp. 66–75.

Hansen, Anne. 2003. "The Image of an Orphan: Cambodian Narrative Sites for Buddhist Ethical Reflection," *Journal of Asian Studies* 62.3 (August), pp. 811–34.

Hara, Minoru. 1973. "The King as a Husband of the Earth (*mahipati*)," *Asiatische Studien* 27, pp. 102–3.

Harris, Townsend. 1959. *The Complete Journal of Townsend Harris, First*

American Consul and Minister to Japan. Reprint ed. Rutland, Vt.: C. E.
Tuttle.

Heine-Geldern, Robert. 1956. *Conceptions of State and Kingship in Southeast
Asia.* Ithaca: Cornell University, Southeast Asia Program, Data Paper
Series.

Hewison, Kevin. 1992. "Thailand: On Becoming a NIC," *Pacific Review* 5.4,
pp. 328–37.

Heyzer, Noeleen. 1986. *Working Women in South-East Asia: Development,
Subordination and Emancipation.* Philadelphia: Open University Press.

Higham, Charles. 1989. *The Archaeology of Mainland Southeast Asia from
10,000 B.C. to the Fall of Angkor.* Cambridge: Cambridge University
Press.

Hirschman, Charles, et al., eds. 1992. *Southeast Asian Studies in the Balance:
Reflections from America.* Ann Arbor: Association for Asian Studies.

Hirshson, Stanley P. 1969. *The Lion of the Lord: A Biography of Brigham
Young.* New York: Alfred A. Knopf.

Hodges, Ian. 1998. "Western Science in Siam: A Tale of Two Kings," *Osiris*
13, pp. 80–95.

———. 1999. "Time in Transition: King Narai and the Luan Prasoet Chronicle
of Ayutthaya," *Journal of the Siam Society* 87.1 and 87.2, pp. 33–44.

Hong Lysa. 1984. *Thailand in the Nineteenth Century: Evolution of the
Economy and Society.* Singapore: Institute of Southeast Asian Studies.

———. 1991. "Itsaraphap kap khwampentua khong tua eng khong
phuying khon nung nai sayam kho so thi 19 [Freedom and autonomy of
one nineteenth-century woman in Siam]," *Junlasan thai khadi suksa* 8.1,
pp. 5–8.

———. 1998. "Of Consorts and Harlots in Thai Popular History," *Journal
of Asian Studies* 57.2, pp. 333–53.

———. 1999. "Palace Women at the Margins of Social Change: An Aspect
of the Politics of Social History in the Reign of King Chulalongkorn,"
Journal of Southeast Asian Studies 30.2 (September), pp. 310–24.

———. 2002. "Indian Policy Subalterns in King Chulalongkorn's Kingdom:
Turn of the Twentieth Century Bangkok Pantomime." In *Khu phumjai*
[With pride], ed. Sirilak Sampatchalit and Siriphorn Yotkamolsat, pp.
453–73. Bangkok: Sangsan Press.

———. 2003. "Extraterritoriality in Bangkok in the reign of King
Chulalongkorn (1868–1910): The Cacophonies of Semi-colonial
Cosmopolitanism," *Itinerario: European Journal of Overseas History*
27.2, pp. 125–46.

———. 2004. "'Strangers Within the Gates': Knowing Semi-colonial Siam as
Extraterritorials," *Modern Asian Studies* 38.2, pp. 327–54.

Hutterer, Karl L. 1982. "Early Southeast Asia: Old Wine in New Skins? A Review Article," *Journal of Asian Studies* 41.3 (May), pp. 559–70.

Hutterer, Karl L., ed. 1977. *Economic Exchange and Social Interaction in Southeast Asia: Perspectives from Prehistory, History, and Ethnography.* Ann Arbor: University of Michigan, Center for South and Southeast Asian Studies, Papers on South and Southeast Asia 13.

Iaming, and P. Phitsanakha. 1956. *Somdet phrajao taksin maharat* [King Taksin the Great]. Bangkok.

Iijima Akiko and Koizumi Junko. 2003. "Engendering Thai History: 'I do not wish my people to be *that*,'" *Asian Research Trends* 13, pp. 21–46.

Irvine, W. 1984. "Decline of Village Spirit Cults and Growth of Urban Spirit Mediumship: The Persistence of Spirit Beliefs, the Position of Women, and Modernization." In "Spirit Cults and the Position of Women in Northern Thailand," *Mankind* 14.4. Special issue no. 3, ed. Cohen and Wijeyewardene, pp. 315–24.

Jackson, Peter A. 1989. *Male Homosexuality in Thailand: An Interpretation of Contemporary Thai Sources.* Elmhurst, New York: Global Academic Publishers.

———. 1997. "Kathoey < Gay < Man: The Historical Emergence of Gay Male Identity in Thailand." In *Sites of Desire/Economies of Pleasure: Sexualities in Asia and the Pacific,* ed. Lenore Manderson and Margaret Jolly. Chicago: University of Chicago Press.

———. 1999. "An American Death in Bangkok: The Murder of Darrell Berrigan and the Hybrid Origins of Gay Identity in 1960s Bangkok," *GLQ: A Journal of Lesbian and Gay Studies* 5, pp. 361–411.

———. 2000. "An Explosion of Thai Identities: Global Queering and Re-imagining Queer Theory," *Culture, History and Sexuality* 2.4, pp. 405–24.

———. 2002a. "Offending Images: Gender and Sexuality Minorities, and State Control of the Media in Thailand." In *Media Fortunes, Changing Times: ASEAN States in Transition,* ed. Russell H. K. Heng, chap. 9. Singapore: Institute of Southeast Asian Studies.

———. 2002b. "Thai-Buddhist Identity: Debates on the *Traiphum Phra Ruang.*" In *National Identity and Its Defenders: Thailand Today.* ed. Craig Reynolds, pp. 155–88. Revised edition. Chiang Mai: Silkworm Books.

———. 2003. "Epilogue." In *Buddhadasa: Theravada Buddhism and Modernist Reform in Thailand.* Chiang Mai: Silkworm Books.

Jackson, Peter A., and Gerard Sullivan, eds. 1999. *Lady Boys, Tom Boys, Rent Boys: Male and Female Homosexualities in Contemporary Thailand.* Binghamton, New York: Haworth Press.

Jakobson, Roman. 1972. "Linguistics and Poetics." In *The Structuralists from Marx to Lévi-Strauss*, ed. Richard and Fernande DeGeorge, pp. 85–122. Garden City, N.J.: Doubleday & Company, Anchor Books.

Jenkins, Richard A., and Bryan Kim, "Cultural Norms and Risk: Lessons Learned from HIV in Thailand," *The Journal of Primary Prevention* 25.1 (September), pp. 17–40.

Ji Giles Ungpakorn, ed. 2003. *Radicalising Thailand: New Political Perspectives*. Bangkok: Chulalongkorn University, Institute of Asian Studies.

Jit Poumisak [Somsamai Srisudravarna, pseud.]. 1957. "Chomna khong śakdina thai nai patjuban [The real face of Thai saktina today]." In *Nitisat 2500 chabap rap sattawatmai* [The Faculty of Law yearbook of 2500 to greet the new century]. Bangkok: Thammasat University, Faculty of Law.

———. [Sitthi Sisayam, Thipakon, et al.]. 1975. *Nirat Nongkhai wannakhadi thi thuk sang phao* [Nirat No'ngkhai: Literary work burned by decree]. October. Ramkhamhaeng Students Association.

———. 1980. "Nirat Nongkhai wannakhadi thi thuk sang phao" [Nirat Nongkhai: Literary work burned by decree]. In *Bot wikhro moradok wannakhadi thai* [Analytic essays on the heritage of Thai literature], pp. 158–270. Bangkok: Sattawat.

Jiranan Phitpricha. 1975. *Lok thi si prawattisat na mai khong ying thai* [The fourth world: A new look at the history of Thai women]. Bangkok.

Jitraphorn Wanatsaphong. 1993. "Samphat chalatchai ramitanon watthanatham chumchon nai krasae lokkanuwat [Interview with Chalatchai Ramitanon: The community culture movement in the age of globalisation]," *Sayamrat Weekly*, 17–23 October, pp. 23–25.

Johnston, D. B. 1975. *Rural Society and the Rice Economy in Thailand, 1880–1930*. Ph.D. dissertation, Yale University.

———. 1980. "Bandit, Nakleng, and Peasant in Rural Thai Society." In *Royalty and Commoners: Essays in Thai Administrative, Economic and Social History*, ed. Constance M. Wilson et al., pp. 90–101. Leiden: E. J. Brill.

Jones, Antoinette M. Barrett. 1984. *Early Tenth Century Java from the Inscriptions: A Study of Economic, Social and Administrative Conditions in the First Quarter of the Century*. Dordrecht, Holland, and Cinnaminson, U.S.A: Foris Publications.

Jones, John T. 1851. "Some Account of the Trai Phum," *Journal of the Indian Archipelago* 5.

Jory, Patrick. 2002. "Thai and Western Buddhist Scholarship in the Age of Colonialism: King Chulalongkorn Redefines the Jatakas," *Journal of Asian Studies* 61.3 (Aug.), pp. 891–918.

Kanjana Kaewthep. 1992. *Itthisat* [Feminism]. Bangkok: Gender Press.

Kasian Tejapira. 1991. Personal communication, 22 April.

_____. 1992. "Pigtail: A Pre-History of Chineseness in Siam," *Sojourn* 7.1, pp. 95–122.

_____. 1994. *Lae lort lai mangkorn* [Looking through the dragon design]. Bangkok: Khopfai Publishing.

_____. "'Globalisers' vs. 'Communitarians': The Current Intellectual Scene in Thailand." Unpublished paper, n.d.

_____. 2001. *Commodifying Marxism: The Formation of Modern Thai Radical Culture, 1927–1958.* Kyoto and Melbourne: Kyoto University Press and Trans Pacific Press.

_____. 2002. "The Postmodernization of Thainess." In *Cultural Crisis and Social Memory: Modernity and Identity in Thailand and Laos,* ed. Shigeharu Tanabe and Charles F. Keyes. London: RoutledgeCurzon.

Kathirithamby-Wells, J., and John Villiers, eds. 1990. *The Southeast Asian Port and Polity: Rise and Demise.* Singapore: Singapore University Press.

Kennedy, J. 1977. "From Stage to Development in Prehistoric Thailand: An Exploration of the Origins of Growth, Exchange, and Variability in Southeast Asia." In *Economic Exchange and Social Interaction in Southeast Asia: Perspectives from Prehistory, History, and Ethnography,* ed. Karl L. Hutterer, pp. 23–38. Ann Arbor: University of Michigan, Center for South and Southeast Asian Studies, Papers on South and Southeast Asia 13.

Kennedy, Victor. 1970. "An Indigenous Early Nineteenth Century Map of Central and Northeast Thailand." In *In Memoriam Phya Anuman Rajadhon,* ed. Tei Bunnag and Michael Smithies, pp. 315–48. Bangkok: The Siam Society.

Keyes, Charles F. 1976. "Towards a New Formulation of the Concept of Ethnic Group," *Ethnicity* 3, pp. 202–13.

_____. 1984. "Mother or Mistress but Never a Monk: Buddhist Notions of Female Gender in Rural Thailand," *American Ethnologist* 11.2, pp. 223–41.

_____. 1986. "Ambiguous Gender: Male Initiation in a Northern Thai Buddhist Society." In *Gender and Religion: on the Complexity of Symbols,* ed. C. W. Bynum et al., pp. 66–96. Boston: Beacon Press.

_____. 1987. *Thailand: Buddhist Kingdom as Modern Nation-State.* Boulder and London: Westview Press.

_____. 1992. "A Conference at Wingspread and Rethinking Southeast Asian Studies." In *Southeast Asian Studies in the Balance: Reflections from America,* ed. Charles Hirschman, pp. 9–24. Ann Arbor: Association for Asian Studies.

——. 2002. "National Heroine or Local Spirit?: The Struggle over Memory in the Case of Thao Suranari of Nakhon Ratchasima." In *Cultural Crisis and Social Memory: Modernity and Identity in Thailand and Laos*, ed. Shigeharu Tanabe and Charles F. Keyes, pp. 113–36. London: RoutledgeCurzon.

Khajorn Sukkhaphanit. 1965. *Kao raek khong nangsuphim nai prathet thai* [The beginnings of journalism in Thailand]. Bangkok.

——. 1975. "Thanandon phrai [The status of Phrai]." In *Prawattisat lae kanmuang nangsu anprakop wichaphunthan arayatham thai* [History and politics: A reader on the fundamentals of Thai civilization], ed. Khukrit Parmote et al., pp. 115–20. Bangkok: Thammasat University.

Khana anukammakan phoephrae ekkalak khong thai [Subcommittee for the propagation of Thai identity]. 1983. *Raingan phon kansammana ruang watthanatham thangphasa khongthai* [Thai linguistic culture: Seminar proceedings]. Bangkok: National Identity Board.

Khana kammakan chat ngan sompot krung rattanakosin 200 roi pi [Bangkok bicentennial celebration committee]. 1982. *Prawattisat krung rattanakosin pho so 2475–patjuban* [History of Bangkok, 1932–present]. Bangkok.

Khin Thitsa. 1980. *Providence and Prostitution: Image and Reality for Women in Buddhist Thailand*. London: Change International Reports (Women and Society).

Khukrit Pramote. 1961. *Farang sakdina* [European saktina]. Bangkok: Kaona.

——. 1964. "Rabop śakdina nai prathetthai [The saktina system in Thailand]." In *Khwamru khu prathip chut kao* [Knowledge is illumination of the past], pp. 4–39. Bangkok.

——. 1975. "Sangkhom ayutthaya [Ayutthaya society]." In *Prawattisat lae kanmuang nangsu anprakop wichaphunthan arayatham thai* [History and politics: A reader on the fundamentals of Thai civilization], ed. Khukrit Pramote et al., pp. 45–67. Bangkok: Thammasat University.

Khurusapha Press. 1963. "Phongsawadan yonok [The Yonok chronicle]." In *Prachum phongsawadan* [Collected chronicles], vol. 4. Bangkok: Khurusapha Press.

Kirsch, A. Thomas. 1967. *Phu Thai Religious Syncretism: A Case Study of Thai Religion and Society*, Ph.D. dissertation, Harvard University.

——. 1975a. "Economy, Polity and Religion in Thailand." In *Change and Persistence in Thai Society: Essays in Honor of Lauriston Sharp*, ed. G. William Skinner and A. Thomas Kirsch, pp. 172–96. Ithaca: Cornell University Press.

——. 1975b. "Modernizing Implications of Nineteenth Century Reforms in the Thai Sangha." In *The Psychological Study of Theravada Societies*, ed. Steven Piker, pp. 8–23. Vol. 8 of *Contributions to Asian Studies*, ed. K. Ishwaran. Leiden: E. J. Brill.

———. 1976. "Kinship, Genealogical Claims, and Societal Integration in Ancient Khmer Society: An Interpretation." In *Southeast Asian History and Historiography: Essays Presented to D. G. E. Hall*, ed. C. D. Cowan and O. W. Wolters, pp. 190–202. Ithaca and London: Cornell University Press.

Klum Phuan Phuying, comp. 1990. *Khu mu asasamak songsoem sitthi satri* [Handbook for women paralegals]. Bangkok: Samakhom sitthi seriphap khong prachachon.

Klum Phuying Sipsathaban. 1976. *Thana lae botbat satrisakon* [The position and role of women everywhere]. Bangkok.

Kobkua Suwannathat-Pian. 1988. *Thailand's Durable Premier: Phibun Through Three Decades, 1932–1957*. Kuala Lumpur and Singapore: Oxford University Press.

Koenig, J. G. 1894. "Journal of a Voyage from India to Siam and Malacca in 1779," *Journal of the Straits Branch of the Royal Asiatic Society* 26 (January), pp. 59–201.

Koizumi, Junko. 2000. "From a Water Buffalo to a Human Being: Women and the Family in Siamese History." In *Other Pasts: Women, Gender and History in Early Modern Southeast Asia*, ed. Barbara Watson Andaya, pp. 254–68. Honolulu: University of Hawai'i at Manoa, Center for Southeast Asian Studies.

Kulap Kritsananon. 1913. *Prawat jaophaya aphairacha (m.r.w. lop) jaophaya bodintharadecha (m.r.w. arun)* [Biography of Jaophraya Aphairacha and Jaophraya Bodintharadecha]. Bangkok.

———. 1939. *Prawat yo tam lamdap tamnaengyot akkharamahasenabodi (lae) senabodi jatusadom ru athibodi lae phu rang tamnaeng senabodi krom ru krasuang 6 haeng* [A brief account according to rank of the prime minister and the four chief ministers as well as the ministers of Krom, namely, the six ministers]. Bangkok.

Kulap Saipradit. 1978a. *Kamnoet khropkhrua* [Origins of the family]. Bangkok: Phi phi.

———. 1978b. *Rabiap sangkhom khong manut* [The human social system]. Bangkok: Phi phi.

Kulap Saipradit, et al. 1976. *Prawattisat satri thai* [History of Thai women]. Bangkok: Chomrom nangsu saengdao

Kulke, Hermann. 1978. *The Devaraja Cult.* Ithaca: Cornell University, Southeast Asia Program, Data Paper 108.

———. 1986. "The Early and the Imperial Kingdom in Southeast Asian History." In *Southeast Asia in the Ninth to Fourteenth Centuries*, ed.

David G. Marr and A. C. Milner, pp. 1–22. Singapore: Institute of Southeast Asian Studies; Canberra: Research School of Pacific Studies.

_____. 1991. "Epigraphical References to the 'City' and the 'State' in Early Indonesia," *Indonesia* 52 (October), pp. 3–22.

Kullada Kesabunchoo. 1988. Personal communications, April.

Kwa Chong Guan. 1998. "From Melaka to Singapura: The Evolution of an Emporium." In *Port Cities and Trade in Western Southeast Asia,* ed. Sunait Chutintaranond et al., pp. 107–35. Yangon: Universities Historical Research Centre; Bangkok: Chulalongkorn University, Institute of Asian Studies, IAS Monograph 53.

Landon, Kenneth P. 1968. *Siam in Transition: A Brief Survey of Cultural Trends in the Five Years since the Revolution of 1932.* Reprint edition. New York: Greenwood Press.

Latham, Michael E. 2000. *Modernization as Ideology: American Social Science and "Nation Building" in the Kennedy Era.* Chapel Hill: The University of North Carolina Press.

Law, B. C. 1925. *Heaven and Hell in Buddhist Perspective.* Calcutta.

_____. 1936. *The Buddhist Conception of Spirits* (2nd ed.). London: Luzac & Co.

Leach, E. R. 1965. *Political Systems of Highland Burma.* Boston: Beacon Press.

Leonowens, A. 1953. *Siamese Harem Life.* New York: Dutton.

_____. 1991. *The Romance of the Harem.* Edited and with an introduction by Susan Morgan. Charlottesville and London: University Press of Virginia.

Lerner, Daniel. 1958. *The Passing of Traditional Society: Modernizing the Middle East.* Glencoe, IL: The Free Press of Glencoe.

Lieberman, Victor B. 1984. *Burmese Administrative Cycles: Anarchy and Conquest c. 1580–1760.* Princeton: Princeton University Press.

_____. 2003. *Strange Parallels.* Vol. I: *Integration on the Mainland, Southeast Asia in Global Context, c 800–1830.* Cambridge: Cambridge University Press.

Likhit Dhiravegin. 1988. "Nationalism and State in Thailand." In *Ethnic Conflicts in Buddhist Societies. Sri Lanka, Thailand, and Burma,* ed. K. De Silva, pp. 92–106. London: Pinter Publishers.

Lingat, R. 1931. *L'esclavage privé dans le vieux droit siamois.* Paris: Les Editions Domat Montchrestien.

_____. 1935. "Les trois Bangkok Recorders," *Journal of the Siam Society* 28.2 (Dec. 1935), pp. 203–13.

_____. 1952–55. *Les regimes matrimoniaux du Sud Est de l'Asie. Essai de droit compare indochinois.* Paris: L'École Française d'Extrême-Orient. Publications, vol. 34. Tome I, *Les regimes traditionnels.*

_____. 1962b. "Time and the Dharma: On Manu 1, 85–86," *Contributions to Indian Sociology* 6, pp. 7–16.

_____. 1973. *The Classical Law of India*. Berkeley: University of California Press.

Lingat, R. [Ro Laengka], ed. 1962. *Kotmai tra sam duang* [Laws of the Three Seals]. 5 vols. Bangkok: Khurusapha Press.

Lithai, Phraya. 1972. *Traiphum phraruang* [The three worlds cosmography of Phraruang]. Bangkok: Khlang Wittahaya Press.

_____. 1973. *Les trois mondes (Traibhumi Brah Rvan)*. Paris: L'École Française d'Extrême Orient. Publications, vol. 89. Trans. G. Coedès and C. Archaimbault.

_____. 1982. *The Three Worlds According to King Ruang: A Thai Buddhist Cosmology*. Trans. F. E. Reynolds and M. Reynolds. Berkeley: The Center for South and Southeast Asian Studies, Berkeley Buddhist Studies Series 4.

Lockard, Craig A. 1989. *The Rise and Changing Status of the Southeast Asian History Field in the United States: An Analytical Study*. Madison: University of Wisconsin-Madison, Center for Southeast Asian Studies, Papers on Southeast Asia 17.

Loos, Tamara. 1998. "Issaraphap: Limits of Individual Liberty in Thai Jurisprudence," *Crossroads* 12.1, pp. 35–75.

_____. 2005. "Sex in the Inner City: The Fidelity between Sex and Politics in Siam," *Journal of Asian Studies* 64.4, pp. 881–909.

Lord, Donald C. 1969. *Mo Bradley and Thailand*. Grand Rapids, Michigan.

Lovejoy, Arthur O. 1973. *The Great Chain of Being: A Study of the History of an Idea*. Reprint edition. Cambridge: Harvard University Press.

Luce, G. H. 1969. *Old Burma–Early Pagan*. Vol. 1. Locust Valley, New York: J. J. Augustin for Artibus Asiae and the Institute of Fine Arts, New York University.

Mabbett, Ian W. 1969. "Devaraja," *Journal of Southeast Asian History* 10.2 (September), pp. 202–23.

_____. 1977a. "The 'Indianization' of Southeast Asia: Reflections on the Historical Sources," *Journal of Southeast Asian Studies* 8. 2 (September), pp. 143–61.

_____. 1977b. "Varnas in Angkor and the Indian Caste System," *Journal of Asian Studies* 36.3 (May), pp. 429–42.

_____. 1978. "Kingship at Angkor," *Journal of the Siam Society* 66.2 (July), pp. 1–58.

_____. 1983a. "Some Remarks on the Present State of Knowledge about Slavery in Angkor." In *Slavery, Bondage, and Dependency in Southeast Asia*, ed. Anthony Reid, pp. 44–63. St. Lucia: University of Queensland Press.

———. 1983b. "The Symbolism of Mount Meru," *History of Religions* 23.1 (August), pp. 64–83.

———. 1985. "A Survey of the Background to the Variety of Political Traditions in Southeast Asia." In *Patterns of Kingship and Authority in Traditional Asia*, ed. I. W. Mabbett, pp. 69–84. London: Croom Helm.

———. 1986. "Buddhism in Champa." In *Southeast Asia in the Ninth to Fourteenth Centuries*, ed. David G. Marr and A. C. Milner, pp. 289–313. Singapore: Institute of Southeast Asian Studies; Canberra: Research School of Pacific Studies.

McCloud, Donald G. 1986. *System and Process in Southeast Asia: The Evolution of a Region*. London: Westview Press.

McCoy, Alfred W. 1982. "Baylan: Animist Religion and Philippine Peasant Ideology." In *Moral Order and the Question of Change: Essays on Southeast Asian Thought*, ed. David K. Wyatt and Alexander Woodside, pp. 338–408. New Haven: Yale University, Southeast Asia Studies, Monograph Series 24.

McVey, Ruth T. 1978. "Introduction: Local Voices, Central Power." In *Southeast Asian Transitions: Approaches through Social History*, ed. Ruth T. McVey, pp. 1–31. New Haven and London: Yale University Press.

———. 1984. *Southeast Asia*. Edited by Lim Joo-jock and Vani S. Singapore: Institute of Southeast Asian Studies, Regional Strategic Studies Programme.

Macknight, C. C. 1983. "The Rise of Agriculture in South Sulawesi before 1600," *Review of Indonesian and Malaysian Affairs* 17 (Winter–Summer), pp. 92–115.

———. 1993. *The Early History of South Sulawesi: Some Recent Advances*. Clayton, Victoria: Monash University, Centre of Southeast Asian Studies, Working Paper 81.

Mahanama. 1920. *Mahawong Lem* 3 [The Mahavamsa, vol. 3]. Bangkok.

Maier, Hendrik M. J. 1988. *In the Center of Authority: The Malay Hikayat Merong Mahawangsa*. Ithaca: Cornell University, Southeast Asia Program, Studies on Southeast Asia.

Malcolm, Howard. 1839. *Travels in South-Eastern Asia, Embracing Hindustan, Malaya, Siam and China*. Vol. 2. Boston: Gould, Kendall and Lincoln.

Manas Chitakasem. 1972. "The Emergence and Development of the Nirat Genre in Thai Poetry," *Journal of the Siam Society* 60.2, pp. 135–68.

Manas Chitakasem, and A. Turton, eds. 1991. *Thai Constructions of Knowledge*. London: University of London, School of Oriental and African Studies.

Manderson, Lenore. 1992. "Public Sex Performances in Patpong and Explorations of the Edges of Imagination," *Journal of Sex Research* 29.4, 451–75.

_____. 1997. "Parables of Imperialism and Fantasies of the Exotic: Western Representations of Thailand – Place and Sex." In *Sites of Desire/Economies of Pleasure: Sexualities in Asia and the Pacific*, ed. Lenore Manderson and Margaret Jolly, pp. 123–44. Chicago: University of Chicago Press.

Manguin, Pierre-Yves. 1986. "Shipshape Societies: Boat Symbolism and Political Systems in Insular Southeast Asia. " In *Southeast Asia in the Ninth to Fourteenth Centuries*, ed. David G. Marr and A. C. Milner, pp. 108–207. Singapore: Institute of Southeast Asian Studies; Canberra: Research School of Pacific Studies.

_____. 1991. "The Merchant and the King: Political Myths of Southeast Asian Coastal Polities," *Indonesia* 52 (October), pp. 41–54.

_____. 1993. "Palembang and Sriwijaya: An Early Malay Harbour-City Rediscovered," *Journal of the Malaysian Branch of the Royal Asiatic Society* 66.1, pp. 23–46.

Marcus, S. 1977. *The Other Victorians: A Study of Sexuality and Pornography in Mid-Nineteenth-Century England*. Reprint edition. New York: New American Library.

Marr, David G., and A. C. Milner, eds. 1986. *Southeast Asia in the Ninth to Fourteenth Centuries*. Singapore: Institute of Southeast Asian Studies; Canberra: Research School of Pacific Studies.

Masson, Joseph. 1942. *La religion populaire dans le canon bouddhique pali*. Louvain: Bureaux du Museon.

Medhi Krongkaew, ed. 1995. *Thailand's Industrialization and Its Consequences*. Houndmills: Macmillan; New York: St. Martin's Press.

Melchers, K. William. 1986. "The Thai Invasion of Kengtung During the Reign of King Rama III." In *Anuson Walter Vella*, ed. Ronald D. Renard. Honolulu: University of Hawaii Press and Centre for Asian and Pacific Studies.

Mendelson, E. M. 1965. "Initiation and the Paradox of Power: A Sociological Approach." In *Initiation*, ed. C. J. Bleeker. Vol. 10 of *Studies in the History of Religions*, supplements to *Numen*. Leiden: E. J. Brill.

_____. 1975. *Sangha and State in Burma, A Study of Monastic Sectarianism and Leadership*. Ed. J. P. Ferguson. Ithaca: Cornell University Press.

Michaelsen, Helen. 1990. "Modern Art in Thailand: An Outline of its Development from 1932–1960," *SPAFA Digest* (SEAMEO Regional Centre for Archaeology and Fine Arts) 11.3, pp. 32–38.

_____. 1993. "State-building and Thai Painting and Sculpture in the 1930s and 1940s." In *Modernity in Asian Art*, ed. John Clark, pp. 60–74. Broadway, NSW: Wild Peony.

Miksic, John. 1990. "Settlement Patterns and Sub-Regions in Southeast Asian History," *Review of Indonesian and Malaysian Affairs* 24 (Winter), pp. 86–129.

Mills, M. B. 1992. "Modernity and Gender Vulnerability: Rural Women Working in Bangkok." In *Gender and Development in Southeast Asia*, ed. Penny Van Esterik and John Van Esterik, pp. 83–96. Montreal: McGill University, Canadian Asian Studies Association.

Milner, Anthony. 1982. *Kerajaan: Malay Political Culture on the Even of Colonial Rule.* Tucson: University of Arizona Press, Association for Asian Studies, Monograph 40.

————. 1995. *The Invention of Politics in Colonial Malaya: Contesting Nationalism and the Expansion of the Public Sphere.* Cambridge: Cambridge University Press.

Moffat, Abbot Low. 1961. *Mongkut, King of Siam.* Ithaca: Cornell University Press.

Mongkut, King. 1968. *Prachum prakat ratchakan thi 4* [Collected decrees of the fourth reign]. 2 vols. Bangkok.

Montesquieu, Baron de. 1914. *The Spirit of Laws.* Trans. by Thomas Nugent. Vol. 1. London: G. Bell and Sons.

Morell, D., and Chai-anan Sumudavanija. 1981. *Political Conflict in Thailand: Reform, Reaction, Revolution.* Cambridge, Mass.: Oelgeschlager, Gunn and Hain.

Morris–Suzuki, T. 1992. "Women in Japanese Economic Development." In *Gendering Japanese Studies*, ed. Vera Mackie, pp. 65–70. Clayton, Victoria: Monash University, Japanese Studies Centre.

Muang Boran (MB). 1994. "Jak 'lokanuwat' thung 'lokawibat' nai sangkhom thai [Thai society: From 'globalisation' to global catastrophe]," *Muang Boran* 20.1, pp 6–12.

Mulholland, Jean. 1987. *Medicine, Magic and Evil Spirits: Study of a Text on Thai Traditional Paediatrics.* Canberra: Australian National University, Faculty of Asian Studies Monographs, n.s. 8.

Mus, Paul. 1975. *India Seen from the East: Indian and Indigenous Cults in Champa.* Translated by I. W. Mabbett. Clayton, Victoria: Monash University, Centre of Southeast Asian Studies, Papers on Southeast Asia 3.

Muzaffar, Chandra. 1979. *Protector?: An Analysis of the Concept and Practice of Loyalty in Leader-Led Relationships within Malay Society.* Pinang: Aliran.

NA. 1926. National Archives, Seventh Reign files. Mahatthai 2.1/22 *Bettalet bukkhon chaothai* [Miscellaneous, individual Thais]. Correspondence of October 1926 (B.E. 2469) and enclosures.

Nader, Laura, ed. 1996. *Naked Science: Anthropological Inquiry into Boundaries, Power, and Knowledge.* New York and London: Routledge.

Nagtegaal, Luc. 1996. *Riding the Dutch Tiger: The Dutch East Indies Company and the Northeast Coast of Java, 1680–1743.* Leiden: KITLV Press.

Nakayama, Shigeru. 1969. *A History of Japanese Astronomy: Chinese Background and Western Impact.* Cambridge: Harvard University Press, Harvard-Yenching Institute Monograph Series 18.

Nakkharin Mektrairat. 1982. "Kanplianplaeng kanpokkhrong 2475 khong sayam: phromdaen haeng khwarnru [Siam's change of government in 1921: The state of knowledge]," *Warasan thammasat* 11.2 (June), pp. 7–52.

———. 1992. *Kan patiwat sayam pho so 2475* [The Siamese revolution of 1932]. Bangkok: Textbook Project for the Humanities and Social Sciences Foundation.

Nanthira Khamphiban. 1987. *Nayobai kiaw kap phuying thai nai samai sang chat khong jomphon po phibunsongkhram pho so 2481–2487* [Policies dealing with Thai women during the nation-building period of Field Marshal P. Phibunsongkhram, 1938–1944]. M.A. thesis, Thammasat University.

Naowarat Suksamran. 1993. "Selling Political Dreams," *Bangkok Post*, 18 July.

Narathip-praphanphong, Prince. 2001. *Witthayathat phra-ong wan* [Knowledgeable insights of Prince Wan]. Bangkok: Narathip-praphanphong-worawan Foundation.

The Nation. 1984. "Crowd Locked out of Sulak's Hearing," 7 November.

Natthawadi Chanachai. 1986. *Satri nai sangkhom thai samai mai suksa korani satri sung prakop achip phayaban (pho so 2439–2485)* [Women in modern Thai society: A case study of women in the nursing profession, 1896–1942]. M.A. thesis, Chulalongkorn University.

Natthawut Sutthisongkhram. 1962. *Somdet jaophraya borommaha sisuriyawong mahaburut.* Vol. 2. Bangkok.

———. 1963. *Sam jaophraya* [Three jaophraya]. Bangkok.

———. (1977). *Phu sang wannakam* [The creators of literary art]. Bangkok: Rungruangsan Kanphim.

Neale, Fredrick. 1852. *Narrative of a Residence at the Capital of Siam.* London: National Illustrated Library.

Nidhi Aeusrivongse. 1976. "Devarja Cult and Khmer Kingship at Angkor." In *Explorations in Early Southeast Asian History: The Origins of Southeast Asian Statecraft,* ed. Kenneth R. Hall and John K. Whitmore, pp. 107–48. Ann Arbor: University of Michigan, Center for South and Southeast Asian Studies, Papers on South and Southeast Asia 11.

———. 1984. *Pak kai lae bai rua* [Quill and sail]. Bangkok: Amarin Kanphim.

———. 1992. "Thini ham krang baep nimnim [No swaggering of the feminine variety allowed here]," *Sinlapa watthanatham* 13 (5), pp. 154–58.

———. 1994. "Watthanatham yuk lokkanwat [Culture in the globalizing epoch]," *Sinlapa watthanatham* [Art and culture] 6, pp. 92–94.

————. 2002. *Wa duay phet* [On gender]. Bangkok: Matichon. Special issue of *Art and Culture*.

NN. 1955. See *Phatthanaphongphakdi* 1955.

Nisbet, Robert A. 1969. *Social Change and History: Aspects of the Western Theory of Development*. New York: Oxford University Press.

Nordholt, H. Schulte. 1981. "Negara: A Theater State?" *Bijdragen Tot de Taal-, Land en Volkenkunde* 137.4, pp. 470–76.

————. 1996. *The Spell of Power: A History of Balinese Politics, 1650–1940*. Leiden: KITLV Press.

————. 2004. "Locating Southeast Asia: Postcolonial Paradigms and Predicaments." In *Asia in Europe, Europe in Asia*, ed. Srilata Ravi, Mario Rutten and Beng-Lan Goh, pp. 36–56. Singapore: Institute of Southeast Asian Studies.

O'Brien, K. 1988. "Candi Jago as a Mandala: Symbolism of its Narratives" (pt. 1), *Review of Indonesian and Malaysian Affairs* 22 (Summer), pp. 1–61.

————. 1990. "Candi Jago: A Javanese Interpretation of the Wheel of Existence?" *Review of Indonesian and Malaysian Affairs* 24 (Winter), pp. 23–85.

————. 1993. *Means and Wisdom in Tantric Buddhist Rulership of the East Javanese Period*. Ph.D. dissertation, University of Sydney.

O'Connor, Stanley J. 1985. "Metallurgy and Immortality at Candi Sukuh, Central Java," *Indonesia* 39 (April), pp. 53–70.

Office of the National Culture Commission, Ministry of Education. n.d. *Organizational Structure*. Bangkok.

O'Hanlon, Rosalind. 1988. "Recovering the Subject: 'Subaltern Studies' and Histories of Resistance in Colonial South Asia," *Modern Asian Studies* 22.1, pp. 189–224.

Osborne, Milton, and David K. Wyatt. 1968. "The Abridged Cambodian Chronicle: A Thai Version of Cambodian History," *France-Asie* 22.2, pp. 189–203.

Pajarayasara. 1987. "Khwamphit than min phraborommadechanuphap kap kanpokkhrong rabop prachathipatai thi mi phramahakasat pen pramuk [The crime of lese-majesty and the constitutional monarchy]," *Pajarayasan* 14.6, pp. 12–45.

Pallegoix, Jean-Baptist. 1896. *Dictionnaire siamois français anglais*. Bangkok.

Pandey, G. 1992. "In Defense of the Fragment: Writing about Hindu-Muslim Riots in India Today," *Representations* 37 (Winter), pp. 27–55.

Peleggi, Maurizio. 1996. "National Heritage and Global Tourism in Thailand," *Annals of Tourism Research* 23.2, pp. 432–48.

————. 2002a. *Lords of Things: The Fashioning of the Siamese Monarchy's Modern Image*. Honolulu: University of Hawai'i Press.

_____. 2002b. *The Politics of Ruins and the Business of Nostalgia.* Bangkok: White Lotus.

_____. 2004. "Royal Antiquarianism, European Orientalism and the Production of Archaeological Knowledge in Modern Siam." In *Asia in Europe, Europe in Asia,* ed. Goh Beng Lan, Srilata Ravi and Mario Rutten, pp. 133–61. Leiden: International Institute of Asian Studies; Singapore: Institute of Southeast Asian Studies.

Pelley, Patricia M. 2002. *Postcolonial Vietnam: New Histories of the National Past.* Durham, N.C., and London: Duke University Press.

Pemberton, John. 1994. *On the Subject of "Java."* Ithaca: Cornell University Press.

Perera, L. S. 1961. "The Pali Chronicle of Ceylon." In *Historians of India, Pakistan and Ceylon,* ed. C. H. Philips, pp. 29–43. London: Oxford University Press.

Phatthanaphongphakdi, Luang (Thim Sukkhayang). 1955. Nirat Nongkhai. Cremation volume for Khun Santhatwutthiwithi (Suan Santhatwutthi). Bangkok.

Phimruthai Chusaengsi. 1990. *Khwamkhit khong phuying nai nittayasan phuying pho so 2500–2516* [Women's thought in women's magazines, 1957–1973]. M.A. thesis, Thammasat University.

Phitthayalapphruttiyakon, Krommamun. 1964. "Prawat thao worajan." In K. Phitthayalapphruttiyakon, *Chumnum niphon* [Collected writings]. Bangkok.

Phonnarat, Somdet Phra. 1923. *Sangkhitiyawong, phongsawadan ruang sangkhayana phratham phrawinai* Translated by Phraya Pariyattithammathada. Bangkok.

Phrapinklao Jaoyuhua, Phrabatsomdet. 1970. *Tamra punyai* [Artillery manual]. Cremation volume for Uthai Wongwiradet. Bangkok.

Phra Sadet, Jaophraya (Pia Malakun). 1987. *Sombat khong phudi* [Characteristics of a properly behaved person]. Bangkok: Office of the Secretary to the Prime Minister, Office to Promote National Identity.

_____. 1999. *Nangsu katun sombat khong phudi* [Characteristics of a properly behaved person: Cartoon edition]. Bangkok: Samnakngan khanakammakan watthanatham haeng chat.

Phunphit Amatyakul, Nai Phaet. 1980. *Sakdina rama.* Bangkok: Bannakit.

Phutthajan (To), Somdet Phra. 1967. *Thamma* [Dhamma]. Bangkok.

Pigeaud, Th. G. Th. 1977. "Javanese Divination and Classification." In *Structural Anthropology in the Netherlands: A Reader,* ed. P. E. de Josselin de Jong, pp. 64–82. The Hague: Martinus Nijhoff.

Pollock, Sheldon. 1985. "The Theory of Practice and the Practice of Theory in Indian Intellectual History," *Journal of the American Oriental Society* 105, pp. 499–519.

Poole, Ross. 1999. *Nation and Identity*. London: Routledge.

Prachum phraratchaputcha phak 2 pen phraratchaputcha nai ratchakan thi 1 [Collected royal questions, pt. 2: the royal questions of the first reign]. 1923. Bangkok.

Prajaksinlapakhom, Prince. 1925. *Sayam praphut; Tuayang nangsu sayam praphut khong krommaluang prajaksinlapakhom* [An example of Prince Prajaksinlapakhom's magazine, Sayam Praphut]. Bangkok.

Praphat Trinarong. 1962. *Somdet Phrasangkharat haeng krung rattanakosin* [Supreme patriarchs of Bangkok]. Bangkok.

Prasong Sunsiri. 1984. "Phasa thai kap khwam-mankhong haeng chat [Thai language and national security]." In *Phasa thai kap sangkhom thai* [Thai language and Thai society], Samnakrigan Soemsang Ekkalak Khong Chat [National Identity Board], pp. 245–51. Bangkok: Office of the Prime Minister.

Prathip Chumphon. 1998. *Prawattisat kanphaet phaen thai kansuksa jak ekkasan tamra ya* [The history of Thai medicine: A study of the pharmacological manuals]. Bangkok: Fine Arts University, Institute for Research and Development.

Prebish, C. 1974. "A Review of Scholarship on the Buddhist Councils," *Journal of Asian Studies* 33.2, pp. 239–54.

Preecha Juntanamalaga. 1988. "Thai or Siam?," *Journal of the American Name Society* 36.1–2 (March–June), pp. 69–84.

Pressman, Douglas Harold. 1993. *Thai Modernity: A Study in the Sociology of Culture*. Ph.D. dissertation, Brown University.

Quinn, George. 1975. "The Javanese Science of Burglary," *Review of Indonesian and Malayan Affairs* 9.1, pp. 33–54.

Radhakrishnan, R. 1992. "Nationalism, Gender, and the Narrative of Identity." In *Nationalisms and Sexualities*, ed. A. Parker, pp. 77–95. New York and London: Routledge.

Rafael, Vincente L. 1988. *Contracting Colonialism: Translation and Christian Conversion in Tagalog Society under Early Spanish Rule*. Ithaca and London: Cornell University Press.

Raktham Rakthai [pseud.]. n.d. *Kao ratchakan haeng ratchawong jakri* [Nine reigns of the Jakri Dynasty].

Rama I. 1913. *Traiphum lokkawinitchai*. Bangkok.

Rattanapanna Thera. 1968. *The Sheaf of Garlands of the Epochs of the Conqueror*. Translated by N.A. Jayawickrama. London: Luzac & Company Ltd. for the Pali Text Society.

Rawi Buranachai. 1982. Interview with Rawi Buranachai in *Sangkhomsat* (Chiangmai University), 6.1 (April–September 1982), pp. 225–26.

Reid, Anthony. 1988a. "Female Roles in Pre–colonial Southeast Asia," *Modern Asian Studies* 22.3, pp. 629–45.

———. 1988b. *Southeast Asia in the Age of Commerce.* Vol. 1: "The Lands below the Winds, 1450–1680." New Haven: Yale University Press.

———. 1993. *Southeast Asia in the Age of Commerce, 1450–1680.* Vol. 2: "Expansion and Crisis." New Haven and London: Yale University Press.

———. 1999. "A Saucer Model of Southeast Asian Identity," *Southeast Asian Journal of Social Science* 27.1, pp. 7–23.

Reid, Anthony, and Lance Castles, eds. 1975. *Pre-colonial State Systems in Southeast Asia: The Malay Peninsula, Sumatra, Bali-Lombok, South Celebes.* Kuala Lumpur: Malaysian Branch of the Royal Asiatic Society, Monograph 6.

Reid, Anthony, and David Marr, eds. 1979. *Perceptions of the Past in Southeast Asia.* Singapore: Heinemann Educational Books (Asia) Ltd. for the Asian Studies Association of Australia.

Reynolds, Craig J. 1973. *The Buddhist Monkhood in Nineteenth-Century Thailand.* Ph.D. dissertation, Cornell University.

———. 1979. *Prawattisat sangkhom khu arai* [What Is Social History?]. Bangkok: Thai Khadi Research Institute. In Thai and English; Thai version reprinted 1984.

———. 1991. "The Plot of Thai History." In *Patterns and Illusions: Thai History and Thought,* ed. Gehan Wijeyawardene and E. C. Chapman, pp. 313–32. Canberra: Australian National University, Research School of Pacific Studies.

———. 1992. "Authenticating Southeast Asia in the Absence of Colonialism: Burma," *Asian Studies Review* 15. 3 (April), pp. 141–51.

———. 1994. *Thai Radical Discourse: The Real Face of Thai Feudalism Today.* Reprint edition. Ithaca: Cornell University, Southeast Asia Program.

———. 1996a. "Thailand." In *Australia in Asia: Communities of Thought,* ed. Anthony Milner and Mary Quilty. Melbourne: Oxford University Press, 1996.

———. 1996b. "Tycoons and Warlords: Modern Thai Social Formations and Chinese Historical Romance." In *Sojourners and Settlers: Histories of Southeast Asia and the Chinese, A Volume in Honour of Jennifer Cushman,* ed. Anthony Reid, pp. 115–47. London: Allen & Unwin.

———. 1997. "Sino-Thai Business Culture: Strategies, Management and Warfare," *The Asia-Pacific Magazine,* nos. 6 and 7, pp. 33–38.

———. 1999. "On the Gendering of Nationalist and Postnationalist Selves in Twentieth-Century Thailand." In *Genders and Sexualities in Modern Thailand,* ed. Peter A. Jackson and Nerida M. Cook, pp. 261–74. Chiang Mai: Silkworm Books.

―――. 2003. "Review Article: Tai-land and Its Others," *South East Asia Research* 11.1 (March), pp. 113–30.

Reynolds, Craig J., ed. 2002. *National Identity and Its Defenders: Thailand Today*. Revised edition. Chiang Mai: Silkworm Books.

Reynolds, Craig J., and Hong Lysa. 1983. "Marxism in Thai Historical Studies," *Journal of Asian Studies* 43.1 (November), pp. 77–104.

Reynolds, Frank. 1972. "The Two Wheels of Dhamma: A Study of Early Buddhism." In *The Two Wheels of Dhamma: Essays on the Theravada Tradition in India and Ceylon*, ed. Bardwell L. Smith. Chambersburg, Penn.: American Academy of Religion, Studies in Religion 3.

Rhys Davids, T. W., and C. A. F., trans. 1971. "Dialogues of the Buddha, pt. III, ch. XXVII." In *Sacred Books of the Buddhists*, vol. 4, ed. T. W. Rhys Davids. London: Luzac & Co. for the Pali Text Society.

Riggs, Fred W. *Thailand: The Modernization of a Bureaucratic Polity*. Honolulu: East-West Center Press, 1966.

RKBS. 1878. *Ratchakitcanubeksa* [Royal Thai government gazette]. Vol. 5, no. 161, part 21.

Robinson, Geoffrey. 1995. *The Dark Side of Paradise: Political Violence in Bali*. Ithaca and London: Cornell University Press.

Roeské. 1914. "L'enfer cambodgien d'après le *Trai Phum (Tri Bhumi)* 'Les trois mondes'," *Journal Asiatique* 4 (11th series), pp. 587–606.

Royal Institute, comp. 1919. *Phraratchaphongsawadan krung thonburi phaendin somdet phraborommaracha thi 4 (phrajao taksin)* [Royal chronicle of the Thonburi King, Lord Taksin]. Bangkok.

Ruang nai kulap editoe sayam praphet riang ru taeng prawat somdetphrasangkharat [On whether Mr. Kulap, editor of Sayam Praphet, compiled or composed the biography of the supreme patriarch]. n.d. Bangkok.

Rungwit Suwan-aphichon. 1982. "Wannakhadi kanmuang kap sangkhom rattanakosin (rawang pho' so' 2418–21): korani suksa jak nirat nongkhai [Political literature and Bangkok society (1875–78): A case study of Nirat Nongkhai]," *Sangkhomsat* (Chiangmai) 6.1, pp. 22–46.

Ryan, Michael. 1982. *Marxism and Deconstruction: A Critical Articulation*. Baltimore and London: The Johns Hopkins University Press.

Samnakngan khana kammakan watthanatham haengchat [Office of the National Culture Commission]. 1988. *Watthanathamprajamchat* [The national culture]. Bangkok: Ministry of Education.

Sanga Luchaphatthanaphom and Athom Techathada, eds. 1981. *Wikkarittakan thang ekkalak banthuk khong khon run mai* [Identity crisis: A report from the younger generation]. Bangkok: Pajarayasan.

Sangermano, Father. 1966. *A Description of the Burmese Empire*. Translated by William Tandy. Reprint edition. London: Susil Gupta.

Sangop Suriyin. 1967. *Thianwan*. Bangkok.

Sathian Canthimathon. 1982. *Saithan wannakam phua chiwit khong thai* [The flow of Thai art for life]. Bangkok: Chaophraya.

Sawat Chanthani, Nawa-ek. 1966. *Nithan chao rai* [Tales for country people]. Vol. 6. Bangkok.

Sawer, Marian. 1977. *Marxism and the Question of the Asiatic Mode of Production*. The Hague: Martinus Nijhoff.

Schweisguth, P. 1951. *Étude sur la Literature siamoise*. Paris.

Scott, James C. 1977. "Protest and Profanation: Agrarian Revolt and the Little Tradition," *Theory and Society* 4.1, pp. 1–38.

_____. 1998. *Seeing Like a State: How Certain Schemes to Improve the Human Condition Have Failed*. New Haven and London: Yale University Press.

Scott, William Henry. 1982. *Cracks in the Parchment Curtain*. Quezon City: New Day.

_____. 1984. *Prehispanic Source Materials for the Study of Philippine History*. Revised edition. Quezon City, Phil.: New Day.

Sears, Laurie. 1993. "The Contingency of Autonomous History." In *Autonomous Histories, Particular Truths: Essays in Honour of John Smail*, ed. Laurie Sears. Madison: University of Wisconsin, Center for Southeast Asian Studies, Monograph 11.

Sedov, Leonid A. 1978. "Angkor: Society and State." In *The Early State*, ed. Henri J. M. Claessen and Peter Skainik, pp. 111–30. The Hague, Paris, New York: Mouton.

Seksan Prasoetkun. 1989. *The Transformation of the Thai State and Economic Change, 1855–1945*. Ph.D. dissertation, Cornell University.

Seri Pongphit. 1992. "Popular Wisdom and the Search for Identity in Northeast Thailand." In *Proceedings to Present the Results of Projects Funded under the Toyota Foundation's International Grant Program*, pp. 138–42. Tokyo: The Tokyo Foundation.

Shankman, Paul. 1984. "The Thick and the Thin: On the Interpretive Theoretical Paradigm of Clifford Geertz," *Current Anthropology* 25.3 (June), pp. 261–80.

Sharma, R. S. 1965. *Indian Feudalism, 300–1200*. Calcutta.

Shorto, H. L. 1963. "The 32 Myos in the Medieval Mon Kingdom," *Bulletin of the School of Oriental and African Studies* 26.3, pp. 572–91.

_____. 1967. "The Dewatu sotapan: A Mon Prototype of the 37 Nats," *Bulletin of the School of Oriental and African Studies* 30.1, pp. 127–41.

Sihadet Bunnag, Phan-ek. 1980. *"Sakdina" kap kanbonthamlai khong fai trongkham* ["Sakdina" and subversion by the opposing side]. Thesis, Thai Army College.

Sillitoe, Paul. 1998. "The Development of Indigenous Knowledge: A New Applied Anthropology," *Current Anthropology* 39.2 (April), pp. 223–52.

Sinlapa Watthanatham. 1994. Editorial in *Sinlapa watthanatham* 15.10, pp. 14–16.

Siripanyamuni (On), Phra. 1968. *Mongkhonsut plae doi phitsadan samnuan thetsana* [The Matigalasutta: Complete translation for preaching]. Bangkok: Fine Arts Department, revision.

Skinner, G. William. 1957. *Chinese Society in Thailand: An Analytical History.* Ithaca: Cornell University Press.

Smail, John R. W. 1961. "On the Possibility of an Autonomous History of Modern Southeast Asia," *Journal of Southeast Asian History* 2 (1961), pp. 72–102. (Reprinted in *Autonomous Histories, Particular Truths: Essays in Honor of John Smail*, ed. Laurie J. Sears, pp. 39–70. Madison, Wisconsin: Centre of for Southeast Asian Studies, 1993.)

Smith, Anthony D. 1986. *The Ethnic Origins of Nations.* Oxford and New York: Basil Blackwell.

Smith, B. L. 1972. "The Ideal Social Order as Portrayed in the Chronicles of Ceylon." In *The Two Wheels of Dhamma: Essays on the Theravada Tradition in India and Ceylon*, ed. Bardwell L. Smith. Chambersburg, Penn.: American Academy of Religion, Studies in Religion 3.

Smith, Harold E. 1973. "Polygyny and Marriage Registration in Thailand," *Southeast Asia: An International Quarterly* 2.3 (Summer), pp. 291–99.

Smith, R. B., and W. Watson, eds. 1979. *Early South East Asia: Essays in Archaeology, History, and Historical Geography.* New York and Kuala Lumpur: Oxford University Press.

Snodgrass, Adrian. 1985. *The Symbolism of the Stupa.* Ithaca: Cornell University, Southeast Asia Program.

Sombat Chantornvong and Chai-anan Samudavanija. 1980. *Khwamkhit thang kanmuang thai* [Thai political thought]. Bangkok: Bannakit.

Somchintana Thongthew-Ratanasam. 1979. *The Socio-cultural Setting of Love Magic in Central Thailand.* Madison: University of Wisconsin, Center for Southeast Asian Studies, Wisconsin Papers on Southeast Asia.

Somkiat Wantana. 1983. "Traiphum phra ruang din kon diaw nai dindaen [The Traiphum Phra Ruang: A mere chunk of earth in the land]." In Phra Ratchaworamuni, *Traiphum phra ruang ittiphon to sangkhom thai* [The Traiphum Phra Ruang and its influence on Thai society], pp. 73–100. Bangkok: Thammasat University, Chumnum Suksa Phuttasat lae Phrapeni.

Sommot Ammoraphan. 1965. *Prakat kanphraratchaphithi* [Announcements of Royal Ceremonies]. Vol. 1. Bangkok: Khurusapha Press.

Sommot Ammoraphan and Damrong Rajanubhab. 1969. *Ruang tang jaophraya krung rattanakosin* [On the appointments of Jaophraya in the Bangkok period]. Bangkok.

Soraj Hongladarom. 2002a. "Cross–cultural Epistemic Practices," *Social Epistemology* 16.1, pp. 83–92.

———. 2002b. *Witthayasat nai sangkhom lae watthanatham thai* [Science in Thai society and culture]. Bangkok: Institute of Academic Development.

Spellman, J. W. 1964. *Political Theory of Ancient India*. Oxford: Clarendon Press.

Srisakr Vallibhotama and Pranee Wongthes. 1993. *Zhuang: The Oldest Tai* (in Thai). Bangkok: Silpakorn University.

Staal, Fritz. 1994. "Pānini." In *The Encyclopedia of Language and Linguistics*, ed. R. E. Asher, pp. 2916–18. Oxford: Pergamon Press.

Stallybrass, Peter, and Allon White. 1986. *The Politics and Poetics of Transgression*. London: Methuen.

Stein, Burton. 1975. "The State and the Agrarian Order in Medieval South India: A Historiographical Critique." In *Essays on South India*, ed. Burton Stein, pp. 64–91. Honolulu: University Press of Hawaii.

———. 1977. "The Segmentary State in South Indian History." In *Realm and Region in Traditional India*, ed. Richard G. Fox. Delhi: n.p.

———. 1980. *Peasant State and Society in Medieval South India*. Delhi: Oxford University Press.

Steinberg, D. J., ed. 1987. *In Search of Southeast Asia: A Modern History*. Revised edition. Sydney and Wellington: Allen & Unwin.

Stivens, M., ed. 1991. *Why Gender Matters in Southeast Asian Politics*. Clayton, Victoria: Monash University, Centre of Southeast Asian Studies, Papers on Southeast Asia 23.

Streckfuss, David E. 1995. "Kings in the Age of Nations: The Paradox of Lèse-Majesté as Political Crime in Thailand," *Comparative Studies in Society and History* 37.3 (July), pp. 445–75.

———. 1998. *The Poetics of Subversion: Civil Liberty and Lèse-Majesté in the Modern Thai State*. Ph.D. dissertation, University of Wisconsin-Madison.

Streckfuss, David E., ed. 1996. *Modern Thai Monarchy and Cultural Politics*. Bangkok: Santi Pracha Dhamma Institute.

Stuart-Fox, Martin. 2000. "Political Patterns in Southeast Asia." In *Eastern Asia: An Introductory History*, ed. Colin Mackerras. 3d edition. Longman.

Stuart-Fox, Martin, and Mary Kooyman. 1992. *Historical Dictionary of Laos*. Methuen, New Jersey, and London: Scarecrow Press.

Subrahmanyam, Sanjay. 1986. "Aspects of State Formation in South India and Southeast Asia, 1500–1650," *The Indian Economic and Social History Review* 23.4, pp. 357–77.

Suchat Sawatsi, ed. 1994a. *Lophanuwat* [Greed]. Bangkok: Changwannakam.
————. 1994b. *Phokhanuwat* [Consumerism]. Bangkok: Changwannakam.
Sudradjat, Iwan. 1991. *A Study of Indonesian Architectural History*. Ph.D. dissertation, University of Sydney.
Sujit Wongthes. 1986. *Khonthai yu thini prawattisat sangbkom lae watthanatham khong chao sayam nai muangthai* [The Thais were always here: A social and cultural history of the Siamese people in Thailand]. Special issue. Bangkok: Sinlapa watthanatham.
————. ed. 1988. *Jaruk phokhun ramkhamhaeng khrai taeng kan nae* [Who really wrote the King Ramakhamhaeng inscription?]. Special issue. Bangkok: Sinlapa watthanatham.
Sukhumbhand Paribatra, M. R. 1988. "Joy and Apprehension over the Thai Monarchy," *Far Eastern Economic Review*, 21 January.
Sunait Chutintaranonda. 1990. "'Mandala,' 'Segmentary States,' and Politics of Centralization in Medieval Ayudhya," *Journal of the Siam Society* 78.1, pp. 89–100.
Supatra Kopkitsuksakun. 1993. *Sen thang nang ngam phuak thoe ma jak nai la pai nai phua khrai* [The path of the beauty queens. Where did they come from? Where are they going? Who will benefit?] Bangkok: Dokbia Publishing.
Suphot Dantrakun. 1985. *Thai ru sayam* [Thai or Siam?]. Nonburi: Santitham Publishing.
Surin Phitsuwan. 1988. "The Lotus and the Crescent: Clashes of Religious Symbolism in Southern Thailand." In *Ethnic Conflicts in Buddhist Societies. Sri Lanka, Thailand, and Burma*, ed. K. M. De Silva, pp. 187–201. London: Pinter Publishers.
Sutherland, Heather. 1974. "Notes on Java's Regent Families: Part II," *Indonesia*, no. 17 (April), pp. 1–42.
Suthilak Ambhanwong. 1966. "Major Periods in Thai Printing," *Journal of Library History* 1 (October), pp. 242–47.
Suwadee Tanaprasitpatana. 1990. *Thai Society's Expectations of Women, 1851–1935*. Ph.D. dissertation, University of Sydney.
Tai, Hue-Tam Ho. 1988. "Six Essays on Vietnamese History: A Review Article," *Vietnam Forum* 11, pp. 81–91.
Tambiah, S. J. 1970. *Buddhism and the Spirit Cults in North-East Thailand*. Cambridge: Cambridge University Press.
————. 1973. "Dowry and Bridewealth, and the Property Rights of Women in South Asia." In *Bridewealth and Dowry*, ed. Jack Goody and S. J. Tambiah. Cambridge: Cambridge University Press, Cambridge Papers in Social Anthropology 7.

_____. 1985. *Culture, Thought, and Social Action*. Cambridge: Harvard University Press.

Tan Liok Ee. 1988. *The Rhetoric of Bangsa and Minzu: Community and Nation in Tension, the Malay Peninsula, 1900–1955*. Clayton, Victoria: Monash University, Centre of Southeast Asian Studies, Working Paper 52.

Tana Li. 1998. *Nguyen Cochinchina: Southern Vietnam in the Seventeenth and Eighteenth Centuries*. Ithaca: Cornell University, Southeast Asia Program, Studies on Southeast Asia.

Tanabe Shigeharu. 1991. "Spirits, Power and the Discourse of Female Gender: The *phi meng* Cult of Northern Thailand." In *Thai Constructions of Knowledge*, ed. Chitakasem Manas and A. Turton, pp. 183–212. London: University of London, School of Oriental and African Studies.

Tarling, Nicholas, ed. 1992. *The Cambridge History of Southeast Asia*. Vol. 1, "From Early Times to c. 1800." Cambridge: Cambridge University Press.

Taylor, Charles. 1991. *The Ethics of Authenticity*. Cambridge: Harvard University Press.

Taylor, Keith Weller. 1983. *The Birth of Vietnam*. Berkeley, Los Angeles and London: University of California Press.

_____. 1986a. "Authority and Legitimacy in Eleventh-Century Vietnam." In *Southeast Asia in the Ninth to Fourteenth Centuries*, ed. David G. Marr and A. C. Milner, pp. 139–76. Singapore: Institute of Southeast Asian Studies; Canberra: Research School of Pacific Studies.

_____. 1986b. "Review of Wheatley 1983," *Journal of Southeast Asian Studies* 17.2 (September), pp. 366–70.

_____. 1993. "Nguyen Hoang and the Beginning of Vietnam's Southward Expansion." In *Southeast Asia in the Early Modern Era: Trade, Power, and Belief*, ed. Anthony Reid, pp. 42–65. Ithaca and London: Cornell University Press.

Taylor, Philip. 2001. *Fragments of the Present: Searching for Modernity in Vietnam's South*. Crows Nest, NSW: Allen & Unwin; Honolulu: University of Hawai'i Press.

Terweil, B. J, "The Five Precepts and Ritual in Rural Thailand," *Journal of the Siam Society* 60.1 (Jan. 1972), pp. 333–43.

_____. 1975. *Monks and Magic: An Analysis of Religious Ceremonies in Central Thailand*. Scandinavian Institute of Asian Studies, Monograph Series 24. London: Curzon Press.

_____. 1983. *A History of Modern Thailand*. St. Lucia: University of Queensland Press.

Thak Chaloemtiarana. 1979. *Thailand: The Politics of Despotic Paternalism*. Bangkok: Thammasat University, Social Science Association of Thailand and Thai Khadi Institute.

Thak Chaloemtiarana, ed. 1978. *Thai Politics: Extracts and Documents, 1932–1957*. Bangkok: Social Science Association of Thailand.

Thamsook Numnonda. 1977. *Thailand and the Japanese Presence, 1941–45*. Singapore: Institute of Southeast Asian Studies. Research Notes and Discussions Series 6.

————. 1978. "Pibulsongkram's Thai Nation-Building Programme during the Japanese Military Presence, 1941–1945," *Journal of Southeast Asian Studies* 9.2 (September), pp. 234–47.

Thapar, Romila. 1961. *Asoka and the Decline of the Mauryas*. London: Oxford University Press.

————. 1984. *From Lineage to State: Social Formations in the Mid-first Millennium B.C. in the Ganga Valley*. Bombay: Oxford University Press.

Thawit Sukhaphanit. 1988. "Huajai mai mi suan koen: prawattisat phua mia [No love to spare: The history of spouses]," *Ban mai ru roi* 4.4, pp. 51–58; 4.5, pp. 84–92; 4.6, pp. 69–80.

Thiphakorawong, Jaophraya. 1960. *Phraratchaphongsawadan krung rattanakosin ratchakan thi 1* [Royal chronicles of Bangkok: The first reign]. Bangkok: Khurusapha Press.

————. 1961. *Phraratchaphongsawadan krung rattanakosin ratchakan thi 4* [Royal chronicles of Bangkok: The fourth reign]. Vol. 2. Bangkok: Suksaphan phanit.

————. 1965–74. *The Dynastic Chronicles, Bangkok Era: The Fourth Reign, B.E. 2394–2411 (A.D. 1851–1868)*. Trans. Chadin (Kanjanavanit) Flood. 5 vols. Tokyo: The Centre for East Asian Cultural Studies.

————. 1965. *Kitjanukit* [A book explaining various things]. Reprint edition. (Originally published Bangkok, 1867.)

Thirayut Bunmi. 1993. *Jut plian haeng yuk samai* [A pivotal moment]. 2d printing. Bangkok: Winyuchon Publication House.

————. 1994. *Sangkhom khem kaeng* [A vigorous society]. Bangkok: Mingmit Press.

————. 2003. *Khwamkhit lang tawantok* [Post-western thought]. Bangkok: Saisan Press.

Thomas, Keith. 1971. *Religion and the Decline of Magic: Studies in Popular Beliefs in Sixteenth and Seventeenth Century England*. London: Weidenfeld & Nicholson.

Thongchai Winichakul. 1994. *Siam Mapped: A History of the Geobody of Siam*. Honolulu: University of Hawai'i Press.

————. 2000a. "The Changing Landscape of the Past: New Histories in Thailand since 1973," *Journal of Southeast Asian Studies* 26.1 (March), pp. 99–120.

_____. 2000b. "The Others Within: Travel and Ethno-Spatial Differentiation of Siamese Subjects, 1885–1910." In *Civility and Savagery: Social Identity in Tai States*, ed. Andrew Turton, chap. 2. Richmond, Surrey: Curzon Press.

_____. 2000c. "The Quest for '*Siwilai*': A Geographical Discourse of Civilizational Thinking in the Late Nineteenth and Early Twentieth Century Siam," *Journal of Asian Studies* 59.3 (August), pp. 528–49.

Thorbek, S. 1987. *Voices from the City: Women of Bangkok*. London: Zed Books Ltd.

Tichelman, Fritjof. 1980. *The Social Evolution of Indonesia: The Asiatic Mode of Production and Its Legacy*. The Hague: Martinus Nijhoff.

Tran Quoc Vuong. 1986. "Traditions, Acculturation, Renovation: The Evolutional Pattern of Vietnamese Culture." In *Southeast Asia in the Ninth to Fourteenth Centuries*, ed. David G. Marr and A. C. Milner, pp. 271–77. Singapore: Institute of Southeast Asian Studies; Canberra: Research School of Pacific Studies.

Tri Amatyakul. 1962. "Phutaeng nangsu phraratchaphongsawadan chabap phim 2 lem [The author of the two-volume royal chronicles]," *Sinlapakon* 5.6, pp. 43–50, and 6.1, pp. 25–34.

Turton, Andrew. 1972. "Matrilineal Descent Groups and Spirit Cults of the Thai-Yuan in Northern Thailand," *Journal of the Siam Society* 60.2 (July), pp. 217–56.

_____. 1980. "Thai Institutions of Slavery." In *Asian and African Systems of Slavery*, ed. James H. Watson, pp. 251–92. Oxford: Basil Blackwell.

_____. 1984. "Limits of Ideological Domination and the Formation of Social Consciousness." In *History and Peasant Consciousness in South East Asia*, ed. Andrew Turton and Shigeharu Tanabe, pp. 19–73. Osaka: National Museum of Ethnology, Senri Ethnological Studies 13.

_____. 1991. "Invulnerability and Local Knowledge." In *Thai Constructions of Knowledge*, ed. Manas Chitakasem and Andrew Turton, pp. 155–82. London: University of London, School of Oriental and African Studies.

Turton, Andrew, ed. 2000. *Civility and Savagery: Social Identity in Tai States*. Richmond, Surrey: Curzon Press.

Udom Sisuwan [Aran Phrommachomphu, pseud.]. 1979. *Senthang songkhomthai* [The path of Thai society]. Bangkok: Akson. (Reprint of *Thai kung muangkhun kung sakdina* [Thailand: Semicolonial and semifeudal]. Bangkok, Mahachon, 1950.)

Ungar, E. S. 1986. "From Myth to History: Imagined Polities in Fourteenth Century Vietnam." In *Southeast Asia in the Ninth to Fourteenth Centuries*, ed. David G. Marr and A. C. Milner, pp. 177–86. Singapore:

Institute of Southeast Asian Studies; Canberra: Research School of Pacific Studies.

Uppakit Silpasarn, Phya. 1979. *Lak phasa thai* [Principles of the Thai language]. Bangkok: Thai Wattana Panich.

Uraisi Varasarin. 1984. *Les éléments khmers dans la formation de la langue siamoise.* Paris: S. E. L. A. F.

Vajiravudh, King. 1951. "Latthi aoyang [The cult of imitation]." In *Pramuan phraratchaniphon nai phrabat somdet phramongkutklao jaoyuhua* [Collected essays of King Mongkutklao]. Bangkok: Cremation volume for Major General Phraya Anirutthewa.

Vajiranana varorasa, Prince. 1979. *Autobiography: The Life of Prince-Patriarch Vajranana of Siam, 1860–1921.* Trans. Craig J. Reynolds. Athens, Ohio: Ohio University Press.

———. 1971. "Ruang nikai [Concerning monastic orders]." In *Phraniphon tang ruang* [Miscellaneous writings], pp. 5–33. Bangkok: Mahamakut Ratchawitthayalai.

Van Esterik, P. 1982. "Laywomen in Theravada Buddhism." In *Women of Southeast Asia,* ed. Penny Van Esterik, pp. 55–78. Dekalb: Northern Illinois University, Center for Southeast Asian Studies, Occasional Paper 9.

———. 1992. "Thai Prostitution and the Medical Gaze." In *Gender and Development in Southeast Asia,* ed. Penny and John Van Esterik, pp. 133–50. Montreal: McGill University, Canadian Asian Studies Association.

———. 2000. *Materializing Thailand.* Oxford and New York: Berg.

Van Esterik, Penny, and John Van Esterik, eds. 1992. *Gender and Development in Southeast Asia.* Montreal: McGill University, Canadian Asian Studies Association.

Van Leur, J. C. 1967. *Indonesian Trade and Society: Essays in Asian Social and Economic History.* The Hague: W. van Hoeve.

Van Lierc, W. J. 1980. "Traditional Water Management in the Lower Mekong Basin," *World Archaeology* 11.3, pp. 265–80.

Van Naerssen, F. H. 1963. "Some Aspects of the Hindu-Javanese Kraton," *Journal of the Oriental Society of Australia* 2.1, pp.14–19.

———. F. H. 1977. "The Economic and Administrative History of Early Indonesia." In F. H. van Naerssen and R. C. de Longh, *The Economic and Administrative History of Early Indonesia,* pp. 1–84. Leiden: E. J. Brill.

Van Naerssen, F. H., and R. C. de Iongh. 1977. *The Economic and Administrative History of Early Indonesia.* Leiden: E. J. Brill.

Vella, Walter E. 1978. *Chaiyo! King Vajiravudh and the Development of Thai Nationalism.* Honolulu: University Press of Hawaii.

Vickers, Adrian. 1986. "History and Social Structure in Ancient Java: A Review Article," *Review of Indonesian and Malayan Affairs* 20.2 (Summer), pp. 156–85.

Vickery, Michael. 1974. "A Note on the Date of the Traibumikatha," *Journal of the Siam Society* 62.2 (July), pp. 275–84.

_____. 1976. "Review," *Journal of the Siam Society* 64.2, pp. 207–36.

_____. 1998. *Society, Economics, and Politics in Pre-Angkor Cambodia, the Seventh-Eighth Centuries.* Tokyo: The Toyo Bunko, Centre for East Asian Cultural Studies for Unesco.

Vivadhanajaya, Prince. "The Statement of Khun Luang Ha Wat," *Journal of the Siam Society* 28.2 (Dec. 1935), pp. 143–72, and *Journal of the Siam Society* 29.2 (April 1937), pp. 123–36.

Wacharaphon, P. 1963. "K.S.R. Kulap." In *Khon nangsuphim* [Journalists]. Bangkok.

Wales, H. G. Quaritch. 1931. *Siamese State Ceremonies: Their History and Function.* London: Bernard Quaritch, Ltd.

_____. 1951. *The Making of Greater India: A Study in South-East Asian Culture Change.* London: Quaritch.

_____. 1957. *Prehistory and Religion in South-East Asia.* London: Quaritch.

Wang Gungwu, 1968. *The Use of History.* Athens, Ohio: Ohio University, Papers in International Studies, Southeast Asian Series no. 4.

Wanwaithayakorn Worawan, Prince. 1951. *Chumnum phraniphon* [Collected writings]. Bangkok: Thammachedi.

Warasan Thammasat. 1994. "Lokanuwat lokantaranuwat lokawiwat," *Warasan thammasat* 20.1, pp. 101–24.

Warder, A. K. 1961. "The Pali Canon and Its Commentaries as an Historical Record." In *Historians of India, Pakistan and Ceylon,* ed. C. H. Phillips, pp. 44–56. London: Oxford University Press.

Warren, Carol. 1990. "Rhetoric and Resistance: Popular Political Culture in Bali," *Anthropological Forum* 6.2, pp. 191–205.

Warren, James Francis. 1981. *The Sulu Zone, 1768–1898: The Dynamics of External Trade, Slavery, and Ethnicity in the Transformation of a Southeast Asian Maritime State.* Singapore: Singapore University Press.

Watson, Burton. 1958. *Ssu-mka Ch'ien: Grand Historian of China.* New York: Columbia University Press.

Webb, Malcolm C. 1975. "The Flag Follows Trade: An Essay on the Necessary Interaction of Military and Commercial Factors in State Formation." In *Ancient Civilization and Trade,* ed. Jeremy A. Sabloff and C.C. Lamberg-Karlovsky, pp. 155–209. Albuquerque: University of New Mexico Press.

Wenk, K. 1965. *Thailandische Miniaturmalereien nach einer Handschrift der indischen Kunstabteilung der staatlichen Museen Berlin.* Wiesbaden: Franz Steiner Verlag GMBH.

————. 1968. *The Restoration of Thailand under Rama I, 1782–1809.* Translated by G. Stahl. Monographs and Papers of the Association for Asian Studies 24. Tucson: University of Arizona Press.

————. 1986. "Some Remarks about the Life and Works of Sunthon Phu," *Journal of the Siam Society* 74, pp. 169–98.

Wheatley, Paul. 1966. *The Golden Khersonese: Studies in the Historical Geography of the Malay Peninsula before A.D. 1500.* Kuala Lumpur: University of Malaya Press.

————. 1979. "Urban Genesis in Mainland South East Asia." In *Early South East Asia: Essays in Archaeology, History, and Historical Geography,* ed. R. B. Smith and W. Watson, pp. 288–303. New York and Kuala Lumpur: Oxford University Press.

————. 1982. "Presidential Address: India Beyond the Ganges—Desultory Reflections on the Origins of Civilization in Southeast Asia," *Journal of Asian Studies* 42.1 (November), pp. 13–28.

————. 1983. *Nagara and Commandery: Origins of the Southeast Asian Urban Traditions.* Chicago: University of Chicago, Department of Geography, Research Paper 207–8.

Whitmore, John K. 1986. "'Elephants Can Actually Swim': Contemporary Chinese Views of Late Ly Dai Viet." In *Southeast Asia in the Ninth to Fourteenth Centuries,* ed. David G. Marr and A. C. Milner, pp. 117–37. Singapore: Institute of Southeast Asian Studies; Canberra: Research School of Pacific Studies.

Wicks, Robert S. 1992. *Money, Markets, and Trade in Early Southeast Asia: The Development of Indigenous Monetary Systems to A.D. 1400.* Ithaca: Cornell University, Southeast Asia Program.

Wiener, Margaret J. 1995. *Visible and Invisible Realms: Power, Magic, and Colonial Conquest in Bali.* Chicago and London: University of Chicago Press.

Wijeyewardene, Gehan. 1990. "Thailand and the Tai: Versions of Ethnic Identity." In *Ethnic Groups Across National Boundaries in Mainland Southeast Asia,* ed. Gehan Wijeyewardene, pp. 48–73. Singapore: Institute of Southeast Asian Studies.

Wilkinson, Endymion. 2000. *Chinese History: A Manual.* Revised and enlarged edition. Cambridge, Mass.: Harvard-Yenching Institute.

Wira Amphai. 1983. *Khwampenthai* [Thainess]. Bangkok.

Wilson, Constance M. 1987. "The Northeast and the Middle Mekong Valley in the Thai Economy: 1830–1870." In *Proceedings,* International Conference on Thai Studies, 3–6 July, pp. 169–90. Vol. 3. Canberra: The Australian National University.

Wittfogel, Karl A. 1957. *Oriental Despotism: A Comparative Study of Total Power.* New Haven: Yale University Press.

Wolf, Eric R. 1982. *Europe and the People without History*. Berkeley, Los Angeles and London: University of California Press.

Wolters, O. W. 1968. "Ayudhya and the Rearward Part of the World," *Journal of the Royal Asiatic Society*, pts. 3 and 4, pp. 166–78.

_____. 1974. *Early Indonesian Commerce: A Study of the Origins of Srivijaya*. Reprint edition. Ithaca and London: Cornell University Press.

_____. 1976. "Le Van Huu's Treatment of Ly Than Thon's Reign (1127–37)." In *Southeast Asian History and Historiography: Essays Presented to D. G. E. Hall*, ed. C. D. Cowan and O. W. Wolters, pp. 203–26. Ithaca and London: Cornell University Press.

_____. 1979a. "Historians and Emperors in Vietnam and China: Comments Arising out of Le Van Huu's History Presented to the Tran Court in 1272." In *Perceptions of the Past in Southeast Asia*, ed. David G. Marr and A. J. S. Reid, pp. 69–89. Singapore: Heinemann Educational Books (Asia) Ltd.

_____. 1979b. "Khmer 'Hinduism' in the Seventh Century." In *Early South East Asia: Essays in Archaeology, History, and Historical Geography*, ed. R. B. Smith and W. Watson, pp. 427–42. New York and Kuala Lumpur: Oxford University Press.

_____. 1979c. "Studying Srivijaya," *Journal of the Malaysian Branch of the Royal Asiatic Society* 52.2, pp. 1–32.

_____. 1988. *Two Essays on Dai-Viet in the Fourteenth Century*. New Haven: Yale University, Center for International and Area Studies.

_____. 1994. "Southeast Asia as a Southeast Asian Field of Study," *Indonesia* 38 (October), pp. 1–17.

_____. 1999. *History, Culture, and Region in Southeast Asian Perspectives*. Revised edition. Ithaca: Cornell University Southeast Asia Program; Singapore: Institute of Southeast Asian Studies.

Wood, William M. 1859. *Fankwei, or the "San Jacinto" in the Seas of India, China and Japan*. New York: Harper.

Woodside, Alexander B. 1971. *Vietnam and the Chinese Model: A Comparative Study of Vietnamese and Chinese Government in the First Half of the Nineteenth Century*. Cambridge, MA: Harvard University Press.

Worsley, Peter. 1986. "Narrative Bas-Reliefs at Candi Surawaria." In *Southeast Asia in the Ninth to Fourteenth Centuries*, ed. David G. Marr and A. C. Milner, pp. 335–67. Singapore: Institute of Southeast Asian Studies; Canberra: Research School of Pacific Studies.

Wrangel, Marc. 1993. "A Geometry Lesson," *Manager*, October, pp. 34–38.

Wyatt, David K. 1969. *The Politics of Reform in Thailand: Education in the Reign of King Chulalongkorn*. New Haven: Yale University Press.

————. 1976. "Chronicle Traditions in Thai Historiography." In *Southeast Asian History and Historiography: Essays Presented to D. G. E. Hall*, ed. C. D. Cowan and O. W. Wolters, pp. 107–22. Ithaca: Cornell University Press.

————. 1982. "The 'Subtle Revolution' of King Rama I of Siam." In *Moral Order and the Question of Change: Essays on Southeast Asian Thought*, ed. David K. Wyatt and Alexander Woodside, pp. 9–52. New Haven: Yale University, Southeast Asia Studies, Monograph Series 24.

————. 1984. *Thailand: A Short History*. New Haven and London: Yale University Press.

————. 1994. *Studies in Thai History*. Chiang Mai: Silkworm Books.

Yakhop [Chot Phraephan]. 1992. *Samkok chabap wanniphok* [Three kingdoms: The mendicant storyteller's version]. Reprint edition. Bangkok: Dokya Press.

Yule, Henry. 1968. *A Narrative of the Mission to the Court of Ava in 1855*. Kuala Lumpur and New York: Oxford University Press.

Yuval-Davis, N., and F. Anthias. 1989. *Woman-Nation-State*. Basingstoke: Macmillan.

Index

Index

publications of, 64;
unauthorized Sa biography,
66–71, 78n13, 78n15
Kulap Saipradit, 109, 134
Kulke, Hermann, 14, 25, 42
Kuomintang, 293
Kurusapha, 236
Kwangsi, 5

La Galigo, 217
Labor history, 134
"Lady White Blood", 125
Lak phasa, 226
Language: assimilation of foreign
terms into Thai, xv; Central
Thai as dominant, 251–52;
class and proper speech, 95;
feudalism as term in Asian
usage, 104; grammars, 218,
225–27; history of *siwilai*,
301–2; nation as term of,
263–64; and national security,
271; power and, 80, 84, 99–
100; used for social change,
111–12; vulgar, 94–95, 100
Lao (people), 170
Laos: Thai military campaigns
into, 85–86, 170; Thai
relations with, 82, 144, 193,
283; Thai territorial claims in,
260; warfare manuals, 229
Law(s): Civil and Commercial
Code (*1935*), 185, 207;
Cullom Bill (U.S., *1969*),
213n9; in Islam, 204; on
marriage, 124, 185, 189–92,
198; National Cultural
Maintenance Act (Thailand,
1940), 249, 254; National
Culture Acts (*1942, 1943*),
254; on opium, 200; on

polygamy, 185, 204;
Prescribing Customs for the
Thai People, 250; on the
sangha, 145, 159; on slavery,
132; Three Seals Code (*1805*),
153, 185, 189–90
Le Van Huu, 48
Leach, E. R., 193
Legge, John, 4
Leonowens, Anna, 132, 213n4
Lese-majesty: as charge in
discussion of regicide, 105;
charges against Nai Thim of,
92–93; defined, 80, 93–94;
foreign view of prosecutions
for, 81; terms for discussion
of, 81; Thai law regarding, 94;
violations of literary genres as,
95–96. *See also* Sedition
Leur, J. C. van, 18–19
Linga cults, 193
Lintel, stolen, 260, 266, 291
Lithai, King, 154, 165–67, 170,
188
Loanwords, 108
Local agency, 300
Local culture, 290
Local genius, 19–20
Local identity. *See* Thai national
identity
Local knowledge, 215, 223, 240,
242n8, 292
Local statements, 21
Local wisdom, 300. *See also Phum
panya*
Locke, John, 44
Lokanuwat, 285–86, 290
Lokaphiwat, 285–86
Lokawibat, 286–87
Lokawiwat, 286, 288
Lophanuwat, 286

Mormonism, 206, 213n8
Morocco, 43
Mot Amatyakul, 57, 174
Muang Boron, 268, 287
Muang Singh, 267
Mud on Our Wheels, 292
Mulasasana, 146
Multinational enterprises, 292
Mus, Paul, x, 8, 10
Myanmar. *See* Burma
Myths of rural abundance, 133

Nagasena, 173
Nagtegaal, Luc, 43
Nakhon Ratchasima, 59
Nakleng, 131, 139n11
Nanchao, 262
Nangsu lamok, 124
Narai, 34
Naresuan, King, 40, 230, 270
Narit, Prince, 55
Narit Worarit, Prince, 68
National Culture Commission,
    256, 273
National Culture Council, 254
National Education Plan, 256
National Identity Board, 256–57,
    270, 273, 275n11
National Museum, 268
National security, vii–viii, 249,
    269–72
National Security Council, 271–72
National Thai woman, 124
Nationalism: components of, 258;
    cultural, 294–95; feudalism as
    a classification in promotion
    of, 104; Kulap's effect on, 74;
    territorial, 262
Nationality, 297
Native wisdom, 300. *See also*
    Phum panya

Natthawut Sutthisongkhram, 83,
    101n3
Nawa-ek Sawat Janthani, 134
Negara (theater state), 26, 43–45,
    99, 264
Network states, 43
Networking, 221
New Industrialized Countries
    (NICs), 258
Nguyen dynasty (Vietnam), 49
Nguyen Hoang, 49
Nidhi Aeusrivongse, 127, 291–92,
    294
*Nine Reigns of the Chakkri
    Dynasty*, 120
Nirat Nongkhai, 83–84; charges
    and sentencing over, 92–93; as
    emblematic of censorship,
    83–84; military campaign related
    in, 85–92; as subversive to
    authority, 97–101; as violation
    of literary genre, 95–96
Nirat poetry genre, 87
Nirat Tangkia, 85
Nongovernmental organizations
    (NGOs), 287
Norarat, Jaophraya, 61
Norholdt, H. Schulte, 29
Nu, U, 155, 157–58

Obstetrics, 173
O'Connor, Stanley, 9
Old City of Bangkok, 268
Opium, 200
Oracle bones, 224
*The Organization of Thai Society
    in the Early Bangkok Period*
    (Akin), 116
Oriental despotism, 31, 34–35, 44
Origin myths, 125
Orthodoxy, 216

Vajirarana Library, 60, 66, 72, 180
Vajiravudh, King: cultural heritage
of Thailand, 267; Cultural
Mandates, 251; education in
England, 236; ethnic Chinese,
259, 282; nationalism of, 253;
opposition to Western cultural
influence, 292–93, 300; on
socialist utopias, 180
Vajirunahis, Crown Prince, 66
Varasethasuta, Princess, 192
Vedas, 230
Vernacular languages, 4–5, 24
Vessantara, Prince, 136
Vessantara Jataka, 89, 136
Vickery, Michael, 35, 160n6
Vietnam: AMP paradigm, 37;
desinicization in, 22–23; as
dynastic state, 48–50; family
in, 189; feudalism as term
used in, 102, 104; mandala
paradigm, 39; as part of
Southeast Asia, 10; state
formation in, 16; Tai peoples
in, 298
Village life, 34–35, 299
Vinaya, 148, 154, 241
Visayas, 10
Vishnu, 216
Vulgarity, 94–95, 100

Wachirayan, 76
Wachirayan Literary Society, 64
Wachirayan Warorot, Prince, 55,
68–69
Wachirayan wiset, 58–59
Wales, H. G. Quaritch, 19, 23, 300
Wallerstein, Immanuel, 288
Wan, Prince, 218
Wannapho, T. W. S., 69, 76
Warfare, 52

Warren, Carol, 274
Warren, James, 42
Wealth, 33–34, 164
Weaving, 138n6
Weber, Max: religion, xiii; study of
the state, 31, 44, 51
Wet–rice technology: at Angkor,
35–36; and growth of
kingdoms, 13–14; in Java, 35;
as Southeast Asian cultural
element, 8–9
Wheatley, Paul, 11, 13
Whitmore, John K., 22
*Why Gender Matters in South
East Asian Politics*, 125–26
Wichit Watthakan, Luang: how-to
books by, 238–39; national
security, 270; nationalism,
253, 259, 261; on the *1932*
coup, 113
Wijeyewardene, Gehan, 261
Wild Tigers, 293
Wittfogel, Karl, 35, 44
Wolf, Eric, 33
Wolters, O. W., x, 6, 20–21, 25,
37, 38–41, 43, 46
Women: bilateral kinship systems
and, 10; Buddhism's role for,
128–29, 138n8, 186–87; in
colonial-era historiography, 8;
as different from men, 204–5;
in economic studies, 126–27;
emancipation of, 197–99;
etiquette manuals for, 236–37;
in historical studies, 127–28;
in the Inner Palace, 132,
194–95, 197–98, 213n4; as
legal equivalent to water
buffalo, 191, 198; marketing
of beauty, 131; Marxism on,
191; as mediums, 129;